LIFE ON THE ABBAGADASSET

The Dunlap family in the dooryard of their farm on the Abbagadasset, 1912.
From left: Genevieve, Al, Jeannette, Al's wife Martha (Robinson) holding daughter
Eleanor, Lois, Vining, Mother [Annie Belle (Williams)] and Pa [James Albert Dunlap],
with Bert in front of Mother and Pa, and Snipe in front of all. Only Minerva is missing.
[Photographed supposedly by Walter Ingram.]

LIFE ON THE ABBAGADASSET

Memories of Boyhood on a Bowdoinham Farm

by

ALBERT A. DUNLAP
1902 - 1978

Edited by Sarah Dunlap and published at this time by the daughters of Albert Atkinson Dunlap to coincide with the 250th Anniversary of the incorporation of the Town of Bowdoinham, Maine, and the restoration of the old Jellerson one-room schoolhouse by the Bowdoinham Historical Association.

ISBN 978-0-615-66198-8
LC in progress

Layout by Jeffrey Crawford

Printed by King Printing Co., Inc., Lowell, MA.

Cover images: Skiff on the Abbagadasset and Burt Hunting Ducks.

If not otherwise credited, photographs were among the papers of Albert A. Dunlap. Many were negatives, discovered and scanned by his granddaughter Rebecca Vaughan.

DEDICATED

to the

Inhabitants of Bowdoinham

TABLE OF CONTENTS

FORWARD

Albert Atkinson "Bert" Dunlap was born on October 31, 1902, in Bowdo-inham, Maine, the seventh child in the farming family of James Albert and Annie Belle (Williams) Dunlap. When he died on October 12, 1978, he was typing what he hoped to be the final draft of the book he had worked on for years, the story of growing up on a farm on the tidal Abbagadasset River.

The family has always treasured this manuscript. One of us (Helen) finished typing it from his edited draft soon after his death and had a few bound copies made. Then in 2003, his granddaughter Jennifer Vaughan Almeida re-typed it onto a computer and made copies on discs. Both versions were distributed to family members. The 250th celebration of the incorporation of the Town of Bowdoinham and the renovation of the Jellerson Schoolhouse provide us with the perfect op-portunity to offer this evocative portrait of rural Maine life in the early twentieth century to a wider audience.

As did most of his siblings, Bert attended Bates College in Lewiston, Maine, graduating in 1923. He went on to receive his Masters' (1927) and Ph.D. (1929) in Plant Pathology and Physiology from Yale University. Awarded one of the cov-eted National Research Council Fellowships in 1929, he carried out research at the University of Wisconsin, at the New Haven Agricultural Experiment Station in Connecticut, and at the Johns Hopkins Institute in Baltimore, Maryland. From 1938 to 1950, he was first a research scientist and then on the faculty at Texas A & M College, serving as head of the Department of Plant Pathology and doing extensive research at their Agricultural Experiment Station. His focus was disease prevention in crop seedlings, and his discoveries included the many benefits of sand culture. His numerous scientific publications detail an expertise on diseases in everything from cotton to live oaks to tomatoes to tobacco.

Bert met Marjorie Bodwell, a fellow lifelong naturalist from Stamford, Connecticut, and a Masters' candidate in Botany at Mount Holyoke College, at sci-entific meetings in Amherst, Massachusetts, and they were married in 1934. They had four girls, born from 1936 to 1945: Anne and Linda in Connecticut, Helen and Sarah (known in the family as Peggy and Ginny) in Texas.

In 1950, he left Texas and, with other scientists on the federal government's American Agricultural Redevelopment Commission, traveled to South Korea to help their farmers, a project foiled by the simultaneous onset of the Korean War. Plans to retire eventually to a farm in New England were thus fast-forwarded, and Bert spent the rest of his life on a dairy farm in Dracut, Massachusetts. He was a fulltime farmer until 1968, when, responding to an effort by the American Institute of Biological Sciences to get retired professors back in the classroom, he returned to teaching biology at Fitchburg State College, serving as Department Chair for several years. Even after retiring from that position, he held field courses in botany, sponsored by Fitchburg, at his farm every summer. He died in Merredin, Western Australia, while accompanying his then son-in-law, Dr. Eric Pianka, on a desert ecology field trip.

This will be his second published nonscientific work. The first, "Altruism on the Abbagadasset," (one of many short stories and accounts he worked on even as he farmed) was published in *Yankee Magazine* in May 1965.

We gratefully acknowledge all of those who have helped inspire and bring this project to fruition, especially our cousins Ronald Burrell and Roberta Rello (Jeannette's son and daughter), Brad Blake (Al's grandson), Rebecca Vaughan (Anne's daughter), and Elizabeth Steen of the Bowdoinham Historical Society. They have resurrected negatives, reproduced, scanned, and shared their large collections of images as well as identified persons and locations. Anne recently became friends with people from Bowdoinham, learned of the upcoming celebrations, and initiated the production of this edition. Sarah did minimal editing of Bert's words.

Anne Dunlap Vaughan, Linda Dunlap Miller,
Helen L. Dunlap, and Sarah V. Dunlap
July, 2012

INTRODUCTION
by Albert A. Dunlap

Dorsal fins of herring were breaking the water in the fish pound as we approached the weir that morning in early May. "That's a good sign," Pa said, "I'll bet we'll make a good haul today. There ought to be a few shad in there, too, with all those herring." We paddled the skiff through the outer entrances of the weir and pushed through the mouth of the fish pound. There we used our seine to boat the day's catch. It was tip-top high tide at nine o'clock that morning. We had been up for three hours already, first doing the farm chores, then eating breakfast of fried potatoes and fresh herring rolled in corn-meal batter, before going to the river.

It was a beautiful spring morning with no wind to ripple the river's surface. The first Canadian warblers with shiny yellow breasts and black necklaces had arrived in the alders at our shore, and young crow fledglings were squawking for food in the evergreen woods across the river. Willows on the "beaver dams" stood out with their new leaves of pale yellow green. It was Saturday and for two days there would be no school. So far everything had gone smoothly that morning, which was unusual for the start of a new day on the farm. There had been almost a small disaster when I caught my paddle over the bow of the skiff and was nearly pulled overboard by the boat's momentum, on the way to the weir. Pa had cautioned me a number of times about dipping my paddle ahead of the square-ended skiff.

Part-time fishing of this sort was a moonlighting extra for our family. Farming was our main pursuit. Although it was always fun to be on the river, our life ashore was often exciting, too. In pre-school days, before I was given chores to do, I spent many hours in a favorite spot on our Maine farm – a small wooded ridge not far from our house that we called Up-under-the-Hill. It was a wildish area, a hundred yards from our backyard, unsuitable for plow or pasture, but just the spot for a boy to play. Beneath the tall red oaks on the east side of the hill was a mossy mound where I used to sit as a five-year-old and gaze towards the wooded horizon in the town of Woolwich, beyond the hidden Kennebec two or three miles away. In the foreground was our river pasture with its narrow gully and marshy "meadow." Thick coniferous woods stood between the nearby Abbagadasset, eastern boundary of our farm, and the wider Kennebec behind the trees. In the distance to the northeast, on a hill in Dresden, I could see the big white house where Pa was farmed out to work for his keep at the age of ten.

It was the day of tall ships. One morning I watched the tops of a schooner's masts move steadily along above the canopy of fir and spruce. Out of sight, the four-master, with sails furled, was being towed up the veering channel of the Kennebec. The tugboat's position was marked by a wisp of smoke in front of the topmasts, barely visible above the trees. Could it be the *Seguin* – the tug with a gilded rooster on the pilothouse – that we had sometimes seen on the way to Bath? I watched the masts till they passed out of sight behind some tall pines towering above the hemlocks in Kil Maxwell's woods. Behind me, to the westward, a stake-driver made his liquid call, hidden by tall grass in Cromwell's swamp at the foot of the hill beyond the road. A red squirrel chattered from one of the few evergreens on our wooded hill. I stayed a while longer to watch a pair of red-shouldered hawks circling above the Old Pine on the farther bank of the Abbagadasset. They nested every year in a tall white birch in the woods below the pine. It was approaching noon on a calm and sunny day in June. Pa would be returning soon from his weekly trip to town, possibly a bit provoked by the horse's antics if, by chance, he had met an automobile along the way. Mother would be calling any moment now. It was nearly time for dinner.

Some of our most pleasant moments of family life were spent during the evening in our small kitchen after dark. Pa usually sat in his rocking chair after supper with his feet on the stove hearth, often chewing tobacco and whittling kindling wood or smoking his white clay T.D. pipe. Mother did her mending of everyone's clothes, knitted, or read her church magazine, *Sign of the Times*. My brother Vining and my two youngest sisters, Genevieve and Jeannette, studied their homework at the table. Conversation was frequent – about any subject that happened to come up. Mother cautioned us about counting our money after dark. "You never know, someone might be looking in the window," she said. Likewise she cautioned us about putting coins in our mouth, saying, "There's no telling who's been handling money nor where it's been." If it was a Sunday evening, Mother would be writing her weekly letter to my oldest brother Al. He always wrote so that we got his letter on Saturday. As Mother started a letter one fall, she dated it "11/11/11." "I won't be able to write another date like that until a year from next month," she said. "Then that will be the last time for me – there are only twelve months in a year!"

What a change seventy years have brought! That section of the Kennebec along the Woolwich shore has seen no schooner for nearly half a century. The countryside, of which we were once a part, no longer has its cows and sheep; the chickens, pigs, and horses have vanished, too. Pastures once closely grazed and fields mowed every summer for their hay have grown up to mini-forests of log-sized trees. The comfortable mound where I watched the moving masts is still there but there is no longer any view. No glimpse of the shining Abbagadasset can now be had, upstream nor down, like there used to be. As growing trees have blotted out the view, so will the years erase memories of that nearly-forgotten period in our rural American life. In time, our only records may be dim pictures in black-and-white, together with scattered memoranda by the written word. Time fades so many things, they say. Is it not fitting to record our experiences during those early years, before memories stored in the fragile archives of the human mind may, through deterioration or irreversible demise, slip beyond recall?

In all those years, our quiet sixty-acre farm was the site of many interesting happenings when we were young. The whole neighborhood had its share of homely events – many humorous, some unbelievable – and so often those unpredictable things did happen. Although there was always work to be done – chickens to feed, weeds to pull, hay to pitch, or wood to cut – farm life was ample and rewarding. It was all the more exciting because of proximity to the river. A river, especially a tidal one, so enhances the attractiveness of an area with its boating, fishing, and winter's ice, that life along its banks can be a more memorable experience than living in a streamless land.

Chapter One

The Dunlap Farm

Our farm was located two and a half miles east of Bowdoinham Village, between the Maine Central tracks and the Abbagadasset River. Its varied topography provided a variety of wildlife habitats. Hayfields and grassy pastures were interspersed with swamps, gullies, ledge outcroppings and patches of mixed woods. A short, rocky peninsula, that Pa called the Point and the rest of us called the Shore, extended into the river at the northeast corner of the farm. Its sloping ledge made the best boat landing on the river. Mature hardwoods covered most of the Point and also the higher ground Up-under-the-Hill. Our only pure stands of conifers stood in scattered groups near the alder swamp in our west pasture, not far from the railroad. They were mostly balsam firs and spruce, with an occasional white pine and the kind of cedar that is known as arbor vitae. There was an alluvial sandy area in our level east field near the river. Higher areas of the farm had a heavy loam that was underlain with the bluest of all blue clays. It was this sticky subsoil that made our hillside roads so slippery after a rainstorm or a summer shower.

Pa complained that the buildings on our farm were located too close to the boundary line; our chickens were always foraging on Amasa Williams' property. Our story and a half house, painted white with dark green shutters, with its end-on extension housing the kitchen and woodshed connected to the stable and barn, stood half way between railroad and river. A two-hundred-foot, tree-lined driveway connected the buildings with the dirt highway that ran straight across the farm. From our south window we looked down the lower reaches of the Abbagadasset and across a goodly portion of Merrymeetng Bay. It was a restful view. A notable feature of the landscape was the dark, pine-covered Bluff Head that protruded into the Bay from its western shore. Far across the Bay was the wooded highland of North Bath. To the southeast, through a gap in the woods we had a glimpse of the Chops – a narrow place in the Kennebec where bay and river made exit towards the sea. Since our barn and stable were in the way, we had to step outdoors whenever we wanted to see the orchard, our low east field, and that part of the river or the woods beyond. Through our north windows we looked across the field, gully, and river pasture to the Shore. Through a fringe of trees on the riverbank we could see the swampy, one-acre island, girdled by beaver dams, overgrown with alders, with a stately elm on its eastern tip, directly across the channel from our shore. Upstream we looked at open water as far as the bend at Kil Maxwell's Point. Past that point, part of the railroad embankment was visible across the swamp on the old Hall farm. Tall oaks Up-under-the-Hill prevented us from seeing the old Cromwell house directly north of us. Northwestwards we had a more open view. Another railroad dike crossed Cromwell's meadow. Beyond the swamp, George Hackett's hayfield sloped unevenly upwards to his yellow buildings at the top of the hill. Due west, our grassy pasture covered the hillside across the road. In the distance, Fred Beals' house and barn sat unpainted close to the skyline, against the woods. To the left, we saw the white spire of the church on the other road. The wooded hill extended southward with, here and there, an ancient pine tree standing tall against the sky. Of the dozen or so farms that surrounded ours, we could see the buildings on only a few; most of them were screened from view by the wooded horizons that hemmed us in.

Of the many views we had through our twelve-light windows with their nine-by-thirteen inch panes of glass, those of the river we thought were the prettiest and best. Everyone beheld the Abbagadasset as an attractive, interesting stream – changing from hour to hour, day to day, and season to season. It was a winding river with almost continuous woods along its eastern bank, and much cultivated farmland along its western shore. It flowed far enough from the ocean so that its waters had only a slight salty taste in prolonged periods of summer drought, yet near enough to have a six-foot rise and fall of normal tide. The gentle flood came in until high-water-slack occurred, followed by a stronger ebb until the shallowest depths at low-water-slack were reached. Next day the same thing happened, except the time of tide was an hour later than the day before. Two weeks passed before high tide occurred at that same hour of the day again.

Tidal fresh-water streams attract and support a variety of plant and animal life. The intertidal zone along the shore provides a favorable environment for wild rice, pickerel weed, and many semi-aquatic plants. At low tide one can see the band of eel grass waving in the current close to the water's edge. Muskrats make their burrows just above the tide and dig roadways in the soft mud below high water mark. In May, when the shadbush blooms and thrushes sing at evening on the wooded banks, herring and shad, accompanied by predatory lampreys, come in from the sea to spawn. Bald eagles and ospreys make their appearance, too, splashing down to catch a shallow-swimming fish. An occasional herring gull flies up and down at tree-top height looking for some morsel from a predator's repast. Late in the year, after the maples have shed their leaves and the water becomes too cold for mist to rise on frosty mornings, smelts and tomcods enter to lay their eggs. Why do fishes leave the vastness of the ocean to spawn in an inland stream? Like all good parents, they try, without a doubt, to provide the best for their tender offspring. Perhaps their instincts tell them that their young could have no better place for growing up. As children we found it so.

Chapter Two

Some Dunlap Family History

We never asked Pa why he bought the farm on the Abbagadasset; it was obvious that farming was the life style he preferred. We knew that he took pride in growing excellent crops of vegetables and good yields of hay. He liked cattle, too. My oldest brother, Al, told us he was skilful in handling oxen and that he had won load-pulling contests with his white-faced pair at Topsham Fair. Having been born on a farm in the town of Windsor, April 30, 1858, he must have enjoyed some of the attractions of farm life at an early age. He was the only boy in a large family that Grandfather Dunlap, impaired in health, was unable to support. Because of the family's impoverishment, Pa was sent as a young boy to work for King Reed in Dresden, some twenty miles from home. There he learned a lot about farming as there was much work to be done on the hundred acre farm. "The Reeds were hard-working people," Pa said. "They ate breakfast by candlelight and supper by candlelight the year round. I battered a new straw hat all out of shape fighting mosquitoes while hoeing corn late into the evening. When they had a boiled dinner, they gave me the cabbage stumps." After a few years with the Reeds, Pa rejoined his family that had moved to Wiscasset. Following the loss of this home by fire, they moved to Bath. Pa completed eighth grade but never attended high school. Over the years, he learned the carpenter's trade.

After moving from Bath to Bowdoinham, Grandfather Dunlap's last job was manager of John Harward's dairy farm that extended from the Kennebec near the south end of Swan Island to the Abbagadasset, half a mile up river from our shore. While living there, Pa became well acquainted with our part of town. He told us how good the farmland west of the Abbagadasset looked to him as he was hunting ducks in Preble Creek with his muzzle-loader. Inasmuch as he liked the whole area, there may have been another reason for his attraction to the neighborhood. At a party in Loyal Brown's house on Brown's Point, Pa met Annie Belle, one of Deacon Williams' daughters, who lived four houses down the road from the farm he would later purchase. "At first, I took such a deep dislike to the name Dunlap," Mother told us.

Mother's childhood was quite different from Pa's. She was born in a low, one story house, overlooking one of the river's cross-channels, on September 29, 1861 – "the year the glorious, glorious war begun," they used to say. Grandfather Williams worked part of his eighty-acre farm and kept some cows, a few sheep, chickens and turkeys. He was also deacon of the Old School Baptist church near the top of Clay Hill at the edge of the village. There were several girls in Mother's family; of the three boys only one, Uncle Everett, lived to maturity. Due to the illness of an older daughter, Grandmother Williams needed Mother's help at home and she attended high school only briefly. Mother lived all of her eighty years in Bowdoinham except for a season she spent as a teenager in Reisterstown, Maryland, with a married sister. Smilingly, she quoted an old saying, "Deacons' daughters and ministers' sons are the biggest sinners that ever run." But Mother was a faithful church member all her life.

On Thanksgiving Day, 1879, Pa sailed for Charleston, South Carolina, on the maiden voyage of the 1491-ton, square-rigged, lumber-laden *Sea King*, the last vessel built at the Bowdoinham Village shipyard. As the youngest member of the crew, he was given the honor of unfurling the first topsail. He returned by train during the winter, with his canvas seaman's bag over his shoulder. He remembered how disagreeably cold it was in New York City the day he changed stations there. The next summer, with financial help from his father, he bought our farm at public auction. Ben Sedgeley, a bachelor, was the seller. He was born in the house that once stood on the cellar hole in our orchard. Ben was one of Mother's admirers. He was heard to say, "I would have married Belle if Jim had kept out of the way." Pa and his parents soon moved into the newly-purchased home. Next-door neighbor, Jere Cromwell, who had aided Pa in transacting the farm papers, helped with the moving and assisted in accumulating some necessary livestock. It was now only a short walk to Deacon Williams' place and Pa saw Mother frequently during the next year or two. On September 24, 1883, they rode with Pa's bay horse, Dick, to Elder Campbell's home fifteen miles away on Maquoit Bay in Harpswell, where they were married. It was nearly fifty years before they saw the place of their marriage again. In the summer of 1932, my sister Minerva and I drove with them to the old, unpainted house where the minister had lived. Pa pointed to the corner near the fireplace and said, "We stood over there by the window for the ceremony." Some twenty years after that, Minerva and I found the site of the Campbell homestead, but the old house had been replaced by another dwelling.

Starting from scratch, it was never easy for a newly-wed couple to make ends meet on a Maine farm. Although both of my parents worked hard, Pa always seemed to find it necessary to supplement the farm income by working away from home. He told us about working "on the ice" when he and Mother were first married. The work was available only during the short days of winter when there were many farm chores to do. After an early breakfast, they milked the cows by lantern light. Then he walked through the snow across the Abbagadasset and through the woods beyond, before daylight, to the Norton Ice Company on the Kennebec, a distance of over a mile and a half from home. There he put in ten or twelve hours a day stowing away heavy blocks of ice in the tall storage house, for a dollar and a quarter a day. "It was tiring work," he said. "We used to stretch out on the stored ice to rest, whenever there was a minute before the next block came up the ramp. If anyone wanted to quit his job, there was always a group of Canadians waiting to take his place. Nowadays, labor unions have done away with that sort of thing." Returning home after dark, Pa and Mother did the evening chores before supper. Mother deserved much credit for her part during those early years of their marriage. She did the daytime chores while Pa was away, in addition to her housework and, eventually, caring for a small child or two. During those early years, Mother contributed to the family income by sewing men's coats for a clothing concern in Boston. The cloth, cut to pattern, was sent to Bowdoinham by railway express.

Mother made finished garments from this material, even to the sewing on of buttons. My parents bought a new, foot-pedal Davis sewing machine for this work. It had a special attachment for making buttonholes.

Eventually, there were seven children in our family, with dates of birth spread over a period of eighteen years. The oldest, James Albion (called Al), was born August 6, 1884. He was followed by two girls – Lois Ann on September 2, 1886, and Minerva Frances on March 13, 1888, during the notorious blizzard. My next older brother, Vining Campbell was born on April 17, 1893. He was followed by two more sisters – Genevieve on January 19, 1895, and Jeannette Dunning on December 4, 1896. It was Halloween of 1902, when I first saw the light of day. My arrival must have been too spooky for Grandmother Dunlap to endure. She passed away the next morning. They say that Pa remarked how unusual it was for a birth and a death to occur in the same family within a twenty-four hour period.

Of the many abilities of the human brain, the capacity for long-remembrance is one of the most amazing. It is truly marvelous that we can dip back into the fringes of memory and recall such distant events as those of early childhood. One Sunday, over seventy years ago, members of Mother's church were invited to an all-day service in the meetinghouse at Bowdoin Center, five miles to the west in an adjacent town. I was four years old. As we entered the church, Mother pointed to Grandfather Williams' picture hanging in the vestibule. I have not seen his picture since but to this day I can see the bearded, solemn face surrounded by a molded wooden frame. At noon that day the guests were invited to dinner in the nearby home of Miss Viola Coombs. To make room for everyone at the table, Pa held me on his knee and we ate baked beans from the same plate. I have thought about that day many times since then.

Another long-remembered incident happened down at the river, probably the same year as the church event. I am quite certain it was a Sunday forenoon, most likely in September, when Pa, Al, and Vining took me with them on a brief walk to the shore before dinner. The tide was high and a duck was seen swimming in the thin grass close to the opposite shore, a little way upstream. As far as I know, Maine has never legally permitted hunting on Sunday, but this was an opportunity to make sure of something for dinner next day. Taking advantage of the situation, Al unlocked the fish house and secured Pa's shotgun that they kept at the shore much of the time during hunting season. We crossed the river in our skiff and went ashore, out of sight from the duck, in a small cove directly across the river from our point. The three older members of the family made their way cautiously along the old wood road that followed the low riverbank. I tagged along and kept the others in sight until I came to a fallen tree that I couldn't climb over. Apprehensive that I might start crying and frighten the duck, Vining came back and lifted me over the obstacle. Next came a loud bang and a few minutes later, Al appeared with his retrieved waterfowl. I don't know why I have always remembered this experience as happening on a Sunday. It may have been the relaxed atmosphere that characterized our day of rest on the farm.

Quite likely it was that same fall that I rode in the hayrack with Pa to get a load of cornstalks for the cows. At that time of the year the pasture feed became short, so the cows were given freshly-cut corn stalks as supplemental roughage in the barn before milking. We had a patch of sweet corn that year in the narrow strip of open land between our road and the picnic ground, on the west side of the woods Up-under-the-Hill. From the road we reached the corn field by a low, wooden bridge over the roadside ditch. After the hayrack was nearly filled with corn stalks, Pa lifted me to the top of the load for a ride back to the barn. Approaching the road, the cart wheels bumped over the old bridge and I slid from the slippery stalks, through the rungs, and landed on weeds in the dry ditch. Pa lifted me onto the load again and held me beside him while I cried most of the way to the house. In the kitchen, Mother brushed me off and tried to console me by saying, "When you fell off the load, the cat heard it way down here. He jumped clear up onto the shelf over the woodbox."

My two youngest sisters, Genevieve and Jeannette, took a keen interest in birds and I got to know many of the common ones at an early age. All three of us had our own "bird book" – a five-cent school notebook with thin brown covers – in which we kept a list of birds seen each year with date of earliest sighting of each species. We often included colored drawings of recently-listed birds. My first bird book goes back to January, 1907. Probably it was that year that I recall watching a chickadee flitting about in low alders near the mouth of our gully. My parents were digging potatoes in our north field as I slipped under the barbed-wire fence to play in the adjacent pasture. It was possibly that same fall, while Pa was away at work, that Mother took me with her when she pulled and stacked bean plants in our east field. There had been a heavy rain, for pools of water stood here and there in the level field. A long-legged bird about the size of a robin lit at the edge of a puddle. I don't remember how long was the bird's bill, so I cannot now say whether it was a Wilson's snipe or a yellow-legs which we also called snipe. But the image of the new bird standing there in the shallow pool remains distinct today. Another interesting bird appeared when I was just tall enough to see over our kitchen windowsill. It was in the winter and our front yard was covered with snow. I asked Mother to come see the funny-looking thing sitting on the sloping water spout a foot above the ground, at the corner of our porch. "That's an owl!" she exclaimed. "We don't see them very often in the daytime. They come out at night. They can see in the dark, like our kitty." Late in the afternoon, when Vining and my sisters came home from school, they found the owl perched on the stairs in our stable. It was probably a saw-whet, possibly a screech owl. I cannot recall whether it had ear tufts or not.

On pleasant, pre-school days in spring, when I was the only child at home, Mother allowed me to play by myself Up-under-the-Hill. The patch of woods was near enough so that she could call me when it was time to come home. It was also far enough from the river that I would not wander near the shore. As children, we were sternly cautioned never to go near the river unless we were accompanied by a grown-up; slippery banks and swift tide made the stream too dangerous for any youngster. The hardwood trees and scattered pines Up-under-the-Hill had broken understories of various shrubs and herbaceous plants. My brothers and sisters had played there years before. Old, weather-beaten boards nailed to trees for seats and shelves showed where they had make-believe living quarters. No doubt, Mother appreciated having a fairly safe playground for us so near at hand. It must have been a relief for her to have the small fry out from under foot while she was performing her many household duties and doing farm chores when Pa was away at work. "We used to play up there as if we'd never have a care in the world," Genevieve once said. But one day I lost one of my favorite playthings Up-under-the-Hill. It was an old heavy brass padlock, with a few links of chain attached, such as was used by the railroad to lock the steel compartment at the base of signal towers. The lock's mechanism was badly worn. After snapping, it could be opened easily without a key. I thought I'd lost the padlock while climbing a small pine tree, but, search as I might in the litter beneath the tree, I couldn't find it.

Some forty years later, I showed my four young daughters the tree and told them about the padlock. We raked and probed the ground beneath the pine. After a few minutes, one of the girls sat on a low ledge outcrop a few feet away and waited for us to get through with our digging. While there, she poked half-heartedly into the decaying leaves and pine needles with a piece of dead limb. She struck something hard and removed it from the spongy humus. "What's this?" she asked. She held up a dirt-covered lump with a rigid, crooked arc projecting from it. When we scraped away the adhering humus from the somewhat corroded metal, the inch-long, rectangular, brass cover, that once swung over the keyhole to keep out freezing rain, came off in our hands. Its steel pin on which it hinged had rusted, like the five links of iron chain.

Chapter Three

Local Geography and History

The town highway that ran south to north across our farm was a narrow, often muddy and always rutted, dirt road, typical of both the area and the times. It began on Center's Point, a neck of land that jutted into the Cathance channel on the west side of Merrymeeting Bay, and ran due north to the County Road in Richmond, a distance of eight or ten miles. We always called it Abbagadasset Road, but late years the Town has named it Carding Machine Road. This latter name was formerly applied to a lonesome road, now abandoned, that branched off from our road, crossed the creek-like headwater of the Abbagadasset a mile or so above tidewater, and continued eastward to the Kennebec. The carding machine building no longer stands on the shallow brook that furnished power for combing wool, but the latest name for our road commemorates a former service to the community.

There were no abandoned farms on our road when I was a boy. They all produced something, adding their bit to the country's GNP. At the lower end of the road, the Center farm, with a big, colonial house overlooking the placid Bay, had dairy cattle and a flock of sheep. When I was in grade school at the Corner, there were six farmers – Sam Raymond, John Welch, Jim Pratt, Jim Allen, George Blair, and George Weymouth – with small acreages of level cultivated land next to the Bay between Bluff Head and Amasa's mill, and a wooded hillside west of the road. With good husbandry and a lot of work, they made a modest living from the fertile sandy soil. Along the East Bowdoinham Road, just north of the Corner, lay the hundred acre Call farm, the ancestral home of the Jellersons. The one story brick house stood diagonally across the highway intersection from our relocated Jellerson District grade school. A rectangular depression near the road marked the spot where a barn once stood. At recess time, we ran across the road to get a pear from the tall old tree that stood near the corner of the former barn. At that time, a Jellerson descendant, elderly Mrs. Call, lived there with another elderly lady, who acted as housekeeper, in the only brick house on our road. One afternoon in winter they cleaned out the fireplace and dumped the ashes in the attached ell where their wood was stored. Disposal of wood ashes within a building is always hazardous because they tend to maintain live coals for some hours after the fire has died out. An hour before daylight the next morning, Pa awakened me to see the southern sky lighted by a fire. From his bedroom window we saw the tips of the flames above Uncle Ed's barn. "That must be Mrs. Call's house," Pa said, "there's no other building in that direction." The partially collapsed walls of the one story house stood for several years until my brother Al bought the place and built a retirement home on the old granite-block foundation in 1954.

The next farm north of the old Jellerson place belonged to Scott Davis. Like the Jellerson's, Scott's farm had a wooded hillside west of the railroad, and it extended eastward as far as the Abbagadasset. There was a peninsula-like bank along the river we called Scott's Point. It was separated from the rest of the farm by a muddy inlet, Scott's Creek, that drained a swampy corner of the Jellerson farm. All of the buildings were a weather-beaten gray. A one story house and a stable stood east of the road and a vertically-boarded barn was propped up in the west field. The farm once supported a herd of dairy cattle but as far back as I can remember there was only a single grizzled brown horse. Scott always seemed to be too frail a man for a farmer. He was a quiet, white-haired man who walked with a pronounced stoop. He lived with his unmarried daughter, Ina. The only time I heard Scott speak was one morning when Rena Kimball and I were walking past his house on the way to school. A moment before, I had tossed a small stone in the direction of Scott's horse grazing in the field west of the road. I believe the old nag was waiting for an excuse to move into the apple orchard behind Scott's house. He was nuzzling a bag of apples at the base of a tree when Scott appeared from behind the stable. "You can't leave anything alone, can you?" he shouted. Rena and I quickened our steps towards school with the knowledge that Scott could talk. During mealtime conversation sometime later, Pa mentioned the fact that Scott no longer spoke to him when they passed on the road to the village. The reason was, Uncle Ed had told him, "Your boy drove his horse into the apple orchard." Scott drove to Bath once in a while, ostensibly to sell some item of produce and do some shopping. Everyone knew that Bath was the nearest place that had a saloon. Rumor had it that on one occasion, having almost reached home from one of those trips, Scott drove straight ahead when he reached Jellerson's Corner, instead of turning up our road towards his home. He ended up on the river's thin ice at the public landing near the sawmill. They said the horse swung back to the road and brought Scott to his house.

Oddly enough, the families living on the three farms between Scott Davis' and ours were all related to Mother in one way or another. The southernmost of these was Mother's old home place, the Deacon Williams farm, with a tall Balm of Gilead tree in the front yard and a tight hedge of old cedar trees across the road from the house. This was the home of Aunt Abby and Uncle Ed Denham and their three daughters. The oldest of these cousins, Edna, was a year older than Al; Georgia was the same age as Lois; and Helen was a year younger than Jeannette. Aunt Abby was a small, almost frail lady, two years younger than Mother. As children, we were somewhat awed by large-framed, six-foot Uncle Ed, with his short, black beard and loud voice. In his blue denim overalls and knee-length rubber boots, he looked every bit the part of farmer-butcher that he was. Uncle Ed was considered one of the most affluent men in our section of town. He was the only dairy farmer on the road that shipped his milk to Turner Center Creamery. With a small slaughterhouse beneath his stable, he supplemented his farm income through the sale of dressed beef, pork and lamb.

Mother's only living brother, Uncle Everett, didn't have to look far for a farm to buy when he decided to leave home. He purchased the former Cushing place next door. The low, one story, white house sat near the road and close to the south line. It faced the back of Uncle Ed's stable. To screen out the unsightly slaughtering activities, a cedar hedge was planted along the farm line at the edge of the front yard. Uncle Everett was an athletically-built man with a roundish, smooth face and wavy, gray hair. His wife, Aunt Etta, was a short, stooped lady with a pronounced back deformity which, I believe, resulted from a childhood accident. They had two boys and two girls who were away from home by the time

I knew them. Uncle Everett and Aunt Etta were a religious couple who attended church regularly in the Village. As I was leaving for school one May morning, Pa handed me a half dozen of his first smoked herring of the season. "Give these to Everett on your way to the corner," he said. Through their open front door as I crossed the porch, I saw Uncle Everett and Aunt Etta kneeling in prayer beside their chairs at the breakfast table. I was temporarily embarrassed and hesitated to knock at the door. Uncle Everett saw me very soon, however, and came to the door.

Between Uncle Everett's place and ours was a hundred acre farm that belonged to Amasa Williams, our next-door neighbor on the south. It was really two farms with no trace remaining of the line fence that originally separated them. The southern part once belonged to Amasa's father, a half brother of Grandfather Williams. Known to us as Uncle John, he lived in a small gray house not far from Uncle Everett's, on the west side of the road. I can barely remember Uncle John. His long gray beard captured my attention. He allowed me to walk around the kitchen with his varnished knotty cane. Amasa's two story yellow house with a wide porch across the front and along one side stood a hundred yards up the road from Uncle John's, on the east side of the highway. It was directly across the field from us, so from our front yard we looked at the rear of his house and long barn. Amasa was the only one on our road to give his farm a name. A large sign fastened across the front gable of the barn read ABBAGADASSET FARM. Amasa and Ella, a large, white-haired lady, had two sons both of whom had left for the New York City area before I got to know them. Charles Holbrook, a middle-aged bachelor, helped Amasa run the sawmill and the steamer, *Nellie G.*, and lived with him. Charles' room was upstairs in the northeast corner of the house. When Mother saw a light in his window late in the evening she said, "Charles must be reading tonight." Amasa and Ella also raised an orphan girl, Rena Kimball, who was in the class after mine in school. Amasa was a dark-complexioned man with the only sideburns in our part of town.

Along the half-mile stretch of road north of us, between our farm and the railroad at Pratt's Crossing, there were three farms, two of which were small ones. The old Cromwell place next to ours was the largest of the three. It was owned by Sherman Denham, a brother of Uncle Ed, and his wife, the former Abby Cromwell. It was a bit unusual for us to have two close neighbors with the name Abby. We never got the two confused, however, since we called one Aunt Abby and the other was referred to by her maiden name, Abby Cromwell. Elderly Mrs. Cromwell lived with her daughter and son-in-law on the old home place. Sherman and Abby had no children. They were sort of foster parents to two teenage State-ward girls for whom they furnished room and board. Abby had a nephew, Merton Webber, who lived in the Village and came for long visits during school vacations. Merton and I went swimming and fishing a lot together. The original once-white Cromwell house stood close to their south line, near our woods Up-under-the-Hill. A hundred feet north of the house was an old windowless barn, with all vestiges of paint washed from its up-and-down boards. The only well on the farm was in a most unusual spot – barely ten feet from the side of the road. There was no pump of any kind. All of the water used in both house and barn was drawn from the well with bucket and rope by hand.

The old Cromwell farm had a well-known landmark on the river – a granite precipice, known as Cromwell's ledge, that rose straight up from the mud flats. High tide lapped its base. Half way up the ledge a narrow path led beneath a shoulder-high ceiling. A pair of phoebes built their nest beneath the massive overhang. There was also a shallow cave we called the Bear's Den. While fishing near the ledge in 1739, a son of Samuel Adams, an early settler in Bowdoinham, was captured by the French and taken by boat to Quebec. Learning of his son's whereabouts, the father joined the Colonial Army, fought on the Plains of Abraham and rescued his son from prison.

With the exception of ours, all of the farms on our road northwards from Jellerson's Corner as far as and including Cromwell's had land west of the railroad. At one time our farm also extended beyond the tracks but that part had been sold to the Hacketts before Pa bought the place. The Jellerson's, Davis', Uncle Ed's and Amasa's farms had nothing but woodlots west of the railroad. Barways in the fences and thick planks nailed between the iron rails allowed vehicular access to their wooded hillside. In addition to a woodlot, Uncle Everett had open pasture land beyond the tracks. When the railroad was put through, the former owner was given the choice of a filled-in grade crossing or an underpass for his cattle. He opted for the underpass. Since it was in a swampy area the underpass could not be used for transporting heavy loads. Uncle Ed let Uncle Everett use his crossing when there were logs and firewood to haul from the woods. On the Cromwell farm, however, all of the pasture land lay beyond the railroad. Consequently, Sherman had to drive his cows through a lane in the west field, across the swamp on a log-and-gravel dike we called Cromwell's Bridge, and finally across the tracks. Midway across the swamp, a gap in the dike marked the remnant of an old channel that was once a headwater of Pratt's Creek. Travel across this boggy place was by means of a floating bridge made from discarded railroad ties with a few planks nailed across them. Heifers were skittish about crossing the shaky footing the first few times; they made it only after much hesitation and several false starts. When the cattle reached the railroad, Sherman listened for a train before opening the bars and allowing them to enter his partially wooded pasture.

For a period of several years, beginning some time before I can remember, Sherman and Abby lived in Bath where they kept a boarding house near the Bath Iron Works. During this time they rented the house and farm to Alden Avery who lived with his mother and, frequently, with some of his relatives. The Averys gave board and room to Mary Ann Elliot, a widow, who used to live a mile up the road at Hall's Corner. Alden was a shiftless fellow who made weak attempts at farming. He earned most of his living by trapping and fishing. All the same he had considerable self pride. One year Pa planted potatoes in the narrow field by the picnic grounds, in front of their house. Having harvested the bulk of the crop, Pa told Mrs. Avery, "You can have those small potatoes I've left if you want to pick them up." She and Mary Ann had their pails half full when Alden came to see what they were doing. He forbade them to gather any more. "We don't need to eat those pig potatoes," he said.

The first of the two small farms north of the Cromwell place belonged to Old Santy Pratt. It had fifteen acres of land, a faded brown four-room house that may have been painted red at one time, and a small barn. Old Santy was not a' farmer. All the farming he did was to plant a small garden and cut some hay for his horse. With the river flowing past his limited acreage he depended mainly on the fortunes of fishing for his meager income. Old Santy had had two or three wives but all had died. He lived alone most of the time except for occasional visits from one of his sons, Young Santy, who was somewhat of an inebriate. Now and then Pa or Vining called on Old Santy for an evening's friendly chat. One evening a day or two after Christmas, when I was about eight, Pa took me with him. The day before Christmas my sisters had taken the old gentleman a few home-made goodies. Soon after we arrived he gave me two popcorn balls, saying, "My teeth are not good enough to handle these." For Snipe that evening, he took and iron skillet from the stove and placed it on the floor for the dog to lick.

The tiniest of the three farms between us and the railroad crossing was the ancestral Pratt place where Old Santy was born. It was bounded on three sides by the crooked channel of Pratt's Creek and by the Cromwell farm on the south. The five-room four-gabled house must have been attractive when it was new, with its fancy outside trim and fine interior woodwork. So near the railroad it was surely a noisy homesite; every train that passed whistled for the grade crossing which was only a stone's throw from the front yard. The last occupant was Francis Hutchins, a bachelor, who raised chickens there for several years. But a more recent owner allowed the buildings to fall into disrepair. Finally, the windows were broken out to disqualify the buildings as taxable property. With a leaky roof the house eventually collapsed.

Just beyond Pratt's Crossing, our road dipped to a swampy area, becoming a stone-and-gravel fill dike that led to a wooden bridge over Pratt's Creek. This piece of road always brings to mind my first town meeting. During a high school noon hour in early March one year, three or four of us went to the nearby Town Hall to watch the annual proceedings. As we listened to the discussions, an agenda item that had been submitted by our neighbor, Sherman Denham, came up for consideration. It proposed that fifty dollars be appropriated for gravel to raise the surface of the road along this alder-lined dike. "I don't know where this section of road you're talking about is located," a taxpayer complained. At that point Dr. Irish, one of the selectmen that year, arose from his chair on the stage and described the piece of highway "a mile north of Jellerson's Corner in East Bowdoinham. The road across the swamp is so low that it is covered with water whenever they have a freshet tide." As I remember there was considerable lack of interest when the voice vote was taken but the item was approved. The short bridge over the creek, like the adjacent dike, was a low one. Several times, when the tide was high, I had to lie flat on my back in the gunning float and pull the boat through the bridge by grasping log spanners overhead one after the other.

From the north end of the bridge, the rutted road ascended to higher ground through a washed-out cut in the clay bank. Even when it was only moderately wet, as it would be after a summer shower, this low steep hill was practically impassable for automobiles without chains. In mud-time spring only a horse could climb the bank. The summer that I learned to ride a bicycle I came down the hill before I had mastered the use of the brake. Heavy rain had washed a foot-deep ditch across the road at the bottom of the hill. The front wheel hit the ditch full tilt and I landed ten feet beyond, underneath the bicycle. After pushing the bike the rest of the way home, Al laughed at my predicament and reset the handlebar.

Near the top of this hill was the driveway to the scenic Hall house that lost its original charm when they put the railroad through. A hundred yards farther, our road crossed the east-west Richmond to Brunswick highway; the intersection was known as Hall's Corner. We hurried there when we had an important letter to mail and we had missed the carrier at our mailbox. It took him half an hour to deliver along the Kennebec, so we had time to meet him at the corner on his way back to the Village. In the northeast angle of Hall's Corner was a solitary, yellow barn – all that was left of a former set of Elliot buildings. A hayfield sloped eastward to the river and ended in a grove of tall hardwoods, Elliot's oaks, just above the big road bridge. Close to the road in front of the yellow barn was Elliot's spring – a clear pool where horses paused to have their check-rein unhooked so that they could drink their fill. During a severe drought one summer we brought our household water from the spring to save the low level of water in our well for the livestock, hens and washday.

Beyond Hall's Corner the road went up a high fairy steep hill. John Maxwell's house at the top had a magnificent view of the lower Abbagadasset and most of Merrymeeting Bay. Pa once inferred that John was a mean cuss. He blamed John for causing Uncle Al Hillman to have a possibly serious accident. He said it must have been John who cut the reins on Uncle Al's harness so that one of them broke when he tried to hold back his horse while going down the hill. Uncle Al had been calling on one of Pa's sisters while she was working at the Maxwell's house. Fortunately Uncle Al survived the spill and married Aunt Carrie after all.

From Maxwell's hill northwards to the Richmond line were several farms in the highest and most heavily wooded part of town. George Hall with his two sons, John and Joe, moved to one of these when they left the old home place near Pratt's Creek. Pa helped them build a new barn. While shingling the roof one clear day in October, they looked far to the northwest and saw Old Mount Blue in the town of Weld some seventy miles away. "We looked for the White Mountains but couldn't make them out for sure," Pa said. Past the Hall's our road continued on to the north and ended at the County Road in Richmond, in a swampy area know as Goshen where the Abbagadasset took its origin. Close to the town line lived one of our distant neighbors, Amandus Borjesson, on a woodsy farm of low hills and many gullies. It was Amandus who met Pa at the hay market in Bath one winter day, when Pa had gone for two weeks without shaving. "Glad to see you again, Jeemy," Amandus said. "And am wheeskers goin' to be high in de spring?"

Like many highways that followed the contours of rural Maine, our road had its seasonal problems. When the frost came out in late March or early April, the dirt thoroughfare became somewhat of a quagmire over a stretch of lowland just north of Jellerson's Corner. Here for a week or two, the tough, partially dried surface buckled under one's weight and molasses-thick mud oozed from holes and cracks. If wagon wheels cut through this flexible surface layer, the driver often had to alight and help the horse pull the carriage from the morass. Under such conditions our postman sometimes left his buggy at the corner and delivered the mail up our road on foot. During dry spells in summer a cloud of dust arose behind every vehicle, even though it may have been travelling no faster than a horse's slow trot. The few motorists often wore long lightweight coats to protect their clothing from the billowing clouds of dust that frequently enveloped their open autos. In winter months heavy snowfalls caused the biggest problems. To keep the roads open, someone in the neighborhood was engaged by the Town to break out certain highways after every storm. The contractor's equipment was his own – usually a horse sled with a short piece of timber lashed at an angle in front of the runners to push some of the snow out of the road. The usual result, however, was a packing down of the snow so that a horse could move along easily and a sleigh, pung, or sled slide over smooth and slippery tracks. Come spring, the roadbed might be a foot or two of well-packed snow.

Chapter Four

Schools

The country schoolhouse a mile down the road played an important part in our young lives. Two or three generations living near the lower reaches of the Abbagadasset had been taught their three R's in the Jellerson District one-room elementary school. For years the white clapboarded building stood in the corner of a spruce-pine-fir woodlot on the west side of the road across from George Blair's house. Mother attended school there in the days when nine years were usually spent in elementary before the student entered high school. The sturdy building with its cedar-shingled roof had a shed attached to one end that housed the toilet with one small window close to the eaves, and a windowless one-door woodshed. It stood against the dark evergreen background, with its tall white flagpole attached to one gable, and an ample grassy playground between the schoolhouse and the road. It was an attractive setting for a school. Children marked off their make-believe living rooms between the trees and collected hard pink globules of gum from the spruces. One of the older boys showed us how to make another kind of chewing gum by setting fire to the pitch that oozed from a wounded pine and collecting the melted resinous liquid with a stick as it ran down the trunk. Another attractive feature of the school's location was Weymouth's open pasture adjacent to the schoolyard on the north. For some distance back from the road, a level area was sparsely covered with pink-blooming lambkill shrubs – the only ones we knew to grow in our part of town. In the back end of the pasture was a steep hill where we slid in wintertime. In springtime a shallow brook ran across the pasture in firm soil at the base of the hill, with a single gray plank for a bridge where a foot-path crossed. This was a favorite spot to visit during noon hour on warm spring days. Black tadpoles were easy to catch in the quiet brook.

Jellerson schoolhouse was an old building when I started school early in September, 1909. After years of wear, protruding knots in the spruce flooring stood smooth and shiny a fraction of an inch above the softer wood around them. The whole building had a musty odor all its own. The first day at school I sat beside my youngest sister Jeannette at a double desk in the back row. She was beginning her last year at Jellerson's and would enter high school in the Village the following year. Our teacher was Mrs. Hortense Cannon, wife of a not-too-close neighbor living on the Brunswick-to-Richmond road beyond the railroad. As soon as school opened that first morning, she gave each of us a slip of paper on which to write our name and age. I wrote may name, then asked Jeannette what to put down for my age since I would be seven in another month. She wrote '6' on the cover of her tablet. The school had no grade system as such at that time; grades were introduced the following year. Because I knew the alphabet, could write fairly well and do some simple arithmetic – the result of sisterly instruction at home – I was placed in a beginner's class by myself. Mrs. Cannon started me off with a second-year reader and the middle of the six-times multiplication table. This seemingly advanced math assignment pleased Pa a great deal; he was always proud of his ability to cipher.

Two somewhat younger boys, Charlie Allen and Harold Blair, started school the same day. Neither of them had received much pre-school instruction at home, so the teacher placed them in another class for beginners. She began their education by teaching them the alphabet as she sat in a chair with a book in her lap and the two youngsters standing beside her. She asked Harold, "What letter is that?" Harold looked at the letter and then at the teacher with a vacant gaze. Seven seconds of silence was all that Charlie could stand. With a pitying smile he looked at Harold and said, "Don't you know what that is? That's Eee."

Surely there were many advantages in starting school with an older sister. I realized this good fortune but also felt there were certain drawbacks as well. On occasional mornings we were late in leaving the house and I found it difficult to keep up with Jeannette who disliked having tardy marks on her report card. "Do you have to be such a slowpoke?" she asked. Other obnoxious experiences took place during the noon recess. As soon as we had eaten our lunches, Charlie and I were taken in tow by Jeannette and our cousin, Helen Denham, as their adopted children. We had to do everything just as our foster mothers told us to. There was a feeling of relief the next year when Jeannette had left for high school and I was on my own.

In the summer of 1910, between my first and second years at school, the schoolhouse was moved a few hundred yards up the road to the current location at Jellerson's Corner. The new site was closer to home for most of the students, and there were no woods nearby. The plot of ground on which the building was placed was sold to the Town by George Weymouth; it was the northwest corner of his hay-field. George was a retired farmer in his seventies, with a mottled gray beard and dark eyebrows. He was a reserved man, seldom speaking to children and thereby giving the impression that he possibly disliked youngsters. It was surprising that he would sell a piece of his property for a schoolyard. The Town's offer must have been too tempting. He first put up a single strand of smooth wire around the school grounds, which proved totally ineffective in keeping the children out of his field. To solve the problem once and for all, he built a seven-foot, no-see-through, board fence all the way around the two sides of the yard adjacent to his property. I'm not sure that the fence was as effective as George would have liked. We made a beaten path behind the fence. The two horizontal two-by-fours on the back of the fence enabled us to climb to the top from the back side. We may have spent nearly as much time behind the fence as in the schoolyard.

At the start of my second year of school in the fall of 1910, a system of grades was set up in the elementary schools of our three-town superintendency – Bowdoin, Bowdoinham, and Richmond. Surprisingly enough, I was assigned to the fourth grade, with Eric Blair who was a year older. After we were class-mates I got to know Eric better than anyone else in school. When they moved the schoolhouse that summer, they removed the old double desks with two separate chairs and replaced them with individual desks and bench-type seats that were wide enough to accommodate two persons for a short time. Eric and I sat together quite frequently between recitations. We asked permission of the teacher to make such visits by raising our hand with two fingers extended. (One finger meant we wanted to leave the room.) The teacher usually granted us permission to sit together upon the assumption there would be mutual benefits during the study period. Many of the things we talked about, however, were far removed from any subject ever taught in public schools of the State of Maine. But nobody questioned us as to what it was we were whispering about. I often wondered where Eric got all of his knowledge of animal behavior including that of humans. A likely source was George Weymouth's fifty-year-old bachelor son, Willie, since their homes were relatively near one another and Eric probably saw Willie a few times each weekend. Eric's precociousness coincided with his intense interest in sensual things and his thoughts turned constantly in those directions. After we finished seventh grade I saw Eric only occasionally. Instead of allowing him to finish eighth grade at Jellerson's, his mother decided that he should attend Bliss Business College in Lewiston – a diversion of his liberal education that proved unrewarding to Eric. He returned home the next spring and we entered high school together that fall. But soon Eric dropped out of the freshman class.

From the time I started school until I finished high school, several thousand miles were covered travelling between school and home. During the six years that I attended Jellerson's practically all of this travel was on foot. In good weather the walk along our country road was unusually pleasant. It was particularly exhilarating on frosty mornings in the fall when there might be a flock of Canada geese heading southwards high overhead. Flocks of red-winged blackbirds and bobolinks emitted their metallic chinks as they hurried past in their undulating flight. Black ducks were migrating, too, and every now and then one heard the popping of shotguns in Merrymeeting Bay. At that time of the year every kind of tree had its own shade of brilliant color. Even in winter, it was fun following the horses' path in the center of the snow-packed roads. On cold, calm mornings the smoke from farmhouse chimneys rose straight up and disappeared in a cloudless sky. But spring mornings were the best of all. Long before the leaves appeared, the last remaining faded-red fruits still clung to the light gray thorn bushes beside the road. Soon after the last vestiges of snowdrifts behind stone walls had disappeared, we looked for chipmunks along the roadside and watched an early woodchuck searching for something green on the brown hillside of the Call and Davis farms. With the sun still quite low in the east, those April mornings were made cheerful by the songs of birds so recently returned and the tattoo of a flicker on a dead limb high in a nearby tree. It seemed as if our road had an excitingly attractive environment most any time of year.

Notwithstanding all of the interesting things to see and hear on the way to the Corner, I remember some mornings when I had definitely depressed feelings. There never seemed to be any good explanation for those unpleasant moments, like the morning I wanted to cry because of a guilty feeling about the lunch in my red lunch box, usually containing two buttermilk biscuit sandwiches, a piece of pie, and a small bottle of milk. I felt that I was taking away the food that Pa and Mother had worked hard to provide. I often wondered why such feelings bothered me only for a short time in the morning – never at school or on the way home in the afternoon. Anyway, the spells were often quite brief. I felt all right as soon as I met someone to walk with along the way. They always wore off as soon as school was reached and things seemed cheerful enough on the way home. And neither after the sixth or seventh grade, nor during high school, can I remember having dejected moments on the way to school.

High school was more than twice as far from home as the elementary. To cover this longer distance when the roads were good, we brought Al's old heavy-framed bicycle down from the shed chamber where it had been stored for a dozen or more years. Al took apart the rear axle for cleaning and added fresh lubricant to the front one. The inner-tube tires had become brittle with age, so we bought a pair of tubeless tires at Fish & Ferber's shop in Bath. For the rear we got a white wall tire with rough red tread and for the front wheel a less expensive smooth black tire. While Al was mounting the tires on the rims at the workbench in our stable, I asked him if it was Mr. Ferber who sold us the tires. "No, that was Fish," he replied, "Ferber's dead." I ordered a luggage carrier and wire basket by mail from Sears Roebuck in Chicago, for carrying my books and lunch box. The old bike's heavy frame was too tall for my legs to reach the pedal in lowest position. Al remedied the situation by removing the seat post and clamping the saddle to the top frame. I rode the bicycle all four of the high school years, in spring and fall whenever the road was reasonably dry, making the distance in less than half an hour. Since there was no convenient safe place at school to leave the bike, I parked it in a stable in the Village and took the sidewalk.

When our dirt roads were too slippery for a bicycle and during winter months, I walked across our pasture to the railroad and followed the tracks into town. I cannot recall ever having walked to high school via our public road. The railroad offered a much shorter route and, although it was not the easiest walking in the world, I was able to adjust my steps to the spacing of the ties, covering a mile in fifteen minutes. When the snow became too deep for easy walking over our pasture, I wore snowshoes as far as the railroad, hid them beneath junipers near the fence and used them again on the way home. No matter how deep the snowfall, the Maine Central kept its tracks clear with its snowplow consisting of an engine and caboose with a heavy, V-shaped steel blade in front. Whenever we used the word snowplow we referred to the one used by the Railroad. On school days during the winter, I was often the first one up in our house. After eating a bowl of oatmeal from the double boiler that Mother had placed on the airtight stove the night before, I was usually on my way to high school before anyone else had come downstairs. Walking along the railroad on winter mornings was invigorating and sometimes even inspiring. During the short days of January the sun was just rising behind the woods east of the Abbagadasset as I was crossing our pasture. It was serenely quiet those cold mornings save for occasional cawing of a crow, the call of a blue jay, crowing of a neighbor's rooster, or the whistle of a distant train. The only continuing noise was the crunching of frosty snow beneath one's feet.

Chapter Five

Raising Chickens

Money was always a scarce item in our household. Pa kept most of it tucked away in his leather pouch-like wallet, in an inside pocket that he kept closed with a safety pin. It might as well have been stored in Fort Knox. Once a month Pa sat by the kitchen window on a Sunday afternoon and counted his money by spreading it on his lap. One day when I was four or five he dropped a coin that rolled beneath the table. I picked it up and ran into the next room.

"Bring it back and I'll give you a coin to keep," Pa said, not knowing the denomination of the one he'd dropped.

I hesitated.

"Yes, give the money to your father," Mother prompted, in obvious cooperation with Pa.

I gave Pa his quarter and received in return a shiny nickel to put in my perforated-tin-can piggybank through a slot in its red cover. Pa continued as the family treasurer until I was in high school, when, following much complaining by Genevieve and many arguments, Pa turned over all of the butter and egg money to Mother. After that, Mother paid for the groceries, kerosene, medicine, and the telephone bill. She helped buy clothing for my two youngest sisters with whatever money was left. Pa paid the big bills such as fire insurance, taxes, repairs to buildings, new equipment or livestock, and Vining's college expenses from other farm income that included sale of hay, vegetables, poultry and livestock, and also from his off-farm earnings as a fisherman and carpenter.

Two sisters in high school and a brother in college made a drain on our family income. They had first call on any surplus funds and it was nip and tuck for me to get any spending money. I'd have to look to my own resources for the wherewithal to buy many of the things I wanted, including items of clothing. There were two possibilities. One was to keep a small flock of hens, if I could persuade my parents to let me have a few of the farm layers. The other was to trap fur-bearing animals that were abundant in our area. Ever since I had been old enough to carry a lard paid full of water and a few quarts of oats or cracked corn, I had tended the hens and younger chickens much of the time. I had also kept four or five Peking-mallard ducks in the ledge pool back of the house during the summer and confined them to the barn cellar in the winter. Since I had this background and experience, my folks allowed me to keep twenty hens in the hen house Up-under-the-Hill, starting in March the year I was in the seventh grade, for whatever profit in eggs I could make from them. After the first year with this flock, Pa and Al built me another, smaller henpen near the old one. Thereafter I had two small flocks confined to separate yards at the southeast corner of the Hill. Both of the buildings were within sight of the house a short distance beyond our northern field. Unfortunately I had no income from the hens during the winter, for soon after Thanksgiving I returned them to the farm flocks where they could be adequately cared for during inclement weather.

This seasonal transfer of hens to and from the hen house Up-under-the-Hill had been the usual procedure for several years. They were carried after dark, a few at a time in a shorts sack over the shoulder. After the hens were brought back to the pens near the house in the fall when I was in fifth grade, an interesting incident took place. Having returned from school one pleasant afternoon in November, I noticed one of our pale-red hens foraging by herself in the field near the hen house Up-under-the-Hill. Realizing that the hens had been brought down from there a few weeks earlier, I went to see if she had gone back to lay eggs in her usual nest – a tendency that all hens seem to have. As I got near to the hen in the field, she ruffled her feathers and started clucking nervously. This behavior indicated that she was at least broody and possibly may have been sitting on a nest for some time. The hen door was open so I checked the nests inside. To my surprise I found, in a deep nest box nailed to the back wall, six fluffy, yellow baby chicks. They were all standing with their heads raised as if they may have been trying to climb out of the deep nest. Apparently they had been hatched for two days or more since they were much lighter in weight than day-old chicks that had not yet consumed the nu-trients stored in the yolk. Returning to the house for a basket, I told Mother about the find. We placed the small family in a low coop in the backyard surrounded by chicken-wire fence. They all ate a hearty meal of bread crumbs, cracked corn and milk. Being late in the fall and relatively cool weather, the chicks grew their feath-ers quickly. Before snowfall they were placed in the barn floor where they became mature birds by spring.

From the time I was in the seventh grade until I left for college in the fall of 1919, I made modest profits from my small flock of hens. I kept count of the eggs from my layers and packed them in the family case for shipment to Boston. Mother paid me for the eggs as soon as Pa cashed the egg check at the grain store. I seldom bought a hundred-pound bag of grain for my own use. Instead I weighed out a week's supply at a time from the farm grain barrels and Mother deducted this cost from the money she paid me for the eggs. I would have liked to receive the money that my hens brought when they were sold in Bath, but all income from dressed poultry went to Pa. I remember a single exception, however. It was an overly-fat hen that stayed on the roost most of the day. "She's liable to drop dead anytime," Pa told me, "you'd better dress her out and I'll take her to Cornish's for you." I got paid for that one.

One thing that made the making of money from poultry a nip and tuck proposition was poor egg production by our flocks during fall and winter when prices were high. Our hens laid well in spring and early summer when eggs brought only thirty cents per dozen, sometimes even less. The birds started to moult in September or October and, except for small eggs laid by early-hatched pullets, production remained low until March or April. Apparently other peoples' hens didn't lay too well in the fall and winter either, for one November we received the unheard-of price of seventy-five cents a dozen for a small shipment to Boston. A mid-January incident when I was in one of the lower grades at school impressed upon me the seriousness of our meager egg production in wintertime. Genevieve's birthday was the nineteenth of the month and Mother wanted to make a cake for the occasion. We probably had over fifty hens at the time but Mother had found only one egg that week, which she was saving for the cake. After completing the barn chores on the morning of the nineteenth, Pa came in for breakfast before going across the river to cut wood. He faced a long forenoon of heavy work. "Is there an egg in the house that I could have to go with the fried potatoes and salt pork?" he asked. Mother cooked him the earmarked egg and Genevieve had no cake that year.

A few winters later, while I was caring for a small flock that had the run of the barn floor, tie-up, scaffold and haymow, I noticed one hen that laid quite regularly during winter months. For weeks at a time, she laid a large brown egg every other day, sometimes oftener. Her predominantly white color, with a lacework of black around her neck and with black tail feathers plus a double comb, marked her as mostly White Wyandotte. But a wash of reddish brown along her back showed that she was of mixed breeds. I wondered why more of our hens didn't lay eggs in winter as well as this one. I got some ideas as to something that might be tried by listening to Vining who was in college. He spoke of the importance of inheritance and of the improvements in plants and animals through selective breeding. He also emphasized the contribution of the male parent to the quality of the offspring. It might be a good thing to do, I thought, to raise some of the white hen's chicks and keep one of them for the farm rooster.

My folks were in the habit of saving a rooster from one of the last flocks of chickens hatched each year. By so doing they avoided the expense of feeding a full-grown bird for two or three months when he wasn't needed. Chickens hatched in early summer would be plenty old enough for breeders the following spring. So I waited until school was ended in June before saving half a dozen eggs from the old white hen for hatching. By that time the barn floor flock had been moved to the barn cellar and the white hen was laying in a nest beneath the seat of an old sleigh parked in a dark corner. Other hens used the same nest but since our flocks were made up almost entirely of mixed breeds, no two hens laid look-alike eggs and I was able to recognize the good-sized brown egg laid by the hen that produced so well the previous winter. The need for formal trap-nesting of the desired layer was thereby avoided.

A hen is able to care for two or three times as many chicks as she can hatch in a single clutch of eggs. Taking advantage of this capability we usually "set" more than one hen at a time and consolidated all of the baby chicks in a single flock. The other hens from whom their chicks were taken were either given a new nestful of eggs to sit upon for another three weeks or they were placed in the "setters' coop" to overcome their broodiness and return to laying. Sometimes we ran into the problem of a mother hen refusing to accept a chicken of a color that was different from any of her own hatching. We might get around this difficulty by placing any off-colored chicks under the desired mother at night before the brood was removed from the nest. Occasionally we had to try two or three of the potential mothers before finding one that would own all of the chicks. Had our flocks been composed of a single, full-blooded strain of poultry there would have been little variation in the color of the chicks and the mothers would have been unable to tell one from another.

A few days before collecting the last of the six eggs from the old white hen, I transferred two broody hens from the big henpen back of the stable to nests in a quiet part of the barn where they would not be disturbed while incubating. A few poultry men in town were using kerosene-heated incubators, but we depended entirely on broody hens for our hatches. The setters were confined to their new nests on a few wooden eggs for a day or two so that they might become accustomed to their surroundings before they were given fertile eggs for hatching. Grain and water were kept nearby, along with a shallow box of wood ashes for the hens to dust in and keep down infestations of lice. While on the nest a setting hen is about the quietest creature in existence. She may raise her feathers and squawk a bit when something approaches and then settle back to perfect calmness. Once in a while she rises slightly and turns the eggs with her bill. But off the nest she is the fussiest thing alive – clucking continuously, fluffing every feather, and objecting to everything that comes near. It is easy to understand how the expression "mad as a settin' hen" came into popular use.

Within a few days the transplanted setting hens became sufficiently attached to their new nests so that both of them returned to their artificial eggs voluntarily after each feeding. It was then that I marked the white hen's six eggs with a pencil and placed them under one of the setters. To complete the nestful of eggs for hatching I added seven randomly selected eggs from our farm flock. The second hen was given the customary clutch of thirteen of these run-of-the-mill eggs. Fortunately our flocks of poultry were made up mostly of so-called heavy breeds that usually make good setters. We had none of the lightweight, white-egg-laying, Mediterranean breeds, like the Leghorns, that became broody rather rarely and were too high-strung to sit still long enough to hatch a chick. Our setters were conscientiously devoted to their task; they remained glued to the nest until the eggs hatched. I don't know how long they'd have kept it up if they had a batch of infertile eggs. Domestic chickens are derived from jungle fowl that were ground nesters and soil moisture provided favorable humidity conditions in the nest. To prevent the incubating eggs in our dry nests from drying out too much before hatching, we sprinkled them a few times with warm water during the last two weeks of incubation. If the setting hen had a mean disposition, we often received pecks on the hands while lifting the hen from the nest in order to sprinkle the eggs.

When the hens had sat upon their nests for nineteen or twenty days, the eggs showed the first signs of hatching. Pipping of the shell near the larger end of the egg by the chick's bill armed with a whitish egg tooth on its tip, accompanied by peeping from within the egg, was an early step in the birth of a chick. This was followed by rotating motion of the chick within the shell as the larger end of the eggshell was completely cut free like a lid and the newborn chick kicked himself clear of the confining shell. It was at this point that I was kept on my toes for a day or two, checking frequently on the emerging chicks so that I knew for sure which ones had hatched from the marked eggs. On the last visit to the nest one night I noticed three pipped eggs from which the chicks might emerge before I got around in the morning. To help in later identification of each individual, I removed a bit of the shell around the pipping place and, with the aid of a flashlight, noted whether the unhatched bird had a single or a double comb and at the same time got some idea as to the color of down on the face of the chick. These bits of information were helpful the next morning in identifying any dry, fluffy chickens that had hatched during the night. Since our poultry flocks were made up of different breeds, the hens showed much variation in color and markings and their offspring varied a great deal in appearance. All of this helped in the identification of chicks hatched from the marked eggs. Everything was not left to memory, however, as I kept a list of all numbered eggs placed under setting hens showing which hen laid each egg. When one of these eggs hatched a notation was made on the record sheet regarding the color and individual markings of the newborn chick, and also noting whether it had a single or double comb. None of us knew anything about telling the sex of a baby chick by anatomical examination. We had to wait a few weeks until they were partially feathered out before we could begin to tell the pullets from the roosters. With our heavy breeds, young pullets became covered with feathers at an earlier age than roosters.

In the secluded nest beneath the seat of the sleigh, all but one of the six marked eggs from the old white hen hatched. One might have expected that some of the chicks would have been yellow at first, showing that they would be mostly white like their mother at maturity. Instead they were all dark colored – two with a tinge of chestnut and three were mostly black. The black ones had an irregular white spot on their heads indicating that they would have barred feathers like our Plymouth Rocks when they grew up. Only two of the five chicks had double combs. The dark color of all five chicks provided good evidence that they were sired by our Plymouth Rock rooster. We had two roosters that year; the other one was a White Wyandotte with a trace of some other blood that gave his white feathers a yellowish tinge. But the Plymouth Rock was cock of the roost. I saw him defeat the white one earlier that summer in the most decisive battle between two roosters that I had ever witnessed. After several minutes of sparring and spurring, the Barred Rock got in a solid peck to the white rooster's head that flattened him for half a minute. I've seen many rooster fights but this was the only time there'd been a knock-out. The Wyandotte got to his feet and disappeared into the barn cellar. Instead of giving chase, the winner of the fight stood stock-still in the arena and crowed lustily several times. This encounter probably resulted in no consorting between the white rooster and the white hen and the five chicks were black or nearly so.

A full-blooded Barred Plymouth Rock rooster has an overall color tone of light gray. Our rooster had the barred markings on his feathers but his general color was a dark gray, almost blackish. This color pattern indicated that his mother may have been one of our Rhode Island Red hens and his father a Barred Rock. We knew from experience that mixing of these two breeds gave a lot of pure black offspring and that the black color was dominant and persistent in later generations. Mother remarked about the earlier broods of chicks we'd hatched that year before I saved the six eggs from the white hen, "We have more black chickens this year than you can shake a stick at." If I saved a farm rooster from one of the five dark chicks that had just been hatched, we'd probably have predominantly black poultry for the next few years. My parents would not object to this too strenuously. They had noticed that black hens usually made good layers. "Seems like the first pullet to start laying in the fall is one of the black ones," Mother noted. However, when it came to preparing dressed broilers and roasting fowl for market, black birds made more work for the womenfolk since every black pinfeather was very conspicuous and had to be removed. Pa liked to see bright yellow shanks on the dressed poultry we sold, in preference to the sooty scales on the legs of black fowl.

I kept close watch of the five selected white hen's chicks as they grew up in the flock with fifteen others that hatched at the same time under the two setting hens. Since there were no two chickens of the same size, shape, and color in this small flock, I had no trouble keeping track of the selected ones. When young chicks start feathering out, a few days can make quite a difference in their appearance so I watched the flock daily and took pains to identify each of the five special chicks as they underwent their developmental changes. The setting hen that we selected from the pair of broody ones that hatched the eggs proved to be a good mother to all of the chickens from both clutches. She accepted both batches of chicks as if she'd hatched them all herself. Being steady and not too nervous, she had not stepped on and crushed any of the fragile chicks while hovering over them during their first clumsy days out of the shell.

Of the five chicks hatched from the six selected eggs, three turned out to be pullets, leaving only two roosters from which to select a breeder for the next year. Two of the pullets were black with white markings when they became completely feathered; the third looked much like her Barred Rock father except she had more whitish feathers around her neck. The two roosters also resembled their male parent but the barring of the feathers was less distinct than his and there was a more general tinge of silver. Three of the five offspring had single combs like our Barred Rock rooster; only two of them inherited their mother's double comb, a pullet and, happily, a rooster.

This matter of comb type was of prime importance to our poultry because of frequent subzero temperatures on cold winter nights. Comb freezing was particularly hazardous for the male breeders. Mature chickens often tuck their heads beneath a wing while sleeping on the roost at night to keep their combs and wattles from becoming frostbitten. A hen can lose most of her comb from frostbite and continue to function as a good layer of fertile eggs, but a rooster that has lost his comb to low temperatures is useless as a breeder. He seems to have plenty of libido and enthusiastically mounts a receptive hen but he just sits there apparently unable to consummate the sexual act. He can't ejaculate. Seemingly it's a case of the spirit being willing but something's missing in the flesh. The tall, serrated, single comb of a rooster may be mostly exposed to the cold even when the bird has his head partly buried beneath his wing. Consequently single-combed roosters are prone to frostbite. A thick, compact, double comb retains body heat efficiently. I have never seen a double comb turn black, nor any portion of it slough off, even after exposure to subzero temperatures that often occur on winter nights in Maine.

Chapter Six

Trapping Fur Animals

As compared with income from eggs, it was "clearer" money that I earned by trapping. When the egg check came, I had to pay for the grain the hens had eaten. With trapping there was not even a license fee to be paid in those days. The biggest expense was the purchase of a new steel trap or two every few years. When I started to catch the local furbearers in the fall of 1910, Vining was away from home for the first time – a freshman at college. He would be home only for an occasional week-end and would have no further use for our ten or twelve traps; so I took over. Trapping was nothing new to me by that time. I had been catching rats around our farm buildings for a few years already. Two years earlier, Pa had showed me how to make a highly successful "set" for house rats. He used a light, wooden patent medicine box with dovetailed corners that he got for free at the drug store. The box was about six inches square, eight inches tall and open at the top. One of the smaller sizes of trap, a Blake and Lamb No. 1, was set and a piece of cotton placed in the bottom of the box and covered with cornmeal. The wad of cotton kept the cornmeal from slipping beneath the trencher and preventing a rat from springing the trap when he jumped into the box. A few crumbles of suet or small pieces of pork fat were scattered over the meal to make the set more tempting. On one or two occasions, I caught two young rats in the same trap when both jumped into the box simultaneously.

One problem that I encountered when I started trapping at the age of seven was my inability to set some of the new traps that had strong springs. I chose the older ones whose steel springs had become somewhat weakened through years of use.

"When would be the best time to start trapping this fall?" I asked Al before he left in September for his principalship in Greenville. "About the 20th of October, I'd think," he replied. "Most furs won't be worth much until they become prime about that time. Muskrats don't get really prime until winter, but they'll buy the ones caught in the fall, at a lower price."

On the last Saturday in October that year, I picked out five or six traps that I could set and went down to our swamp in the west pasture and set two or three of them around old muskrat houses. I set another in a hole in the top of the dike on Cromwell's meadow. With two or three traps left, I boldly crossed our east swamp to the outer beaver dam along the river. There I found an abandoned muskrat hole on the river side of the beaver dam a foot below high water mark. I set a trap in it. The weather that fall had been mild enough so that I was still going barefoot that day. It remained mild for a while and I was able to visit the traps the next day, Sunday, and also after school on Monday and Tuesday. All of the traps were undisturbed. But the middle of the week brought one of those cold northeast rainstorms with gale force winds that the folks called the "line gale" which, they said, would determine the direction of the prevailing wind for the remainder of the fall and the coming winter. It was followed by a light freeze that put an end to going barefoot for that year. I could get the traps in our west swamp and on Cromwell's Bridge with the shoes and rubbers I wore to school, but without rubber boots I was unable to get across our flooded east swamp to the trap at the edge of the river.

"You wouldn't be going down river past the Old Pine today, would you?" I asked Pa as he sat by the kitchen stove while I was leaving for school on my birthday the following week. "I set a trap the other day in a hole on our outer beaver dam right across from the cove below the Old Pine and haven't been able to get to it since the rain."

"How far down the beaver dam is it?" he asked.

"About half way to our south fence," I replied. "It's right close to a young willow that's growing on the dam. I think it's the only muskrat hole in that section of the dam."

"M-m-m," was the only response from Pa. He looked at me from beneath his eyebrows as much as to say, "What were you doing setting traps around in places where you can't get to them?" Taking my lunch box from the kitchen table, I left for school.

Pa was standing in the stable door when I returned that afternoon. I put books and lunch box on the table and walked towards him to get feed for the hens from the alleyway.

"You had a mink in that trap," he said. "I've stretched the skin on a board upstairs. He was a medium-sized one – not very dark. You ought to use a stouter stake to fasten your traps – that was a little withe, no bigger than your finger." The fact that such a small stake was adequate to hold the mink demonstrated the advantage of setting traps below the high water mark. An animal caught at high tide would drown immediately; or if caught at low tide, would drown with the incoming tide.

There was an interesting sequel to the catching of that mink. It came about as a result of our practice of feeding the carcasses of the furbearers we caught to the hens after chopping them into small pieces, or tossing the skinned animal to the pigs. That day Pa gave the mink to the hundred-fifty-pound pig we were raising for our winter pork. The pig became ill the next day. As he slowly recovered during the next several days, the margins of his ears and the distal half of his tail turned black. In the course of a week or two the blackened, necrotic tissues sloughed off, with no more apparent ill effects to the pig and we ate him that winter. There must have been something poisonous about the possibly overripe mink carcass. The pig's symptoms resembled those of cattle that have grazed on ergot-infested grasses – they often lose parts of their extremities also. After that experience, we buried any mink we caught as soon as we had removed the skin.

Open season for trapping came during those seasons of the year when school was in session. I was therefore restricted in my activities to make a little money from this source to early morning, late afternoon, weekends, and vacations. Tending muskrat traps before and after school on weekdays, in the fall and spring, was limited to a few days every two weeks when the tide was low mornings and evenings, because some of the best muskrat holes and roadways were well down towards low-water mark. On those days when low tide occurred around six o'clock, I got up early and tended traps in Pratt's Creek. After school those same days, I looked after traps set along the river. Since the time of tide came an hour later each succeeding day, I could set traps three, or at the most, four days at a time on these bi-weekly periods. In between, when the morning and evening tides were too high for muskrat trapping, I brought the traps ashore and set them for skunks in their upland holes. In the winter there was no way to trap muskrats along the ice-covered river. During those months, I caught a few of them in their swamp houses. Later it became illegal to catch muskrats in their houses. Also in the winter I watched for skunk tracks in the snow during thaws and tried to make some catches before the weather turned cold again. I also set a number of weasel traps baited with frozen tomcod at likely nearby locations. In our collection of traps were two large ones with double springs we called fox traps. I set them a number of times but was never successful in catching one of those crafty animals.

I caught my first skunk one weekend in the fall of 1911. The trap was set in an abandoned woodchuck hole on Uncle John's Island – a low peninsula that protruded into the swamp in Amasa's east field, within shouting distance of our house. When I discovered on a Sunday morning that I had trapped a skunk, I called to Vining who was home from college for the weekend and happened to be in our dooryard at that moment. He came to my aid with Pa's 10-gauge, double-barrel loaded with a light charge, black-powder shell that Pa had prepared for shooting rats in the barn cellar. After dispatching the animal, Vining returned to the house, saying, "You'll have to skin him yourself, I guess. I have to take the train back to Lewiston this afternoon and I can't get all smelled-up." With my brass-lined, rosewood-handled jackknife from Sears Roebuck, well-sharpened, and having skun [sic] several muskrats, I had little difficulty in removing the pelt from the skunk. It must have been a "broad-striper" with a lot of white on its back, since I have an invoice slip from G. R. Hunnewell, the fur dealer in Auburn, dated December 19, 1911, listing a #4 skunk for forty cents. A nearly black, #1 skunk with only the white patch on top of its head brought about two dollars at that time.

After that first skunk, I trapped the smelly animals for several years before I had the inevitable misfortune of getting splattered with their scent. It was in mid-March of one of my last years in high school, during spring vacation, with the accumulated snows of winter three or four feet deep under trees. I was on snowshoes in the woods on the other side of the river when I came across and followed the skunk. He was freshly out of his hibernation den and the footprints in the damp snow were easily followed because of a conspicuous trace of brownish soil along the meandering trail. The tracks led to a snowy hole at the base of two large hemlocks growing on a common stump in Kil Maxwell's woods not far from Aunt Emma's former home on the Kennebec. There were no skunk footprints going away from the opening. With a hatchet, I cut a small spruce sapling that had died from over-shading by the taller trees and slipped the ring on the end of the trap chain over the larger end of the knotty pole.

The next morning, after another snowshoe walk through the woods, I found the trap pulled into the mouth of the burrow. Gently withdrawing the pole, I felt a counter movement at the far end. With the single-shot .22 in my right hand, I used the other to pull the trap and its contents into view. First the trap chain appeared and then the trap, partially concealed by the tail of a skunk. Slowly withdrawing the trap a little closer, I saw one of the skunk's eyes looking at me from the semi-darkness of the den. I was maneuvering for a vital shot when, suddenly and with no warning, a squirt of the yellowish liquid struck me precisely on the forehead. Fearful for my eyesight and thankful for the abundance of heavy snow, I washed my face several times to get rid of the odoriferous substance. I remembered at once what Mother had told me about Aunt Susan Buker who was sprayed in the face by a skunk one evening when she reached into a barrel to gather eggs; her eyesight, Mother had said, was not affected. Thank Heavens! Relieved that I was still able to see, I proceeded to complete the task at hand. This incident delayed my coverage of the trap line that morning and I was late for dinner. My parents and Minerva had nearly finished their meal when I entered the kitchen. Trying to appear nonchalant, I hung my outer garments near the door and walked between the table and stove on my way to wash up at the kitchen sink. As soon as I had passed the table where the folks were eating, Minerva straightened in her chair and exclaimed, "Fury! Good Heavens! What did you get into?" As I began to wash thoroughly my face and hands, she continued, "That smell is terrible! Do we have to put up with this sort of thing?" My parents, always pleased to have me earn some money by trapping, made no further comment. I wore a cap that day that belonged to Al. It was a heavy dark blue woolen cap, with fur ear-lappers. Al told me that following summer that I could have the cap. For several years, during periods of damp weather, the cap gave off that still-strong unmistakable odor.

My experience under Kil Maxwell's hemlocks that day settled some arguments that a few of us boys at school had been having about the mechanics of how a skunk threw its scent. Since the skunk usually held his tail over his back when he went into action, Bill Trufant claimed that the bad-smelling substance was thrown by switching the tail – the same way some thought a porcupine threw his quills, or more like the way farmers applied water suspensions of lead arsenate to their potato plants with a whisk broom. Merton Webber claimed that the scent was expelled as a concentrated fog cloud that expanded larger and larger as it neared the target. After that day in March, I knew that neither theory was quite right.

The amount of money I made from trapping depended on the abundance of the furbearers in our locality that year, the success I had in catching them, and the price of furs. Every fall while I was in the fifth to eighth grades and while in high school, I caught about forty muskrats in late October and November. In the early years, muskrats brought from thirty to fifty cents for an average fall-caught skin. In later years, during the latter part of World War I, and for a year or two after the Armistice, the same quality of furs brought a dollar or a dollar and a half. It seemed that muskrats did not have fully prime fur until mid-winter or early spring, when their skins were worth the most. One spring, shortly after the war, I received as much as four dollars for a single muskrat caught after the ice had left the river. I have an old invoice received from G. R. Hunnewell after I sent him the mink I caught on our beaver dam which reads as follows:

November 25, 1910
14 Rats, fall ......@ .35 ....4.90
1 #2 mink, unprime 4.50
                    Total 9.40

Life on the Abbagadasset

It was October 31st that Pa found the mink in my trap. The four and a half dollars was the biggest birthday present I had that year. It was a lot of money – as much as Pa received for two days' work as a carpenter. During my senior year in high school, I received nine dollars for a single mink pelt – the highest price I was ever paid for a skin of this species. Each year that I was trapping, I usually caught one or two mink – all of them were caught accidentally in traps set for muskrats in the fall. These fall catches of mink and muskrats were followed by winter catches of four or five white weasels – called ermine in finished furs. Also four to five skunks were usually caught from fall to spring each trapping season. About ten muskrats were taken each winter from their swamp houses. The last catches of the season consisted of from five to ten muskrats in late March and early April. It was a big thrill, as a farm boy, to receive a check in the mail for furs I had sent to dealers in Auburn or Lewiston. Some of the checks were deposited in my account at the Bath Trust Company, were I was saving up money for college. We tried sending a few furs to St. Louis a couple of times with unsatisfactory results – the prices they paid, we thought, were lower than those we could expect from our buyers in Maine. We sent the furs to market by mail, a few skins at a time. The odor of the raw furs in shipment was sometimes a problem in containment. One time, a few days after we had sent a package containing several muskrats and a skunk by mail to Hunnewell in Auburn, the local postmaster met Pa on the village street and told him, "You ought to tell your boy to wrap more newspaper around the skins he sends through the mail. The last package he sent smelled so strong we had to keep it in the window until train time."

After I entered college, I continued to pick up a little money by trapping on weekends at home and during vacations. One Sunday in January, I returned to college with a single weasel skin that I had caught a couple of weeks earlier. I also took back to the dormitory enough sandwiches, turnovers, and apples to last a day or two, so I could delay eating at the College Commons until Tuesday night or Wednesday. After sharing some of the things with my roommate, the food ran out after breakfast on Tuesday of that week. As soon as my last class was over Tuesday afternoon, I took the weasel pelt to the nearest dealer, T. J. Murphy & Sons, at the corner of Lisbon and Ash streets in Lewiston. One of the Murphy sons was doing the buying that afternoon. He smoothed the fur of the weasel on the counter and held it up to the light for close examination.

"That's a medium size. It's pretty badly stained. I'll pay you sixty cents."

"I'd hoped to get a little more than that," I replied. "That's a pretty good-sized weasel. They all have a little yellow on their hind parts."

Mr. Murphy laid the skin on the counter and brushed it again. I was prepared to take it across the Androscoggin to Mr. Hunnewell in Auburn if necessary, to get top price.

"Well, how much do you want for it?"

"I think it's worth seventy-five cents."

"Okay, I have to catch a train to New York," Mr. Murphy said, as he handed a slip to his secretary. "Pay him for this," he told her.

I have forgotten the name of the cafeteria that was diagonally across Lisbon Street from the Murphy establishment. Maybe it was Longley's. Anyway, I went there immediately and had the big meal for the day – a bowl of beef stew with bread and butter, for fifteen cents.

Chapter Seven

Sounds

Although our farm was situated in rural countryside, a supposedly quiet environment, there were many noticeable daytime sounds and noises in the night. Most of the audible things were pleasant, some meaningful, some melodious, and others mystifying. Some of the things we heard were animate, others inanimate but wholly natural, and some, often the loudest, were inanimate, man-made and plainly mechanical. One of the rarest and faintest, yet so gratifying to hear, was the distant moan of the foghorn near Seguin at the mouth of the Kennebec. We heard this far-away warning only on those rare occasions when atmospheric conditions were just right to bring the sound waves up the river. It was a mournful noise, a low moan suggestive of a metal buoy swinging captive over some treacherous ledge, whose presence it was betraying to passing ships. A similar, slow and plaintive but somewhat louder sound was the distant whistle of trains on the line between Bath and Brunswick across the Bay; or, if more from the southeast, on the Bath to Wiscasset line. Nearer at hand, we paid less attention to the louder, noisy trains and their shrill whistles that were sounded on the way past our farm. We told the approximate time of day by passenger trains. On days with northwest wind, when the warning blasts of an eastbound train was sounded for Pratt's Crossing while it was crossing Cromwell's meadow, the noise reached our house with undiminished loudness, sharp and clear. Aside from their whistles, the long heavy freight trains made a lot of clatter, as compared with the faster, smoother Flying Yankee or the Bar Harbor Express. Blasts from the automobile horns were uncommon when I was growing up, and the noise from airborne traffic was more than unknown in the clear blue sky.

A very imposing whistle came from Amasa's sawmill a mile down the river at the west end of the lower bridge. We never failed to hear its two or three long blasts, sounded on weekdays at seven o'clock in the morning, twice at noon, and again at knocking-off time later in the day. The peacefulness of Sundays was enhanced by the quiet of the mill. We could also hear the less audible puffing of the steam engine and the hum of the circular saw as it sliced a board from a moving log. Finally the end of the log was reached and the hardest work for the saw was over and the carriage paused before returning to make another board. At this point, there was a rapid throbbing sound the engine made, temporarily relieved of its sawing load. That noise sometimes confused me while hunting in the woods. On quiet days, when I was hunting partridge within earshot of the mill, the sudden throb of the engine often gave me a sudden start. It sounded like some wise old grouse flushing somewhere ahead of me, out of sight behind the trees.

As for making any noises of its own, the Abbagadasset, when free of ice, was in all respects a quiet stream. It's true the tide flowed fast on the strength of flood or ebb – fast enough to make ripples around a midstream stake, and dozens of whirlpools in the eddies behind a rock or bridge. But even when it was fastest flowing, the water made no noise that was easily perceptible to the human ear.

However, if a wind was blowing, the slap-slap of the waves against the square upturned bottom of a skiff made this type of boat quite useless for hunting ducks. But here was frequent man-made noise along the river, such as the ker-chunk, ker-chunk of oars and oar-locks as Old Santy rowed his heavy skiff against the tide. In the years before Al built his motorboat, the river's quiet was now and then broken by the slow putt-putt of Charlie Blair's towing engine in his "naphtha boat," as we called it because of the fuel used. Making a lot of noise, Charlie often towed a raft of logs with his twenty-five foot "towboat" up-river to Dinsmore's sawmill. A few days later, he'd bring back the freshly-sawed lumber on his scow in tow.

Each year, at the approach to fall, one morning was extra noisy. It was opening day on waterfowl. The first year or two that I was big enough to hunt ducks, the season opened the first day of September. But later, beginning with the fall I was a sophomore in high school, the State Legislature, at the last moment and only a day or two before everyone expected the shooting to begin, pushed back the opening day two weeks. Since then there have been a number of steps taken to curtail the hunting season still further in view of the diminished numbers of wildfowl. Opening day in Merrymeeting Bay sounded like a giant celebration of the Fourth of July. For an hour or two after the legal shots were fired, there was a continuous popping of shotguns all over the Bay and up and down our rivers as far as one could hear. When Vining went to France with the A.E.F. in 1917, his first letter after arriving at the Western Front described the noise of battle as much like that of the first day of duck hunting in Merrymeeting Bay.

Some seasonal sounds were signs of enterprising activities. In winter, the steady chopping of a woodsman's axe could be heard in nearby woods and on a day, now and then, the baying call of Hal Cheney's foxhound broke the chilly silence. In early spring, after the frost was out of the ground, one could hear the thump of a heavy, wooden maul as Uncle Everett stood in his horse cart and drove replacement stakes into his pasture fence. The stakedriver bird in some swamp might answer. A few weeks later, Uncle Ed turned his cows to pasture and we could hear him shouting at them night and morning. Pa said he could tell by the exuberant hollering which days he had been to Bath. "He hollers louder after a drink or two," he said. On hot forenoons in July, the chatter of horse-drawn mowing machines could be heard in the hayfields around our home. This was followed in the afternoon, after there had been time for the new-mowed hay to dry a bit, by the rattle of high-wheeled tiger rakes that made a loud clatter as they came to a windrow and dropped their loads.

Occasionally we heard another noise that resembled distant thunder and shook our house a bit. I first heard this booming sound as a five-year-old coloring pictures in my bird book on the kitchen floor.

"What's that noise?" I asked Mother.

"That's blasting," she replied.

"What's blasting?"

"Oh, they have a feldspar mine down in Topsham and they use explosives to break up the rock so that they can haul it to the mill and grind it to a powder."

"What do they do with feldspar?"

"They use it for making dishes, like our plates, and cups and saucers."

"Do they make our glasses with it, too?"

"No. Glass is made from sand."

"Oh."

Sometimes when a train was going by, a loud bang not unlike the report of a gun was heard. Mother told me that was caused by the train running over a torpedo that workmen had left on the rail to warn the engineer that there were people working on the tracks ahead.

Another noise heard on the coldest winter nights within the confines of the house was a muffled boom followed sometimes by a very slight vibration in the walls. It was a startling, often scary sound. Pa said it was the frost "starting a roof nail in the rafter." It seems that temperatures zero or below caused a contraction of the iron nail so that its sharp end was pulled from the dry rafter. At the same time, the roof board that had been pulled tightly against the rafter by the contracting nail sprang back to its former position when the nail "let go." A somewhat similar but duller sound was heard at times in the Maine woods on extremely cold days, especially early in the winter, when a limb or a small tree was burst by freezing of the water within the "green" wood.

"The telephone wires are singing tonight," Pa said as he returned from the barn after giving the cattle a late snack of hay on a particularly cold night in midwinter. Even before we had a telephone installed, we could hear the whistling vibration of the wires stretched between poles along the road. It was a clear penetrating sound, that we could hear in our bedrooms late at night when the temperature was low and the wind was right.

In winter, the noisiest and most frequent of all the natural sounds around our country place were those made by the ice on the Abbagadasset. We heard the noise as soon as the river froze over, usually around Thanksgiving time, when, at low tide, pieces of shell ice, formed at high tide above the thicker ice on the high flats, broke off in loose plates and slid down across the smooth ice of the channel with every lowering tide. We could hear this continuous noise clearly most anywhere in our house on calm cold nights. The wind and interfering noises kept us from hearing sliding ice during the day. I remember listening to it in the evening stillness of our cold bedroom until I fell asleep. That was the time of year, too, when foxes liked to yap at night in the woods across the river. Unfortunately, the chorus of sliding ice lasted for two weeks at the most. It ended with the first snowfall, when the snow then prevented any sliding of the window glass plates of broken ice.

Later in the winter, when the ice had thickened to a foot or more, less frequent but louder and more sinister noises emanated from the river. The giant ice sheets slipped and bumped each other in their fight for space as the flood tide raised them into a narrower space from shore to opposite shore. After low-water-slack and the tide was on the rise, the big, central sheet of ice which spanned the channel wedged against ice sheets left lying on the flats when the tide went out. All the time, whenever the temperature was well below freezing point, the big sheets of ice, super-chilled by the cold, grew constantly in width from accretions at the edges where water surfaced and froze in the cracks formed when the ice sheets, lying on the channel bank, cracked at low tide. By February, after weeks of sub-freezing weather, the increments resulted in broken layers pushed straight up or on a slant. We heard the effects of this frigid struggle, transmitted across the snowy field in a heavy code of icy scrapes and thumps, or often a prolonged and cracking noise. With the rise and fall of tide, we often heard a progressive cracking sound as a huge ice sheet tried to bend too much and fissured for a distance of possibly a hundred feet or more. From the sound, it was easy to visualize a two-foot layer of ice cracking, not all at once, but starting at some tension spot and continuing for perhaps a full second, or even longer, to some distant edge, maybe a hundred yards up or down the stream. Such icy thuds, creaks and groans may be not at all unlike the movements of earth crust plates along some fault, that cause earthquakes here and there. We could hear all this in our living room on frosty nights. It was as if Nature were presenting, with the cooperation of tide and temperature, and the tidal river as the stage, a frosty midwinter audio-visual show. We slept within its sound.

Among other inanimate sounds we listened to, there was one we heard least often that delighted us the most. It was a tiny, seasonal waterfall a goodly distance away on the other side of the railroad, yet near enough to be clearly heard if one listened, after a heavy rain, on calm evenings in early spring. It was located in a shallow wooded gulch in Hackett's field beyond the tracks on Cromwell's meadow. The steep sides of the shallow gully formed a trough that drained a large area of hillside sod. In the bottom of the gully was a ledge with an exposed width of only a foot or so and with a perpendicular two-foot drop near the gully's mouth. We called it the Falls. For most of the year, no water at all flowed over the rocks, but while the snow was melting in the spring or after a copious fall of rain, there was a miniature torrent coming down the small ravine. We used to stand in our dooryard at dusk, listening swampwards to our neighborhood's lone water cascade.

In retrospect, the most pleasant sounds of our countryside in Maine were animate ones – like the songs of birds and the springtime choruses of frogs and toads. The small brown wood frogs with a black band through the eye – we called them "croakers" – were the first amphibians to punctuate the stillness of vernal air. They started croaking in the pools beside the railroad where the tracks went through some low spot in the woods. A day or two later, the peepers began to sing. These little tree frogs, with a dark X on their backs and a tiny suction cup on each toe, filled the evening air with music by their high-pitched call. It took me quite a while one night with my newly-acquired flashlight to find the maker of this shrill noise in our swamp at the foot of our west-pasture hill. I brought him home and left him in a jar of water on the kitchen table with some blades of swamp grass, on which the frog climbed for a perch. At breakfast time next morning, he startled us with his piping whistle. We were all amazed at the size of the air sac that inflated from his throat when he made his call. It seemed as large as the tiny frog himself. A few nights later, we heard the leopard and green frogs in the swamp. Then the trill of the common toad joined the chorus. The toad often sang during daylight hours, too. Like the peeper, the common toad inflated a big bubble beneath his chin when he made his noise. Later on, from the last of May until late July, we heard the deep jug-o-rum of the bullfrog coming from Amasa's pond.

Among the birds, the cumulative efforts of hundreds of red-winged blackbirds in the trees around our house made their chorus most welcome so early in the spring. When we heard the blackbirds, we were sure that spring had come at last. The swallows arrived the last of April and kept our barn filled with their song until after the mows were filled with hay. One of the prettiest songs was that of the wood thrush singing in the woods across the river near sundown on quiet nights in May. Although the honking of a goose was nothing new, we always went outdoors to spot the V-shaped flock of Canada geese passing high overhead, either in fall or spring. There was one natural sound which I thought to be mechanical the first time I heard it. One Sunday afternoon in May, when I was seven or eight, Vining took me for a row up river in the skiff. As we approached the Mill Pond, I heard a repeated noise like someone trying to start a balky motor of some sort. It gave a few putts then abruptly stopped. I remarked, "The Halls are having difficulty getting their stationary engine started." "That's a partridge drumming," Vining said. I had heard the noise before in the woods near our house.

There was a sound coming from overhead we used to hear on calm evenings in April, but for years we never knew what made it. It was a short undulating noise, lasting only a few seconds, and sounding something like a sheet flapping in the wind on the clothes line. It came from the sky, as if made by some spirit up among the clouds. It was several years later before I knew the maker of this strange sound. One cloudy day, in broad daylight, I watched a Wilson's snipe make the noise every time he made repeated dives accelerated by erratic wingbeats. It was the bird's mating call, often known as winnowing.

There is a sinister cry of a big bird that I always wanted to hear, but never have. It is the blood-curdling screech of the great-horned owl. Pa heard it at midnight once when he was towing a raft of lumber from Dinsmore's Mill past Cromwell's ledge. It had been dark and quiet all the way since he had left the Mill Pond at the head of the river. He was almost home, with our shore just around the bend, when suddenly there was a terrific scream from a tall pine near the ledge. "It was the damnedest noise I ever heard," he said. "I was glad that I was close to home. Someone told me afterwards that those big cat owls make a noise like that once in a while." Great horned owls were always plentiful in the thick, coniferous woods of our neighborhood. I occasionally saw them on heavily overcast days or towards nightfall along the river. The distinctive hoot of this owl: Whoooo - whoooo -whoo-whoo - whoo-whoo, was heard after nightfall the year round. But after all the hours of darkness I have spent along the river, I have yet to hear the great horned owl's unearthly cry, described by some as being like the scream of a woman in distress. Crows frequently held their noisy "town meetings" when they found one of the big predators hiding in some dense treetop in the daytime. One night in August, as I was sitting on the ledge at the tip of our point, one of the big birds swooped low directly over me – a huge, dark shape, maybe ten feet overhead, against the faint light of the moonless sky. The bird came from the direction of the same pine near Cromwell's ledge and disappeared silently in the darkness.

With dark woods of mixed pine, hemlock, spruce and fir not too far from home, it took only the active imagination of a ten-year-old boy to fill the shady recesses of those fancied forests with aggressive predators, some of which surely might be dangerous to man. My heart skipped a number of beats at supper one midwinter night when Genevieve told me something she had heard at high school that day. Helen Wildes, her classmate from our part of town, had told her that "Ira Allen saw a long, gray animal cross the road while he was driving to work in the Village just at daylight one morning that week. It was near the foot of the second of the three hills. He thought it was a mountain lion." Such a report, although the animal might have been a dog, was all that was necessary to start some speculative thoughts. The three hills were between Jellerson's Crossing and Clay Hill. We took that road every time we went to the Village. It was flanked with habitationless woods on both sides for half a mile. By the time the dishes were washed and dried, I saw those woods as the home of a prowling panther, of powerful build and dangerous. Fortifying my speculations was the fact that, the fall before, Mr. Bremner, who lived in Aunt Emma's house on the Kennebec, had caught a Canada lynx in a trap set for a fox. To claim his bounty the animal was taken to the Village, where it was viewed with excitement and awe by many of the local residents. Then, too, hadn't I heard strange noises coming from our woods at night?

No sooner than the iron skillet was hung in the cabinet beneath the kitchen sink, and Pa had settled into his rocking chair before the stove with his clay T.D. pipe, but I got on my sweater and went out to the chilly porch to listen for sounds in the distant woods. Sure enough, from the direction of those wooded hills where Ira saw the animal, I heard every once in a while a strange call that echoed slightly through the woods. It was a somewhat prolonged call, that could, with some imagination, easily be classified as a screech. More proof, I was sure, that some unfriendly beast, probably a cougar, was prowling the woods around us, unbeknownst to the local folks. Trying to appear not too excited, I returned to the kitchen and attempted to tell what I had been hearing. No one paid much attention to my story. After a couple of minutes, Pa arose slowly from his chair, slipped on his heavy felt boots, sheepskin jacket, woolen cap and stepped outside. I followed feeling elated that Pa had taken that much interest in my observation. We listened for a moment in the cold, wintry silence. "Hear that!" I said. "That's it!" After hearing the noise two or three times, Pa made a seemingly unconvinced, "Mm-m-m," and returned to the warmth of the cookstove. Relaxed again in his chair, Pa told the others, "There is some kind of noise over there around Jellerson's Crossing." "Could you tell what it is?" Mother asked. "Nope, I dunno what it is. Could be an owl or maybe a fox; they make queer noises once in a while," Pa replied. Nevertheless, since I was too young to have a gun, I avoided the woods entirely for the remainder of the winter. When I tended my muskrat traps in Fred Beal's swamp and in our swamp near the railroad, I took the long way around, across the open stretch of Cromwell's meadow, to avoid the clump of spreading white pines on Beal's Point and the patch of evergreens in our west pasture. My only weapon was Pa's light shingling hatchet that I used for cutting through the grass, cat-tail stems and mud with which the muskrats built the walls of their houses. It would be inadequate, I felt, for meeting the lunge of some hungry cat that might be lying on some horizontal limb. My fears of a mountain lion in our area never were substantiated, although there were some places in New England where these large animals were thought to exist. As in my case, solid evidence of their presence was usually lacking.

I heard John Maxwell tell Pa how puzzled he was by a noise he heard one dark, overcast night in May when he went to seine his weir in the small hours of the night. The weir was located up river from John's boat landing, in the second cross-channel above the big road bridge. He had paddled out to the weir and found that the tide was still coming in strongly. It would be fifteen minutes or so before tip-top high water and the weir was probably catching more and more fish by the minute. John decided to wait until the tide slackened before seining. He took a couple of half hitches with the boat's painter around the stake in the weir's leader and sat down in the stern of the skiff. Except for the noise of a few frogs in the alder swamp to the north, everything was completely quiet along the river. There was light enough in the sky for John to see the tops of the trees against the horizon and some of the tallest stakes in the weir a few feet away. The rest was darkness and silence. As he sat there John heard an animal drinking at the river's edge on a wooded point less than fifty yards up river. John listened, motionless. Whatever the animal was, John decided it must have been a stealthy one. "I heard no sound like a foot being pulled out of the mud nor any sloshing of footsteps in the water. No snapping of twigs, nor nothing to make so damn much noise while he drank." John seined his weir, with the knowledge that he was not the only creature prowling the Abbagadasset that moonless night.

Pa and I once heard a strange inanimate noise that we could not identify. We heard it first one pleasant afternoon in August of 1919, soon after leaving the Shore on our way to the house. We had little doubt that it was made by some sort of combustion motor. By the time we climbed the pasture bars, it sounded loud and clear. It seemed to be something approaching the railroad down by the Davis farm. On the hill by the Big Rock, we stopped for a moment to get a better fix on the source of the noise that was getting louder all the time and seemed to fluctuate in volume from one moment to the next.

"It's coming up the railroad," Pa said. "Must be one of them motor hand-cars the section crew ride on."

We hurried across the field towards the road so that we could see whatever it was when it crossed Cromwell's swamp along the tracks. The noise now came directly from the west but there was nothing on the railroad in that direction.

"Must be a threshing machine or something over at Hackett's, seems to be coming from that direction," Pa added. But we could see no activity of any sort around any of the farms on the other road. Pa finally concluded, "It must have been something on the railroad that went by before we got there to see it."

The sound, most like that of a gasoline motor, now seemed to come from the northwest behind the woods Up-under-the-Hill. It grew steadily weaker as it faded away in the northeast. We returned to the house and thought nothing more about the unusual noise. After supper that evening, Mother had one of her frequent telephone chats with Aunt Abbie. We were sitting on the front porch when she finished her conversation. After Mother joined us, she said, "They saw a flying machine go over this afternoon. They thought it followed the railroad up towards Augusta." Pa looked at me. "That was the noise we heard!" For failing to look skyward, we had missed seeing our first airplane.

Chapter Eight

Sources of Energy

Had there been an energy crisis while I was growing up, we would have scarcely noticed it on the farm. I was always amazed at the hours of hard work we could get from our horse after he had eaten only a pitchforkful of hay and two quarts of oats. The horse's enormous capacity plus our own muscular efforts, which we referred to as elbow grease, provided most of the energy we needed in our many and varied activities on the farm. According to twentieth century standards, these would be regarded as slow energy sources; but they were plentiful and inexpensive, entirely sufficient for the jobs we had to do. Firewood was the answer to all our heating needs. This fuel provided our energy for cooking too. A five-gallon can of kerosene furnished us with light for a few months – even in wintertime. In the spring, a cupful or two of this fuel was used to fill a tin can into which handpicked potato bugs were dropped, and for saturating a rag wrapped around the end of a pole with which at night we put the torch to tent caterpillars massed in their nests at dusk.

Aside from our limited usage of kerosene, and before Al's gasoline-powered boat came upon the scene, our annual use of petroleum products was very small. Pa bought a gallon of liquid fly-killer once a year for spraying the cows as soon as they were brought in from the pasture. It kept their tails quiet and out of our faces at milking time. A quart of machine oil once a year was sufficient to lubricate the mowing machine, hay rake, grindstone and "wheel-barrer" bearings, plus rust-prevention coatings on our iron tools. The mowing machine had small oil cups with flip-covers, cast in the housing of its main bearings. In order to make each application of oil last longer we placed in each oil cup a small wad of sheep's wool that we collected from Amasa's barbed-wire fence. The wool retained the oil and released it slowly to the bearing, providing the essential lubrication for a half-day's work at cutting hay. A one-pound can of mica axle grease kept our wagon and horse cart from squeaking for a couple of years. We kept a five-cent jar of Vaseline petroleum jelly on the kitchen mantelpiece for use on burns, sunburn, chapped hands and cold sores. Pa had a ten-cent jar of the same material in the tie-up to use as ointment for the cows. For removing grease spots from clothing we kept a small bottle of naphtha on a shelf in the pantry cabinet, away from the stove.

The long, cold winters in Maine required a lot of heat to keep us warm. This energy was entirely supplied by wood. For providing the heat we needed, we had two types of wood-burning stoves and two "airtights." The kitchen cookstove provided all of our heat for cooking and much of our space-heating needs throughout the year. Two sources of hot water were the teakettle on the kitchen stove and an eight-gallon, lid-covered tank attached to the end of the stove opposite the firebox. One of our airtight stoves stood in the sitting room, close to the kitchen door. A taller, fancier but seldom-used airtight provided heat on special occasions in the parlor. Some years, the one in the parlor went the entire winter without being used.

In the first years after Pa bought our farm, he built the attached ell which contained the kitchen, the woodshed and an unfinished shed-chamber overhead. He did not extend the cellar underneath this new addition. Pa later regretted this omission and said, "This kitchen's the hardest room in the house to keep warm; its floor stays so blamed cold." Consequently, after supper on the coldest nights, we let the fire in the cookstove die down and everyone moved into the sitting-room with all doors closed. A good fire was maintained in the airtight stove all evening. Pa may have had an ulterior motive in making this move on cold nights because there was a round flue in the ceiling, directly above the airtight stove, that opened into his bedroom above. The difficulty in keeping the kitchen warm, however, was demonstrated in the morning by the window-glass thick ice on the pails of water on the shelf by the kitchen sink. Mother took advantage of the flat top of the sitting-room stove and placed her double boiler full of oatmeal there before going to bed. It would be hot and well-cooked in the morning for our breakfast before going to school.

To make sure that we never ran out of fuel for comfort and for cooking, we tried to maintain an ample woodpile the year round. Sources of firewood were as varied as the different kinds of wood we burned. Previous to 1914, when Aunt Emma sold her Kennebec farm, Pa was thankful for her permission to take all the wood we needed from her woods which extended westward to the Abbagadasset almost directly across the river from our Shore. Each winter while I was in grade school, Pa kept a snow road open to Aunt Emma's woods across the river. On nearly every Saturday in winter, every year, I accompanied him on his trips to the woods. Here we spent an hour or more felling an old beech or maple, nearly two feet in diameter at the butt, and cutting it into such lengths as we could roll onto the horse sled with the aid of skids and cant dogs. Back to the woods, after we had felled a large tree on the weekend, Pa returned while I was at school the follow-ing week and brought back the smaller portions of the trunks along with the larger branches.

It was slow work sawing through the frozen hardwood trunks with a cross-cut saw. Genevieve once complained to my folks that I would become round-shouldered from bending over so much with the two-man saw, but Mother replied, "Fiddlesticks. A little work never hurt anyone." We brought the hardwood logs to our backyard where we sawed off stove lengths and split them into stove-size pieces at our leisure during warmer months. Near the river bank, on the way home, we stopped in a stand of young gray birches and cut several of them to be chopped into stove lengths at home for the kitchen stove that evening. Although "green," this birch wood with its oily bark burned well in the cookstove, with a lot of heat. There was one difficulty, however, in burning green wood. The volatile creosote and steam from such fuel condensed in our brick chimneys in cold weather. The brown liquid seeped through the chimney bricks and ran down the brickwork and, in spite of all the rags we placed around the chimneys upstairs, some of the creo-sote seeped through and stained the whitewashed plaster ceiling above the stoves.

We gleaned a lot of our fuel from the river. Driftwood was a constant source of firewood for us. During the ice-free months, the tide was continually bringing logs, old timbers of a bridge or wharf, and various other kinds of wood such as pulpwood sticks, into the Abbagadasset. One spring someone must have lost a cord or two of maple cordwood, maybe from near Bath or perhaps from the Androscoggin. That year we picked up several skiff-loads of seasoned, four-foot wood, some of it already split for easy handling. Possibly, too, it may have been that someone's scow had grounded on a sloping bank when the tide was high, and, as the tide went out, the scow tilted sharply and the cargo of cordwood may have slid into the drink. Another time we salvaged two forty-foot spruce wharf-logs that had drifted in from some abandoned pier on the Kennebec, maybe from some town like Gardiner, Richmond or Bath. The old logs, nearly two feet in diameter, had lost their bark long ago and their outer sapwood was worn away from years of wear and tear, plus friction from tide and ice, but they were "sound as a nut" all the way through. We would have liked to have had them sawed into boards, but remnants of nails, spikes and iron rods that once held the logs in place as part of a busy wharf made them unacceptable at the mill. Carefully avoiding embedded iron, we sawed the logs into stove lengths with our crosscut. Although spruce is considered one of the tougher members of the coniferous group, the big logs were remarkably straight-grained and the fifteen-inch chunks were easily split with an axe. They made big piles of firewood.

One Sunday morning in the summer, Pa, Al, Vining and I went across the river in the skiff and were walking around along the cove below the Old Pine. We came upon a small area close to the riverbank where the surface of the mud had a corrugated appearance – a lot of low, parallel ridges several inches apart. "What makes all these humps?" Al asked as he kicked the mud from one of the ridges. He exposed the top of a good-sized log embedded in the flats. Each ridge, we found, was a water-soaked log settled almost completely out of sight in the mud and covered with several years' accumulation of silt. Pa recalled that Amasa and Charles had bought all of the white birch trees in Stephen Preble's nearby woodlot many years before. They dragged the logs to the river and left them on the ice to be towed to their sawmill for making hardwood flooring, after the ice went out. "They did saw a lot of them," Pa said. "But they must have forgotten these." By the time we found the logs, the sawmill had burned down and Amasa and Charles were no longer in the lumber business. Since the logs were across the river from our meadow and only a short distance below our Shore, Pa decided to try to get them for wood. We made several trips there with the skiff at high tide and brought back a single log at a time. A hardwood log will rarely float and these had long since lost any slight degree of buoyancy they might once have had. It was necessary, first, to pry each log from the mud one end at a time. The log was then raised to the surface, lashed to the side of the skiff with a rope, and towed to our landing at the Point. We found over a dozen of the partially buried logs. They were so smooth, wet, and slippery that Dandy had no difficulty in snaking them onto dry land. When sawed and split, the once attractive, fine-grained wood that was intended for someone's white birch floor had become a homely gray. But after it had dried, though mud-stained, it made excellent fuel for our stove.

In the years before the sawmill burned, Pa used to buy an occasional load of short slab wood for fires. Amasa charged fifty cents for a horse cart load. Practically all of this was soft wood: pine, hemlock, fir and spruce. Since the slabs had just been sawed from freshly-cut logs, many of which had been brought to the mill by water, the wood was mostly green and heavy with wetness. We used to split the foot-long pieces and leave the wood in a pile on the ledge back of the house to dry for a few weeks before burning. When there was no dry wood available, we filled the oven with wet wood whenever Mother was not using it for cooking. This gave us at least a few sticks of dry wood for use next morning. The pieces of hemlock seemed to give more heat than the other soft woods but it popped a lot while burning – a characteristic that makes hemlock undesirable for fireplaces but causes no problems in stoves such as ours.

After Aunt Emma sold her farm, it seemed as if Pa made less effort to maintain an over-abundant supply of wood. He limited his tree cutting to an occasional over-age oak Up-under-the-Hill and once we cut an oak tree that was on the Cromwell farm line, while Sherman was out of town for a few days. About that time I assumed an increasing share of the work of wood gathering. I started to apply some elementary forestry practices to the conifers in the far end of our west pasture. Here I trimmed low limbs from the pines and spruces and cut many of the crooked alders at the edge of the swamp for wood. Most of the sizeable trees were balsam firs, which, like poplars and gray birches, are short-lived species and hence there were many dead ones. I chopped down all of the dead firs each year, limbed them with the axe, and hauled the trunk sections to our backyard in the hayrack. One clump of firs was on the far side of our swamp near the railroad and it was necessary to wait until late summer when the mud dried up to haul logs from there.

Before World War I, there was a stand of tall red oaks on Elliot's riverbank just above the big road bridge. It was an attractive spot, where Pa said he once watched a brood of full-grown partridges work their way up from the shoreline and take wing, one at a time, when they reached the field at the top. During WWI, the trees were sold to provide timber for Bath shipyards. Only the lower limb-free portions of the trunks were taken for making ship material. The upper parts of the trees were left where they fell. Some of them landed in the mud below high water mark close to the main channel of the river. After a year or two, the bark dropped off, leaving dry, hard oak wood that makes one of the hottest fires. It was apparent that no one cared anything about the fallen tops. Some of them were, in a way, a hazard to river traffic since they could be pulled into the channel when attached ice sheets moved in the spring. One summer I made several trips up river to bring back, one at a time, several of the oak tops for firewood.

Although my taking of the discarded tree tops could hardly be considered as pilferage, I didn't want to appear too nervy about the matter, and for that reason restricted such work to the dusk of evening. The tree tops were within view of the big road bridge, but at that time of the day my presence was not noticeable from the highway. As oak tops with branches attached could easily be dislodged from their bed of mud only when the tide was high, there were only two or three evenings, every two weeks, to secure an oak top during the hours of approaching darkness. An axe made too much noise, so I used a saw for removing any interfering limbs, before prying, rolling, and sliding the oak top into deep water. Once moved to the edge of the channel, the heavy, water-soaked wood sank immediately to the channel's bank. The top was raised and lashed to the skiff for transportation down river with the help of the new ebb tide. It was after dark by the time the highway and railroad bridges were reached a hundred yards downstream. With the boat acting as a sounding board, it gave one an eerie feeling to hear the scraping and feel the slight vibrations when ends of branches dragged over boulders the bridge builders placed on the river bottom. It told me there was something solid down there, ten feet beneath the tide. My rowing helped to move the boat and tree top downstream a little faster than the tide would carry us, and the oars were useful in keeping the boat in the channel and thereby avoid running aground at bends in the river in the darkness. The oak top was finally landed on the mud flats beside our Point, and next day the horse pulled it out to dry.

Closely associated with the necessity of wood for fuel was our need for lumber to use around the farm. Some of this we salvaged from the river in the form of boards, stray planks, and even larger timbers. The hard pine sills in both the boat- and icehouses that Pa built on our Point were discarded cross timbers from a railroad bridge, dumped into the Abbagadasset when section crews made repairs. We also used some of these durable timbers as replacements for extra posts beneath the barn. Before Amasa's sawmill burned down, Pa took a small raft of logs each spring and fall to be sawed into boards, two-by-threes, two-by-fours, and two-inch planks of varying widths. This lumber was largely used for repairs around our buildings and an occasional new hen house. Pa always kept a lot of new lumber stashed away on the collar beams in the stable chamber and another large pile in the barn cellar. No matter what carpentry need arose, he could usually find the right piece of lumber for the job.

The small rafts of eight or ten logs that we towed to the mill with the skiff were a motley assortment accumulated from various sources. In the spring, the rafts were made up of some logs that Pa had cut in Aunt Emma's woods while we were cutting firewood the previous winter. They were brought out to the river by sled and left tied to the bank until the ice went out. Some years, we included a pine log from Up-under-the-Hill and one or two big fir logs from the west pasture. In keeping with our characteristic thriftiness, however, we cut our own trees sparingly when we could get saw logs and firewood from other sources. During the months when the river was open, we frequently found logs here and there that seemed to belong to no one in particular. Assuming that finders could be keepers, we pushed these logs into some obscure creek or cove at high tide, where they would be out of sight of persons paddling the river. In the fall, the hidden logs were rounded up and made part of a mill-bound raft. A few logs found their way into our river that we usually carefully avoided. They were so-called "river-logs" that had floated away when a boom broke on the Kennebec. These logs had a Roman numeral mark cut into their sapwood with an axe. Pa told us that such marks were registered in Augusta and that "anyone caught monkeying with a marked log might get a stiff fine or even end up in jail." Each year, it was a common practice for lumber companies to send men in motorboats into the Bay and adjacent rivers to recover any of their marked logs they might find. They failed to see them all. We chanced upon a large pine log in the oat grass on our high flats one summer before the searchers came, which they missed. Pa and I shoved it into a brushy gulch behind the beaver dam were it could not be seen from the river. Two months later we brought it to our Shore. Knowing that Amasa's men at the sawmill would not think of sawing a marked log, we cut about four feet from the end that bore the river mark. Pa smeared flats mud on the freshly-cut end of the slightly shortened log making the cut appear as if it had been made at least a year ago. That fall, we added the twelve-foot butt-cut to the raft that went to the mill. The short section of the log with the mark was sawed into foot-lengths immediately, split into stove-size sections and tossed onto the woodpile. "I'll challenge anyone to put that river mark back together," Pa said.

One colorful afternoon in early October, when there was no school because of a teacher's convention, Pa and I salvaged a boatload of white oak planks from a derelict mill slip grounded on Hall's meadow up river. The slip had been the ramp on which the logs were pulled from the pond into Dinsmore's mill at the head of the tidewater. The entire ramp was pulled free from the mill's super-structure by the ice and rushing water during an early April's heavy rain. The slip, including the logs that served as its support, drifted down river a quarter mile and blew ashore on the south side of Hall's cross-channel. We first noticed the marooned slip on a motorboat ride up river that summer. The structure had not budged when we saw it in September while hunting ducks. It took more than an hour of prying with a crowbar for Pa to remove most of the bone-dry planking. I stacked the planks in the skiff without removing the big, 60-penny nails that had held them to the slip's frame. A pied-billed grebe kept diving and reappearing just below us in the river, acting very much as if it were keeping an eye on our operation. We used Al's launch to tow the loaded skiff back home. We salvaged many board feet of used white oak planking that were used in several places around the farm.

Chapter Nine

Water

Along with food and fuel needs, an adequate water supply was a prime necessity for living on a farm. There were always millions of gallons of water in the Abbagadasset, but not even in the driest summers, when our well sometimes ran low, did we ever consider hauling water from the river. This was, however, an ever-present source of water for our young cattle in the river pasture. When our Little Pond and nearby swamp dried up, the milking herd went to the railroad culvert for drinks. The river water contained so much sediment that we never would have considered using it for washing clothes; the Kennebec and Androscoggin were so badly polluted with mill and sewage wastes that water from none of our rivers was safe to drink. Tom Wildes came down with typhoid fever after taking a drink from the Bay while hunting on a warm fall day. Except for our rain barrel, and occasional trips to the Cromwell's roadside well or to Elliot's spring during a prolonged summer drought, we depended year-round on our fourteen-foot dug well near the northeast corner of the barn for most of our water. An earlier well was located in our field east of the orchard. It was the source of water for the original Sedgeley house that stood on the old cellar hole in our orchard between two Bellflower apple trees. While we were loading hay, Pa showed us the depression in the east field where he had filled in the old well years before.

Our family well had already been dug when Pa bought the farm. At that time the barn stood on the ledge behind the house; the well was a considerable distance to the southeast and not in the line of drainage from that early building whose wastes drained to the north and westward. When the time came for Pa to build the stable, the attached privy, and later the barn, the only convenient locations were within a hundred feet or less from the well. The stable was built directly up-hill from the well, while the barn was on the same level with it. In those days, people were little concerned with bacteriological problems. Soon after the new barn was built, a well-driller from Gardiner made an offer to Pa to drill a well through the ledge back of the house for $100. But that was a lot of money. Why pay so much for a new well as long as the one they had had never gone dry? After I was through college and away from home, the folks began to notice an unsightly scum forming on kettles of boiling water. Undesirable seepage apparently had finally contaminated the soil all the way from the stable and barn to the well. Minerva sent a sample of our well water to the State Department of Health in August for laboratory tests. They reported a high coliform bacteria count and other evidence of pollution such as might be caused by nitrogenous wastes. It was then that a new artesian well was drilled in the front dooryard close to the front porch.

When Pa built the barn, he planned a watering facility for the cows in the open part of the tie-up in the southeast corner of the building. He laid an inch and a quarter iron pipe from the well, four feet underground, diagonally across the barn cellar as far as this part of the tie-up. Here, the water pipe rose vertically to a tall, cast iron hand pump enclosed in a tight insulated closet in one corner of the tie-up. The long-handled pump had a sort of spherical swelling in the casting near the spout. On the side of this bulge was the name Douglas along with the raised figure of a swan. To keep the water in the upright pipe in the barn cellar from freezing in cold weather, Pa enclosed it in a three-foot-square box, filled with sawdust, from the ground to the tie-up floor. When the livestock were watered, the water was pumped through a wooden trough projecting from the side of the pump house into a wooden tub that was made by sawing a molasses barrel in two. The old pump lacked any means of allowing the water within it, when pumping stopped, to be returned to the well and there was danger of the water freezing solid on cold nights. To prevent this, before going to bed in coldest weather, Pa plugged the spout with a rag and poured a teakettle full of hot water in it to keep it warm for the night. With the pump closet closed tightly, the hot water prevented any serious freezing before Pa got to the barn in the morning. The first thing he did on cold mornings was to pump out enough water so that it came "fresh from the well, without any frost on it."

Once, on a bitterly cold night, the water in the pipe somewhere between the well and the pump in the barn did get too much frost in it. The preceding fall that year had been unusually dry and winter found water in the well at a lower level than usual. It would not get real full again till spring. That left the pipe to the barn exposed for three or four feet above the water in the well. One night, I remember, while I was doing high school homework, it came near to Pa's bedtime and he bundled up for the trip to the barn with the teakettle. He returned in a few minutes and replaced the full teakettle on the stove. "I can't get any water out of that pump in the barn," he said. "Could you slip into your things and help me thaw the pipe? It must be frozen down in the well. I'll have to pour some hot water on it. I'm afraid if we let it go till morning it might burst the pipe." The sharp north wind hit our faces as we went around the end of the barn. Pa lifted the wooden well curb together with the pump and its housing and pushed it to one side. He lowered himself into the well by carefully placing his feet against protruding rocks that lined the well. "Let me have the teakettle," he called from six feet down, "and hold the lantern so I can see that pipe." Pa poured hot water on the horizontal pipe that protruded two feet into the well beyond the stones. The iron elbow and the vertical pipe going down to the water got warmed up, too. "That ought to do it," he said, and climbed out of the well. "I had to do that trick once before, one winter 'way back before you were born." Back in the barn, water soon flowed into the tub as Pa worked the pump handle. The pipe was freed of ice. Our water supply was again available. Returning to the well, we replaced the curb and banked it with snow to prevent the wind from circulating more cold air into the well and freezing the water in the pipe again. After that, Pa banked the well curb with brush every fall to catch some snow and insulate the interior of the well against cold wintry blasts of arctic air.

We had an outdoor pump installed on the well curb that we used a lot in the warmer months. It was factory-made but I can't remember seeing its maker's name. In appearance, it was a tall wooden box-like structure, one foot wide, two feet long, and four feet high, with a hood-like, hinged cover. To make it work, one turned a crank on one side of the box. The crank's shaft rested on rollers and turned a sprocket wheel in the center of the box. It was a peculiarly-shaped sprocket in that the prongs on the margin of the wheel were in the form of Y's which held an endless chain. The pump chain was made of closed links with small leather cups, about two and a half inches in diameter, spaced a foot and a half apart along the closed chain. Another unique feature of the pump was its long riser pipe which extended from the spout almost to the bottom of the well. This pipe had been made from a piece of four-by-four pine with a hole bored in its center for its entire length, big enough to allow tight passage of the leather cups. The endless chain passed upward through the vertical wooden pipe. When the crank was turned, the chain raised a succession of the leather cups in the pipe, bringing to the spout the water trapped above each cup. At ordinary speed, the pump delivered a bucketful of water in less than a minute. Like the barn pump, the one on the well could also "stick" in cold weather. If we went to the well for water in the winter, we took along some hot water to pour down the wooden pipe and thaw loose any of the cups that might be frozen to its wall. After years of use, the links of the rather heavy chain tended to wear thin at their ends. Now and then the old chain broke and dropped to the bottom of the well. When this happened, we borrowed an old eel spear they kept in Cromwell's barn, and fished up the broken chain. It was replaced in the wooden pipe and made endless again by removing the broken link and rejoining the adjacent ones. I have never seen another pump like that one.

To fulfill our household needs, water had to be carried in pails to the kitchen sink. I remember the two shiny red "pulp-pails" on a nearby shelf which we children were supposed to keep filled with water. These rather attractive pails were made of a material that resembled pressed cardboard and they were made waterproof by a lacquer-like coating. They had the distinct advantage of not rusting or springing a leak. They held about twelve quarts each. Before I was big enough to carry these big pails filled with water, I was given a two-quart lard pail for keeping the kitchen pails filled by making as many trips to the pump as necessary. During the months when there was little or no snow, Mother wanted me to bring water from the well; she thought water from the barn acquired too much iron from the pipe it passed through. Pa thought water from the chain-pump at the well had a better taste than that from the barn, even though it all came from the same well. During the winter, however, I was permitted to get the water from the barn, since that did not involve getting out of doors. In the course of a year, we must have lugged tons of water for use in the house alone. Besides this, we carried a few gallons a day to the hens.

We had another somewhat intermittent water source besides the well. This was the rain and melting snow on the roof. Since our well water was quite hard, Mother preferred rainwater for washing clothes. We liked it for our face and hands, too. Sometimes there was enough for a bath. We kept an old vinegar barrel under the downspout at the end of the porch that caught the run-off from the south roof of the stable. When it rained, we collected additional rainwater in tubs placed under other downspouts. I was always happy to see an abundant supply of rainwater on hand for washday, for it meant I would not have to bring so much from the well. Wash day required many gallons of water for the wash-boiler on the kitchen stove, and for the wash and rinse tubs in the shed. For a near-at-hand supply of hot, soft water in the house, we kept the tank on the kitchen range filled with rainwater, as long as it was available. During the winter, we sometimes melted snow in the tank to maintain a soft water supply.

In the wintertime, our biggest consumers of water were the livestock. They drank many gallons every day. To meet this need, we were fortunate to have an indoor pump in the barn. Many farmers in the neighborhood watered their cattle by turning them outdoors and bailing water from a well into a drinking trough. This was a hardship procedure during the coldest weather. Furthermore the practice was a dangerous one since severe injury could result to cattle from slipping on the smooth ice. After our cattle were confined to the barn for the winter, we had to spend about an hour every day, usually soon after dinner, performing the chore of "watering-up." This involved turning loose each of the cows and the horse separately and driving them to the enlarged end of the tie-up where the pump and tub were located. It was too risky turning the bull loose when Pa was not around, and the young cattle were too difficult to get back into their stanchions, so we carried water in pails to these individuals. Some of the cows were reluctant to begin drinking immediately upon arrival at the tub; they insisted on flicking the cold water for a minute with their tongues before starting to drink. As the cows drank, we pumped more water into the tub, thus keeping it full while the animal was drinking. During the coldest weather, we had to chop a hole in the ice of the tub before starting to "water-up." After a month of freezing weather, a solid wall of ice had formed all around the inside of the tub. By late January, this ice became so thick that only a basin-like hole about a foot in diameter and a foot deep was left in the center of the tub – the cow's drinking space. With a space of such small volume, it was necessary to pump slowly and continuously while the cow was drinking. Along in late March or early April, the heavy ring of ice started to thaw and became loosened in the tub. Pa and I lifted it from the tub and carried it outdoors. There it lay, some years for two weeks or more, before the spring sun melted it completely.

On the wooded hillside on Mrs. Call's farm, beyond the railroad, one fall day I came across an iron pipe partially buried in the humus. The upper end lay in a spring – the other end reached the railroad. "That's where the engines used to take water in the old days," Pa said, when I told him about the discovery. "They had an elevated tank just north of Jellerson's Crossing, where trains used to stop and fill the locomotor boiler."

Compared with the mechanism and labor involved in providing our farm and family with water, the disposal of liquid waste was relatively simple. At the end of the weekly wash, the murky contents of the two wooden tubs in the shed were poured around the iris, daffodils, golden glow, roses and current bushes in front of the house. The only plumbing involved in our wastewater disposal was a slightly curved, four-foot length of inch and a quarter lead pipe – the sink spout – that ran from a bowl-like depression in one end of the kitchen sink, through the cabinet below, and extended less than a foot beyond the outside clapboards a bit above the foundation of the house. Putty was packed around the spout in the hole where it came through the boarding to keep out the cold northwestern wind. A long wooden drain spout was made from two narrow boards nailed together to make a V-shaped trough that carried the effluent from the sink spout to a spot nearly twenty feet from the house. Here a wet spot remained all year beneath a clump of flowering currents and not far from the three big willows back of the house. These woody plants shared the nutrients and water that collected in the puddle and was without doubt responsible for the first of the three willows being much larger than the other two. This simple disposal system took care of all of the dishwater and any solids it might carry from the area of the kitchen. A few of our more knowledgeable hens seemed happy as they scratched for tasty morsels that missed being scraped into the dog's dish or the pig's pail but made it to the muddy place where the effluent finally landed.

The sink spout had one annoying feature, however, in that it was prone to freeze up solid at its lower end during the coldest weather. We kept a five-foot butt portion of flexible carriage whip in the cabinet beneath the sink for punching out blockages in the lead spout. I can remember one or two occasions in mid-winter when the outer end of the spout became solidly frozen soon after the supper dishes had been washed. To thaw the spout, Pa reluctantly put on all of his outdoor duds and with the teakettle poured boiling water on the exposed end of the lead pipe. In a few seconds, he pulled out the curved ice plug. Upon returning to the kitchen, he asked us to "be sure to wipe the sink dry and squeeze all of the water out of that rag before you put it over the spout every time you use the sink these cold nights. A little water keeps running down and it freezes when it hits that cold air out there. It doesn't take much water to freeze up that sink spout when the weather is as cold as this."

Chapter Ten

Old Santy Pratt

Old Santy Pratt was probably the most legendary character who ever roamed the Abbagadasset. It was his father, Uncle Charles Pratt, who told Pa he once saw a white-faced bear in the woods near Fred Beal's home. Santy was born in the 1840's, in the story and a half house with high, pointed gables that stood on the west side of the road near Pratt's Crossing. Pratt's Creek branched off from the river in front of the house, and, after passing under the Little Railroad Bridge, circled southwestward behind the house towards its origin in Cromwell's meadow. The creek, so near home, must have been a big attraction to a growing boy. When Santy was seven or eight, he was playing on the railroad one afternoon in Hall's Cut close to the east end of the Little Railroad Bridge. Frightened by the sudden appearance of a freight train coming towards him over the dike on Hall's meadow, Santy dashed towards home. He was about to cross the bridge over the creek when the train, bearing down upon him, gave a frightening blast from the locomotive's whistle. Almost paralyzed with fear, he threw himself down on the edge of the bridge and, grasping the lengthwise timber that was bolted to the end of the bridge's cross-timbers, Santy hung by his hands above the water. As he hung for dear life, Mrs. Buker, a neighbor who lived in a shanty at the Pratt's shore, noticed the boy's predicament. She started shouting, "Santy's going to be killed! He'll drown." Santy's mother, who had been keeping an occasional eye on her small son, heard Mrs. Buker shout and dashed from her house. She yelled first, "Get back in your house, you Buker bitch." Then to Santy she shouted, loud enough to be heard above the rumble of the train, "Hang, Santy!! You can hang a week as well as a day." The train rattled past and Santy pulled himself back onto the bridge.

In his youth, Santy apparently was an independent, somewhat unruly young man. I was too young to remember much about Old Santy as he plied his calling on the river, or to listen to his own recounting of his colorful experiences. But Al and Vining related things about Old Santy frequently and I learned about his exploits and idiosyncrasies that way. Also, Pa had learned a lot about Old Santy, either from seeing him in action or listening to his tales. All we knew about the early years of his life was gleaned from the incidents he told Pa, Al or Vining when they called at his home for an evening. He told them that during the Civil War he was called up for duty in the Union Army, along with another Bowdoinham youth named Lithco Allen. They were ordered to report to an Army camp near Augusta. Arriving at the camp late in the day, they were told at the mess quarters that they were too late for supper, that the last meal of the day had been served. Old Santy related to Vining how he held an iron skillet over the cook and ordered him, in his peculiar, individualistic way of speaking, "Do you get us something to eat, and that mighty quick, too!" Some days later, Santy and Lithco were exercising with their squad in a field adjacent to a patch of woods. When the order to relax was given, the two Bowdoinham "volunteers" headed for the woods. They passed a guard who ordered them to halt. According to Old Santy's own account, he told the guard, "If you do not want to see me, do you look the other way." After the two men were out of sight, the cry "Skeddaddlers!" went up from the camp. According to Silas Adams' History of the Town of Bowdoinham, Lithco Allen served in the 24th Maine Regiment for nine months and was discharged for disability on January 8, 1863. But Augusta (Maine, not Georgia) was as far as Santy got in the War between the States. I once asked Pa why they never arrested him as a deserter or returned him to the Army. Pa's reply was that "the Army may have figured they were better off without him."

At one point in his younger years, Old Santy must have been an inquisitive experimenter of sorts, with considerable interest in steam as a power source. He told about the experiment he performed with a teakettle on his parents' cookstove. With the teakettle half full of water, he tied a cloth plug tightly into the spout and jammed a strip of cloth into the narrow space around the cover. With the kettle directly over the wood fire, he held the cover down with a length of broken broom handle set against the ceiling. With a hot fire in the stove, the steam began to hiss through tiny escape holes around the cover of the teakettle. Santy stepped back and watched with interest. Suddenly the teakettle's cover shot upwards and the broom handle penetrated the plaster ceiling. Following these convincing results, Santy took a job one winter as fireman at a Kennebec icehouse. He operated the steam engine that moved the cakes of ice from the river up the long incline into the spacious storage house. One day, the foreman suggested to him, "Can't you give us a little more steam, Santy? The ice isn't moving very fast." Santy's pride was injured by the remark. He tied down the safety valve and fed more wood into the firebox beneath the boiler. The ice slid up the ramp much faster and the supporting structure began to tremble and vibrate. The foreman returned to see what was going on. Many years later, we saw Old Santy still firing a boiler. During recess time at Jellerson School, we often ran to Amasa's sawmill to watch the big circular saw in action. There was Old Santy feeding green slabs and sawdust into the glowing chamber beneath the sawmill's big, brick-covered boiler.

According to a story he told to Al, Old Santy was, for a while, a locomotive engineer on the Lackawanna. All went well until, one day, he brought his train into the terminal fifteen minutes ahead of time, making definitely possible a serious mishap. Old Santy was accused of taking one too many drinks that day. "The supervisor of our line called me into his office," Santy told Al, "and told me they would not need my services anymore."

Old Santy said he once joined a fraternal group, and, as he expressed it, "They did give me the title of 'Venerable Sage'."

Like many residents of the Abbagadasset, Old Santy felt that local people should have priority over others in harvesting the river's resources. He resented having out-of-towners fish or trap in his domain. Outsiders were fair game for any tricks that might be played upon them. It gave Old Santy much pleasure one moonless night in May when, near the Spar Landing, two shad fisherman from Bath asked him the location of the channel where they could cast their drift net. The tide was high and Preble Creek reflected what little light there was from the northeast sky. The course of the main channel of the river lay in the shadow of the woods. Old Santy directed the strangers into the relatively shallow creek, where they then cast their net. A flimsy drift net is notorious for collecting submerged debris from shallow areas, making it very difficult to cast them again until they have been taken ashore and the entangled grass, twigs and leaves removed.

Another night, at the height of the shad run, the river was crowded with fishermen. Old Santy was sitting in his skiff alongside Sam Wildes who was throwing out his net at the Spar Landing for a flood-tide drift up the reach to the Old Pine. The moon was bright. Sam paused in his heaving of his net and turned to look down river. "What'n hell is that coming 'round the bend?" he asked Santy. In the moonlight, they could see a long line of white buoys drifting towards them with the tide. The binnacle light on the owner's boat could be seen in the distance coming around the bend in the river. "Had I better pull anchor and drift out of the way, Santy?" Sam asked. "Do you keep on throwing out, Sam," Santy replied. "I will fix those jokers." It was an unwritten law of the river that no one should allow his net to drift around a bend from one reach into the next. When the forward end of the drift net came to the end of the reach into which it had been cast, the owner was expected to haul his net back into the boat and return to throw it out again. These out-of-town fellows, Old Santy thought, were breaking a hard-and-fast rule of drifting etiquette. He rowed a few boat lengths downstream from Sam's anchored skiff and dropped anchor in midstream. The maverick net waving deep in the water below the buoy-line soon made contact with Santy's painter and its buoys began to cluster beneath his boat. Santy waited until the owners of the net were getting near to pull his anchor rope with one hand and, walking to the end of his skiff, to bend over and slice away the entangled netting with his long-bladed jackknife in the other. One of the strangers recognized Old Santy and said, "What do you say, Santy?" Continuing to slash away at the accumulated net, Old Santy replied, "I do not say anything. I am just trying to get my keelic."

I remember Old Santy as a large, well-built man, with broad shoulders and a short thick neck. In his prime, he probably stood a little less than six feet; the years had produced a slight stoop in his posture. He walked with a determined gait, his body bent forward a little, suggesting that he be given room to pass. He had the misfortune of losing two wives, to whom he referred as his "sparrows." I knew two of his sons, one of whom, Jim Pratt, lived on the shore of the Bay below the sawmill. Jim had two grown boys in the Jellerson School during the first few years I attended there. Jim's half-brother, Young Santy, was somewhat of an inebriate who was away from home most of the time while I was growing up. I think it was for this son that Old Santy said the judge gave him a writ of "hoppus coppus."

Although he never gave any indication of fearing any of his fellow men, Old Santy was afraid of bulls. The fact that Pa had one or two bulls on the farm most of the time was disturbing to him. He once told Al, "I do believe your father loves bulls." Santy's fear of these animals caused him no little annoyance in those years when Pa had a job away from home and he and Pa built a weir in partnership. Our Shore, including the boat landing and the fish house, was an unfenced enclave within the river pasture where the heifers and young bull were confined every year from spring to late fall. Old Santy wanted to call off his agreement to be a fishing partner after an experience one spring, a few days after cattle had been placed in the pasture. He was packing shad in the old fish house when he turned around to see the yearling bull, out of curiosity, standing with his head in the open door. The fish house was a small building with but one door and no windows. Old Santy felt trapped and he was greatly frightened. When the tide was high, Old Santy came to our Shore by boat, thereby avoiding having to walk through our pasture. But when the tide was down, his skiff was often grounded on the muddy flats and he came by shank's mare through the pasture. One day, Pa and Vining were at the Shore when Old Santy came via the upland route. He held his .32-caliber revolver in his right hand, which he said "was for long distance." In his other hand he carried a four-tined pitchfork "for close range."

One night in late summer, the young cattle got out of the river pasture and someone told us the next morning that they were in the road above Cromwell's. Pa and I went to drive them back home. I was about ten years old and barefoot. With a four-foot gray birch stick, I ran ahead to intercept the cattle before they had time to reach the railroad crossing. They were grazing along the road near Old Santy's house. I quickly rounded up the group, which included a young Jersey bull, and chased them down the road towards home. Later that day, Pa and I were driving past Old Santy's house on the way to meet someone at Harwards Depot. As we passed his house, Old Santy came out to our wagon to talk with Pa. The first thing he said was, "You should not let that boy get so near to that black bull of yours. Those critters are too dangerous."

Old Santy had a sense of humor and enjoyed playing tricks even in his later years. One day down at the Shore he said to Vining, "Do you watch me give that squirrel a flip," as he stepped quickly on one end of a long weir stake that was lying across a log with a chipmunk sitting on the far end. One spring, while Old Santy and Pa were fishing partners, Pa was confined to the house for a few days with an asthma attack. Old Santy came to the house after seining the weir to tell Pa about the catch that day. He entered the kitchen with a dejected look and said to Pa, "We may as well pull that ghostly weir and bring it ashore. I got only four-teen shad and a couple hundred herring just now." Four or five shad and a hundred herring would have been a good catch for one day. Old Santy was also adept at rigging mechanical devices. His bedroom was so cold on wintry nights that he had to use a number of blankets and comforters on his bed in order to keep warm. The weight of the bedclothes was excessive. In order to make it easier to crawl into bed and to prevent the bedding from sliding to the floor during the night, Old Santy showed us how he had fastened a small pulley to the ceiling directly over the bed, through which a length of clothes line was passed. He could then raise the bedding like a tent and lower it after he got into bed. The rope, which was fastened to the bed coverings near the center, also kept the bedding from slipping off the bed when he rolled over during the night.

I was too young, while Old Santy was living in his house up the road, to visit him during the evening as Al and Vining often did. I did go up to his house one summer evening, however. It was one of those times when I thought I had been mistreated by some sibling while we were gathered on the porch after supper. "I'm going up to see Old Santy," I said, and took off on foot. Old Santy was seated on his doorstep enjoying the cool of the early night when I arrived. I remember his bare ankles as he relaxed with his trouser cuffs raised half way to his knees. He wore shoes but no socks – Vining said Santy once told him he often went barefoot in summer "to get electricity out of ground." We passed a few words of greeting when bashfulness overcame me. I said, "I'll have to be going," and returned home. A few days later, Old Santy told Vining that I had come up to his place but did not stay.

As far back as I can remember, Old Santy was hard of hearing, or at least he claimed he was. No one ever knew just how deaf he was. He often leaned forward and cupped a hand behind his ear when someone spoke to him in ordinary tones. Pa was certain, however, that Santy sometimes heard what was being said even in low tones when the other parties did not want him to hear. But Ira Allen was convinced that Old Santy could not have had very good hearing, especially the afternoon Ira rescued Santy when the elderly gentleman broke through early-spring ice down by Scott's Point. It was a warm, pleasant day in late March and Old Santy had walked down the road to see his son, Jim. At that time of the year, a week or two before the ice broke up, the snow-ice on the flats was still thick and solid but, in the channel, only the lower blue layer was left. The bright sun had honeycombed the surface of the blue ice reducing the danger of slipping and making for easy walking. Since the channel ice was always level, and hence not difficult for the old man to navigate, Old Santy took to the river when he reached the mill on the way home that afternoon. He made his way up river for a couple hundred yards above the bridge. Approaching the bend a little way above Scott's Point, he came to an area of weak ice and broke through. Ira was crossing the bridge a few minutes later and heard Old Santy shout, "Help! I'm in the river!" Ira left the road and ran along the east shore of the river to where Old Santy was struggling amidst pieces of broken ice. With the aid of a long spruce sucker net stake, which Ira was able to shove under one of Santy's arms, he was helped ashore. "If Old Santy hadn't been so deaf," Ira said, "he would have heard the weak ice cracking all around him." As a sequel to this accident, although it may have been coincidental, there was an unusually poor run of shad in the river that spring. Local fishermen blamed it all on Old Santy.

The last time we saw Old Santy was during the summer before he died. He had left his house up the road from ours and was living in a one-room cabin at Jim's place on the Bay. One Sunday in August, some of us went for a boat ride in the motorboat and we landed at Jim Pratt's shore for a brief call. Pa, Al, and I visited Old Santy in his cabin for ten minutes or so. He showed us a smoked shoulder he was baking in his oven. That winter Pa and Mother picked me up at school one day on their way home from Old Santy's funeral.

Chapter Eleven

Caterpillars and Other Pests

In the early part of the present century we had a severe outbreak of the brown-tail moth. It began around 1906 and the infestation became increasingly serious for several years – finally reaching a point where most of the oak trees in our area were completely defoliated by early summer. The insect got its name from the brown, egg-containing, posterior portion of the abdomen of the females of this inch-long, snow-white species. The female moth deposited a mass of fertilized eggs on mature leaves near the tips of smaller branches in late summer. Red oak, apple and wild cherry were most severely attacked in our area. Soon after the egg masses were laid, they hatched into tiny, hairy larvae that started to feed immediately on nearby leaves. Within a few weeks, the group of young larvae that hatched from the single egg mass wove a few leaves tightly together for a nest that they fastened to the twig by whitish, silky threads, to prevent its dropping when the leaves would fall in autumn. This was their home in which they hibernated. The Town, for a few years, paid a bounty of a penny each for all the brown-tail nests that were brought to the Town Treasurer's office. I helped Genevieve and Jeannette collect the nests during the two or three years that the Town supported the program of control. In a few years, the pest became so numerous that the bounty was discontinued. One spring during the bounty period, the treasurer was tardy in destroying the nests that had been brought in. With the first warm days in late April, the burlap bags containing the larval nests became covered with the fuzzy squirming quarter-inch worms.

During these years when the brown-tail infestation was at its height, we borrowed Uncle Everett's sprayer and treated our apple trees with a suspension of powdered lead arsenate. The sprayer was considered a modern one at the time. It consisted of a hand pump attached to the inner rim of a metal barrel. We placed it in our horse cart and drove close to each fruit tree. I worked the pump handle while Pa thoroughly sprayed the trees with a short spray rod attached to the pump by a long rubber hose. For those two or three years, we were worried that the oak trees in our area might be killed. They had all of their leaves stripped clean by mid-summer but were able to grow some new foliage after the larvae had stopped feeding. Fortunately they survived the epidemic. The brown-tail moth larvae were sparsely covered with short, bristly hairs; very noticeable and helpful for identification were a few tufts of short, bright orange hairs on their backs. As the larvae approached full size, they shed most of their protective hairs and took on a smooth appearance, resembling somewhat the larval stage of the eastern tent caterpillar. We were told these brown-tail moth hairs were the cause of a skin allergy in some people. I was never noticeably affected but some of our friends who went with us to pick blueberries in Woolwich, where there were a lot of defoliated oak trees overhead, developed an unpleasant rash on their neck and arms.

The period of heavy infestation by the brown-tail moth in our area ended more abruptly than it started. We believed at the time that the end of the outbreak was associated with a lethargic stage in the life history of the insect. After the larvae had fed on the tree's foliage for some time and full size was reached, they gathered in broad patches on the trunks of the trees where they had been feeding. The worms remained in this close contact for at least a few days. One year, sometime around 1912, we had a northeaster and a period of cold wet weather at the time the larvae were clustered together on the bark. Within a week after the weather cleared, Pa came up from the Point one day and casually told us during supper that "the patches of worms on the oaks near the fish house are all dead. Some of them have fallen to the ground but most of them are still on the trees. A lot of them are still stuck to the bark with their heads and tails bent backwards. That cold rain we had must have been too much for them." Later on, I remember seeing the dried remains of many larvae still marking the spot where the original cluster had swarmed together weeks before. Since that year, I have never seen a tree stripped of its leaves by the brown-tail moth.

It was only a few years later, after the leaves had dropped in the fall, that I found three or four brown-tail moth nests with the tell-tale white, silky strands holding them to the twigs. There was no mistaking that kind of worm's nest; there was nothing else like it in our area. The numbers I found in our orchard were almost as many as the few that we collected for a cent apiece several years before, when the big infestation started. "Here we go again," I thought. "A few years more and they'll be back in numbers." But for some reason no such infestation ever built up again. We heard that an entomogenous fungus, working in extremely favorable wet weather, became very active in attacking the brown-tail larvae clustered on the tree trunks and that the damp weather so greatly enhanced its spread that the worms were killed over the entire area. That may well have been the case. However, I could not understand how fungus spores could remain in the countryside for several years in sufficient quantity to prevent even a noticeable re-infestation after the moth made its reappearance.

(The clustering of brown-tail moth larvae when they have reached their full growth is a bit of insect behavior that entomologists would like to see certain other species incorporate into their life histories, to make possible more effective methods of control. One of our graduate school professors, Dr. G. F. Clinton, was sent to Japan in the first decade of this century to collect and bring back a fungus that caused disease among silkworm larvae. The United States Department of Agriculture sponsored the project with the hope that a fungus parasite might be introduced to combat another destructive tree-defoliating worm, the gypsy moth. Dr. Clinton found his fungus and started home with a collection of infected larvae and a supply of green leaves that they relished. Travel by ocean liner was relatively slow and the food supply for the worms had seriously deteriorated by the time he reached Hawaii. He was successful, however, in reaching New Haven with the fungus in viable condition. Attempts to create an epidemic among gypsy moth larvae in the wild resulted in failure, largely, he thought, because of the rather solitary habits of the insect. Had this pest gathered in groups, sometime or other, like the brown-tail moth, the tent caterpillar, or the fall web-worm, the parasitic fungus Dr. Clinton brought from Japan might have raised havoc with it.)

The complete disappearance of the brown-tail moth from our area made me wonder, at the time, if there might not be some unseen factor interfering with the reproductive processes of a species when the population of that species becomes too numerous for its own good. It never seemed quite in keeping with the processes of nature to have a parasitic fungus wipe out so completely an insect population that had attained such tremendous proportions. The question of the complete demise of the brown-tail moth raised the same doubts in my mind that I had entertained about the over-hunted theory in the case of extinction of the passenger pigeon. Pa remembered seeing the huge flocks of wild pigeons that darkened the entire sky when he was working on the Reed farm in Dresden. Less than ten years later, in North Bath, he told about seeing an elderly hunter waiting for a few stray birds to come for peas he had scattered on the ground as bait. It always seemed that it should have been possible for enough individuals to have escaped here and there into the vastness of our wilderness to perpetuate the species. I wondered, too, about the thousands of black ducks that used to leave Merrymeeting Bay in a huge swarm every morning to spend the day away from the hunters watching the open area. The immense flocks took wing with a roar like Niagara Falls, at the first sign of light in the eastern sky, and they came back to the Bay each night. They did this for a month or so during fall migration. Such numbers must have consumed most of the wild rice and other available food in the Bay and over-taxed the provisions that Nature makes for them. Might not Nature have some subtle way we've not discovered yet of limiting or possibly exterminating a species when its population gets too large? Workers who have tried to perpetuate desperately endangered species have often found fertility rates to be disappointingly low. Could there be some lethal factor, undetected yet by science, that creeps into the chromosomal make-up to do a species in?

Chapter Twelve

River Dangers

Everyone saw the Abbagadasset as an attractive, peaceful stream. And so it was. Yet its waters were more than deep enough, for most of its length and most of the time, to drown a man who couldn't swim. In the channel at our Shore, the water was nearly five feet deep on a lowest, drain-out tide, and around eleven feet when the tide was high. There were many deep, washed-out places in the river bed, such as those found at sharp bends or just below a bridge where the swirling ebb tide dug deep basins in the river's floor. The predominantly swift current, plus many steep slick clay banks, and slippery silt-covered rocks or ledges here and there, were dangerous spots for those unaware of the hazards and uninformed of the power inherent in a flowing stream. As children we were continuously cautioned never to go close to the river's edge nor to step into a boat unless some grown-up was near. Al and Vining frequently took me into the water with them after I was five years old. The first time they brought me along when they went for a swim, I waded onto the high flats bedside our Point, where the water came up to my waist. I pulled up all of the wild rice plants within reach, trying to keep my balance and remain upright. It was some years later that I took my first dog-paw strokes in a washed-out pool about five feet in depth, below an old abandoned highway bridge behind the railroad on Pratt's Creek. Merton Webber helped to get me started. He was a year older and had already graduated to the more sophisticated breast stroke.

Fortunately, none of us children, as far as I know, ever came close to getting drowned. The closest to an accident of this sort had to be, I guess, the night Pa fell overboard from the skiff while he and Al were drifting for shad. Pa was trying to locate the bank of the channel before dropping anchor and casting out the net just below the Old Pine. He was probing the depth of the water with an oar across the low flats when he came to the steep channel bank and his next jab failed to reach bottom. Losing balance, he pitched headlong into the river from the stern of the boat. He surfaced after a few seconds, however, and with Al's help climbed back into the boat, thoroughly drenched and his hip boots filled with cold water.

There had been two accidental drownings on the Abbagadasset which our parents told us about in detail. They probably wanted these unfortunate incidents to serve as warnings for us to be careful around the river. One day Pa had taken us up river in the skiff and we were returning at low tide, when he called our attention to a large, oval, mud-covered rock near Elliot's oaks that was completely covered at high tide. "That's the rock," Pa said, "that the Dinsmore boy slipped off of into the river when he was drowned a number of years ago. He couldn't swim and the tide was running so strong that the other boys couldn't get to him to help. A diver come up from Bath and found the body down there aways, just this side of the bridge." The second tragedy took place near Amasa's sawmill. They had recently launched the *Nellie G.* and Charles Holbrook was getting the steamer ready for its summer service at Boothbay Harbor. Amasa and Ella frequently had teenage girls from New York City as boarders at the farm during the spring and fall and one of them was with them for a couple of weeks. There were not many things for the girls to do in the quiet countryside. They spent some of their time watching the mill in operation and helping tidy up the ferryboat, which was hitched to its mooring in the Abbagadasset channel a short distance below the sawmill. One afternoon, Charles and the girl had been working on the *Nellie G.* for an hour when she told Charles that she was going ashore for awhile to watch the sawing of logs. Charles was working below deck in the engine room. The girl told him, "I'll be back in a little while."

Charles worked on the engine half an hour or so longer before going on deck. He saw the tender tied to the stern of the steamer but the girl was not around. He looked through the passenger quarters and in the pilot house. Nobody there. Charles hurriedly went ashore and questioned the workmen in the mill. No one had seen the girl that afternoon. Charles immediately drove back to the farm to get Amasa. After a thorough search, they came to the depressing conclusion that the girl may have done something that is altogether too easy to do – she must have pushed the light tender away from the big boat when she stepped into it, lost her balance and fallen into the river. She had never learned to swim. Tom Walker Wildes, a young man working at the mill at the time, was a strong swimmer and a good diver. He volunteered to search the river bottom. After several dives, he located the body in the middle of the channel not far from the *Nellie G.* Pa accompanied Amasa on the steamer to Bath that evening, where the undertaker met them at City Wharf and took the remains for shipment to New York by rail.

While in high school, during the last days of school in June, I had an experience that had all the makings for a tragic accident like the sad case of the Dinsmore boy near Elliot's oaks. It happened on the Branch – a small stream that flowed northwards from the Cathance on the east side of the Village. About five or six of us decided to go swimming that warm, sunny day after school. We went to the rocky shore of Kendall's sheep pasture, just above the highway and railroad bridges at the foot of Clay Hill, far enough from traffic that we needed no bathing suits. The only fellows I remember to be in the group were Bill Trufant and Chester Carr, although there were two or three others. When we reached the riverbank, the tide was quite high but still coming in strongly. I was swimming near the ledge when suddenly Bill, who could not swim, was either pushed or he slipped from the rocks. He immediately found himself in water that was over his head. I tried to keep his head above water with one hand but Bill grasped my wrist and we both went under. The tide was carrying us upstream away from the ledges. As the situation began to look desperate, between several submersions and a few mouthfuls of water, I called for help from the others. Chester, a good swimmer, was first to reach us. He offered his back to Bill and headed towards shore. I swam for a boat that was tied close to the ledges. By the time I reached the boat, Chester and Bill were almost ashore. Bill stumbled out of the water. His face had a bluish tinge that I had never seen before. If the nursery rhyme daughter didn't know how to swim, her mother's admonition to stay close to the hickory limb was good advice.

Sometime before I can remember, we lost a cousin about Minerva's age in a boating accident on the Kennebec at Bath. She was a daughter of Aunt Melissa, one of Pa's sisters who lived on the Woolwich shore below the Chops. The teenage cousin had gone to Bath with Wilbur Howe in his small sailboat to visit the circus. When they were leaving for home, someone on the wharf advised Wilbur to wait until the highway ferryboat Hockomock had reached shore before casting off. Wilbur ignored the warning. The sailboat was too difficult to control with both wind and the tide to contend with. It was struck near midstream by the powerful ferry and our cousin was drowned when the much smaller boat capsized.

Chapter Thirteen

War

The outbreak of war in Europe in the August of 1914 caused a lot of excitement in our family and, to me at least, it came as a big surprise. We had been led to believe that war was a thing of the past, and that I probably would never see one. That in our advanced state of civilization, nations had learned to live in peace. As an eleven-year-old boy, the sudden outbreak of hostilities left me shocked and puzzled. I remember having a kind of dread of wars; a feeling that may have resulted from a visit with Pa and Mother a few years before to a cemetery in Windsor where two of Pa's cousins were buried. One of them, Lieutenant Marcellus Vining, aged 22, died on May 19, 1864, from wounds received at Spotsylvania, Virginia, a week earlier. The other, Reuben, a brother of Marcellus, aged 18, was killed at Petersburg, Virginia, on June 16, 1864. Both were serving in the Union Army for other persons who had paid Pa's uncle $300 each to allow his sons to go to war in their stead. Such buying of substitutes, I was told, was a legal procedure in the military set-up of the time. "I remember Marcellus," Pa recalled as he stood before the stone, a single one that marked both graves. "He was going to receive a promotion in a few weeks."

Al and Vining were at home when the war broke out. Although it would be nearly three years before the United States entered the conflict, they talked of the possibility that we would become involved and they speculated as to which ones of us might see service. I was entirely omitted from consideration. A lot of our dinner table conversation was centered around the war. Pa noted that he was living between two wars. "I was too young for the Civil War and am now too old for this one," he said. Apparently he disregarded the Spanish-American War since the manpower drain was not great. Al had a family to support and felt rather safe from any soldier draft that might be instituted. Vining was two months out of college and single. They figured that he would be among the first in line for military duty if the U.S. joined the fray.

Another frequent topic of table conversation involved arguments as to which side should win. The difference of opinion within our own family on this point was surprising. Pa was impressed with Germany's high degree of military preparedness as a result of their compulsory training, but I got the feeling that he would rather see England and France prevail. He may have had a kindly feeling towards Kaiser Wilhelm since they were both were born in 1858. Al was decidedly pro-British and expressed his feelings forcefully. "Why do you want to see them win?" he asked Vining pointedly in countering some remark in favor of Germany. I asked Mother one day whose side she was on. She made the neutral reply, "Oh, I don't know. I always liked the German people." Jeannette and I talked about which side should win the war. She expressed the view that maybe England had ruled the roost long enough; that she could be defeated because we had done it in the Revolution. At that early point in the conflict, I may have held a somewhat sympathetic feeling for the Central European powers in their fancied position of underdog.

In the spring of 1915, after several months of trench warfare in Europe and all sorts of war activities on the high seas, I was allowed for the first time to go hunting by myself. With some trapping money I had bought Vining's single-shot .22-cal. rifle, when he left to become high school principle at Harrington, Maine, after spending the fall and winter at home. An incident we learned about one pleasant afternoon in early May of that year was typical of the events that helped to turn our feelings in favor of the Allies. I had been hunting woodchucks in our east field and had missed three or four shots at one standing motionless near the edge of the bushes a short distance from the highland in Newell's meadow. I must have had chuck fever. The rodent left in disgust. Back at the house, Pa had returned home from working in the Village and had brought a copy of the *Boston Post*. The newspaper was lying on the kitchen table, with big headlines: "*Lusitania* Sunk." The front page told the story about the big liner being torpedoed by a U-boat off the coast of Ireland with a loss of over a thousand lives, more than a hundred of them Americans.

To keep informed of the progress of the war in Europe and of the military attitude in the United States, Pa felt we should have a daily newspaper. He subscribed to the *Boston Post*, which was delivered by mail. We really preferred the *Globe* because it gave the prices dairy products and eggs were bringing on the Boston market. But the *Post* was a one-cent newspaper, the *Globe* cost two. For months, the paper had daily maps of both Western and Eastern fronts. Heavy black lines showed the latest positions of the trenches and dotted lines showed where they had been before some local drive had taken place. Arrows indicated the location and direction of current offenses.

Our interest in the war continued for two and a half years, but in 1917 our concern became much greater. President Wilson declared war on Germany and the drafting of men for the armed services began soon after. Vining had been studying for an advanced degree in the Cornell Graduate School for two years when registration for the draft took place. He was on vacation at home when the first fish-bowl drawing occurred in Washington that determined the order in which the draftees would be called. From the newspaper the next day, he learned that his was one of the relatively early numbers drawn in the draft lottery. "I've been lucky sometimes in lotteries," he said. "Maybe this is my luck continuing – if you can see it that way." Vining returned to Ithaca sooner than he had planned, to report for his physical examination in connection with the draft. He wrote us a few days later that he was still awaiting orders, and that his major professor, Dr. Rowles, had offered to appear before the local draft board in his behalf, if he so wished. While Mother was writing a reply, Pa said to her, "You'd better tell him to let the Professor get him exempted if he can. If the war were in this country, it would be different. I'm not much in favor of going all the way to Europe to fight for someone else." Word came back from Vining in a couple of weeks that they had excused from immediate duty, in the first draft call at least, those students who were involved in research that might lead to increased food production. With this information, he was settling down to work for his degree.

During the first year or two of the war we had a tendency to imagine ourselves more closely involved than we really were. Frequently, in previous years, we had heard loud booming sounds way off in the distance somewhere. We were told that we were hearing coastal batteries, like Fort Popham, testing their guns, or some naval vessel having target practice in the nearby ocean. With the war underway, we interpreted such noises as a duel between a British and a German warship somewhere along our coast. Likewise, in the summer of 1915 when it rained so much we had great difficulty making hay, we wondered if the war might be to blame. Pa asked, "Do you suppose all the cannonading over in Europe could be upsetting our weather like this? There's never been so much explosives used anywhere in the world before, you know."

The United States was soon sending large numbers of troops overseas and the need for fresh recruits in the armed services was increasing daily. In February of 1917, Vining received his orders to report for military training. He came home for a week before reporting to Camp Upton, in the pine barrens of eastern Long Island. The Sunday afternoon before he left, Vining and I walked across Cromwell's meadow on the ice, crossed the railroad and followed the channel of Pratt's Creek all the way to the Little Road Bridge. "I used to come up here a lot, trapping and hunting," he said, "probably more than I ever will again."

At Camp Upton, Vining was placed in the Headquarters' Company, 77th Division, an Army division composed largely of draftees from New York City and nearby areas of the state. He was assigned eventually to its ammunition train as a corporal. The demand for more troops in Europe was becoming greater all the time and the training period in this country was often reduced to a very minimum. After a little more than a month in camp and with no furlough, Vining's unit was sent in a convoy of troopships across the submarine-infested Atlantic and landed in Brest, France. It was transported immediately to the front and spent the remaining several months of the war in or near the Argonne Forest.

At home, we were kept informed of the whereabouts of the 77th Division in France through a newsletter issued by a group of officers' wives in New York City. They contacted us soon after the unit went overseas offering to send a copy of each issue if we would contribute a small amount to cover printing and mailing costs. Pa sent two dollars and we received the mimeographed letter every few weeks. The wartime information the group was able to gather about the 77th Division was limited and often meager; however, it was eagerly awaited by us all. Vining's letters were censored and he was able to tell us little about his military activities. The newsletter was also helpful in that it provided contact with others who were also deeply concerned.

During the summer, Vining was promoted to sergeant. He never talked much about his wartime experiences. An incident he did mention occurred one evening when he was taking a ride on one of the horses. Presently he heard men conversing in German and realized he had come too close to enemy lines. The only service-connected injury he received was accidental. "We were unloading a truckload of hard French bread, bucket-brigade fashion, when I dropped one of the loaves. I bent over to pick up the bread and, just as I straightened up, the next loaf arrived on target and broke off two front teeth. I didn't go to the army dentist because he'd only pull both of the broken ones. I waited until we got back to New York and had new caps put on."

"After the armistice was signed, we were sent for a recreation period to nice quarters in Aix-les-Bains. It was difficult to recognize hardly anyone in our outfit, around the table that first night, after we had all washed, shaved, and gotten into some clean clothes. I had the Spanish flu while we were there."

Our quiet town received rumors that World War I was over at least two or three days before the signing of the armistice. After having undergone a period of sugar rationing and using a bran-like product called "Red Dog" in place of flour, everyone became excited at the prospect of an end to the fighting. A premature celebration was held at the Village during the early evening of November 10, which was halted when word was received that the war was not yet over. I went to school on the morning of November 11, but all schools in town were dismissed when official confirmation of an armistice was received. I missed the celebration in the Village later that day, because I returned home late after purchasing a pair of shoes at Philip Nealy's store on Main Street with a check received the day before for a few early-caught muskrat skins. It was a mild clear day and, since the tide was low, I spent the afternoon setting some more muskrat traps along the river.

As far as I know, there was but one death from combat among the seventy or more servicemen from Bowdoinham. Another casualty was John Dewey Brown, who died in an accident aboard one of our destroyers. He was given a public funeral in one of the Village churches and all high school students and teachers were present.

After the war was over, Pa expressed his opinion about the armistice. "I think we let the Germans off too easily," he said. "They stove Belgium and a lot of France all to pieces. The only part of their country that had much damage was some of Alsace-Lorraine. We should have kept going and marched right into Berlin."

We had too many troops in France when the armistice was signed for the Army to bring back in a short time. It was early May of 1919 before the men in Vining's outfit, homeward bound on a slow ship, saw the Statue of Liberty on their return. Following his discharge and a short stay in New York, Vining returned home the last of May. About the same time, Al came from Massachusetts to spend Memorial Day weekend with us. Since Pa and I had been drifting for shad earlier that month, the drift net was wrapped in its burlap sheet and ready for use in the boathouse. Saturday evening was calm and warm. It was also low tide soon after sunset. In a nostalgic tone, Al said to Vining, "Let's go down and cast out on this low-water slack – the shad run's about over but we might catch one." I tagged along for the excitement. We anchored the skiff at the Old Pine, where the ebb tide was still strong enough to carry the net downstream as Al, standing in the stern, cast the net overboard a yard or two at a time. When the last of the net was cast, the long line of white buoys drifted slowly down the reach. As the net went past the mouth of Preble Creek, a snag on the bottom caught it and the buoys started to bunch at that point. While Al pulled upwards on the netting to clear it from the submerged obstacle, I stood behind him and raised the buoy-line out of his way with the blade of the paddle. Vining was sitting close behind me, at the oars. The net was freed and I struggled to withdraw the paddle from some tangled meshes. A sudden backward pull caused the handle of the oak paddle to graze Vining's face. "Watch that paddle," he warned me. "I just got two new teeth. Don't knock them out again!"

Vining continued to be reluctant to talk about his war experiences. He never talked about them and we refrained from asking many questions. I got the impression there were things he would prefer to forget. In the late summer of 1918, Pa and Al had done some repair work on the north roof of our stable. In the course of this re-boarding, they had pulled a lot of old-fashioned cut nails from the roof and thrown them to the ground behind the stable. Someone had shown me how to hold one of the nails across my fingers with my thumb so that it made a loud whistling noise when hurled forcibly in the air. One afternoon, a week or two after Vining had returned, I was idly throwing some of these nails – a few of which went over the house and landed somewhere out in Amasa's field. Suddenly, Vining, who had been reading on the porch, appeared in the back shed door. His face had a pale look, with a faint scowl on his forehead. As soon as he saw what I was doing, he said, "Don't throw any more of those. It sounds just like a shell coming over."

Chapter Fourteen

The Hall House - Eminent Domain

"What do they mean by 'eminent domain' that Pa and Amasa were talking about?" I asked Mother. "That's the right that states have to take someone's land to use for something that would be for everybody's good," she replied. "We had a good example of that right up the road here. The Halls lived in that nice old house up by Pratt's Crossing and when they put the railroad through, they paid Mr. Hall for the right-of-way to lay the tracks across their front yard. Mrs. Hall told me that her home was spoiled when they put the railroad through. She never wanted to live there after that. They finally bought the other farm up the road above John Maxwell's where they're living now."

The ancestral Hall house, near the confluence of Pratt's Creek and the Abbagadasset, must have been an elegant building in its day. It was a story and a half house with a steep roof and three or four gables. It had an expensive appearance. There were tall narrow windows of stained glass on both sides of the front door. The doorsteps were heavy slabs of granite. The site of the home was selected, I am sure, because of the wonderful view from the south windows. They looked down one of the most attractive reaches of the river. One could see water for half a mile downstream, all the way to our Shore. The open field south of the house sloped for fifty yards to a ledge which, at that time, was on the edge of the main channel. They built the railroad half way between the house and river. In order to keep the tracks level, they blasted a cut through the rise of land and underlying ledge directly in front of the Hall's house. Along the house side of the cut, a snow fence was erected of closely-spaced boards on end, six feet high. The board fence alone was enough to spoil the view, and the noise of the trains passing so close must have been unbearable after the previous quiet of the riverfront. The house was probably built in the early 1800's, some years before the railroad came. It was still in good repair, although empty for many years, when I first saw the interior of the house in 1910. One Sunday the Hall brothers showed us the grain they had stored in the downstairs rooms. Carloads of loose grain were delivered to the siding at Harwards Depot, and the Halls shovelled it into their horse cart and brought it to the old house for storage. It was fun walking barefoot through the oats and whole corn spread, wall to wall, to a depth of nearly two feet over the floor. In the summer of 1924, I helped the Halls with their haying and mowed the hay around the house with their two-horse mower. Some of the windows had been broken by then and the shingles were falling from the roof, but the former fancy dwelling still had its air of elegance. I showed the place to my children in 1950. By then the entire building had collapsed into the cellar and the fallen roof was completely covered with woodbine. A group of locust trees still stood tall and healthy in the dooryard, doing their best to preserve the former splendor of the place and keep faith with the young housewife, of a hundred years before, who cherished the beautiful homestead she called her own.

Several years after the railroad was built across Hall's Point and the family had moved to a new house, the river did a bit of taking by a different means. Pa told us that when he first paddled up and down the river, the cross-channel along the north side of Kil Maxwell's woods turned northwards near its western end, passed between two marshy islands and flowed past the rocks of Hall's Point, before turning south past the mouth of Pratt's Creek. It no longer followed this route, and the change in the course of the river robbed the Halls of their deep-water landing, but they no longer cared. It gave them in return a small island consisting of two short beaver dams surrounded by several acres of grassy mud flats, in the ownership of which they found no joy. According to the law, I believe, the middle of the channel marks the boundary line between properties on opposite shores. When the river washed its new course through the low muddy "middle ground" north of Kil's Point, a wide area of mud flats that was bare at low tide, it took away from the Maxwells this miniature island which the Halls acquired. Over a period of many years, the old channel around Hall's Point became filled with muddy ooze and finally aquatic vegetation grew all the way across the "guzzle." Vining thought that the pressure exerted by the long railroad dike across the swamp just east of Hall's Point may have been responsible for the change in the river's course. Perhaps it was. As another explanation, Pa had read that rivers tend to straighten themselves with time. A sharp ox-bow bend was surely eliminated in this case. From an airplane, over certain rivers like the Ohio, for example, one can see cases where an ox-bow has been cut off leaving a landlocked basin at the tip of the former bend.

We used to be concerned about the possibility of the river changing its course in a similar fashion near our farm. If the channel had ever cut through the middle ground between the island near our shore and Aunt Emma's farm across the river, the bend in the river near Cromwell's ledge would have eventually filled in and the tip of our Point would have become a part of Cromwell's farm. This change may have been averted by the direction of the strong ebb tide coming down past Kil Maxwell's Point which had a straight run past the upper end of the middle ground. There was no bend in the river at that spot and the tide merely boiled straight ahead down the established channel; there was no incentive for the tide to change its course southward across the middle ground, and the Point remained our property.

Chapter Fifteen

Chestnut Trees

"The tide's going to be high in an hour or so. We ought to go up river this afternoon and look for chestnuts," Pa said while Mother was taking an apple pie from the oven for dessert. It was Sunday dinner and we had finished eating black duck that Pa shot upstream the day before. "After I got that duck yesterday, I went into the woods north of Walt Dinsmore's Creek looking for partridge and found a few chestnuts under the old tree up there. Maybe if we all went along we could get a pailful." Pa rowed us up the river in a skiff on the last of the flood. It was one of those exceptionally pleasant late fall days at the very end of October, sometime around 1909. There had been heavy frosts the past few weeks; the last one had been cold enough to leave shell ice along the shore in the morning. With the exception of many brown leaves on the oak trees, most of the colored foliage had dropped a week or two before. As we passed Kil's Point, a big flock of Canada geese, flying in an asymmetrical V, passed high overhead, southwards towards the Bay.

If it had stood by itself in a more exposed site, the old chestnut tree would have been a landmark. It was the only tree of its kind we knew anywhere around. To those of us who plied the river, it was a sort of landmark, taller than the birches, oaks, and maples around it, standing back from the river a little ways, not far from the railroad tracks a quarter mile above Harward's Depot. Growing close to the northern limits of its natural range, the old chestnut was somewhat of a neighborhood curiosity. It was the source of the only chestnuts we children ever knew.

Pa pushed the skiff ashore at the edge of the woods half way up Dinsmore's Creek. A lone teal jumped from the grass farther up the creek. We didn't find ducks there very often – it was too close to the noise of the trains. We had only a few yards walk to the chestnut tree. The ground beneath the tree was partially covered with prickly burrs of two or three different yearly crops. We found only a very small percentage of them with meaty nuts. Squirrels and partridge had been looking for the good ones, too. Ten or fifteen minutes' search yielded enough well-developed chestnuts to fill our ten-quart pail perhaps three-fourths full. The old tree was two feet or more in diameter at the base. Having grown in competition with other hardwoods, the lowest limbs were twenty feet above the ground. Pa pointed to a younger tree not far from the parent, and there were scattered seedlings two or three feet high. With the ebb tide flowing strongly, we took turns, two at a time, paddling the skiff back home. Afternoons had already become much shortened and it was nearly sunset when we got back to the house.

It was probably five years later that I returned to the old chestnut tree one day in late April to get one of the chestnut seedlings to plant near our home. I dug up a small tree about three feet high and transplanted it near the big henpen behind our stable. The tree took nicely and started growing right away. By the time I was in college in the early 1920's, it had developed a wide spreading top five or six feet tall. By that time, too, we had noticed that the old chestnut upriver had been cut by the man who bought the Dinsmore farm. He had also cut the smaller one that stood near it and, while hunting there in the fall, we saw the stump with sucker sprouts growing from both. We were happy to have a scion of the old tree growing at home. In our botany class at college, Prof. Sawyer discussed the nature of fungi and told about the parasitic ones and how infectious spores were often spread long distances by insects, birds, and the wind. He called our attention to a lone chestnut tree in front of Libbey Forum. It had been recently killed by chestnut blight. "The fungus spores that infected the tree must have been blown a long distance," he said. "Possibly they came all the way from Massachusetts where the disease has killed practically all of the chestnuts. I've never seen any chestnut trees in the woods around here that could have served as a source of infection for this campus tree." I became worried about my chestnut by the henpen. Since it was a small and isolated tree, I hoped it might be luckier than the one at the college and possibly escape the infection. Much to my dismay, I noticed that summer a couple of reddish sunken cankers that were girdling the main stem of the little tree. There was also a small canker on one of the branches. During wet weather, the discolored bark in the cankers was dotted with small, raised pimples, resembling tiny volcanoes, and from their tops, jelly-like curlicues oozed out bearing millions of microscopic spores that would spread far and wide. These were positive evidence of chestnut blight. My thrifty young tree died the next summer.

With the chestnut up river gone from the scene and with the one I transplanted killed by blight, we considered this kind of tree to be extinct from our locality. We thought no more about them until one October day in the mid-1950's. Al and I were returning from hunting ducks along the upper reaches of the Abbagadasset from Hall's meadow to the Mill Pond one morning. In the early afternoon, we were paddling downstream above Dinsmore's Creek when Al said, "That's where we used to get chestnuts in there. I sort of miss the old, big tree, standing there above the rest." Both of us looked toward the wooded bank north of the creek. Everything looked much like it always had – mostly a soft-wood stand of hemlock, spruce and fir, with a few white birches, aspen and oaks mixed in. "What's that dark green tree in there on the bank?" Al asked. "The leaves look too long for an oak; it's probably a black cherry. Put me ashore and I'll take a look." Since Al was in the stern of the gunning float I said to him, "Put me ashore and I'll take a look." I could hardly believe my eyes. "It's a chestnut," I shouted to Al. It was a fair-sized tree, maybe twenty years old and thirty feet high. It looked perfectly healthy. How could this tree have escaped the blight for so many years? Could it be a blight-resistant individual, like foresters had been hoping for years to find, or had the blight fungus died out from lack of susceptible hosts, as some thought might happen this time?

"Let's take a look back in the woods here a way, where the old chestnut used to stand," Al suggested. We quickly found were the big tree had stood as well as the smaller one close by. A cluster of sprouts several feet tall marked the site of both trees demonstrating the terrific longevity of chestnut roots after the aboveground parts had been cut down or killed. But many of the sprouts were dead. "Let's take a look at the dead shoots," said Al. Sure enough, they'd been killed by the blight! With the disease so near, how had the tree on the river bank escaped so long? We came to the conclusion that it must have had some degree of natural resistance to blight, or else it was a mighty lucky escape. We noticed the riverbank tree whenever we passed during the next two or three years. Its dark foliage stood out against the other species as before. Then, for a period of ten years, we did no hunting along the river. It was not until 1969 that I hunted on foot along the east side of the Abbagadasset in the vicinity of Dinsmore's Creek. I planned my route along the river in order to check on the condition of that tree. I approached the bank from deeper in the woods and had difficulty in locating the tree at first. Then something disturbing caught my eye. Directly ahead, silhouetted against the river's surface, was a standing tree trunk with a lot of sprouts growing from its base. A few steps further brought more bad news. The tree had been killed by blight but, as usual, the roots survived. I found signs of the fungus on some of the sprouts. It was merely another picture of chestnut blight's host-parasite relationship we knew so well. Our coveted chestnut, for whose survival we hoped so optimistically, was just another tree that was susceptible to the blight. It is remarkable that chestnut roots can be kept alive for so many years by a cluster of short-lived sprouts that keep appearing from their crown, attaining sometimes many feet in height before falling victim to the disease. If there is a reward for persistence, the chestnut blight fungus should also receive its share. It has maintained its regrettable presence in our woodlands long after it has killed its last sizeable host trees.

Chapter Sixteen

Weather and Folk Wisdom

"There's a bright star near the moon tonight," Pa said as he blew out the lantern and hung it on a nail outside the kitchen door. He had returned from the barn where he had spread clean sawdust in the horse stall and had given the cows a late forkful of hay one chilly December night. "My folks always said that was a sign of cold weather. Maybe it's what brought on this cold snap. We'll just have to live through it, cold or no cold. All this part of the country is good for is bears and woodchucks, anyway." Observations of such phenomena and deductions made from them have long given farmers the reputation of being better than ordinary forecasters. Attest the popularity of the Old Farmer's Almanac. The things upon which our folks based their prognostications of weather and climate were innumerable. When heavy overcast skies threatened rain for some outdoor evening event we planned to attend, Mother often said, "Maybe the full moon will clear it off." On cloudy days, she predicted, "It will rain by two o'clock if it's going to at all." Another example was Pa's distrust of a brightening sky during a northeast storm. Instead of indicating that the storm might be coming to an end, the brighter sky merely meant, he said, that "it's letting up to get a new hold." "Bath and Brunswick lights are showing on the clouds tonight," was another observation that our parents always thought worthy of mention. They never seemed perturbed about such sky reflections, so I guess they meant there was no bad weather in the offing. Hearing the far-off whistle of a locomotive, especially in the winter, was a sure sign of an impending storm. Those coming from trains running between Brunswick and Bath, beyond the Bay, or those between Bath and Rockland, behind the Woolwich hills, were the ones we listened for when we wanted to get the lowdown on the weather for the next few days. A cuckoo calling or frogs croaking in the middle of the day were good indicators of imminent rain.

There seemed to be no end to things like that, indicating rain was on the way. A dog or cat eating grass, chickens preening themselves while huddled together in the shade, or even cows lying down in the pasture (something they were always likely to do anyway as soon as their stomachs were full), have all been said to be followed by rainy weather. The old sayings: "Rainbow in the morning, sailors take warning; rainbow at night, sailors delight," and "Red sky in the morning, rain before dawning," we always considered as fairly sound forecasting. And no one ever questioned the soundness of the rhyme:

> Evening red and morning gray
> Sets the traveller on his way.
> But evening gray and morning red
> Will bring down rain upon his head.

Cobwebs on the grass made conspicuous with morning dew, and white frosts on three successive nights, were phenomena Mother stolidly believed would shortly bring rain. During a summer shower in haying time, Pa liked to hear the thunder die out quickly after each clap. "That long, rolling thunder," he said, "that takes a long time to fade away in the distance, means that the shower may turn into a general rain." As to the expected duration for a period of rain, my folks based their prognostications on the direction of the wind. A sou'easter usually lasted only a day. Nor'easters were a different breed of cats. They could be expected to last three days. Pa considered anything less from them as a "show of mercy on the part of nature." A mackerel sky was also considered as foretelling rain. I can go along with that one. During my sophomore year at Bates, I arranged my fall schedule so that I had no classes on Monday. This allowed for a long week-end at home. On the high tide, one of those early Mondays in October, I went to the head of the river soon after daybreak. On the way home around ten o'clock, the sky became lightly overcast with a beautiful high curtain of mackerel clouds. Against the pink-tinted background, a large flock of pintails, a rather uncommon species in our area, flew northwards far out of range overhead. The long line of light brown ducks against the mackerel sky was a memorable sight. That afternoon, while I was walking up the railroad tracks to take the four o'clock train at Harward's Depot, the rain commenced.

In the wintertime we viewed with a certain uneasiness those whitish rings around the moon, like the sailors saw on the ill-fated *Hesperus*. They could be the forerunners of a snowstorm, we were told. The greater the diameter of the ring, the bigger the storm, and the number of days it would last might be told by the number of stars within the circle. But the rings were often seen in a hazy sky and it might take a day or two for the storm to arrive; so we relaxed in the belief that perhaps the ring didn't mean too much anyway. More awesome was the yellow streamer that we saw once in a while in late autumn or during the winter, reaching straight upwards from the setting sun. The presence of a bright sundog on the horizon both north and south of the streamer made a combination that we observed with much concern. "Those things could bring us some rough weather," Pa said. "I hope it's not going to be one of those winter blizzards with a howling northwester behind it." Those biting, sixty-mile-an-hour winds with temperatures around zero were the sort of weather that Pa disliked entirely. The gusty winds howling around the back of our house forced the cold right through our buildings. It was difficult to keep the kitchen, pantry and sitting room comfortable and prevent things from freezing anywhere in the barn or in the house cellar. Pa told about one of those cold gales that blew for three days and three nights, continuously. He used to sit close to a hot stove during the evening and mentally record the length of the wind's lulls between the gusts. "When the lulls start getting longer, it's a sign the wind is dying out," said Pa. He never minded too much those cold calm winter mornings when, at sunrise, the smoke from the sawmill's stack and from Uncle Everett's chimney rose straight up against a windless sky. He rather enjoyed even the coldest weather as long as the wind didn't blow. When Pa looked out of the back kitchen window and saw northern lights, he said, "That means we're due for a change of weather." Which, most New Englanders will agree, occurs every day or two, anyway.

Most everyone is always interested in the kind of winter the next one will be. We can put up with a late cold spring, a hot dry summer, or a wet and windy fall, but we'd rather not be faced with a tough winter. We'd give most anything to know that we can expect one of those open winters with a minimum of snow and no extremely low temperatures. By the first of October every year, we began to speculate as to how deep a freeze we were in for during the next four months. If the old heron stayed around the river until it froze over, we could look forward to a mild winter. Likewise, dark opaque keels on the breastbones of the wild game birds that Mother fricasseed were good omens, as was the failure of anyone to see a flock of geese heading south before the middle of October. For some reason we paid little attention to the much-talked-about relative widths of the black and red bands on that kind of woolly bear caterpillar. None of us like caterpillars that much. But we bought an extra pair of long underwear whenever the fall-caught skunks had an extra thick layer of fat beneath their skin, or if partridges had unusually long bristles on the sides of their toes to improve their efficiency as snowshoes. Believing that Nature takes care of its wild creatures in times of stress, we took a dim view of a heavy acorn crop or pine trees loaded with cones. A late-season thunder shower indicated a mild winter coming up. Pa was confused one winter, however, when we heard thunder in January. "I don't know whether they would call this late or early," he said. As for predicting how long a winter might last, we never took any stock in Groundhog Day. Skunks lived in abandoned woodchuck dens and we set traps in them all, regardless of present occupants. We never caught a chuck in any of our skunk traps that were set throughout February every year. It was always late in March before we saw muddy tracks of the wood-chuck on melting snowdrifts. Had they come out of their dens on Candlemas Day, we would have caught one now and then.

As indicators of the prevailing weather we could expect in the approaching winter, muskrat houses were considered one of the most reliable prognostications. To me it always seemed a plausible basis for making predictions. Muskrats build their winter houses in swamps, where semi-aquatic food plants like cattail, iris, sweet flag and sedge are available. They gather the lower stems and roots of these plants beneath the ice and take them into their houses through underwater entrances. Here, they devour the nourishing morsels in an insulated air chamber above the water level of the swamp. Much of their time during the winter, muskrats spend in shoreline dens at the end of burrows in dry land not far from their houses. The entrance to the burrows is also under water at the edge of the swamp. For comfortable living, a muskrat needs a frost-free chamber above the water level in his house to which he can take his food to be eaten. If the winter ahead is to be a steady cold one, they can save some work and materials when building their houses in the fall by constructing a low house with the air chamber not far above November's ice level. If instinct tells them that the winter will be mild, with frequent thaws and a rainstorm now and then instead of a blizzard, they build much taller houses, ones which will be well above the water level even after a foot or two of flooding of the swamp. After observing the height of muskrat houses in two or three swamp locations near our home for several years, I was confused to find some years that there were a few low houses when most of them were tall, and vice versa. Perhaps some muskrats, by mistake, got hold of an outdated issue of the *Old Rodents' Almanac*.

Differences in snow depths in different parts of the State were believed to have an effect some years on the plentifulness of fish in our river in the spring. Fishermen along the Abbagadasset thought it possible to predict how good the shad run would be by noting the difference in final depths of snow between our area and points farther to the north in Maine, around the headwaters of the Androscoggin and Kennebec. Pa explained it this way: "When they get a lot more snow up-country than we do, our run-off is all over while the Androscoggin and Kennebec are still carrying a lot of icy water from the melting snow. This gives the sun a chance to warm up the water in this river while the bigger ones stay cold. When the schools of shad come up the Kennebec from the ocean, they feel the warm current from our river as soon as they get through the Chops and they follow the warmer water right up here. That seems to have been the way it was, years when we've had the best runs of shad in this river. Herring seem to be attracted to the warmer water the same way, too."

One of the most difficult weather elements for us to predict was fog. It often closed in on me with little warning or none at all. In southern Maine, we knew two kinds of fog, sea fog and land fog, besides the wispy mist that arose from the river's surface on frosty fall mornings. Land fog was something like the river mist except that it was usually more dense and extended much higher in the atmosphere. It was pleasant to watch as it formed over low land when the air became cooler after a warm rain in spring or summer. Sea fog often rolled in from the ocean during the night and usually remained until it was burned away by mid-morning sun. In late July, August, and early September, we could sometimes see the approaching fog bank in the southeast during the late afternoon. In haying time, sea fog sometimes kept us from bringing in a load of hay after supper.

For the most part, we considered fog as a sort of nuisance. There were few good things we could say about it. We did welcome fog in wintertime, however, since everyone believed it had a way of "eating" snow. Pa rejoiced at the appearance of a heavy fog after contending with snowdrifts for several weeks. "There's nothing like a good fog for getting rid of a lot of this snow," he said. For those of us who were involved in the trapping of skunks, a period of foggy weather in late February or March was a welcome phenomenon. Not only would the animals come out of their dens in the mild temperatures, but also the loss of snow meant there would be bare spots here and there in the fields and pastures. It was a big relief, after trudging through crunchy snow for a hundred yards, to come to a bare spot where one could get solid footing for a ways – it gave one a lift, like a refund from the IRS.

Flocks of Canada geese often seemed to lose their bearings in dense fog. On some occasions during fall migrations, these birds, honking their heads off, flew low over our house apparently utterly confused as to where they were. They probably had followed the Kennebec southwards to the vicinity of the Bay, where they lost all contact with the earth in the high, thick fog that blocked out all lowland and most of the hills. At times, too, I have noticed an unusual effect of fog on some other game birds, particularly Wilson's snipe and partridge. One foggy morning in September, while I was taking the cows to pasture before going to school, I saw a small flock of these snipe, which are ordinarily secretive and remain hidden in the grass, running about on the exposed mud at the margin of Amasa's pond. They were not at all disturbed by the entrance of the cows to the nearby pasture nor did they take to cover at the clatter of the pasture bars as I slid them into place. On one or two occasions, I have seen the usually timid ruffed grouse fly casually into a tree and perch there motionless when the woods were filled with heavy fog, instead of thundering away through the branches and out of sight as they so frequently are wont to do when the air is clear.

One did not have to be a weather forecaster to predict that the morning after our chicken-picking day in August would be foggy. The fog had been heavy that morning, as it had the day before. Those were the kind of mornings that the Boston boats, upon reaching the mouth of the Kennebec, dropped anchor and waited for the fog to lift. We had scarcely gotten the tubfuls of feathers cleared away in the tie-up and the dressed fowl and broilers hung down cellar to cool, when the soft white bank appeared beyond the Chops. Al was taking the dressed poultry to Bath in his motorboat in the morning. He and Pa became concerned about their being able to follow the channels in the Bay when the fog was thick. They remembered how young Santy Pratt had boasted, "I can find my way across Merrymeeting Bay in the thickest fog that God ever made." They knew that young Santy was staying with his father at the time, and they asked him to navigate the boat to Bath early the next day. "This will give him the chance to show how well he knows the lower Abbagadasset and the Cathance channel," Pa said. By keeping the grass close to the channel in view, they were able to reach the mouth of our river, far out in the Bay, without much difficulty. Here, it was all open water – no more grass. Al lowered the commutator on the engine to slow the boat's speed as they proceeded into what they hoped to be the Cathance channel, which meets the Kennebec at the Chops. After several minutes, we saw tall pines almost directly above us in what appeared to be the clouds. Things always seem much taller in a fog. Instead of going towards the Kennebec, we were in a branch channel that led westward straight to Bluff Head. Our direction of course should have been towards the east. The boat was turned, and, with the aid of a compass, an east-southeast course eventually brought us within sight of the ledges and the oak trees close above the Chops. Here, the fog lifted slightly so that Young Santy was able to see the Kennebec shore the rest of the way to Bath.

Chapter Seventeen

Oxen and Steers

Two heavy ox yokes stood in the corner of our stable chamber along with a lighter one for training steers that Al made from a piece of spruce timber. All were complete with nicely curved ash bows, steel pins that held the bows in place, and a heavy iron ring halfway between the bows for hooking the ox chain that was fastened to the load. Although oxen were a thing of the past in our section of the State by the time I came on the scene, Pa still talked a lot about them. One of the earliest incidents concerned the moving of a house owned by Grandfather Williams from near the sawmill on the West Branch at the edge of the Village to a new site on Clay Hill. He secured the help of many farmers in town, who furnished a total of fifty pairs of oxen. This team was able to move the building only a short distance, on the level, to the first bridge over the Branch. It was a hundred yards further to the foot of the hill, and then the building had to be moved a short distance up the hillside. Grandfather solicited more oxen from three surrounding towns. Finally, with the combined power of one hundred pairs of oxen, the house was moved to its new location. This was said to be the largest oxen team ever assembled in our town.

Oxen were especially useful in harvesting meadow hay. They could haul a load through boggy ground without getting stuck in the mud. In this sort of footing, the big feet of a horse would become mired unless square wooden bog shoes were strapped onto all four feet. Al told me of a frightening experience he had as a teenager one hot August day after he and Pa had been bringing in meadow hay with the oxen. When they quit work for dinner, Pa asked Al to fasten the oxen in their stanchions and give them a forkful of hay. The two oxen stood at the far end of the tie-up, next to the horse's stall. Al fastened the chain around the neck of the first ox and then pushed his way between the other ox and the rough boards of the horse stall to hitch the second one. As Al pushed past the ox's mid-section, the animal started to relieve an itchy place on his side by rubbing against the horse stall. He squeezed Al against the boarding. Try as hard as he could to push the ox away, Al's efforts were futile against the 1800-pound ox. With the last of his air being pressed from his lungs, Al shouted for help. Surmising what the trouble might be, Pa rushed to the tie-up and, with a dung fork, forced the ox to desist with his rubbing. Al was released unhurt.

It was about that time that Uncle Ed had an unfortunate experience with a yoke of young steers that he borrowed from his father. Since Uncle Ed's back woodlot extended nearly to the other highway west of the railroad, not far from his father's farm, he was bringing the steers via the shortcut through the woods. They reached the barways in the fences on both sides of the tracks. While he was opening the bars on the east side of the railroad, the steers that had just crossed the tracks were standing behind him. Suddenly they decided to return home by taking off up the tracks. Uncle Ed was unable to catch up with them and his shouting was to no avail. He heard a freight train approaching beyond the bend at Amasa's woods. The pair of steers paid no heed to the sudden appearance of the oncoming locomotive and the long heavy freight train could not stop in time. Relatives and neighbors came with tubs and baskets to salvage as much of the meat as they could.

Pa had an anxious moment one day in December when his pair of steers broke through the ice where a breakage had started to form. It happened the year before he built the stable. There had been an infestation of green worms in the woods that summer killing nearly all of the spruces. "The worms were dangling everywhere when you walked through the woods," Pa said. When Aunt Emma and Uncle Al Maxwell saw that the spruce on the farm were dead, they told Pa he could have all of them that he wanted to cut. It was a good opportunity to get lumber for the stable. During the fall, Pa went across the river by boat and cut a lot of logs to be snaked out of the woods as soon as he could cross the river with his steers. He would leave the logs tied to the bank shore until the ice went out, then would tow them in a raft to the sawmill with the skiff. Pa wanted to get the logs out of the woods before the snow became too deep. He wanted to get started with this work as soon as the river ice was strong enough to hold his steers. His first attempt to cross the river was a little too soon, or else he picked a bad spot for the crossing. The broad sheet of ice over the main channel was crossed successfully. But near the east shore, where the channel bank was fairly steep, the ice had big cracks from resting on the sloping bank of low tide. Suddenly both animals broke through. The tide was high and the water was too deep for the steers to touch bottom. They struggled to keep their heads above the water. Fortunately the ice was strong enough for Pa to get quite close to them. With his axe he knocked the metal pins from the ends of the oxbows that projected above the top of the yoke. "They really saved themselves," Pa said. "They tried to climb out and in doing so brought the might of their front quarters onto the edge of the ice. The ice kept breaking and the steers worked closer and closer towards shore. They continued this performance until they reached the high flats and were able to walk to shore. One of them was about done for, and he staggered around for awhile and could hardly stand. I've always been careful about crossing those breakage areas after that."

Chapter Eighteen

Cemeteries

Bowdoinham was the seventeenth town to be formally organized in Maine. It was incorporated in 1762. Construction of the first church in town was started in 1765; its site was less than a quarter mile up river from our home. The building was located on level ground near the west bank of the Abbagadasset, a hundred yards north of Cromwell's ledge. Back then, church construction was a community affair. It took several years to complete the building. In May, 1775, when all was finished except the pews, a meeting was held to discuss participation in the Revolution. A few weeks later the church burned – a fire presumably set by the Tories who owned much of the land. "Silas Adams and I found old nails and melted glass at the site, when he came over to see the location one day while he was writing his town history," Pa told us.

Like so many churches, this one had an adjacent cemetery – also the first in town. It was a well-chosen spot for both the church and the cemetery. The first public road in town passed close by and the river was only a few steps away, a convenience in those days to many of the residents who did much of their travelling along the waterways. Townspeople travelled five or six miles to attend services at the church, coming by foot, on horseback, in farm vehicles, and by boat. The site was equally well chosen for the cemetery – the river flowed in and out at the foot of the wooded bank at the graveyard's eastern edge, and thrushes sang at sunset in nearby woods across the river. In his history of the town, written around 1910, Adams states: "Years ago, when the cemetery was quite free from trees and weeds, one could count scores of graves on this side hill, marked only by a flat rock for the head and foot stones. .... This beautiful location has been most sadly neglected for many years, it having been used for pasture and is now grown to bushes and weeds." When I was in my teens, there were small trees growing everywhere in the old graveyard. It was difficult to see more than three or four of the old stone markers from any one point. There were no names, dates or inscriptions – just flat fieldstones standing on edge. Many were badly tilted and some were broken at ground level. After passing through the cemetery one day in late summer on the way home, after seeing Genevieve off on an afternoon train at Harward's, I told Mother I was depressed by the condition of the unmarked headstones, none of which had any means of identification. I described to her the way the ground cover plants were growing above them. Mother had known about the old burying ground since childhood and realized that it had been neglected. She said that two Revolutionary War soldiers were buried there. I remember seeing two Revolutionary soldiers' markers, with tiny flags placed there by the DAR group in the Village on Memorial Day one year. I don't know how they knew at which of the graves to place the markers. Perhaps they, indeed, could not be sure. Regarding the lack of upkeep, Mother said, "The trees will keep a better vigil than some caretaker who might merely be making a dollar or two a day. To those buried there, I'm sure it makes no difference."

Although the cemetery above Cromwell's ledge was the first land set aside for such use by the early settlers, an Indian burying ground near the Abbagadasset point was possibly centuries older. The Indians chose a site on the north shore of Merrymeeting Bay, where the level ground was sandy and much easier for digging than gravelly areas or those of clay. It was to this cemetery that settlers in the block house at the Chops saw Indians ferrying their casualties after a retaliatory raid by twelve whites at Center's Point the night before. (It all started when Thomas McFadden brought his family and cattle from Georgetown and settled on Center's Point in 1720, without making arrangements with the Indians for use of the land. McFadden built a home on the Point and escaped with his family just before it was burned by the Indians. Returning after dark with eleven men, McFadden, and the others fired their muzzle-loaders into the group of Indians as they feasted on one of the cattle.)

The lack of upkeep of public burying grounds led many of the early families to establish private cemeteries on their own land. There were several of these family plots in our neighborhood, about fifty feet square, surrounded by a cast iron fence, and often with a five or six foot monument in the center bearing the family name. The Davis cemetery was located between the road and the orchard back of their house. It had a conical cedar tree in each corner. The Calls had theirs near the riverbank, a short distance above the sawmill. There were two cemeteries belonging to the Puringtons on the ridge west of our schoolhouse. One was near Newell's house not far from Jellerson's Corner and the other, belonging to Norris Purington, was located on a high hill near the far corner of Weymouth's pasture. The old Hall farm, up the road from us, had a large private plot near the river at the roadside where it sloped down toward the west end of the big road bridge. It was close to a clump of large oaks and had hackmatack trees growing in the corners. The Cromwells also had their own private burial plot, although the early town cemetery was adjacent to their land. It was a small fenced plot beneath a large red oak, and only a few yards from the northeast corner of their barn.

Whenever I passed the Cromwell's graveyard, I was always moved to take a closer look at Jere's headstone. Jere was a member of Company D, 19th Maine Division, during the Civil War. He was a tall man and to keep his feet from being in sight of the enemy while lying on his back behind a log, he brought them in towards his body. In this position his knees were raised and one of them was hit by a Confederate sharpshooter's bullet. A Confederate doctor was prepared to amputate the leg but Jere cursed the surgeon and left the operating table. They let him go as a paroled prisoner doomed to death, they thought. But he survived the wound and returned to Bowdoinham. He had been a good friend to Pa and had helped with the legal papers when he bought our farm. A while later, Pa bought his only breech-loading shotgun from Jere, a 10-gauge hammer gun with Damascus twist steel double barrels. I think it was a Parker. Jere was the neighbor to whom Pa went when he needed incidental help around the farm. The inscription on Jere's headstone read:

Jeremiah M. Cromwell
Died Sept. 11, 1886
Age 48 yr. 10 mo.

Pa told us about Jere's untimely and unfortunate accident and death. The eleventh of September that year was a fine early fall day, with comfortable sunshine and a moderately brisk southerly breeze. It was also second week of the duck hunting season. Jere had gone into the Bay that morning with George Jack, locally known as "The Hunter." They were returning in the late forenoon along the east shore of the river with fair wind and tide. A duck rose from the grass in the cove below the Old Pine. With the usual craftiness of a black duck, the bird had waited until the hunters had passed before taking wing. By doing so the duck was able to rise more effectively against the wind and fly out of range down river. Since George was seated up front on the bottom of the gunning float, he could not turn far enough around to bring his gun into play against the climbing waterfowl. It was Jere's chance. When he pulled the trigger, there was only the ping of the hammer. The shell was a dud.

"I'll take that home and put a new primer in it," Jere said as he extracted the loaded shell and put it in his pocket.

"Better throw the thing overboard," George advised him.

Back at Jere's house an hour later, the two hunters were waiting while Jere's wife, Liza, made the final preparations for dinner. It would soon be ready. George was reading a paper in the living room; Jere was around somewhere. Suddenly there was a loud explosion that rattled the windows. Liza was frightened. "Jere, what's that?" she shouted. Jere did not answer. Wisps of black powder smoke drifted through the front door when George opened it. Jere lay motionless at the foot of the low steps just outside. His jackknife with the small blade opened lay on the top step. Jere never regained consciousness. The primer that failed to function when hit by the firing pin was no dud after all. When Jere tried to pry it from the base of the shell, the percussion cap exploded. The ounce and a quarter load of lead shot, in the crimped end of the shell that pointed away from Jere acted, with all of its inertia, like a missile launching pad for the lighter cardboard shell casing and its brass base. With tremendous momentum, the three-inch casing disappeared entirely near Jere's eye. "The lead shot," Pa told us, "only had force enough to scar the wooden doorstep." He warned us, "Unless you know what you're doing, don't go monkeying around with any kind of ammunition; it's too dangerous."

While hunting partridge along the riverbank one fall morning, I came across Young Santy Pratt's newly closed grave, close to Old Santy's south line. The grave was just across the border of Cromwell's upper field where the old town burying ground was located. It was a damp still morning on a Saturday while I was in high school. Burial had been held earlier in the week and I first noticed the mound of fresh soil some distance away. The spot was not a family burying ground; there were no other graves nearby. It was merely an out of the way place in a group of shrubby dogwoods. In the calmness of that damp morning, I noticed a strong, pungent odor arising from the mat of fallen dogwood leaves. The smell was so strong that I was momentarily startled – making me wonder at the time if it might be emanating from the grave. Since then I have noticed the same odor around various kinds of dogwood. The wood of this shrub, even when dead, if freshly cut has that same peculiar sort of aromatic smell. This rather unpleasant odor resembles that of a dog, and it may account for the shrub's name.

Our farm never had a private cemetery but there were two graves side by side on a slight rise of ground close to our south line, half way between the barn and the meadow. They contained the remains of Ben Sedgeley's father and of Ben's sister who had died as a young girl. "When we bought the place, Ben said he would have the bodies moved to the Ridge," Pa said. "But he never has." Pa mowed the grass on the graves each year at haying time, but he carefully avoided them while plowing. "Someday, someone will plow right over them and no-one will know where the graves are any longer." One spring, Pa plowed that portion of the east field along the south line for the vegetable plot. I usually was given a corner in the family garden patch every year to raise some things of my own. That year Pa allowed me to have a small area at each end of the graves. Since I would be doing all of the weeding myself by hand, Pa would not have to drive over the graves when he cultivated his larger portion of the field. I sometimes had a slightly sad feeling while working near the two parallel mounds of raised turf. The fact that one of the graves was that of a child made me wonder if she might have been old enough to have a garden of her own, if she too got chapped feet and shins after wading for tadpoles in stagnant swamp water on those first days in spring that were warm enough for going barefoot, and if her mother cured the chapping by applying ordinary cream.

There was a small cemetery on Amasa William's farm. It was located on a short peninsula with high banks that extended out into the swamp at the lower end of his east field. We could see the two white headstones from our house, underneath three towering elm trees and a bushy, twenty year old white pine near-by. There had been four graves in the cemetery at one time, including those of Grandmother and Grandfather Williams which had been removed before I was big enough to visit the gravesite. When I was about five, I remember Mother watching from the kitchen window as the horse cart bearing the casket moved across Amasa's field to the road. Later, I saw the two empty graves filled with discarded field stones.

During my trapping days, it always seemed as if old woodchuck holes in farm cemeteries were likely places to catch skunks. I got two or three of the animals near Amasa's graveyard, and others were trapped in the Call's plot as well as around both the old and new cemeteries on the Cromwell's farm. The usual explanation was that the burying grounds offered a place where woodchucks could dig a burrow unmolested and, at the same time, be close to cultivated fields. I discovered that holes among those depressions on the bank of the swamp on our Point, where farm animals had been buried in the past, were most likely places for catching skunks. This made me wonder if there might be another reason why these animals were plentiful on burial plots, other than the woodchuck's choice of burrowing site.

Across a narrow boggy swamp from Amasa's cemetery was the tip of an-other somewhat longer peninsula, the south end of which sloped to such low land that freshet tides flowed entirely around the higher part. It was on the piece of Amasa's farm that had earlier belonged to his father, "Uncle John," and hence we called the peninsula Uncle John's Island. It too had several woodchuck holes around its brushy tip, some of which were appropriated by skunks. Here, one Saturday when he was home from college, Vining decided to dig out a skunk den. He used a long limber birch pole with which to find the direction of the burrow and the distance to the first bend. He dug a pit at that point, then used the pole again to find out what direction the burrow took after bending. By dinnertime, he was halfway down the second shaft. In mid-afternoon, Pa said to me, "Let's go down and see how he's making out with his digging." By that time, Vining had reached the nest of dry brown grass in the enlarged chamber at the end of the burrow. The den contained no skunks. "Funny thing," Vining said, "I dug up those bones in this second pit – pretty close to the nest. What do you suppose they could be?" Pa didn't make a guess as to the identity of the nearly foot-long bones. "I don't know of anything ever being buried here," he replied. "John Williams had a hog die one winter but I don't believe he went to the trouble of burying him." The bones looked like those from the legs of some animal; they were too short to be from a mature human. Years later I thought about those bones Vining had dug up while I was deer hunting on state game lands near Millville, Pennsylvania. At the head of a wooded ravine, near the source of a small brook, I came upon a carefully constructed mound with a flat stone set exactly upright in its top. The mound obviously had been built many years ago. Well-established ferns were growing among the moss-covered stones. The surroundings were quiet and comfortable, with high steep hills on three sides and the big opening to the west, where the setting sun shone in. It was the sort of spot someone enamoured of his countryside might have chosen late in life, in which to wait out eternity. The area was old abandoned farmland with stone walls running through the woods. Stone structures such as an old building foundation or a well-built culvert could be found here and there beneath shrubs and vines that partially hid them from view. I thought of Vining and wondered what he might have found if he had dug into the damp interior of the grave-like mound. Perhaps some bones? Possibly only those of someone's faithful horse? Maybe of a "higher" species?

Chapter Nineteen

Predators

Predators presented quite a problem in our farm's economy. Although Pa always said, when a fox caught one of our hens, "We'll have one less hen to buy grain for now – no great loss without some small gain," the dollar or more the hen would have brought at Cornish's store was a lot to us, to say nothing of the profit from the eggs she would have produced before her laying days were over. All sorts of losses like that had to be prevented if we were to make a go of our enterprise. Not only were there bird and mammal predators to control, but also rodents and many insects. I doubt that we would have fared nearly as well if we had been denied use of the gun and steel trap.

An early rather humorous incident involving predator control occurred when my parents were first married. Mother told us about hearing a commotion among the hens in the barn cellar around midnight one dark night. Ordinarily, when darkness falls, chickens are the quietest things on earth after they have gone to roost for the night or, if young, were still sitting on the floor of their coop. Any noise made by them after dark deserves immediate attention. "I happened to be awake long enough to hear the noise," Mother said. "I awakened your father and we went downstairs. He got his shotgun and I went along with the lantern to find out what was going on. We saw a skunk in one corner of the henpen beneath the tie-up. He had driven a setting hen off her low nest near the ground. Your father asked me to hold the lantern close to the gun barrel, so he could see the front sight and the skunk at the same time. I must have held it a little too close to the muzzle. When he fired, it blew out the lantern. I had to go back to the kitchen to get a match to light it again."

A similar event involving another carnivore of the same kind took place years later, except this time Pa didn't get a shot at the skunk. It was one hot summer night when Genevieve had chosen to sleep in the porch hammock. She was awakened sometime before dawn by the excited cackling of a hen down around the south side of the barn. She awakened Pa who, clad only in the lower part of his long underwear that he used like pajama bottoms, hastened to get his gun from the stable. Genevieve said, "He was holding up his pants by the gusset strap." He told her, "Wake Bert up and have him bring his flashlight." By the time I reached the corner of the barn, Pa was peering cautiously into the clump of horseradish that grew close to the barn's stone foundation. "Shine your light in behind that horseradish," Pa said. "I just saw a skunk go in there." The hen was still cackling her head off on the other side of the line fence in the unmowed hay in Amasa's field. I edged cautiously forward towards the clump of tall broad leaves. "He's giving me the ticklish part of this job to do," I thought. I would have preferred to stand back there with the gun. Finally I was close enough to the horseradish to use a stick to push some of the plants away from the building. I neither saw nor smelled the skunk. Pa approached close beside me. "He's gone into the barn cellar through that hole between the rocks," Pa said. "We'll never see him under that pile of lumber in there." We turned our attention to the still noisy hen and found her close to a clutch of eggs where she had stolen her nest away. Next day we moved both the eggs and broody hen to a safer nest in the barn, where she could be shut in at night and hatch her brood in peace, safe from stealthy varmints that prowled at night. The skunk, in a way, did us a favor in discovering the nest. In another week they'd have been mowing Amasa's hay.

One Sunday morning in November, Pa was reading a newspaper in the kitchen after breakfast. Glancing out of the north window he saw a fox sitting at the edge of the woods Up-under-the-Hill. Quickly changing his reading glasses for his regular ones, he went for the shotgun. He tried to remove the shells to see if they were heavy duck loads, but the shells in both barrels were stuck so that they could not be extracted with the fingers. Instead of taking the time to punch out the shells with a cleaning rod, he took a chance that Vining had left the right loads in the gun, and went after the fox. Just as he went out the back stable door, the fox came trotting straight towards the house, possibly to get closer to our chickens around the barn. Pa took aim at the animal and fired. The fox took off towards the river with a burst of speed that allowed no time to discharge the second barrel. There was great dismay in our household when Pa discovered that the gun was loaded with light hand-loaded charges that Vining had used in snipe hunting. They were ineffective against the fox forty or fifty yards away. When we fed the hens that morning, we found that the fox had killed one of them in the field north of the house.

Al told me that he once shot a large mink after it had caught one of the full grown roosters the folks were fattening in the barn cellar henpen. My parents also told of losing twenty young chickens – all in one coop at night – the depredations of a weasel, they thought. "Those blood-thirsty things just kill for the sake of killing," they said. Since I can remember, however, we lost no fowl of any age to either of these predators. Once, a rat killed a full-blooded white Plymouth Rock chicken about two weeks old that I had hatched from one of the eggs purchased from a Pennsylvania breeder. Another time, a rat, or rats, gnawed a hole in the bottom of a coop and killed a black pullet that was half-grown and completely feathered out. Pa told me, "When we lived in Bath, I saw a rat catch one of our chickens. He grabbed it right by the back." One winter, we noticed one of our barn cellar hens with a few drops of blood on her neck. Examination showed a few small punctures in the skin. It was our guess that a mink had tried to capture the hen and was driven off by the rooster using his strong wings and sharp spurs. We brought the hen upstairs and kept her in the tie-up for a few days, where she quickly recovered, whatever the injuries were.

Many of our predatory losses of fowl of any age were due to certain kinds of hawks. Cooper's hawks were the worst ones. They had a habit of slipping slyly into our backyard and making off with a chicken before anybody had time to get hold of a gun. Goshawks were bad, too. They caught several of our hens, mostly during the fall. One summer we lost a couple of nearly full-grown chickens to a pair of marsh hawks that were nesting in Newell's meadow. We never considered marsh hawks as serious predators, however. The few chickens we lost to them were taken in tall grass when the birds were flying low over the field looking for frogs and mice. Red-shouldered hawks nested across the river every year and we always called them "hen hawks" but only once did they catch any of our poultry. That happened early in the spring, soon after these hawks arrived from the south, and the single hen that was caught had wandered quite a long way into the woods Up-under-the-Hill. I was surprised one spring to see a rather small hawk catch one of our week-old chickens and fly off with it dangling in its claws into the field between the house and the woods on the Hill. It turned out to be a male sharp-shinned hawk – the only one of that kind that I was ever sure had caught a chicken. We saw an occasional duck hawk in our area but we never lost any of our poultry to them as far as we knew. Once, however, I saw a pair of green-winged teal alight most precipitously near the mouth of Pratt's Creek, without making their circles to see if the area was free of hunters. Flying higher than the teal and quite a ways behind them was a fair-sized hawk which I presumed, from the way the teal behaved, must have been a duck hawk. One tale about a hawk that we heard as children we never quite knew whether or not to believe. It was told to Pa by Old Santy who said he was once looking out of the window one quiet overcast day in winter and saw a hawk swoop down and carry off Alden Avery's cat that was sitting on a rock behind Cromwell's barn. With rapid wing-beats and its legs stretched straight downwards by the weight of its prey, the hawk flew quickly downhill and disappeared behind Old Santy's woods. If the story was true, and Old Santy was not known to make up stories "out of whole cloth," the attacker in this meeting of two predators, must have been a goshawk. This bird of prey is known to be fiercely aggressive and fearless. Dr. Frederick W. Davis, Professor of Ornithology at Fitchburg State College, told of an incident wherein a goshawk was seen capturing a full-grown wild turkey by fastening its claws to the turkey's back and mauling the larger bird with its sharp curved beak as the victim dashed into the underbrush. Apparently, Pa sought to discourage our taking too much stock in Old Santy's story when he said, "A cat would twist around in the hawk's grip and scratch the guts out of the bird." Still, if the cat was not large and was partially stunned by the hawk's stoop, and if the lungs were pierced by the needle-sharp talons, it might become subdued by a hungry goshawk. The most likely bird of prey that we had that would be capable of carrying off a cat would be the great horned owl. But Old Santy would certainly have recognized one of those large birds and besides they do not capture prey during the daylight hours.

If the truth were known, the great horned owl probably caused more loss among our poultry flocks than any other predator. The thick coniferous woods across the river provided favorable habitat where the big owls could nest in seclusion and hide from pestering crows during the day. They were year-round residents and we heard their distinctive hooting on calm nights almost any month of the year. These nighttime raiders came and went while we slept. We were often unaware that our flocks were being plundered by these big birds unless, by chance, we found evidence, such as a half-devoured chicken in the east field near the meadow. When our chickens in the backyard became half-grown, they preferred to leave their low coops and roost in the trees at night. They were cooler and more comfortable in the trees. On still nights I have heard a noise like the brushing of large wings in the branches as an owl possibly was making off with a chicken. Our flocks were not exceptionally large but there were too many birds for easy, frequent counting. We could lose a number of chickens without becoming aware of their disappearance. These big owls have preyed upon farmers' flocks for years. Mother told us about the turkeys her father raised each year. As soon as the young birds were large enough to fly, the flock roosted on the ridge pole of the barn at night. One moonlit night there was a great commotion among the turkeys and, aroused from bed, her father found that all of them had left their perch. None were missing the next day, but when they dressed the birds for Thanksgiving, they found scars on the back of one where it had been scratched most likely by the owl that caused the disturbance in the moonlight.

One summer evening, an hour after dark, we were sitting around the kitchen talking when we heard a sudden burst of noise in the big henpen north of the stable. There was a huge fluttering that sounded almost like a muffled explosion, then all was quiet. Grabbing the lantern, we went quickly to the henpen and found that all of the hens had left their roosts. They were huddled in the corners and against the walls. We suspected that an owl had flown in the open door in the east end of the henpen, sailed above the roosts, and caused a panic among the hens. Next day, we hung a chick-wire door over the opening and I set a trap on top of a stake several feet away. The following morning Al went to the Shore before breakfast to remove the canvas cover from his motorboat. As he left the skiff at our landing, he heard the faint rattling of a chain in an elm tree on the beaver dam near the boathouse. Investigating the noise, he found a big owl in a trap with the chain caught on a limb in the top of the elm. Returning to the house, we found that the fence staple I had used to fasten the trap to the henyard stake had been pulled out.

It was in the same henpen some years later that my parents had a most baffling experience involving the loss of a full-blooded Plymouth Rock rooster that Al had sent them from Massachusetts. When Mother went to feed the hens one cold morning in the dead of winter, she found the head of the rooster in one corner of the building and his body in another. Most of the neck was missing. Mother and Pa searched diligently for clues. There were no tracks in the deep snow outside the henpen and both doors had been tightly closed. The building had three twelve-light windows on the south side from which a few of the glass panes had been missing for a year or two. Chicken wire netting was fastened over each window on the inside. There seemed to be no way for a predator to get either in or out of the building. My folks wondered about the mystery all day. It was not solved until soon after sunset when Pa looked out of the kitchen window and saw, in the deepening dusk and silhouetted against an unbroken background of snow over the field, the dark figure of a big owl with upright ears sitting on a stake in the henyard fence behind the henpen. He made sure, this time, that his trusty 10-gauge was adequately loaded. The next day, Pa discovered that the wire netting on the side of one of the windows, close to one of the missing glass panes, was not fastened to the casing for a couple of feet. It could be pushed several inches away from the woodwork. "That must be the place where the owl forced his way into the henpen," Pa concluded. It took an even wiser bird to find its way back out than to push its way in. But this owl did both. No one had a good explanation, however, as to why, with forty or fifty fowls to pick from, it chose the one thoroughbred rooster.

Everyone knows that great horned owls prey upon many kinds of wild birds and animals as well as upon farm flocks. Crows hate the big birds because they may fall victim to them after dark. One night, Pa and I saw from the river a striking demonstration by one of these powerful nocturnal predators of an attack on the black diurnal denizens of the coniferous woods. A full moon was shining brightly as we approached our shore after drifting for shad on the high water slack below the Old Pine. Pa said, "Let's put these shad on ice and carry the drift net ashore, then go seine the weir. The tide hasn't dropped but an inch or so and we can seine it easily now. If we get what is in there now, there won't be so many fish for me to handle tomorrow while you're at school, and some might find their way out before tomorrow's high water." It was around one o'clock in the morning when we left the weir and headed for our shore past the east end of the island. There was not a breath of breeze. It was deathly quiet – the noise of both midnight express trains had faded into the distance some time before and there were few freights at that time of the night. The peaceful silence was suddenly broken by a startling sound from the woods across the river. Crows are like chickens in that they never make a sound after dark unless they are violently disturbed. Neither Pa nor I had ever heard a crow holler at night before. There were two crows making their excited calls first. After a second or two, the cawing of one crow diminished and then stopped entirely. In the bright moonlight, we saw a lone crow flying southwards against the sky across the cut-over land on Aunt Emma's farm to the spruce woods on the old Dunning farm. The crow cawed continuously until it reached the dense cover of the spruces. "An owl must have caught one of those crows," Pa said. "I never heard anything like that." After listening to the bit of wild and tragic drama, it was easy to understand why crows gather from miles around to pester an owl in the daytime. I thought of the sentence by Chester A. Reed in his bird guide referring to the way chickadees and kinglets harass the diminutive saw-whet owl during daylight. "Little they know, which one of them may fall victim to him after dusk . . .," he wrote.

Crows were both friend and foe to us. It was pleasant to see them around on cold winter days, giving the impression that there was no need to be overly concerned about sub-zero temperatures. Their cawing early in the morning in late February made us believe that spring was on the way – only a few weeks to the arrival of red-winged blackbirds, grackles and robins. Every time we removed the fish from a sucker net beneath the ice, we left a few tomcods for the hungry crows. One cold winter, when everything was buried under deep snow, Pa threw out some oats for the few crows that came around on the snowdrift that was higher than the roof of our henpen. "Why can't those crows eat the whole oat like hens do?" he asked. "They pick out the meat and leave the hulls. Damned if I'll feed them any more if they can't eat the whole thing. Maybe they can't afford the space for the hulls, though. I don't suppose a crow's crop holds more than a thimbleful. That's why they don't eat any more than they have to."

In late May, while our corn was coming up, crows were a destructive nuisance. Stirring a little tar on the seed before planting and stringing white twine on three-foot sticks around the corn patch were sometimes effective in preventing the crows from pulling the corn seedlings out of the ground and eating the kernels. Pa had a method of control, however, that seemed always to prove effective in protecting the corn. Somewhere in the corn patch, he tied a fresh herring to the top of a stake driven flush with the soil and around the fish he set four or five traps carefully covered with dry dirt. As he finished making the set, Pa said, "There, that's perfect. The morning sun will shine on the herring and the crows will see it first thing." It was necessary to catch but one of the vandals each year. The dead crow was hung from a tall leaning pole in the midst of the corn patch and no more corn was pulled for the rest of the season.

Another kind of varmint ate our cabbages, beans, lettuce and turnips with gusto. Woodchucks were particularly fond of these crops and it took traps and the help of the dog to keep these tough mammals under control. Since their dens could be located easily, we were usually quite successful in preventing extensive losses from these rodents. A still different kind of mammal gave us trouble one year in our recently-planted field of potatoes. The potatoes were planted that year to the north of our driveway, between the house and the road. Since there was a heavy run of late season, run-down herring that spring, Pa decided to use them for fertilizer instead of spending money for the "phosphate" they made at the Village. When the young potato plants started coming up, we saw a problem at hand. We noticed that several of the rows were being dug into here and there every night. In the morning we found many of the potato seed-pieces with their rooted sprouts still attached scattered about. Pa knew right away what was causing the damage. "The skunks have found the rotting herring we put at the bottom of the furrows," he said. "I don't know as there is much we can do about it." There was good moonlight at the time and I volunteered to watch for the skunks on Friday with my .22 rifle. Instead of going to bed at ten o'clock, I began to patrol. "You may have to wait out there quite a while," Pa told me. "I don't know what time of night those critters do their depredations." By midnight, walking up and down the potato rows or resting against one of the driveway trees became monotonous. I brought a box from the stable and sat in the center of the potato patch with the .22 across my knees. About 3 AM, I started seeing skunks entering the cultivated plot every few minutes. The mirage-like sightings became so aggravating that I forsook the potato patch for bed an hour before dawn, without firing a shot. Perhaps my presence that night had a discouraging effect on the skunks for their damage markedly decreased on succeeding nights or the buried herring may have become less palatable to the carrion-loving skunks. At any rate, by going to the trouble of resetting the uprooted plants and hilling up the rows early in the summer, we produced a good crop of potatoes at digging time.

After the great horned owl, the goshawk was probably the next worst predator of our poultry. They usually showed up in October and stayed around until January. One fall afternoon I came home from school at the Corner to find an unsavory task awaiting me. Mother told me that a goshawk had attacked one of our hens back of the stable just after dinner that day. While Pa was getting his gun, the hawk had killed the hen. Since no excess damage had been done to the hen, Pa had hung the bird in the barn for me to pluck and clean for Mother to cook. I complained about the job, arguing that we should not eat poultry that had been killed in such a fashion. But Mother insisted that I dress out the fowl. After a heated protest, I changed into old clothes and went to the barn to undertake my assignment. The hen, I discovered, was old Beauty, Genevieve's pet Rhode Island Red – a friendly bird that approached with a lot of singing anyone who entered the henyard. She was at least eight or ten years old; so old, in fact, that she had laid no eggs for a year or two and had started to change into a rooster. She had developed those shiny sickle-shaped feathers on her back just in front of the tail and she had been heard to make a crowing noise on several occasions.

Immediately I returned to the house and continued arguing with Mother that the hen was too old. She would not be worth the trouble to pick and clean. Mother was unmoved. "Do as you're told," she said. Half an hour later I returned to the kitchen with the scrawny carcass neatly dressed out and ready for Mother to fricassee. "That will be the toughest bird we ever ate," I told her. Mother gave a good look at the bony bird with its shrunken flesh and complete lack of yellow skin color. "I guess you'd better give it to the pig," she said. "I wouldn't have made you dress it in the first place if you hadn't made such a fuss about it."

For one or two years, I had a small flock of ducks that spent summer nights in the front yard between the barn and our porch. They were sometimes frightened into noisy confusion by, we believed, one of the horned owls swooping over them. This happened one evening after everyone else had gone to bed and I was reading by the kerosene lamp in the kitchen. A short time later, I heard an owl hoot in the big elm in our front yard. Sneaking quietly to the stable, I got Pa's 10-gauge shotgun and went to our front porch steps. In the light of a new moon to the west, I could barely see a dark blurry shape leave the upper elm branches and start to fly across Amasa's field. The four and a half drams of black powder made a terrific boom in the quiet of the night and a lot of sparks accompanied the cloud of smoke in the direction of the disappearing owl. We had a lady visiting us that time. She was asleep in the upstairs good room that night, with the front dormer windows open over the dooryard. Next morning, she said she heard the terrific bang and said, "I was never so completely startled in my life. I didn't dare to get up to find out what was going on."

Chapter Twenty

Indians

There was Indian lore associated with our neighborhood. The name of our river was obviously of Indian origin. One version had the name, Abbagadasset, first applied to the point of land that extends into the Bay between our river and the Kennebec, and that the name referred to "shining water." We can vouch for this term being applicable to Merrymeeting Bay. When the light was right, the Bay's surface often appeared from our house as a gleaming sheet of water that shone with extreme brilliance though it was more than a mile away. Another version had it that a settler named Abby killed Dasset, an Indian. Genevieve told me a bedtime story in which both of the men were Indians. "They had shot a deer with bow and arrow near Preble Creek," as she told it. "With the deer in their canoe, on the way back to camp they became embroiled in an argument as to which one actually bagged the game. Anger turned to violence, and Abby shot Dasset in the back." I don't know how true this story was, nor where Genevieve got her information. The true origin of the river's name may never be known.

My folks had been told about a teenage girl whose family, one of the early settlers, lived near Center's Point. She went to visit friends in the Village one day and took the only trail that wound through the woods along the north bank of the Cathance. The girl was never seen again. It was presumed that she was captured by the natives. As a small girl, Mother remembered Indians calling at her house to sell baskets they had made. Pa told us about a group of Indians who camped one winter near Decker's Creek up river. "Ash trees were as scarce as hen's teeth after that," he said. "They cut all of them to make all sorts of things."

Upriver at low tide, Pa pointed to a stone pier-like structure on the east side of the river in the bend of the cross channel, above Maxwell's shore. It was a long mound of rocks of various sizes, well covered with sticky silt. The shore end of the pier had become covered with mud but the stones near the channel's bank were washed by the tide. "I think the Indians must have built that to catch fish from," Pa said. Although we found old settler's relics like pewter spoons and flint-lock parts in our plowed fields, none of us ever found an Indian artifact. I would have thought that, over the years, we would have found a spearhead, or a stone axe, or at least a few arrowheads.

Chapter Twenty-One

Al's Motorboat

The summer of 1910 was filled with excitement. Al and Martha Robinson were married in June and Al was making plans to build a motorboat the following summer. As in the case of most of our momentous matters, we awaited Pa's indication of approval or disapproval. He complained to Mother that Martha was too short to make a good wife for Al. Mother replied that as long as Al was in love with Martha that was all that was necessary. Regarding the motor launch, Pa went along with Al on the idea, although he told us later in the fall after Al had gone back to his school that he thought it was foolish to spend a lot of money on a damned boat. Had it been Vining or I who wanted to build a boat, I'm sure we would have been in for a big argument as to the advisability of the project. Anything Al wanted to do was all right with Pa; few questions were asked. Al had already bought off Martha's brother, Walter, an ancient pine tree that stood on Sprague's Mountain on the Robinson farm near the Topsham line. Walter had cut a twenty-four-foot log from the trunk and hauled it on the snow to Muddy River the previous winter. Charlie Blair towed the log to Amasa's mill where it was sawed when they started the mill in September. Pa hauled the smooth planed lumber home and stacked it to dry in the stable chamber. "That's real punkin pine," Pa said, "soft, and clear as a quill. It takes an old tree to make boards like them." While Al was home for Thanksgiving, they cut a big red oak on the east side of the hill and Pa hauled the butt to the mill on the sled that winter. Lumber from that tree was used for the boat's stem-piece, ribs and transom. It was early spring before Pa brought this oak lumber home and put it upstairs in the stable alongside the pine. "I hope it has time to dry out before they start on the boat," he said.

The following summer, June and July 1911, was a busy one for us. Al came home from Princeton, Maine, as soon as his high school's graduation was over. He immediately made plans to have the motorboat completed by haying time, not later than the middle of July. Building of the boat, as it turned out, involved the entire family, and in varying degrees touched the lives of all of us. Al hired an experienced boat builder, Will Robinson, to take charge of the construction. Will took his meals with the family and was lodged in the spare "good room" upstairs for the two or three weeks while the boat was being built, with everything ready for the launching. He was not related to Martha in any way, although their surnames were the same and he also lived on the Muddy River in Topsham, not far from Martha's home. He was an orphan boy brought up by Seth Holbrook on a small farm just over the Bowdoinham line. Seth had a peculiar manner of speech that Al used to imitate a lot around home. While everyone was working on the boat one day, I started to say something in a mimicking way, copying Al's imitation of Seth as closely as I could. I had not realized Will's close association with Seth. Apparently my rendition of Seth's dialect was close to the real thing. Before I had hardly completed a sentence Al shut me up abruptly.

In order to make room for the new boat in the stable, we moved both of our wagons into the barn. This gave ample space for laying the keel on wooden horses in the middle of the stable floor. The keel was a long strip of white oak, an inch and a half thick, that Al bought from Amasa who had it stowed away in his drying shed at the sawmill. The first addition to the keel was the long tapering triangular skeg that Pa sawed by hand from a yellow birch plank that had been stored in the barn cellar for some time. It was from a log Pa had cut in Aunt Emma's woods some years before. Next came the curved stem. It was made from two pieces of red oak sawed, also by hand, from a four-inch timber milled from the oak cut Up-under-the-Hill. The curved pieces were jointed and securely fastened together with galvanized screws. Finally, there were temporary forms set crosswise, on edge, at two-foot intervals along the keel; something like the septa in a chambered nautilus. The forms were a single board in thickness and rounded properly at the ends to give the sides of the boat a curvature that corresponded with the model. They held the planking and ribs in place, thereby determining the final shape of the boat.

Since the lines of the finished boat would have several graceful bends and curves, the ribs and planking had to be steamed before they could be bent or, in some cases, twisted to fit the forms without cracking the lumber. This was the part of the boat-building that involved the domestic household and most of the work routine of the womenfolk. A twelve-foot long, one-foot square steam box was built to fit at one end onto the wash boiler on the kitchen stove. Pa removed one of the south kitchen windows so that the long steam tunnel could be passed in from the front porch. When a roaring fire was built beneath the wash boiler, the long square wooden tube became filled with hot steam. The smooth one-inch square oak ribs and the twenty-two-foot, six-inch wide strips of pine planking were passed end-wise through the kitchen window from the porch. After several minutes' exposure to the steam, the oak ribs and pine planking could be bent to fit the curves of the boat with little difficulty. The steaming process did present a problem for Mother and my sisters, however, since they had to schedule the cooking, washing and ironing while the steam box was not in use.

Vining helped Pa, Al and Will frequently while they were working on the boat, but I was too small to be of much help. There were only a couple of things that I was permitted to do. When the planking was being riveted to the ribs, I held an iron maul against the rivet's head on the outside of the boat's hull while someone on the inside placed a burr on the copper rivet and headed it on. After the planking was completed, I caulked some of the open, below-water seams with cotton twine, before the first coat of paint was applied. The last steps in the boat's construction involved the fastening of a half-round, yellow birch bumper strip along the gunwales and the installation of a cypress combing board just inside the gunwales. Al had an eye for color when it came to painting the boat. The outside of the hull above the water line was given two coats of gleaming white. Below water, a dark green copper-bearing paint was used. The two small forward and aft decks were bright yellow; inside of the hull was slate, and the floor was painted maroon. Combing and bumper strip were coated with Valspar. This same varnish brought out the beautiful oak grain of the transom.

After the engine was fastened in place, and the brass drive shaft and propeller were attached, Al installed the rudder and steering system. It was at this point that I received an important assignment. Al gave me train fare for a trip to

Richmond and the money to purchase a couple of items for the boat. I took the eastbound two-o'clock local from Harward's and returned at four. At the Richmond store I purchased the strongest clothes line they had for a tiller rope between the steering wheel and rudder post, and a one-inch galvanized pipe cap. I took the cap to the village blacksmith shop at the foot of the Main Street hill on the Kennebec and had a three-quarter-inch hole drilled through it. This would be used to make a packing box on the lower end of a vertical pipe installed in the locker stern, which served as a housing for the rudder post. The blacksmith was perspiring freely when he finished the drilling. He charged ten cents for the job. "Don't you think I earned that much?" he asked.

By the time the second coat of paint was thoroughly dry, the boat was ready for the engine that Al had bought at the factory in Bath. It was an inboard, two cylinder, Kennebec engine manufactured by Torrey Roller Bushing Works, capable of driving the twenty-two-foot boat ten or twelve miles an hour. Compared with speedboats of today, that would be considered a snail's pace, but it was a little faster than most of the motorboats plying our waters at the time. The engine arrived by freight at Harward's Depot. Pa brought it home in the baggage wagon.

In order to get the motor into the boat, a few boards were removed from the stable chamber floor directly above the middle of the boat, so that a block and tackle could be suspended from the high beams upstairs. The engine was hoisted from the crate and lowered to its wooden bed. The engine's two cylinders were entirely separate except for the common base, both standing out tall and round. Two large Oswell spark plugs, containing both plugs and coil, stood up five or six inches above the tops of the cylinders. Electricity for ignition was supplied by two sets of six dry cells each in a covered box fastened to the side of the boat; a switch on the end of the battery box made it possible to change from one set of batteries to the other every hour or so. There was no magneto or self starter. To start the motor one turned the heavy fly wheel by hand. Gasoline was the fuel; most boats had recently changed from out-moded naphtha. Each cylinder had a glass oil cup attached to its side, which slowly dispensed lubricant to the piston. A moveable commutator immediately behind the fly wheel shifted from one side to the other to regulate the speed or to reverse direction.

"We'll have to go across the river and cut a couple of young pines for skids," Pa said when the boat was completed and ready to be moved to the shore. "Sapling pine logs will slide over the ground easier than anything else." A carriage to hold the boat upright was built on top of the skids. With the carriage in place, it was time to move the launch to the river. "I'm not sure that Dandy can haul that big a load all the way to the Point," Pa said. "Maybe we'd better borrow Amasa's horse to help out. He's doing nothing out there in the pasture. His harness is hanging there in the barn." Anyone who has worked with horses knows how difficult it can sometimes be to get two strange horses to pull together. They're often troublesome enough when they're used to working with each other. It required everyone's best efforts to get the boat hauled across the field and inside the river pasture. Two of my sisters and I followed closely and kept picking up the wooden rolls as fast as they were freed by the skids and replacing them in front. The load was too heavy for the two horses to drag any distance over the ground without the continued use of rolls. Inside the pasture a little ways, Amasa's horse Pomp decided he'd done enough work for one day. He lay down close to a small gray birch tree by the side of the path and refused to budge. Pa nicknamed the tree "Horse Birch" after that. Fortunately the distance to the river was not far and the road was level for a bit and then downhill. Apparently relieved by being unshackled from another horse, Dandy pulled harder by himself and moved the boat down to the water's edge with no further difficulty.

The motorboat proved to be both useful and educational for all of us over the next several years. It was a quick and convenient means of transporting freshly killed fowl to Chase's store in Bath. Pa and Al towed the skiff to the sandbar at the mouth of the river in the Bay and brought back bagfuls of clean sand for use in masonry work such as chimney and foundations repair. Before we had the motorboat, the distance was too far to row a heavily laden skiff back home. The launch also gave fast and pleasant transportation to the Woolwich shore where we went for blueberries a few times each August. We took many Sunday afternoon pleasure rides into the Bay and, if the tide was high, up river sometimes all the way to the millpond. Also, when someone came to visit, Al was always generous with his boat rides that never failed to please the company.

The most exciting and pleasureful trips we took in the motorboat were the day-long excursions to Sheepscot Bay. Once every summer, as soon as haying was over in August, Al would say, "Some day this week would be a good time for a trip to the seashore. The tide will be high in the morning. We can have it with us going and coming. If the weather's good, let's plan for Thursday?" Such a suggestion was all that was necessary for Mother and my sisters to start preparing sandwiches, molasses cookies, blueberry turnovers, and a jug or two of lemonade. On the way down river, we stopped at Bath for gasoline and Pa always bought a hand of bananas for the trip. Leaving the city dock at Bath, we crossed the Kennebec and took Back River beneath Hell's Gate Bridge, passed Arrowsic and continued on southwards to Sheepscot Bay. Before reaching the Bay, we passed the precipitous Hockamock Bluff on our left. Mother told us about the way the promontory got its name. Early settlers chased an Indian to the high rocky headland. She had heard that his last words were: "Catch an Injun, catch a fly, Hockamocke jump or die!" It was near there that we began to see the ubiquitous shoreline ledges covered with brown seaweed. At that time there were few cottages on Sheepscot Bay and we had many choices of landing place for a picnic spot.

Al's boat carried six people comfortably and sometimes seven or even eight of us went along on the seashore visits. If possible, everyone who was at home at the time was included in the party. The house was locked and everything left in the care of Snipe. None of us ever wanted to stay at home when the family went "down river" and it was a difficult decision as to who would stay behind on those few occasions when there were too many of us at home for the boat to carry. Genevieve and I stayed at home on one occasion when Aunt Emma and Irving were visiting with us. Aunt Emma was a fairly large woman and Irving stood close to six feet. There was just not enough room in the boat that day for everyone so we were the ones left behind. Genevieve looked after things around the house while I kept an eye on the chickens and cows. In the afternoon I slipped away to do some exploring in Fred Beal's swamp. I had often visited the swamp when it was frozen over and I was looking for muskrat houses, but I had never really investigated the place in the summertime. I was now barefoot and in the channels opened by the muskrats I sank in muddy water up to my knees. After wandering among the cattails where the muskrats had their houses, I came to a somewhat dryer part of the meadow where the footing was firmer, the sedges were less than waist high, and there was only enough water to cover one's feet. There were many swamp grass tussocks in this part of the swamp and as I approached close to one of them I saw a rusty black object slide from the top of the hummock and disappear in the grass. It was too small for even a baby muskrat – more the size of a big field mouse. I looked closer at the tussock. Imbedded in its top was a nest with two recently hatched jet black rail chicks. They were too young to follow their mother from the nest, merely sitting there with their heads raised but not opening their mouths like so many young birds do when someone approaches. I assumed they were Virginia Rails, from the color of the mature bird's back. They possibly could have been Soras since that species was very common during migrations in the fall. However, I used to find mostly Virginia Rails in the adjacent Cromwell's swamp, while the Soras were more abundant along the river. At any rate, I felt not the least unhappy about being left at home that day. Finding the nest in Beal's swamp equalled any joy I could imagine from a trip to the salt water.

Every trip to the seashore was, however, in a way an education in itself. I well remember the first one when I was seven – sighting my first seal, rocks covered with barnacles, black mussels everywhere, and so many kinds of buoyant seaweeds. We had nothing like these things in our freshwater environment. Having become accustomed to the silt-laden semi-turbid water of the Abbagadasset, where one can barely see an object at a depth of two feet, it was a tremendous surprise to be able to see the cunners and sculpins we were catching many feet down in the clear salt water. One year, we had our picnic on the Westport shore near the cottage where Al and Martha spent their honeymoon. Pa, Al and I paid a visit to the cottage's owner at his small year-round house. He showed us a pair of objects which were most unusual for the ocean floor in that vicinity. They were large curved horns of a mountain sheep. "We were dragging just outside the mouth of the Bay last fall when we brought up one of those horns," he said. "The next day we were dragging in the same area and darned if we didn't bring up its mate." The two horns were practically identical in size and shape – one had a tip broken off. There was little doubt that they belonged to the same ram. How the horns of a Rocky Mountain sheep came to rest in deep water off the coast of Maine was a question for which none of us had an answer.

On one trip to Sheepscot Bay we came home the long way, out into the Atlantic, past Bay Point, and into the mouth of the Kennebec. There were high swells that day and it was thrilling when the boat pitched through the crests of the waves, with the motor racing for a moment whenever the stern was out of the water. We saw a four-masted schooner with folded sails at anchor in the mouth of the river waiting for a tugboat to take it to Bath or Gardiner. The strong tide and unpredictable winds in the river made it too dangerous for such large vessels to attempt to sail upstream or down. A few miles above Fort Popham we passed a tug with another schooner in tow; the stout hawser between the two vessels was as taut as a bowstring. Above Bath, we passed one of the big white side-wheeler passenger steamships, the *City of Bangor*, on its return to Boston after an overnight trip to Augusta. Another side-wheeler, the City of Rockland, made the same schedule on alternate days. A third passenger steamer, the propeller-driven *Islander*, a somewhat smaller ship, made daytime runs between Portland and Augusta. The Islander was faster than the side-wheelers; Al used to caution us when we were steering to give the *Islander* wide berth because of the extra-high waves she created in her wake. We could see these large passenger ships from the house when they were passing through the Chops. Often at supper, someone at the table would remark: "There goes the Boston boat." The late afternoon sun reflected brightly from the gleaming white sides of the big boats as they followed the winding channel through the Chops. We first saw the boat just as it approached the Chops. A few minutes later it was even more noticeable when it turned broadside to us in some narrows called "Burnjacket." The big side-wheelers were the same type of vessel as the *City of Portland* that was lost in a northeast blizzard in the 1890's on its way from Boston to Portland on a weekend after Thanksgiving. A resident of the Village carried for years a ticket for that ill-fated voyage that he did not use. Upon arriving at the Boston pier that evening to start the overnight sea journey to Portland, he disliked the looks of the weather and returned to Bowdoinham by train.

On our trips to Bath in the motorboat, we saw many commerce ships that plied the Kennebec. Bath was the largest city on the river. Upstream there were the cities of Gardiner and Augusta, and the town of Richmond, which were served to a large extent by water transportation. Perhaps the most common of the big sea-going boats were the drab coal barges with their two low masts and control house at the stern. Large four-masted schooners were constantly carrying ice from Kennebec storage houses to distant ports. Ice was an important commodity in those days prior to electric refrigeration. I used to watch smaller three-masters being towed across Merrymeeting Bay loaded with nitrates, phosphates and potash from areas of production to the Sagadahoc Fertilizer Company's plant at Bowdoinham Village. Schooners of all sizes brought many articles of commerce, such as structural materials, southern pine, and Oregon fir to all three cities along the Kennebec. Many of the barges brought coal to Maine. One summer, there were two or three huge freighters tied up at a shipyard in North Bath. The big, black vessels had been brought from the Great Lakes for ocean duty. They were so long that it was necessary to cut away part of the stern in order for them to pass through the St. Lawrence locks on their way to the Atlantic. During World War I, we were intrigued by the fantastic camouflage on many of the ships we saw at Bath. The broad zigzag stripes and bands on the ship's sides and superstructures seemed so out of place on vessels at anchor in the quiet waters of a peaceful town. Some of the camouflaged boats were commercial ones performing their wartime duties; others were U.S. Navy destroyers tied up at Bath Iron Works for repairs. Another thing about Bath's waterfront I shall never forget was the high board sign at both ends of cables or water mains laid on the bottom of the river between Bath and Woolwich. The letters, which were several feet tall, warned: DO NOT AN-CHOR – 100 FEET UP OR DOWN. The signs, high above town, were almost as memorable as the two ferryboats – both steam powered side-wheelers that plied back and forth across the Kennebec regardless of tide or weather. The larger of the two was Maine Central's black and white ferryboat, named for Maine's founder, Ferdinando Gorges; the smaller was the brownish vehicular ferry, the *Hockamock*. Both ferries had their names painted in big letters on their sides. Another activity we liked to watch was the horse-drawn hacks that made the rounds of the dock area every so often.

The steering wheel on Al's launch was on the right side, handy to the middle seat. Al usually sat on the forward seat in the bow, where he could keep one eye on the course of the boat and the other on the engine. He rarely did the steering when there was someone else aboard who was qualified for the job. In both the Kennebec and in our river, it was necessary for the helmsman to be familiar with the channel and to know the locations of such navigational hazards as wide low flats, sandbars or protruding ledges. The long sandbar stretching into the Cathance channel at the mouth of the Abbagadasset, far out into the Bay, was a dangerous navigational hazard at half tide. Covered by five feet of water when the tide was high, it was less than a foot above water at low tide. On one of our return trips from Bath, Pa was steering when we had a small accident. Coming through Burnjacket, there was a sudden thump, a brief scraping noise as the bow of the boat dropped a foot for a second or two. "Jeevus, I believe we hit Old Washie," Pa said. "I should have kept closer to the east shore. I thought I knew right where that rock was. I saw a scow loaded with lumber piled right on top of that rock once, years ago." Old Washie was the smooth top of a big rock that showed only a few inches above water at low tide. We often saw a ripple that it made on the surface at half-tide or lower. Several minutes passed and Al noticed that water began to come in around the propeller shaft. This meant that the brass shaft was bent where it entered the packing box in the end of the skeg. Al had it straightened at a marine repair shop the next time he went to Bath. I was steering one day as we came up the river at low tide. Passing the head of the sandbank, a gust of wind blew my hat off. I turned to watch the hat scale away and land in the wake of the boat twenty feet astern. While I was watching that hat, the boat went aground in the soft mud at the bend of the channel. Another time, Al and Martha took two of my sisters and some of our relatives for a Sunday afternoon boat ride into the Bay. Martha was at the helm that day. It was an hour or two before low water when they came up the river and ran aground on the sandbar that extends from Uncle Everett's meadow into the cross-channel a short distance below the Spar Landing. Al reversed the engine and pushed with an oar but the boat's skeg was stuck firmly in the sand. Pa and I could see the predicament of the boat from the house. "We'll have to go down and get them in the skiff," he said. By the time we reached the stranded party, the launch was resting on its side – stuck fast in the sand. Like a good captain, Al stayed with his ship and waited for the flood tide to float the craft just before dark.

Although the motorboat was designated as a pleasure craft, it required attention at times that was something less than pleasant. When Al had to return to his teaching duties early in September, he said, "You and Pa may want to use the boat this fall, so I'll leave it in the river when I leave. You and he will have a chance to pull it out sometime before freeze-up." I'm sure we could have managed nicely without the motorboat. We had little use for it in the fall. One good reason for leaving the boat in the water was that the long period of drying the boat would undergo during weeks of dry fall weather might cause excessive opening of the seams and it would take longer to make the boat seaworthy in June. So, the motor-boat swung at its mooring until late October. On at least two or three unexpectedly cold nights in October of each fall, I accompanied Pa to the Shore, paddled the skiff out to the motorboat at its midstream mooring, and held the lantern while he drained the water from the engine's cooling system, thereby preventing possible damage such as a cracked cylinder or a broken water pump.

"I wish Al had pulled his motorboat out before he left," Pa said to me one day in late September when I returned from school. "Coming home from the Village today, Ed hailed me and wanted to know if I could take him to Bath in the boat tomorrow with a batch of dressed chickens. His road mare's come up lame in a front quarter and he don't want to drive her that far. I didn't want to do it, but he said he'd give me five dollars. I didn't want to turn him down. After I told him I'd do it, I remember how that engine acted up a few times with Al last summer and he had trouble getting the thing started sometimes. I don't know too much about that engine. I'm a little afraid of the thing." Pa had never used the powerboat much when Al wasn't around – only a few short trips, like towing some logs to the mill. The boat was three or four years old that fall and the engine had not been running quite as well that summer as it used to. Pa came in from the barn the next morning as I was about ready to leave for school. "I only got a couple of hours of sleep all night, thinking about going down there today," he said. "Your Aunt Abby is going along for the ride too; that won't make it any less worrisome. I ought to have you go with us, but it's not worth keeping you out of school for. I'll make it one way or another."

"I can miss a day of school, if you want me to go," I told Pa after a pause to mask my eagerness. "I could make it up tomorrow."

"No, you go on to school," he replied. "We'll get there and back some way or other."

Pa was already back home that afternoon when I returned from school. Everything had gone well on the boat trip to Bath. "The motor sputtered a few times while we were going through the Chops," he said. "I told Ed to steer her close to the west side down by North Bath, so in case the engine stopped we could paddle ashore before the ebb tide carried us off down river. The engine ran fine all the way back. That's the last boat-hiring I'm going to do."

Then there was the necessary hauling of the boat out of the water every fall. Pa always chose some Saturday during hunting season when I'd much rather be hunting ducks. The first step in this pulling-out process involved the sliding of the carriage beneath the motorboat while it was afloat in the river. We then dragged both boat and carriage onto dry land with block-and-tackle. Another Saturday was ruined, a week or two later, when we had to roll the boat into the boathouse for the winter. In spite of some extra work it demanded, the acquisition of the motor launch did result in two new buildings at our Point that we might not otherwise have had. A twenty-five-foot boathouse was built first. This also provided ample room for the fishing paraphernalia and other items formerly kept in the old fish house. Consequently, Pa tore down the fish house and used much of the salvaged lumber in building an ice house.

Had it not been for Al's motorboat, we might not have discovered a derelict sucker net half-buried in the mudflats near our shore one summer. Pa, Al, Vining and I were returning from a short boat ride down river on a warm Sunday afternoon in August. It was dead low-water, one of those summer drain-out tides with the water level "down to Death's door." As the motorboat plowed along the narrow channel past the sandbank, the big waves in the boat's wake momentarily exposed some of the shoreline that was ordinarily below low water mark. We had just rounded the bend in the river at the corner of our pasture swamp when the trough of a wave exposed what looked like the arcs of two or three hoops protruding a few inches from the flats' mud. "That's something buried there," Pa said. "Let's investigate." We fastened the launch to its mooring and returned to the spot in the skiff. Pa reached into the shallow water and partially raised a fyke-net hoop with some rotten netting attached. It turned out to be a complete net, wing chain and all, that someone had left in the river too late the preceding fall. The top of the net had become frozen into the ice during the winter. When the ice broke up in the spring, the net was carried to the edge of our low flats before it melted free from the moving ice sheet. The net had been placed in a shallow section of the river and the ice at low tide had crushed several of the larger hoops. Warm water of spring and summer had decayed the white untarred cotton netting but the smaller oak hoops, the buoys, and the brand-new chain were in perfect condition. "I don't know who this net could have belonged to," Pa said. "It may have been Milton Douglas or one of the Pratt boys. Damned if I'm going to try to find out." Pa and Al pulling together were able to extricate some of the wooden hoops, but the heavy iron chain was too firmly embedded in the mud to be easily removed. "Let's let it go now. We'll come down with a pry sometime when the tide's a little higher and pull up that chain."

Several days later, when low tide came in the cool of evening, Pa and I went to salvage the net's chain. We took along a stout weir-leader stake a few feet longer than the skiff and a short piece of strong rope. Both of us stood in the extreme stern of the skiff and tied the chain to the big end of the stake close to the water. Holding the stake shoulder high, we walked to the bow of the skiff and pressed down on the small end of the stake. This raised the skiff's stern a foot or two higher than before and the considerable leverage caused the chain to be pulled from the mud a similar distance. This performance was repeated a number of times and, finally, we had all fifty feet of the relatively new chain in our boat. We had used a similar leverage technique in pulling weir or sucker net stakes that were too firmly stuck in the river bottom to be pulled by hand. By moving from one end of the boat to the other, our combined weights created a tremendous lift at the other end of the skiff. As we paddled back to our point, Pa planned a use for the chain. "That will be just what I'll need to weigh down the fish pound netting on the weir next spring."

Chapter Twenty-Two

Illnesses and Accidents

Over the years, our family must have been relatively free from major ill-nesses and accidents. Mother complained of rheumatism in her hands and fore-arms, which was one reason the folks eventually gave up butter making. She thought that keeping her hands so long in cold water while washing butter aggra-vated the pain. However, I cannot recall a day when Mother was unable to be up and around and doing her daily work. We all had occasional colds, usually two or three times a year, most of them during the winter. Toothache was fairly common. We went by train to Richmond in the winter and by boat to Bath in summer for dental work – most of which involved extractions. Mother and Pa had upper and lower dentures. While I was in grade school, my two upper front teeth appeared through the gums before my first teeth were shed. Al was the first to notice this and Pa took me to Dr. Bates, in Bath, to have the baby teeth removed. With no anaesthetic and with two quick flips of his forceps, the dentist removed the two teeth and I remember no great pain at all. "How much will that be?" Pa asked Dr. Bates. "Nothing at all," the dentist replied. "You should give the boy fifty cents for making no fuss about it." Discussing our dental problems, Mother once said, "You know, for some reason Dr. Irish suggested that we give Vining cod liver oil when he was a baby. As it happened, he is the only one of all you children who has had good teeth. Do you suppose the cod liver oil could have had anything to do with it?"

An asthmatic condition troubled Pa a lot during the years that I was grow-ing up. When this was complicated by a chest cold during the winter, he was often confined to the house for a week or more at a time. The asthma bothered him more or less the year round, often while he was trying to sleep. To alleviate the congestion, he inhaled the smoke from burning paper that had been impregnated with saltpeter. Genevieve had a recurring illness while she was in high school that Dr. Irish was unable to diagnose. As Genevieve curled up in a rocking chair, Mother said, "She has another of her sick spells. She'll have to stay home for two or three days." With abdominal pain, she would curl up in the rocking chair for a day or two at a time. When Vining was a senior in high school, he missed a few days because of jaundice. Black cherry bark tea was the family's remedy for that ailment. "Take a knife and go Up-under-the-Hill and get some black cherry bark," Mother told Jeannette, who soon returned with a lard pail half full of strips of the bark. "That's just fine," Mother praised her. "We'll have him well again in no time." A week later, Vining, with his cheeks back to their normal pink, took a walk Up-under-the-Hill. Upon his return, he told Mother, with an indignant air, "If I'm sick again, don't send Jeannette to get anything for me. She can't tell one tree from another. She stripped the bark off those young choke-cherries at the point of the Hill. It's a wonder it didn't make me worse."

Jeannette was the only one who required surgery. She was operated on in Portland for the removal of a benign breast tumor while she was in high school. Mother thought the growth may have been caused by a basketball in a noontime game. Jeannette recuperated at Aunt Emma's house in Portland for several days after leaving the hospital. Pa withdrew $300 from the bank to pay for it – surgeon's fee, hospital room, and a trained nurse, along with other usual expenses.

I remember the "upset stomach" that I occasionally had for a day or two at a time. Starting in late October every fall, I usually caught my first cold of the season, followed by three or four more before the ice went out. I had probably my most serious illness the year I was a senior in high school. It began the week before Christmas vacation, 1918, the year of the Spanish flu. A girl in the sophomore class from the adjoining town of Bowdoin had died in October when that most virulent influenza first appeared in our area. After tending our traps one Sunday afternoon, I began to have an achy feverish feeling that seemed to first become noticeable while I was crossing Uncle Everett's meadow. I felt worse that evening and stayed home the next day. The folks called Dr. Irish who drove out to our house in his light wagon Monday afternoon. As soon as the doctor had completed his examination, Pa asked, "What's he got, Doctor?" "Oh, it's just this blamed distemper that's going around," Doctor Irish replied. I was given a bed in the sitting room and kept indoors until after Christmas. Minerva, then a high school teacher at Bound Brook, New Jersey, came home for the holidays a few days later. The flu had been so bad in New Jersey that the high school was closed and the teachers acted as nurses in improvised hospitals in churches and armories. On a warm, snowy day, soon after Christmas, I decided I was well enough to venture outdoors, so I went hunting red squirrels with my .22 in Amasa's woods across the railroad. It was a calm cloudy day and the wet snow on the evergreen branches dripped constantly. Returning to the house, I entered the back stable door and went to my bedroom by the back shed stairs. Knowing that I had gone out for some time, Minerva scolded me for leaving the house so soon after the flu and for staying out so long the first time. She had seen several strong middle-aged men recover from the flu and leave the hospital too soon only to return later with fatal pneumonia. "You should know better than to go out at all on a damp day like this," she said. Minerva also told of one humorous experience she had while serving as a nurse. One of her patients was an immigrant chemical worker who spoke broken English. She thought he asked for a pin. After a search, she brought him a safety pin. With a sidewise glance at the object she held, he shouted, "Nein, nein! Eet iss de bedpan I vanted!"

Since farming is usually considered one of the more dangerous pursuits, we were fortunate in meeting with few accidents. It always seemed remarkable to me that we were never gored by a bull or kicked by a horse. The closest to this type of injury we ever had was having a cow step on a foot. Although not too damaging, occasional things like that were sometimes exceedingly painful. We heard many times about Vining breaking his arm from falling from the sewing machine when he was a year old. Dr. Irish set the bone which mended perfectly. That was the only bone fracture in our family. Another incident fraught with potential danger had the folks worried for a day or two when Vining swallowed a broken half of a horseshoe nail, when he was a small youngster playing on the floor. Mother noticed that the nail was missing. It was happily recovered through Mother's watchful waiting next day. A blue ribbon was tied to it and it hung for years on one of the two miniature spires of our clock mantel. Mother kept the clock key on the opposite spire and faithfully wound the old clock every night before retiring.

It must have been one of our most serious accidents when ten-year-old Genevieve stepped on Pa's scythe as it lay on the stable floor. The sharp blade flipped up and cut a gash in the front of her leg bone, halfway between the ankle and the knee. Although frightening to our parents, cuts of that sort were not considered serious enough to require the attention of a physician. After tincture of benzoin and a bandage were applied, they sent for Uncle Ed who had treated many cuts he had received while butchering. He brought his trusted device for treating bad cuts. It consisted of a burner using feathers as a fuel. The smoke was directed against the wound for an hour or so. Perhaps there was some germicidal effect of the gases from the feathers, or perhaps it was the heat. In any case, following this homely therapeutic treatment, Genevieve's wound healed with no serious infection, but it did leave an unsightly scar. Years later she told me she thought a doctor should have taken stitches to close the wound.

As children, we were told about the dire effects of lockjaw, but no precautions were ever taken against this disease. On several occasions as a barefoot boy I stepped on a rusty nail that made a puncture wound. A drop of benzoin was placed on the puncture. I would walk on the side of the foot for a few days until the swelling and soreness wore off. Perhaps we were very lucky, because we always had a horse, and later on we learned that horses often carry and disseminate the lockjaw germs. On two occasions, I received painful burns on the hand. The first time, I placed the palm of my hand against the hot schoolroom stove while we were playing tag during the noon hour. It was during my first year at school when the schoolhouse was located across the road from George Blair's residence. There was no first aid kit at the school, so the teacher sent me to Mrs. Blair, who applied linseed oil to the burned area and placed a bandage on the hand. I returned to school for the afternoon classes. The other burn was received one cold night in winter, while I was playing with the fire through the open damper of the airtight stove – a practice Mother disapproved of because she thought it might make me wet the bed. Pa had filled a pail with glowing coals from the stove one night, using an old saucepan for handling the coals. I carelessly picked up the pan while the handle was still exceedingly hot. This time Mother applied cold chicken fat to the burned skin before bandaging.

I cannot recall any injury caused by our own carelessness or stupidity – like the earache Harold Blair experienced when he was in the first grade. The teacher gave the beginning students each a handful of split peas for forming the outline of some animals or for making letters of the alphabet and also Arabic numbers. Harold got to playing with his peas and stuffed as many as he could into his ears. His father had to get up in the middle of the night to dig out the dry halves that had swelled somewhat and had given Harold a painful earache.

Chapter Twenty-Three

Dairy Cows, Milk and Butter

Butter money was the major part of our family's income. We had no fancy dairy herd. For years we had no cream separator. Our barn never knew the sound of a milking machine. Nevertheless, through careful and energetic manual process, my folks produced a profitable amount of that tasty product – dairy butter. The commodity insured a steady inflow of cash. The fact that dairy butter sold directly to the consumer, in the first decade or two of this century, brought fifty cents per pound helped the farmer to make a comfortable living from relatively few cows. With the returns from a few pounds of butter one could buy a lot of things when I was a boy.

Seven or eight cows were the most we ever had in the milking herd. With a bull or two and a few replacement heifers growing up, we occasionally had from twelve to fourteen head of cattle in the barn at wintertime. When Pa built his new barn in the early 1890's, he made a tie-up that ran the entire length of the south side of the fifty-foot building. Located in the tie-up, from east to west, were two horse stalls, stanchions for a dozen head of cattle, a sawdust bin, and a wider space just inside the tie-up door where we harnessed the horse, watered the livestock, bred the cows, and occasionally built a temporary pen for a freshening cow. Besides, we usually had three or four calves hitched along the walk behind the cows.

The first cow that I can remember was a long-bodied, dark brown animal named Pansy. She was an old cow as shown by more than a dozen rings on her forward-curved horns. Her pedigree was unknown – probably a Guernsey-Jersey cross with something else thrown in. Pansy was the highly-prized individual that dairymen find but once or twice in a lifetime, but which they all hope for with each calf. She gave lots of rich milk, had a calf every year, was never sick, a fairly easy milker, and always gentle to handle. "When she's new-milch she makes a pound of butter a day," Pa said, a performance that was exceptionally good. Pa raised all of Pansy's female calves, none of which ever seemed to equal their mother in milk production nor in her all-round desirable qualities. The poorer performances on the part of Pansy's offspring may have been due to the questionable quality of the bulls that were available for breeding in the neighborhood. Most of the bulls raised were selected because they "looked good" as young calves. Testing prospective herd sires to prove their ability to transmit desirable traits to their offspring involved a period of too many years to be considered by any of the dairymen in our area at the time. Pa did raise one of Pansy's bull calves. He was a large animal, with attractive dark red and white makings, but I cannot remember that any of his offspring became more than ordinary milk producers. Pansy was sixteen years old, they said, when she had her last calf. It was an exceptionally large, two weeks overdue, bull calf that was born dead. "She's getting too old," Pa said. "We won't try to breed her again." They kept Pansy for nearly a year longer. When her production dropped below a couple of quarts at a milking, Pa called Uncle Ed to see how much she would bring for beef. The old cow that had done so much to provide a living for the family then did her final stint – twenty-five dollars on the hoof. "I'm sorry to see her go, Ed," Pa told our uncle as he led Pansy through the tie-up door. "She's been a good one, hasn't she?" Uncle Ed replied. Pa sat in his rocking chair, looking towards the woodbox for half an hour without speaking.

A few years before he sold Pansy, Pa tried to improve the dairy herd by purchasing from a cattle dealer in Topsham three full-blooded dairy heifers that came from registered stock. He was persuaded to make the purchase by Walter Robinson who had attended a short course in dairying at the University in Orono.

"If you're going to make more money keeping cows, you ought to get some pure-blooded, high-producing stock," Walter told Pa. "They'll give a lot more milk than anything you can raise out of grade animals with the scrub bulls they have around here. Talk to Isaiah Morrill down in Topsham. He can get you some young heifers that will start producing for you in a year or so. They wouldn't cost you too much either, if you buy some that haven't been bred."

"What breed would you ask for?" Pa asked.

"Oh, the breed doesn't make too much difference, I don't think," Walter replied. "Since you're making butter, you might want to keep away from Holsteins – most of them have pretty low butterfat. Something in the line of Guernsey or Jersey should be all right, if you can get them at the right price."

Pa dug into the goldbacks tucked away in a seldom-opened compartment of his bag-like leather wallet. He bought three yearling heifers. The largest of the three was a beautiful Dutch Belt, with a broad band of pure white all the way around her mid-section, her head, neck, shoulders, and hindquarters were jet black. Vining claimed this one as his cow and named her Violet. The second heifer, a uniformly brown Jersey, was named Clover by Genevieve. Jeannette's heifer was a Guernsey that she named Buttercup. This one was somewhat lighter brown than the Jersey but with a bit more buffish tinge. She had a perfect, symmetrical white shield on her forehead. I was old enough at the time to realize that all of this grasping of the new cattle by my older siblings left me without a cow I could call "mine." When I complained to Mother, "I don't have any cow," she promised, "You can have the first calf that we raise from any one of these three new ones." That turned out to be a light brown, white-spotted heifer calf with a white forehead shield, born to Violet, a year later. I named her Rosie. Her sire, a bull owned by Uncle Ed when Pa had no bull of serviceable age, must have had some Ayrshire blood in him, judging from Rosie's horns which were tall, sharp and curved straight upwards. Rosie's short legs were her biggest fault; milking was difficult because her udder was close to the floor.

"Violet's lying down out in the pasture and wouldn't get up," Vining told Pa when he brought the cows in late one afternoon in August, only a day after Rosie was born. "She tried to get up a couple of times, but she couldn't get her body off the ground." This was the first inkling of a set-back in Pa's plans for a bigger and better dairy herd.

"That's funny," Pa replied. "Where 'bouts in the pasture is she?"

"Right in the bottom of the gully where the old road went over the brow of the hill."

"Well, I'll get the cows milked and we'll go out and see if we can get her up. I can't see what might have happened to her. She didn't have any trouble calving yesterday and she looked all right when they went out to pasture this morning."

An hour later, Pa and Vining were at Violet's side, prodding her with a stick, trying to make her rise. She attempted to get up several times, only to slump back in abandonment of the effort. "I can't imagine what the trouble with her can be," Pa said. "She doesn't have any marks on her like she'd been in a fight. And I don't see any marks on the bank here, where she might have slipped down. Sure is funny. Well, we won't let her lie here all night. I'll get the horse and drag and we'll see if we can get her into the barn. Maybe she'll be able to get up in the morning."

With everyone's combined efforts, Violet was moved onto the stone drag and finally pulled into her stanchion, where she ate a little hay and drank a pailful of water. Pa made a sling from a heavy coffee bag and put it under her mid-section. With the aid of block-and-tackle hung from an overhead scaffold timber, he was able to hoist the cow for milking. All of this went on for a week, with no improvement on the part of the new-milch heifer. She lost weight rapidly and finally was destroyed. A few weeks later Walter Robinson came to the house to see Lois one evening. Pa told him about the unfortunate loss of the Dutch Belted cow due to a paralyzed condition. "That was a case of milk fever," Walter said. "It's often the best producers that have that trouble. It strikes them right after calving. If you had pumped air into her udder with a bicycle pump, she might have recovered."

This was one of the times when we really needed a veterinarian. There probably was one in Brunswick, twelve miles away. But no one in our neighborhood ever hired a veterinarian in all the years that I can remember. Farmers relied on the few remedies they knew. Many of the cows' illnesses were successfully treated with home methods. One winter, a cow became constipated from eating too much mouldy hay. "She's all bunged up," Pa said. "We'll have to give her a dose of salts." He kept a household whiskey bottle in the barn that we had found floating in the river. A cupful of Epsom salts was dissolved in the bottleful of water and the mixture poured down the cow's throat. With the cow's head held high, Pa placed the bottle neck in a space between the jaws where there were no teeth. Along with a lot of bubbling in the bottle, the medicine flowed out and down the gullet. Pa made dilators from drugstore slippery elm when a cow had an injured teat. They kept the milk duct open until the injury was healed. For treating mastitis of the udder, Pa added tincture of alconite to the cow's grain.

If home treatments were unsuccessful, the animal was written off as a loss and forgotten or sold for beef. It is now known that milk fever is due to a sudden calcium deficiency brought on by the increased milk production at calving time. Nowadays, in cases like Violet's, a veterinarian would have the affected cow intravenously fed with calcium glucaonate. Almost as soon as the last drops of this substance drain from the bottle, the cow gets up and joins the herd, fully recovered. In those rare cases when the calcium injections do not effect a cure, the veterinarian has a hand-operated rubber syringe in his car for inflation of the udder – a modern variant of the bicycle pump.

Clover and Buttercup, along with Pansy, were the backbone of the farm herd for several years. Buttercup became one of our favorite cows and sort of a family pet. Clover, however, was too aggressive – often trying to pick a fight with one of the other cows. One day in winter, while Pa was away at work, Mother found Clover roaming loose in the tie-up, the stanchion chain having become unfastened in some way. Although Pa had previously sawed off the sharp tips of Clover's horns, some of the other cows showed marks on their hindquarters where she had hooked them. Clover displayed her mean disposition on another occasion. I had turned the cows loose and was about to drive them out of the barn into the pasture after the morning milking. No sooner had they reached the dooryard than Clover viciously attacked Rosie and bowled her over. The bigger cow continued to hook the other one as she struggled to regain her footing. Whacks from a stick went unnoticed by Clover. "Pa! Come here! Quick!" I shouted. He came immediately from the kitchen, and, taking the stick I was holding, drove Clover away from her victim. We put Rosie back in the barn for the day, for observation and recuperation, and to allow time for Clover to forget whatever grudge she bore against the other cow. Rosie showed no ill effects from the unprovoked attack.

Pa raised several of Clover's and Buttercup's heifer calves. Although the offspring were a varied nondescript group – a reflection of the scrub nature of the local sires – some of them became excellent milk producers, and our milking herd was markedly improved by them. One summer, when the two cows were about seven years old, they freshened at nearly the same time and Pa, realizing they would never be worth as much again, decided to sell both of them, while they were still young enough to be desirable producers. On his weekly trip to the Village, Pa stopped at the Telephone Company's office and talked with a cattle dealer in Topsham. The dealer showed up at the farm with horse and wagon the next day. I never knew exactly how much Pa received for the two cows; it was probably around fifty dollars apiece. The dealer started for home with the cows in tow. Neither Clover nor Buttercup were accustomed to being behind a wagon and, although their calves were in the back of the wagon, they held back at first against their taut ropes. To keep the cows on the move, Pa and I followed along behind them for awhile until they learned to keep up with the wagon. Uncle Everett saw us passing his house and came out to see what was going on.

"What you got there?" Uncle Everett asked.

"Got a nice pair of new-milch cows," the dealer replied. "You interested?"

"Let's take a look. I've been intending to get one or two," and he started to examine the animals. He ran his hand over both cows to make sure they were steady and squirted milk from their teats to see if they all worked properly. Finding everything up-to-snuff with both cows, Uncle Everett and the dealer stepped to one side to talk prices. Pa and I stayed out of hearing. After talking with the dealer, Uncle Everett returned to the house and reappeared with the money.

"We should have gotten together on this before and saved the dealer's fee," Uncle Everett said to Pa as they unhitched the cows from the wagon.

"Yeup, we should have."

"Be sure not to let that Jersey get loose in the barn. She has a tendency to be a little ugly toward other cows from time to time," Pa cautioned him.

The two calves were not taken in the deal. They would be raised by the dealer for sale at some later time. As we walked back up the road, Pa said, "I doubt if Everett would have bought the cows from us anyway. He would have been afraid that I'd try to pawn a bogus one off onto him. He probably figured if a dealer bought the cows they'd be all right."

Helping to milk the cows, taking care of the milk and cream, and making the butter were chores that Mother performed continuously for many years. After Vining graduated from Bates in 1914, Pa had a little extra money with which to buy a Sharpless cream separator that made some of this work a little easier. But, previous to that time, Mother strained the milk from tin-plated pails through a cotton salt bag into round, shallow pans which were kept overnight in any available space in the pantry or dining room. The tin-plated milk pans lasted a long time but eventually a pin-hole appeared in one now and then. Mother stopped the leak by first making the hole a bit larger with a darning needle, then pulling a bit of cotton cloth into the opening. Some pans were used for a couple of years with cloth plugs in them. I'm not sure what present day bacteriologically-minded dairy inspectors would say about a practice of this sort. But there were no inspectors then. After the milk had stood in the pans overnight or longer, the cream which had risen to the top was removed with a tin skimmer – a sort of a handle-less ladle with a shallow perforated bowl. The holes in the bottom of the skimmer allowed any of the fat-free milk that had been gathered up with the cream to run out. The cream was placed in three-gallon stone jars until churning day. Along with the purchase of the crank-type separator, Pa also bought a new churn – an oaken barrel that was mounted on a standard and was turned end over end by a short crank. For many years before that, we had used an old-fashioned upright churn with a tapering barrel, slightly smaller at the top than at the bottom. The up-and-down handle worked through a hole in the churn's cover. A round board smaller in diameter than the churn was fastened to the lower end of the handle.

I have spent many hours standing beside the old churn, continually moving the handle up and down and waiting to hear the swish of buttermilk inside, which would indicate that the cream had "broken" and the butter had "come." "Don't spend so much time peeking into the churn," Mother said to me as I raised the cover to see if there might be a few crumbly flecks of butter on the lower handle that would foretell an early end to my labors. "You just keep on churning. I can tell from the sound it makes when it's time for you to stop." Depending on certain unknown factors, different churnings required varying lengths of time to bring the butter. From long experience, Mother knew a few tricks that would shorten churning time. One of these was having the cream near a certain temperature when it was poured into the churn. Another was making sure the cream had soured before churning. To meet both requisites during winter it was necessary to leave the stone jars filled with cream on the cooler part of the cookstove for varying periods. In our house, cream soured very slowly in the colder months unless it was kept near the stove.

The butter making process had two by-products that were consumed on the farm – skimmed milk and buttermilk. The former was quickly devoured by our calves, pigs and hens. Most of us enjoyed a few glasses of fresh buttermilk after every churning. Mother always kept a stone jar full of buttermilk on hand for making biscuits. The pigs and chickens drank all they could get of this delicacy and they got the entire surplus. Skimmed milk couldn't be used for raising calves for veal. Uncle Ed would not buy them for slaughter. "They're too damn skinny," he said. "To make a good veal calf you've got to let him have all the whole milk he wants right from the cow for four weeks. He'd be good and fat then and make good veal." In those days farmers never considered it proper to sell day-old calves for butchering, as is the custom today. Such meat was known then as "bob-veal." "I've heard they use it for canning, to be sold as chicken," Pa said. "No matter what you call it, I wouldn't think of eating a day-old calf." However, he did use skimmed milk, fortified with Blatchford's Calf Feed Meal, for raising our replacements for the dairy herd. Young bulls got the same without as much meal. The young animals seemed to grow well on this diet but they never had as much fat on their bones. Pa once said: "I don't know as you can raise a heifer on skimmed milk and have her make the best dairy cow." Yet, we raised a lot of herd replacements that way.

Over the years, Mother must have spent a great deal of her time making butter. Often I have watched her as she washed the newly-churned butter and prepared the commodity for the market. First, she gathered the butter fragments into a large ball while it was still floating in buttermilk in the churn. The ball was lifted into an oval-shaped wooden dug-out vessel made especially for this purpose, and thoroughly washed with several changes of cold water to remove all traces of buttermilk. If the buttermilk was not completely washed out, the butter had unsightly whitish streaks in it. The proper amount of refined granulated salt was then carefully kneaded into the mass of butter while it was in the wooden bowl. For the next step, Mother used her foot-wide, four-foot-long butter board Pa had made from basswood lumber. The board was placed across the corner of the sink where Mother stamped out the one-pound squares. The butter mould, or stamp, was an intriguing piece of equipment that we were never allowed to play with. Essentially it was a shallow wooden box, about six or seven inches square, that came apart in three pieces. Two opposite corners of the box dovetailed together permanently. The other two were held together by brass hooks that slipped over a brass screw in the adjoining side. This allowed the sides of the box to be removed in two pieces. The third piece was the bottom board, a six-inch square with two lines intersecting at right angles, marking the surface into four equal quarters. Each quarter had a flower design cut into the wood. This inner figured surface of the bottom of the box gave an attractive sculptured surface to the top of the finished, ready-for-sale pound of butter. The two intersecting ridges made it possible to cut the pound of butter into approximately a half pound or quarter pound if desired. In stamping out a pound of butter, Mother filled the box mould a little more than full of the washed and salted butter, pressing it firmly into all four corners. With the straight edge of the blade, she scraped off all excess butter that stood higher than the sides. This left exactly a pound in the box. The mould was then placed upside-down on a square sheet of butter paper which they sold by the pound, ready cut at the grocery counter. Mother unfastened the two brass hooks and removed the sides of the box in pieces. The bottom of the box was carefully raised, leaving the pound, with its attractive flower design on top, sitting free. The edges of the paper square were folded smoothly over the butter and it was ready for market.

We had several customers in the Village to whom we delivered butter at their homes every week. When we made more butter than the customers needed, Cornish's store took the surplus at a few cents per pound less than our retail price. Once, one of the store's customers complained to Mr. Cornish that our butter was underweight. "He weighed some of the cakes I took in today," Pa said, "and there were two or three that did weigh a fraction of an ounce under a pound. Some of them were a little over a pound." It was embarrassing to Mother. "I'll have to be a little more careful when I scrape off the butter in the mould," she said. "The blade of that knife I use curves along the sharp edge; I'll make sure to use the top edge after this. It's a little straighter." Another time, Mr. Cornish told Pa about the response of another dairy farmer who lived south of the Village, to a complaint about home-made butter. "One of our customers said she found hair in the butter," Mr. Cornish said. "When I passed the complaint on to the dairyman, he told me to tell the lady that 'a few hairs was a sure sign that it's dairy butter'."

During the late spring and early summer, when pasture feed was abundant, everyone's cows produced a lot of milk and the market for butter was glutted. The store was unable to take the surplus that we made during those months. Instead of stamping it into pound squares after it was washed and salted, Mother "packed it down" in five-gallon stone jars, tightly covered the jars with paraffin paper beneath the heavy lid, and kept them down cellar. We consumed some of this butter later in the year, in place of the fresh product. When butter became less plentiful during the fall and winter, Mother often stamped out some of this older butter and sold it at a slightly reduced price to regular customers or to the store. A few of our customers said they liked the slightly rancid taste of the packed-down butter and asked that we furnish them with that kind whenever we had it. One of the families preferred unsalted butter, so Mother stamped two or three pounds for them, from washed butter before the salt was added.

Chapter Twenty-Four

Cattle and Beef

"I'm going to raise that big Guernsey calf of Pansy's as a steer," Pa said a few days after the pretty pale red and white bull calf was born. "He'll be a fast grower, I'll bet, and make a lot of beef after two or three years." At about the same time, Pa started raising a Jersey bull calf to keep as a herd sire. The two animals grew up together. When they were about two years old, I wondered why the big-bellied Jersey was the one to be turned loose when a cow was bred. The Guernsey steer was a longer, better shaped animal with much more attractive markings than the black-necked dark brown Jersey. Although I was very curious about the continued use of the Jersey, I judiciously refrained from asking any pertinent questions for I surmised the subject came within one of those gray areas – something no one talked about.

When the Guernsey steer was nearly three years of age, he was given cornmeal twice a day for a month to fatten him for slaughter. This took place in mid-December, when Al came home for Christmas vacation. I don't remember seeing any of the dressing-out process; perhaps I had a cold and was confined to the house. However, I did see the dressed carcass hoisted by block and tackle to one of the high beams over the barn floor. "I don't know as we can eat all that beef this winter since there is the pig we killed the other day," Pa said. "I think I'll see if Harry Tarr won't buy half of it." Harry was a part-time butcher in Richmond who peddled the beef he killed, travelling house to house with his horse and wagon. Harry looked at the dressed steer and agreed to buy one side. He came the next day with his meat saw and split the carcass straight down the middle of the back. For easier handling, he sawed his half into quarters. The only weighing device we had was the steelyards, with a maximum capacity of fifty pounds. Harry forgot to bring his scales. "I'll take this side home and weigh it on my scales tonight. I'll pay you when I come by first of the week," he said before heading back to Richmond. "All right, Harry," Pa agreed.

Not knowing how much Harry could be trusted and feeling a bit uneasy about the deal, Pa borrowed George Weymouth's beam scales next day; they handled weight up to a thousand pounds. I don't know how much our half of the steer weighed, but when Harry came by with the money, he figured the weight of the side he bought by some thirty pounds lighter than ours.

"See here, Harry," Pa said to him eye-to-eye, "no steer was ever that lopsided. There's some discrepancy somewhere. You cut that carcass right down the middle of the backbone. There shouldn't be a difference of more than two or three pounds, at the most, between the two sides."

"Well, I dunno. Can you come to my place this afternoon, Jim?" Harry asked. "I've only cut those quarters into six or seven pieces, so's to handle it easier and weigh it on my platform scales. We can weigh it all again and see how it comes out. I could have made a mistake reading the damn scales."

"Well, I don't relish driving way up to your place, Harry, but I guess I'd better," Pa told him. "I'll be there around three."

When they totalled the weighings of all the beef, the weight came out quite close to the poundage for our side of the animal. Pa got paid for another thirty pounds of beef. "I must have left out one of the pieces of flank," Harry told Pa.

Around Thanksgiving time the next fall, Pa decided to have some more beef that winter, to go with the pork. "We may as well eat old Pottle Belly," he said. "I don't care too much for bull beef, but he's in pretty good condition and shouldn't be too tough. Ed Denham sells all the bulls he can to Will Rideout's store and the people in the Village must buy it." I was out in the barn that time after Pa and Vining had finished skinning the animal. It was a cold windy day and the barn doors were all closed. The air in the barn was permeated with the pungent odor of a beef animal's entrails. Mother came out later with a couple of pails to collect the heart, tongue and skirt to prepare for cooking later on. Pa cut the tail into short sections and placed them in an iron kettle. "That will make good ox-tail soup," he said. My folks always saved the stomach for making tripe. After boiling it they scraped the honeycombed inner surfaces of the squarish pieces thoroughly with a sharp knife. The tripe was then soaked in vinegar for several days before it was fried in flour batter. This time there would be no tripe. After Mother brought a small metal tub to get the stomach pieces, Pa cut into the distended stomach – the first step in preparing tripe. "Look at that!" he cried. "That wall's no thicker than paper. It's too thin to try to make into tripe." I don't know whether the folks knew why the bull had such a distended stomach. He may have been given too much liquid as a calf, or the abnormality was possibly an inherited characteristic. Anyway, we had no more hearty meals of tripe that winter.

While I was in high school, Pa slaughtered the last beef animal that we had for our own use. It was a young Jersey cow that had had one or two calves and was unable to have any more. She had an ovarian malfunction that caused what veterinarians call nymphomania, the effect of which seemed to cause the cow to continuously come into heat. Later symptoms often included the acquisition of some male characteristics, like the development of heavy front quarters and the making of low bawling noise like a bull. Veterinarians sometimes can effect a cure by massaging the ovaries. A more certain treatment consists of the injection of chorionic gonadotropin, a hormone they obtain, I believe, from the urine of pregnant mares. But here again, we had no veterinarian handy and the cow that probably could have been saved was turned into beef. Unlike our winter's supply of fresh pork, we did not hang beef in the stable chamber to freeze. Pa place the four quarters on newspaper on the floor beneath the table in our north dining room. It stayed cold enough there to keep nicely until we had consumed it all.

An item of bovine origin that we often bought from Uncle Ed for fifty cents each was the beef haslet. This consisted of the liver, heart, tongue, lights (lungs), and skirt (diaphragm) from a freshly killed animal. The lungs and gullet were chopped to pieces for the hens. We ate the rest. Like the cow herself, we ate the best part first – in this case the lean skirt. Mother fried it in the skillet and we enjoyed this morsel which tasted something like steak.

Chapter Twenty-Five

Fish and Fishing

There were many kinds of fishes in the Abbagadasset and its tributaries. Among the smallest were the two-spined sticklebacks that I grasped when they hid in the mud on the bottom of the shallow overflow ditch between Amasa's pond and our line. Near our south line fence, there was a washed-out basin a little deeper than the rest of the ditch. Here, inch-long sticklebacks lived and guarded their nests. When I tried to catch one, it would scoot to the edge of the ditch and bury itself in the silty debris. On the river flats at low tide, I sometimes caught with my hands a slightly longer and slimmer stickleback that had four dorsal spines. The sticklebacks were year-round residents, like the sucker, pumpkinseed, dace and yellow perch. The mud minnow that we saw swimming in large schools near shore at almost any time of tide also stayed with us year round. Another permanent resident in our waterways was the common eel that spent the winter embedded in the mud along the submerged channel banks. This snake-like fish apparently travelled through the shallow water of a marsh to reach our remote culvert beneath the railroad. Al told me he used to catch them there. I never tried. But I did feel something slip from beneath my bare foot one day while I was wading around the shore of the little pond near the culvert. It was either an eel or a water snake; I'll never know which. Amasa Williams told us, "We found eels in the wet mud when we deepened the pond during that dry fall we had a number of years ago." To reach either of these tiny bodies of water from the river, the eels had to swim up Pratt's Creek until it faded into the cattails and sedges of Cromwell's meadow. From there the culvert and the pond were still several hundred yards beyond the last vestiges of the creek's channel. I've heard that eels are able to travel overland like snakes for short distances, on rainy days when things are sopping wet. "It's funny," Pa used to say, "you never find an eel with eggs in it, not even the big ones. Yet we see little eels just a few inches long swimming in the river." Since then they've learned that the common eel breeds only in the ocean depths southeast of Bermuda. Perhaps many of the small eels we saw in our river were lampreys.

Economically, our most important fish were those anadromous species that came into our waters to spawn. In the springtime, the most abundant of these were the herring, accompanied by much smaller numbers of shad, lamprey eels and sturgeon. In the fall, schools of tomcods and, in some years, good runs of smelts of all sizes came in. "The best eating fish," Pa declared, "are the ones that have just come in from the salt water. After they've been in our river a while, they lose a lot of their firmness and good taste." Occasionally, in the spring, we caught a striped bass in the weir and, even less frequently, pickerel and brook trout. Once in the fall, Pat caught a six-pound salmon in a sucker net below the Old Pine. With our springtime weir, hook-and-line in the summer, and sucker nets in the fall and winter, we kept tabs on the different kinds of fish that swam the Abbagadasset and learned about their length of stay in local waters.

We started to catch fish with a hook and line at an early age. The best place for fishing with a pole was the ledge on our Point. The sediment-coated rocks were slippery at low tide, making it necessary to step with caution. However, we rarely slipped; our bare feet made for surer walking than the best skid-proof soles. Low water slack was the time to fish, when they were biting the best, the same time when the rocks were the most slippery. Fishing rods and bamboo poles were things we had seen in pictures but we had neither on our farm. Instead we used long limber spruce weir stakes – the ones that Pa had selected for making the two wings on either side of the fish-pound's mouth. These stakes had to be slender enough so that the wings could be spread apart when the skiff was pushed through the narrow mouth at high tide seining time. They made fishing poles that would never break. It took one of our largest big eels, a fish that can hold back with amazing force when hooked, to make one of our dry spruce poles bend even slightly. The yellow perch caught with a spruce pole never had a chance.

"It's time to go fishing, now," Amasa Williams said to me one day in April, soon after the ice had gone out. I used to take some salt pork for bait and catch white perch down by the bridge when I was a boy. Somewhat skeptical, I tried fishing at our Shore with salt pork but without success. Although we caught white perch in both weir and sucker net, I never caught one with hook and line. Yellow perch and eels, together with an occasional pumpkinseed and sucker, were the only species I landed at our Shore. Earthworms were our standby bait at all times. We never had difficulty in finding an ample supply of them in our river pasture, usually close to the boathouse. Even in dry periods, we found earthworms beneath dried-up cow droppings ("meadow biscuits") close to our fishing site. Most of our hook-and-line fishing was done in the summer, when some folks said yellow perch were apt to be wormy and undesirable for food. I used to skin the perch and Mother fried them for our main dish whenever there were enough to go round. If perch had parasitic larvae in their white muscle tissues, we never saw them.

Commercial fishing took much of our time during the cooler months of the year. In the spring, the weir and drift net kept us occupied several hours a day. Sucker nets in the fall and winter required daily attention. Although we could not start building the weir until all of the ice in the river had melted, Pa began cutting new spruce stakes in the woods across the river during late winter. He also accumulated a pile of lithe gray birch binders at the Shore during the winter, for weaving among the tops of the stakes in the weir to give the structure more stability. The birch binders woven all the way around the weir, two feet above high water mark, also served as a support for hanging the netting. Many chilly hours were spent on the river on some of those windy, late April days as I was sitting still, holding the skiff in place while Pa staked the weir. "Keep your end of the boat over that way a little further," Pa told me, pointing towards the middle of the river, "while I get this bend of the fish pound staked out. It has to be right on the edge of the channel." The northwest wind made miniature whitecaps on the modest waves. A gray squirrel eating buds high in an elm tree on Cromwell's bank swayed back and forth as he gathered his meal. I was holding the boat with both hands grasping a stake Pa had temporarily stuck in the bottom of the channel. It seemed as if every time I had the skiff in the proper position, a gust of wind would force it somewhere else.

"I wouldn't try to stake a weir when it's blowing like this," Pa apologized, "but those early herring and shad will be coming through the Chops any day now and we want to be ready for them. Those first ones bring the best prices."

When the weir was completely staked out and the tops of the stakes held in place by interwoven birch binders, it was then ready for the netting. At this point I performed one of my most tedious boyhood tasks – tying the heavy chain to the bottom line of the netting. The correct lengths of ten-foot-wide netting, in pieces measured and cut to fit three sections of the weir – pasture, round pound, and fish pound – were stretched out on the ground on our Point. Here was where I put in a couple of spring vacation days of monotonous back-bending work tying on chain. The chain's purpose was to weigh down the netting firmly into the flats mud on the bottom, leaving no holes through which the fish might escape below the net. The heavy iron chain was a discarded ship's anchor chain that Pa had picked up at a ship yard in Bath. Most of it had links three inches long with a sturdy cross bar welded across the middle of each link to prevent it from collapsing under excessive tension. A jammed link in the anchor could cause a kink that would for sure make a troubling snarl while dropping anchor. The old chain was deeply pockmarked by rust after many years of service in ocean brine.

The tying of the chain was tedious because every other link had to be tied to the bottom line of the netting with a short piece of rope-yarn. It was imperative that every knot be a square knot. Pa tried to tell me how to tie a square knot by having "the end come out of the same side," but I never did understand his directions. I took several looks at a square knot Pa had tied and tried to make them all like that one. After I had tied fifteen or twenty feet of chain, Pa walked along the piece of netting to see if my knots were all the right kind. "See here, son; you tied a granny that time," he would say. "A granny knot will come untied when the tide washes back and forth over it. That'll leave a hole for the fish to get out." I was kept home from school once in a while to help stake the weir or tie the chain on, if Pa was a little late in building the weir. It was one of the few times that I was ever kept home from school for any kind of work.

With a single exception, all of the weirs that I can remember were so-called flats weirs. One year Pa built a deep-water weir half way across the main channel on Cromwell's shore. "A flats weir is easier to stake out," he said. "The shallow water doesn't call for such wide netting, and I believe it catches just as many fish." Our weir was located in practically the same spot year after year – on the edge of the middle ground at the upper end of the island. The weir's leader, pasture and round pound were on the low flats where there was little or no water at low tide. The fish pound extended a few feet over the channel's bank, so part of it always had a foot-deep of water, even on "drain-out" low tides. This was sufficient to keep trapped fish alive from one tide to the next. Pa explained to us his designing the weir the way he did. "The fish we're after are migrating up river with the incoming tide," he explained. "When the tide gets high enough so that there are three or four feet of water over the middle ground, they take this short cut across the middle ground instead of following the channel all the way around the island. They come to the weir's leader" – (a straight row of stakes with brushy young untrimmed birches woven into them) – "and head for deep water in an attempt to get around it. This course takes them through the mouth of the weir and into the pasture. Here they discover they're trapped. At this point, shad and herring react the same way: when they think they're cornered they head the tide and look for deeper water. This takes them through the four-foot-wide mouth of the round pound where they're cooped up a little tighter. By continuing to head the tide, they pass through the foot-wide mouth of the fish pound and not many of them find their way out." On tip-top high water, the skiff is pushed through the narrow mouth of the fish pound by bending the limber spruce stakes beside the mouth. Inside the fish pound the fish are seined and landed in the boat. At the height of the spring run, we often got ten or fifteen shad and as many as two hundred herring – the accumulated catch of two flood tides – at a single daily seining. At the height of the runs, to make less work lugging the catch ashore, we sometimes seined the weir on the high water at night as well as during the day. Besides these two salable species we sometimes got a bushel of suckers and a scattering of perch, shiners, and eels. These "trash" fish were fed raw to the pigs, cooked for the hens, or occasionally used for fertilizer.

Frequently we found victims of predation when we seined the weir. Sometimes dead shad were found floating in the fish pound when we arrived for seining. They had a hole in the belly and the entire soft internal organs had been completely devoured. "That's the work of a common eel," Pa told us. "They attack at low tide when there's not much water in the weir and a big fish like a shad may run aground when an eel gets after him. The eel has the advantage then." Every once in a while, we caught a live shad in the weir that had a gaping wound on its back where a lamprey had attached itself with its suctorial mouth and rasped away the flesh. These injured fish would probably die eventually but they were completely alive when we caught them. As children we never felt too unkindly towards either kind of eel because of their predatory acts; the damaged shad were not salable meat and that meant that we had shad to eat instead of boney herring.

Sometimes during the height of the shad run, when it was low tide in the morning, Pa visited the weir to capture any of the valuable fish that might have been caught during the night. He was afraid they might find their way out of the weir on the flood tide, before seining time. He waded into the fish pound in his rubber boots and was usually able to catch the shad with his heavy dip net. One Sunday morning he did the barn chores early and went to the weir at low water, before I was up. He returned shortly and asked me to go with him while he attempted to spear a striped bass he had found in the weir. It happened that it was one of those moderately low tides that morning that did not drain out to the usual low level. By the time we reached the weir, the incoming tide had begun to flow and there were nearly three feet of water in the fish pound. We could see the bass still there, by peeking through the meshes of the netting, but the water was now too deep for Pa's knee boots. "We'll have to leave him there and take a chance on his not getting out before high water," Pa announced, unhappily holding his pitchfork that would have served as a spear. That afternoon, in anxious anticipation, we seined the weir as early as possible, a half-hour before the flood tide had reached full height. As we pulled the puckered seine into the boat, there, among a mass of flopping herring and a few shad, was the prize fish – a seven-pound striped bass, recently arrived from the Atlantic. We never got to know what striped bass tasted like. It brought too much at Cornish's store.

One of my most exciting childhood experiences took place inside the weir when I was about ten years old. It was the middle of June, time to dismantle the weir and get the netting out of the water before it started to decay. Ordinarily, Pa would have had the dried netting already under cover but he was carpentering in the Village. He had been prevented by rainy weather from working on the weir the past two Sundays. It was now up to Al to remove the netting as soon as he came home for the summer. I went with him the day he started the dismantling. It was low tide when we reached the weir and we could see herring swimming in the shallow water of the fish pound. "Why don't you see if you can catch some of those fish, Bert? I'll take the net off the pasture and round pound first. If you can catch enough for a mess, we can have them for supper." I'd never heard a more welcome suggestion. Barefoot, I was wading through the door of the fish pound before Al had reached upwards to unfasten the first piece of netting. My trousers were rolled up well above my knees.

It was a slightly strange feeling to be inside the weir. Skyward, there was plenty of open space but it was a long ways up. I was completely surrounded by eight-foot walls of muddy netting so heavily encased with two months' accumulation of silt and vegetable debris that it was impossible to see through it. The fish, frightened by my presence, stayed in the deepest water on the channel side. They were exceedingly active as well as slippery. It was a few minutes before I got a firm-enough grip on a herring to carry the wiggling fish in both hands and place it in the boat. "You're squeezing that fish so hard its eyes are ready to pop out," Al said. After the water in the fish pound became so roiled that the herring could not see my hands, I was able to catch them more easily. By the time Al had removed the netting from the other parts of the weir, I had caught eight or ten herring. By then the tide had risen so much that the water became too deep to capture any more fish. I sat in the skiff with wet trousers while Al removed the fish-pound netting. We watched the fish that I failed to catch disappear into the deep-water channel. It was not until then that I noticed the many cuts and scratches on my hands from the sharp scale-like points that overlap one another along the thin belly of the herring. Although it was past the spawning season and the herring were what Pa called "run-down," we did enjoy the fried fresh herring that evening. Split down the back, rolled in dry cornmeal, and fried with fresh salt pork, it seemed that the fish I'd had such a time catching tasted even better than those early ones we caught during the last week of April.

Considering the many small bones that herring have, it was not surprising that we got a bone in our throat once in a while. "Swallow a piece of dry bread," Mother told us whenever this happened. It seemed to work, for none of us ever had a bone lodged in our throat for more than a minute at the longest. However, Pa told about the time a herring bone became stuck in his throat at supper one evening when he was a boy. Perhaps his folks did not know about dislodging it with bread, for it was still there in the morning when his father bent a small hook on the end of a knitting needle and removed the bone. Someone said there were families living on Eastern River who ate so many herring every spring that, come summer, some of the menfolks who hadn't changed their undershirts since Christmas couldn't get them off because of fish bones protruding from their backs. Mother had a way of rendering herring bones completely edible and safe and at the same time serving a fine herring dish. She added vinegar to the boiled fish and allowed them to soak in a stone jar for a few days. The vinegar softened the bones so that we ate them, along with the flesh, with impunity. It was just like the softened bones in canned salmon. We called it "potted herring."

Most of the shad that were taken in the weir were held on ice, together with those that were caught in the drift net, until Pa had enough to fill a flour barrel for shipment to Boston. Once in a while, one of the neighbors bought one of our shad, Cornish's store would usually take a few whenever Pa went to the Village, and we sold some to people who dropped by while on a Sunday horse and buggy ride. We sold a few fresh herring in this manner also, particularly early in the season when residents of our area were hankering for some fresh fish after a winter of pork and potatoes.

Because of the large numbers of herring that we caught, most of them were placed in a barrel of salt brine for a few days. After this salting, they were strung on thirty-inch cedar sticks and hung on horizontal parallel poles close to the roof of our small windowless smokehouse Up-under-the-Hill. The smokehouse was an old gray weather-beaten building that Pa bought from Amasa Williams. It used to be a storage building for boating and other items that Amasa kept near his wharf. The smoke was produced by a partially smothered fire in a discarded wash boiler resting on the ground in the center of the smokehouse. A hole punched in one end of the wash boiler, with a piece of tin placed over it to control the draft, served as a damper. We had no hickory trees in our part of the state to provide wood for the supposedly best flavor for ham or fish. We used a mixture of such readily available woods as poplar, oak, alder, gray birch and black cherry. Pa claimed that smoke from black cherry imparted a "better flavor to smoked herring than anyone ever got from hickory." Pa started smoking the herring as early as possible every spring. Smoked fish brought a better price than the fresh ones. Some years the earliest smoked herring brought the fancy price of seven cents apiece. Storekeepers in the Village liked to keep stocked with smoked herring, but they disliked handling the fresh ones. Towards the end of the fishing season each spring, we had a barrel in the stable chamber nearly filled with smoked herring. We covered them with wood ashes to keep out clothes moths, and enjoyed this delicacy throughout the summer and fall.

A lot of painstaking work went into building the weir and, as a partial reward, there was considerable excitement every time it was seined. The seine had a spruce pole attached to each end and one of the poles was placed at the mouth of the fish pound first thing. Pa moved the other pole close to the netting all the way around the inner edge of the fish pound, gathering up everything within the weir. Finally, he wrapped the two poles tightly together, pulled the puckering rope that closed the seine's bottom, then raised the seine, fish and all, into the skiff. There were a few minutes of intense anticipation as we tried to evaluate the catch. With every fish flopping around in the seine, we could estimate how many shad were hauled in from the number of heavy thumps on the bottom of the boat. We tried to answer immediately such questions as: Was there a bass in the catch today? How many eels? Any lampreys? Usually a few small eels had escaped, as seen by the whitish slime on the mesh of the seine where one had squeezed through. Two big white perch had no chance to escape; they'll go good for supper.

For enjoyment, few of our fishing experiences could compare with drifting for shad. It was done most frequently on calm evenings in May, when it was a pleasure merely to be afloat on the Abbagadasset. At that time of the year, peepers were still singing and the trill of common toads arose from the swampy meadows along the river. One could hear the occasional, spirit-like winnowing of the Wilson's snipe coming from overhead and sometimes we heard the squawk of a night heron passing in the night. Here and there, along the eastern shore, one could distinguish a patch of white where shadbush was in bloom against the dark background of thick coniferous woods. We did our drifting after dusk had fallen when the shad could not see to avoid the flimsy white gillnet waving in the tide. On rare occasions we went drifting in the daytime when the water was badly roiled following a heavy rain, so that the shad could not see the ensnaring net.

I was born a few years too late to see shad fishing at its height. Al and Vining were around to help with the boat when drifting had its heyday. At the height of the spring run, they sometimes caught as many as forty or fifty shad between dusk and midnight with a single net. The best catches that I knew were no more than seven or eight shad in one night. I remember how wealthy I felt after returning home from high school one afternoon and Mother handed me a few dollars as my share of the money Pa had received for shad we had caught in the night before. "I don't want the money, Marm," I said. "It's Pa's net and boat. He should keep whatever we get. All I had to do was a little rowing that was sort of fun." "No, you take the money," she replied. "You helped catch the fish and you deserve part of the proceeds. Your father wants you to have it." The last time I went drifting was one pleasant May evening the year I was a freshman in college. Pa and I took the low water slack in the bend at Uncle Ed's shore. It was one of the best fishing spots on the river and the tide was favorable for the best of catches. We caught only one small buck shad that we had for Sunday dinner. The big nights of drifting were over. Something had happened to those good runs of shad. Some said it was too much pollution in the Androscoggin and Kennebec. Others thought too many shad were caught by the big trawlers while the fish were out at sea.

A most interesting piece of equipment amongst the necessary paraphernalia for drifting was the binnacle light. It was essential even on moonlit nights. Every shadding boat had one. In the years when shad were plentiful, Mother often counted twenty or more of these lights that she could see from the house, between the Old Pine and the lower bridge, in a single evening. The light consisted of an ordinary kerosene lantern fastened inside an upright open box called a binnacle. The binnacle had a short piece of broom handle protruding from its lower end, which fitted into a hole in the gunwale of the skiff. This allowed the light to be shined into the boat or over the surface of the water. The box kept the light from blinding

Old James Dunlap house in Windsor, Maine. Both the Dunlap and Vining families moved to the Malta/New Waterford area between 1815 and 1825 and had farms on Windsor Neck.

The *Sea King*, last large schooner built in Bowdoinham in 1879, towards the end of her days in Bath, 1911. When a young man, James A. Dunlap (Pa) sailed on her maiden voyage. [Bowdoinham Historical Society]

Nathaniel Williams' farm, c.1900, childhood home of Annie Belle. [B. Blake]

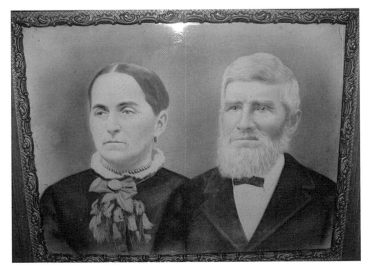

Lois Campbell and Nathaniel Williams, the parents of Bert's
mother Annie Belle. [B. Blake]

Annie Belle Williams holding doll from
Paris, c. 1870.

Legend has it that this was taken at end of October, 1902, while Mother was giving birth to Bert, and while grandmother Lois Campbell Williams was dying. However the leaves on the trees and the lack of winter clothing suggest otherwise.

From left: Lois, Jeannette, Minerva, Aunt Lizzie Card, Vining, Pa, Genevieve, cousin Helen Denham.

Favorite view, the Abbaga-
dasset and Merrymeeting
Bay from the dooryard.
[B. Blake}

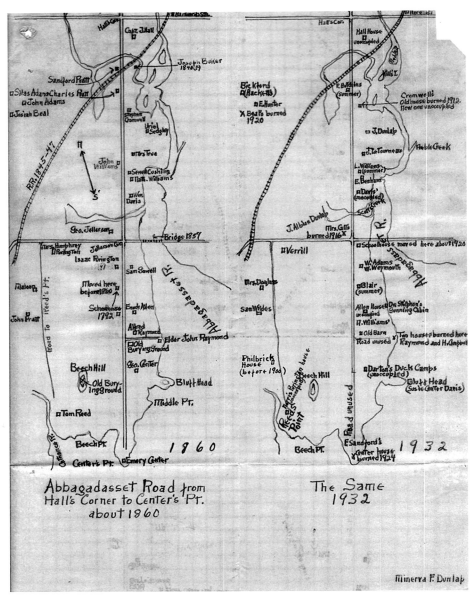

Maps of Abbagadasset Road, 1860 and 1922, by Minerva Dunlap for her booklet of each families' history and genealogy. Note: the Jellerson Schoolhouse was moved in 1910, not 1920. [Bowdoinham Historical Society]

Al, Minerva, Genevieve and Lois,
c. 1899.
[Missing: Vining and Jeannette].
[B. Blake]

Students at Jellerson 1895

FRONT ROW:
1. Gertrude _____?
2. John Thomas Pratt (b. 1888) [m Gertrude Brown b. 1885]
       Father - Sherman W. Pratt; Mother - Jennie M. Record
3. Mellie Williams (Melvina Lizzie) (b. 1/19/1887)
       Father - Everett N. Williams; Mother Henri'etta' Ward
4. Irving Heath
5. Lois Ann Dunlap (b.9/2/1886) [m___ Ingram]
       Father James Albert Dunlap (farmer b Windsor);
                     Mother Annie Belle Williams
6. Mina F. Welch (b.5/11/1888)
       Father - Charles H. Welch (carpenter); Mother - Alice J. Gowell
7. Georgia Nichols Denham (b 11/6/1886)
       Father Edwin Denham (farmer); Mother Abbie Victoria Williams

Jellerson School, shortly after move to Jellerson's Corner in 1910. [B. Blake]

BACK ROW:
1. Horace Smith
2. Florence Brewster, Teacher
3. Emma F. Cromwell (b 2/24/1879)
       Father - Jere (Jeremiah M) Cromwell; Mother - Eliza N. Booker
4. Alice P. Pratt (b 11/22/1885)n [Albert Preble]
5. Albion Dunlap (b 8/6/1884
       Father James Albert Dunlap (farmer b Windsor);
                     Mother Annie Belle Williams
6. Ida Davis
7. Edna Alice Denham (b. 11/9/1883) [m Thomas Ward]

Should Be There?
Minerva Frances Dunlap (b 3/13/1888)

Jellerson School pupils of 1910. Bert is the smallest child, on right in front row, after his haircut.

Jellerson School population, 1912. Bert is the boy wearing a necktie.

Old Bowdoinham High School,
where Al, Lois, Minerva and Vining studied.

Coombs High School,
Genevieve graduated in first class 1912,
then Jeannette in 1914, and Bert 1919.

Unknown man on bicycle on Abbagadasset Road, in front of Nathaniel Williams' house, and the road
stretching away towards the Dunlap
farm. [B. Blake]

The Old Pine Tree on the Abbagadasset. [B. Blake]

Harward's Depot. [B. Blake]

Dinsmore's Mill. [B. Blake]

The *Nellie G.*, 1911, passenger and jack-of-all-trades boat owned by Amasa Williams.
[B. Blake]

Maxwell Farm across the Abbagadasset from the Dunlap Farm, later home of Vining and Lydia Dunlap.

Genevieve with Snipe. [B. Blake]

Pvt. Vining C. Dunlap, c. 1917. [B. Blake]

Minerva, c. 1905. [B. Blake]

Jeannette in sitting room.

Bert, just before his curls were cut off, in dress made for photographic expedition by his sister Lois. Brad says 1908 written on back of seated version.

"She took me to a photographer in Brunswick when I was five years old to have my picture taken before I was to have my curls cut off and wear a 'dutch-cut' instead. I wore my white suit that she and Mother made for me – mostly, I expect, to have 'something nice to have my picture taken in'."

Bert and Snipe, c. 1908. [B. Blake]

Dandy and Bert, c. 1909

Bert, Snipe and Al, September 1, 1915, with results of trip along the river. [B. Blake]

Bert at time of graduation from Bates College, 1923.

Al's motorboat, 1911. [B. Blake]

Outing on the River. Martha and Al in the prow; tall figure on right could be the boatbuilder Robinson or Ed Denham.

Lois, Snipe and Al's boat. Note the rollers and skids used to move the boat on land. [B. Blake]

New ice house and boat house.

Al and Charles Cary preparing to fish from scow, in Merrymeeting Bay, c. 1900. [Bowdoinham Historical Society]

View of Abbagadasset, showing the Point with new ice and boat houses, c. 1912.

Setting the fyke-net in winter. [B. Blake]

On the river with Dandy and old pung. Ice is being cut, either to store it or to make hole to set sucker nets.

Al and Martha's daughter Eleanor, old enough to help out, c. 1915.
[Bowdoinham Historical Society]

Hay load in dooryard, ready to store in haymow. [B. Blake]

Pa with horse Jerry and fully loaded hay wagon at Maxwell
Farm, c. 1910. [Bowdoinham Historical Society]

Pa raking hay, using "tiger" or dump rake. [B. Blake]

Edwin Denham and his cows at the Abbagadasset River. [B. Blake]

Pa watering Jerry, hauling firewood. [Bowdoinham Historical Society]

Bert tending chickens and small smoke house, Up-under-the-Hill.

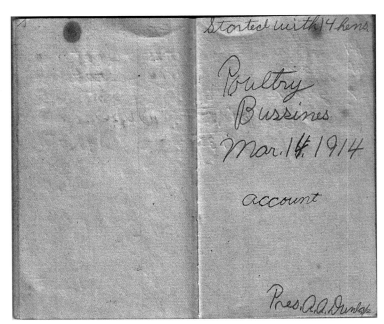

Bert's record book for his chicken business.

Box used to ship eggs to Adams Chapman Co., Commission Merchants, 37 North Market and 37 Clinton St., Boston.
[B. Blake]

Butter mold used by Mother in her butter business. [A. Vaughan]

Walter Ingram's sawmill, c. 1916.

Family reunion, c. 1934.
Back: Minerva, Al, Al's daughter Alison, Pa, Mother, Genevieve's husband Phillip Webb, Al's son Jim
Front: Genevieve, Genevieve's children Marilyn and Dorothy Webb, Al's wife Martha, Jeannette, Vining, Jeannette's son Ron, Bert

Last family picture, c. 1935.
Seated: Jeannette Dunning Dunlap Burrell, James Albert Dunlap (Pa), Annie Belle Williams Dunlap (Mother), and Albert Atkinson Dunlap. Standing: James Albion Dunlap (Al), Genevieve Dunlap Webb, Vining Campbell Dunlap, and Minerva Frances Dunlap.

the fishermen. Although the light from the lantern was not intense, it did illuminate the water's surface for many yards and one could see the long line of white buoys fading away in the darkness. Our drift net was fifty fathoms long – too long, at night, to see the entire string of buoys at once. We had to row the skiff back and forth along the net, watching for any clustering of the buoys which probably meant that something on the bottom had snagged the dangling meshes. "We'll shine that light across the buoys so as to attract the shad into the net," Pa said. We liked to see one or two buoys bob beneath the surface and come up again – a sure sign that a sizeable fish had hit the small twine meshes. When we saw a buoy go under Pa would say, "Back me up to there and I'll take that shad out before he works himself free." He pulled some of the net with the fish into the boat and, with the binnacle facing inwards, held the fish close to the lantern while he untangled its gills from the mesh, dropped the flopping shad onto the bottom of the skiff, and tossed the net back into the river. Vining told me that, on some nights when shad were plentiful, Pa did not take the time to remove individual fish. They merely watched the net float along to make sure it was free from snags and removed the captured shad as the net was taken into the boat at the end of the reach.

One night Pa noticed that a boat from Bath had an unusually brilliant binnacle light. He saw that the exceptional brightness was due to a shiny reflector on the inside of the box. Next day he told Mother about the light. "Do we have something shiny I could line our binnacle box with?" he asked. "The shiniest tin I can think of would be the inside of a new lard pail," Mother replied. With his tin snips, Pa cut open Mother's newest two-quart pail, tacked it inside his binnacle box and enjoyed a much brighter light thereafter.

Slack water at both high and low tide was the most desirable time for drifting for shad. Local fishermen believed that the fish were more active when the current was moving slowly or not at all. Another reason for this preference was the tendency for the drift net to move so fast when the tide ran swiftly that a large mass of tangled net accumulated if it caught on some snag on the river bottom, before the fisherman could reach the spot and lift the net free from the obstruction. For these reasons, shad fishermen often sat out the strength of the flood and ebb, casting the nets into the more moderately moving water. For many years, there was a shanty at the Spar Landing where they gathered to await the slackening of the tide. This interlude provided an ideal opportunity to tell stories, and maybe pass a bottle if someone had been to Bath recently. It is regrettable that there were no tape recorders then to preserve the conversations for later generations to enjoy.

Snags on the bottom of the Abbagadasset channel were dreaded baneful objects that made life miserable for shad fishermen. No one knew for sure just what they were but everyone knew right where they were. There was one spot in the cross channel, about halfway between Uncle Ed's shore and the Spar Landing, where we had to lift the drift net free from a snag almost every time we drifted that reach. "That's where Deacon Williams and Harvey Campbell let their weir freeze in one fall. The ice broke the stakes off and I'll be damned if I ever drifted the length of that reach without getting hung up," Pa said.

One of the daytime chores during shad season was the spreading of the net to remove sticks and drift-hay and to allow it to dry in the morning sunlight. Some years, when strong spring winds had blown most of the old oak leaves from the pasture turf, we spread the drift net on the brow of the hill near the boathouse. When there were too many dead leaves to become tangled in the net, we spread it in the hayfield outside the pasture. This was a job for two people – one to hold the top line while the other straightened the linen meshes, picking out any knots and removing bits of debris that had become tangled in the flimsy netting. Pa usually took this side, keeping his fisherman's needle filled with heavy linen thread in his pocket, ready to mend any torn meshes where the net had been snagged by something in the river. "That hole there must have been torn by the three-foot sturgeon we pulled in last night," he said. "I hate to catch a sturgeon in one of these nets; they've got so many rough places on them to catch on the netting. I can't take the time to make all those new meshes. We'll just close up the hole and let it go at that." After a few hours the net was thoroughly dry. Sometime in the afternoon we piled it carefully on a piece of burlap, the four corners of which were brought together over the net and fastened with a nail. The bundle was placed in the boat and ready for another night's use.

Spreading the drift net was one of the jobs we took pleasure in doing. The air was mild and balmy on those sunny forenoons in May. Barn, cliff and tree swallows flitted about as we straightened the netting. Herring gulls flew up and down the river and red-shouldered hawks uttered their sharp calls as they soared almost out of sight in the deep blue sky.

I was a small boy when Pa made his last drift net. He sent to the American Net and Twine Company in Boston for the woven netting. The white cotton top line was purchased at the Village. Pa used many of the oval white factory-made wooden buoys form a previous net, together with some newly-painted, cylindrical ones that he had made from round cedar fence stakes. The new net was assembled in our kitchen, one portion at a time, with the top line stretched between nails driven into opposite window sills. The job required several midwinter days of work. "Some people put a bottom line on their drift nets," Pa said one day as he fastened the netting to the top line. "Maybe I should put one on this. It gives you something to get hold of when the net gets caught on a snag. A bottom line keeps the net straight up and down in the tide without all that waving from one side of the channel to the other. But another line makes the net that much heavier to handle. Maybe if I ever make another net, I'll put a bottom line on it."

With the decline of the shad came a new fishing enterprise to the Abbagadasset. The lowly sucker became an important commercial fish around 1910-1912. They were abundant in our river where, at dusk, they frightened many a lonesome boatman in their sudden splashing dash from some feeding place on a high flats to deep water. Apparently, suckers enjoyed feeding on the flats at high tide where they became so engrossed with their food that they disregarded the shallower water as the tide receded. When something suddenly frightened them in lonely two or three inches of water, they frantically thrashed their way to the channel. We sometimes ate suckers for one or two meals in the spring. Some years, our weir was completed before the herring arrived and the first seining produced only a pailful of the ever-present suckers. To satisfy our desire for fresh fish, we selected four medium-sized suckers and fried them in cornmeal batter and pork fat as we did the herring a few days later. The fine-grained fish flesh was rather soft and it often had a slightly muddy taste. As soon as herring arrived, we fed the suckers uncooked to the pigs or, after they were boiled in an old iron kettle, they were mixed steaming hot with cornmeal for the hens. Suckers have a membranaceous air bladder, elongated-pear shaped, with a constriction near the larger end. It looked something like a baby zippered up in a hooded sleeping bag. Oddly enough, many of the air bladders survived the boiling, and I rescued them from the kettle to use as navigational buoys in my rock-bound pool back of the house. I tied them with a short piece of string to a small stone that was placed on the bottom of the pool. Sometimes the buoy remained upright for a week, to mark some dangerous underwater ledge in the two-yard-square pool with its peapod boats.

Pa was a year or two late in breaking into the sucker business. When word got around one fall that Milton Douglass and Melvin Pratt had earned eight hundred dollars suckering, from the first of October to freeze-up time in late November, Pa got out the Sears Roebuck catalog and ordered his first fyke net. Catching suckers involved a technique that was quite different from the taking of herring and shad with a weir. Unlike these two fish, suckers do not turn tail and head for the tide when they become entrapped; they merely proceed straight ahead with the tide as far as they can go. The fyke net is well adapted to catch them. The central part of the net consists of a tapering barrel of six wooden hoops covered with netting. The hoops are from four to six feet in diameter at the mouth, and a little less than three feet at the nose or fish pocket. In use, the barrel lies lengthwise to the river in the middle of the channel. Two wings made of coarser netting than the barrel, weighted down by a chain on the bottom and held suspended by wooden buoys on the top rope, angle away from the barrel's mouth to stakes on opposite sides of the channel. The wings guide the suckers into the barrel where they pass through two sleeve-like funnels. After passing through the second, smaller funnel, the fish are held captive in the third chamber of the net until the fisherman unties the puckering string in the net's nose and dumps them out. Fyke nets can be set for either flood or ebb-tide catch, but one set to catch on the ebb catches nothing on the flood tide because the two funnels collapse when the tide turns. Three stakes hold the net in place in the river – two support the ends of the wings on the opposite sides of the river, and the third is driven in the middle of the channel some distance beyond the nose of the net, to keep the barrel in place regardless of the direction of the tide. In the fall, we set fyke nets and tended them with the skiff. In winter, all of this was done through holes in the ice. Low water slack was the usual time to remove the fish, either by boat or on the ice.

There was no market for suckers locally. The Boston market didn't handle them either. They were packed on ice in wooden boxes and shipped by railway express to New York where they were known as "mullet." The prices we received varied from a few cents per pound to as much as twenty cents, depending on how well the market was supplied with this kind, as well as other kinds, of fish that particular week. "During unusually cold stormy weather is the best time, I've found, to ship suckers," Pa used to say. "There's not so many fish coming into New York when the weather is bad." Suckers were a fall and winter deal. We never shipped any that we caught in the weir in the springtime because they didn't keep at that time of the year. "Spring-caught suckers, seems like, have a tendency to get soft and disintegrate on the belly awfully quick. They don't stand shipping when the weather starts getting warm," Pa said. Sometimes he set the nets in September and held the suckers in a board and hardware cloth cage, anchored in the river, until the weather was cool enough to ship them to New York City. In the winter, we held the suckers alive in shorts sacks tied to a rope under the ice, until enough fish were caught to make a worthwhile shipment. Fortunately for us, in those days, many goods were shipped in wooden boxes instead of corrugated pasteboard. Every time Pa went to the Village in summer, he brought back three or four empty boxes that the grocery stores sold him for a nickel apiece. He stored them in the stable chamber for use in fall and winter. In the fall the boxes were harder to find because all of the sucker fishermen were shipping fish and taking the empty boxes as fast as the grocers removed their contents. Pa preferred boxes that they shipped canned salmon in. They were the right size, holding about forty pounds of suckers, and were well-made of straight-grained Oregon fir.

It was fun tending the sucker nets from the skiff in the fall. Pa had me hold the boat in place while he raised the barrel of the net over the side. "I'll bring in these bigger hoops," he said as he hooked an ice pick onto the tallest one, "just to make sure no sunken stuff has gotten caught in there and see that there's no holes in the netting." The biggest hoops were then dropped back into the water and the smaller end with the entrapped fish was lifted aboard. "Not a bad catch today," Pa said while untying the puckering string in the nose of the net. "Got two eels, didn't we? It's about time they started bedding in the mud." There was a peck of tomcods along with fifty pounds of suckers. Late in the fall, along towards freeze-up time, we often got a few large smelts every time we pulled the net; we caught only the biggest smelts in the sucker net, since the smaller ones slipped through the one-inch mesh. A few yellow perch also showed up in the catch nearly every day. "Had a good-sized salmon in the net today," Pa told me as I rode home from school with him one late afternoon in October. "First one I ever caught in a fyke net. Sold the head half to Ed Denham for a dollar. Your mother's cooking the rest for supper." One day we pulled the net into the skiff and, instead of the expected hundred or so fish, there were less than a couple dozen. "Now, how do you account for that?" Pa asked. "Suppose someone fished the net before daylight? Yesterday we had a good haul, and look at it today." As Pa untied the puckering string, he noticed a six-inch hole big enough for a shad to get through in the puckering netting near the tip of the barrel. "There's the answer – a cursed muskrat chewed his way out there and most of the fish found the hole."

Tending the sucker nets through the ice in winter was an entirely different procedure. On calm days when it was not too cold, it was pleasant, but in blustery frigid weather it was a chilly task. The entire barrel of the net was pulled onto the ice, big hoop first, through a four-by-six-foot hole. The net often froze stiff in a few minutes if the day was cold. We poured the fish from the net onto the cold ice that was often covered with snow. We had to keep the suckers alive until shipping day, so we shoveled them at once into a shorts sack, and hung them in the water immediately. They would freeze stiff if allowed to lie on the ice more than a very few minutes, with the temperature around 20° F or lower. Plastic gloves had not been invented at that time and rubber mittens were too expensive, so we carried an extra pair of woolen mittens just for handling the wet fish and net. The mittens became quickly frozen but, even so, they kept our hands warm no matter how cold the weather.

Only two stakes were required for each fyke net in the winter. These held the ends of the wings on opposite sides of the channel. A long rope attached to the nose of the net was passed downstream beneath the ice, fished up through a hole with an ice pick, and tied to a stake across the hole. This held the barrel of the net extended along the river bottom. Thus the need for a third stake, as was the case in the fall, became unnecessary. One of the hazards of winter fishing was the tendency for the stakes to freeze solidly to the ice at slack water on either high or low tide. To prevent this freezing of the water in a stake hole, we banked the stakes with spruce brush and shoveled snow into the brush. This provided sufficient insulation to prevent freezing of the water around the stake except on the very coldest nights. One morning, after a bitterly cold night in late January, Pa scraped a hole in the frost on the kitchen window to see how the stakes had fared overnight. "We've got two pulled stakes," he said. "One on the net by Preble Creek and another in the cross channel. They're sticking up high in the air. Froze in on low water slack." Sucker net stakes frozen in like that at low water could be easily reset by chopping away at the new ice that held the stake and pulled it from the bottom mud when the ice sheet rose with the tide. Had they become frozen in at high tide, they would have been rammed into the mud and broken when the ice sheet lowered on the ebb tide. Another hazard involved in the setting of sucker nets beneath the ice was the crushing of the larger hoops when the depth of the river became too shallow on the lowest drain-out tides. On this account, Pa finally bought only four-foot nets, after ice crushed his first one that had a hoop five feet high. "Except for the deep hole in Cromwell's bend, I have to set all of the nets somewhere below the Old Pine," Pa said. "Otherwise I'd have a lot of hoops broken by the ice at low tide." The first winter after graduating from Bates, Vining stayed at home and fished in partnership with Pa. They set one net up river in the deep hole just below the big railroad bridge, where the water was more than deep enough even for the tall five-foot net. That was the farthest spot upriver that we ever set a sucker net beneath the ice.

Heavy rain in winter made for undesirable conditions for sucker nets beneath the ice. It washed silt and drift hay into the river, badly clogging the nets. Sometimes we had to pull the entire net onto the ice, shake off the accumulated debris, and reset the net. It was an unpleasant task. "Rains in the spring, when they're supposed to come, are all right," Pa said. "They only roil the water so that we can go drifting in the daytime. But rain in the winter does nobody any good."

One or two fishermen on the Abbagadasset shipped our common eel to the Boston market. They caught most of them in eel pots baited with chunks of fish, a method quite similar to techniques used by lobstermen along the coast. Since eels can be kept alive for extended periods in captivity, many of them were caught in the summer and held in submerged wooden bins, called "cars," until conditions were favorable for marketing them when the weather became cool. Another popular method for taking eels involved the use of a special type of spear. An eel spear is a sort of several-tined fork with a long slim handle. The tip of each tine is bent upwards into a short sharp hook that faces the tine next to it. On our river, eels were speared from a boat during the late fall after they had embedded for the winter in the mud along the channel banks. Later they were speared through holes cut in the ice. Unlike a fish spear, the tines of the eel spear do not penetrate the fish. Since the eel is more or less immobile in the flats mud, it is squeezed between the tines by the thrust of the spear. The squirming eel is prevented from slipping away from the spear by the hooks on the ends of the tines which hold him fast. An experienced fisherman can feel the vibrations in the handle of the spear caused by the wriggling of the captive eel, and thereby tell when he should empty the spear of its catch. The winter he spent at home, Vining bought our only eel spear from Sears Roebuck and mounted it on a slender weir stake. Nearly all of us tried our hand at spearing eels but with poor success.

Everyone in our family had an inherent dislike of wiggly crawling things like tent caterpillars, earthworms and snakes. Consequently it was only natural that we never ate eels, although we had heard that they were a delicious morsel. I have yet to taste eel, but I did try once to pass one off onto the folks. It was the next weekend after Pa had set the first sucker net in the fall. We had caught no smelts as yet and we all wanted some fresh fish after eating smoked herring all summer and fall. Mother asked, "Why don't you skin out a few of the best tomcods and I'll fry them for supper? Some fresh fish will taste good for a change." I complied with her wishes right away. As it happened, there was a medium sized eel in the catch that day and I got the bright idea of trying to get someone in the family to try a piece of it along with the tomcod for supper. I cut out and carefully skinned a section from the middle of the eel about the same length as a tomcod. Mother washed the fish I prepared, rolled them in cornmeal and fried them as usual. I kept my eye on the piece of eel lying on the platter's edge in the center of the table, along with the crisply-fried tomcods, hoping that I would not be the one to be served the slightly thicker piece of fish and wondering what I'd better do if Pa did put it on my plate. When he served the third person, Pa came to the atypical tomcod. Raising it on the serving fork, he meticulously placed it on the far edge of the platter. "That's an eel," he observed.

Maine farmers had a special use for the eel skin. It was so tough that it was used as a flexible hinge on homemade flails that were used in threshing beans and peas. The long handle of the flail was fastened to one end of the heavy, thirty-inch length of three-inch round hornbeam by a dry eel skin. The leathery hinge withstood years of vicious pounding.

Although the eel is a predatory fish, I saw one being preyed upon by a small mammal. As I was sitting in our boathouse door one rainy afternoon in June, I saw a mink emerge from the shallow water on our grassy flats with a foot-long eel in her mouth. The mink dragged the eel quickly across our Point to a pile of weir stakes beneath the oaks, where she presumably had young ones to be fed.

A somewhat unusual fish that we caught rather frequently in the weir, less frequently in the drift net, and very rarely in a sucker net, was the sturgeon. We never caught a very large sturgeon, like the one that Deacon Williams caught in his weir. Mother said that one was so long that its tail extended beyond the body of the oxcart when they hauled it up to the house from the shore. On warm summer evenings, we used to see the lights of fishermen drifting for big sturgeon on the Kennebec. One spring, I kept a foot-long sturgeon in the rock pool back of the house for a couple of weeks as a pet. It was a little too large for the small pool, so I transferred it to our Little Pond in the west pasture until Al came home and could go along with me while I took the fish to our deep culvert beneath the railroad, where the water was deep enough for the fish to grow and prosper. When we went to the Little Pond to transfer the fish, the cows had washed in the water too often and roiled it so badly that the sturgeon had died. Most of the sturgeons we caught were from two to three feet in length. "I keep hoping we won't catch one of them in the drift net," Pa said. "With all those humps along their backs, it's hard to free them without breaking a lot of the meshes once they get all tangled up in the webbing." Vining thought we should try eating a sturgeon so he prepared a small one for Mother to cook. On the table at mealtime, as I remember, the sturgeon had a peculiar yellowish-orange tinge and a slightly oily texture. The taste was a bit bizarre. It was one of the few items of food that reached our table and did not get eaten. The other tentative morsel was a fish-eating sheldrake that Pa shot just before Thanksgiving one fall. A third unpalatable item was the first breakfast Mother prepared using some of a new five pounds of oatmeal that was contaminated with grain-moth larvae. Vining was the first one to notice the cooked insects as he sprinkled sugar on his breakfast cereal. "Let's have some molasses to go with these steamed biscuits, Marm. We can make out a good breakfast without the cereal," Vining said. "I'll take that oatmeal right back to Mr. Cornish," Pa insisted. "It's probably from a barrel they've had setting in the store for six months."

Aside from some unusual fish, at least one uncommon animal was caught in a weir on our river. Old Santy had the rare experience of boating a seal in his seine one spring. Apparently the animal had followed the schools of herring all the way from the ocean and eventually into the fish pound of Old Santy's weir. It may have been the same year that Ira Allen was surprised and much disturbed when "the funniest face you ever saw bobbed up out of the water" not far from his skiff as he rowed upriver one April day. One damp morning Pa brought me a pied-billed grebe that he'd seined from the weir before I was up. "He's in a shorts sack in the stable," Pa told me when I came downstairs. After breakfast, I took the sack to my fish pond back of the house. As I extracted the bird from the bag, it gave me a vicious peck on the back of my hand with its sharp bill. I dropped the bird immediately. It fluttered over the ledge and took off, flying across the field back to the river.

As for real danger of damage to his weir, Pa worried most about logging traffic on the river. For several years, when the sawmill at the head of the tide on our river was in operation, Owen Emmons towed rafts of logs on the Abbagadasset up-stream to the sawmill. One day, Pa returned hastily from the Village after learning that Owen was on his way with a raft. He was crossing the Bay as Pa rounded Jellerson's Corner. "I'll get this horse unhitched and go down to the weir as quick as I can," he said. "If he sees someone there, he'll swing wide enough to clear everything. If one of the logs of that raft catches on the weir, he might tear it in two."

Chapter Twenty-Six

Thieves, Vandals and Their Ilk

"I can't imagine whatever happened to some dry wood I left beside the chopping block last evening," Mother said as we sat down to dinner one summer noon. "Vining split some of Amasa's slab wood yesterday and I used a little of it for cooking supper last night. Then, this forenoon, when I went for some to bake biscuits with, there wasn't any there." We suspected the family that was renting the Cromwell house at the time. This was the only case of loss by theft of anything from our farm that I can remember during the years that I was growing up. On at least two occasions, however, the Village post office was broken into as the townfolk slept. The thieves were cautious about awakening them for they covered the safe with a blanket before "blowing" it. In both cases, the robbery was not discovered till morning. Returning one night from Brunswick, Al took the midnight train that did not stop at Harward's. He walked home from the Village along the railroad. As he approached Uncle Ed's pasture, he heard voices of people coming towards him along the tracks. To avoid passing strangers in so lonely a spot at that time of night, he left the railroad and entered the pasture to wait among concealing alders. Two men soon arrived at the barway and stood there a minute. One said, "He went in here." They continued on down the tracks. The next day, our folks heard that the tiny depot at Harward's, a mile up the tracks from where Al saw the men, had been broken into during the night. The railroad station at that time also housed the East Bowdoinham post office. The robbers took postage stamps together with all the cash they could find. One spring after Eric Blair dropped out of high school, he along with a pal from Bowdoin broke into Rideout's store in the Village by cutting a hole in the door with a glass cutter. The two were later arrested after their loot, mostly canned goods, was found hidden in the railroad underpass in Uncle Everett's pasture. Aside from these incidents, few burglaries were committed in our neighborhood in spite of the fact that every day hoboes walked the railroad, some of whom came to our house to ask for food. The habit many farmers had of keeping a loaded shotgun near at hand for hawks and skunks may have been a factor maintaining low crime rates.

Even in the good old days of the early 1900's, vandalism was not unheard of in our town. One day, after I had thrown a stone at a telephone pole, Pa told me there was a fine for breaking those glass insulators at the top. An irresistible target for stones, however, was Mrs. Shepard's house that stood close to the railroad embankment south of Jellerson's Crossing. It might have seemed that the railroad was in cahoots with the boys since it embedded the cross-ties in crushed white granite of convenient throwing size. At suppertime one evening, while Vining was in high school, our meal was suddenly interrupted by a sudden outburst of barking by Snipe. We looked out the window in time to see Mrs. Shepard hurry past the dog, come up the porch steps and burst into our kitchen without pausing to knock. "That's him! Right there!" Mrs. Shepard shouted as she pointed her finger at Vining seated at the far corner of the table. "You threw those rocks at my house this afternoon!"

"I didn't throw any rocks at your house," Vining said, arising from his chair.

"Do you mean to stand there and say you didn't throw a rock through my window?"

"Yes, I'll say it standing up or I'll sit down and say it," Vining replied.

After a minute or two of accusations and denials, there was a lull in the shouting which gave Pa the chance to ask Mrs. Shepard how much it would cost to replace the broken glass. "Fifty cents," she replied. Pa withdrew his wallet from a hip pocket, obtained a fifty cent piece, and, reaching across the table, placed it in the lady's outstretched hand. "Thank you," she said as she turned and abruptly left the house. At school the next day, Vining and Genevieve learned that Mrs. Shepard had visited two other families that evening, creating a similar scene each time. Even in the case of vandalism, history may repeat itself. During my freshman year in high school, nearly ten years after the incident of which Vining was accused, four or five of us boys were on the way home along the railroad past the house where Mrs. Shepard still lived with Les, her middle-aged retarded son. I think it was Eric's throwing arm that was accurate that afternoon. At the shattering of the glass, all of us dashed down the back side of the embankment and ran its entire length, out of sight of the Shepard's house. We had no visitations from the elderly lady that evening but I had a distinctly unpleasant feeling that I was, in a way, a participant in an ungentlemanly act. Next day, Roland Hall and I were walking home along the highway as far as Jellerson's Crossing instead of taking the railroad. Mrs. Shepard's next door neighbor, elderly John Woodsum, was seated in front of his house. He beckoned to us as we went by. We approached within talking distance. "You know," he said, "it's bad business throwing rocks at people's houses. We hadn't ought to be doing things like that." Neither Roland nor I had anything to say in reply to the white-haired gentleman. We nodded agreement and continued on our way, thinking that Eric should have been there to hear what Mr. Woodsum had to say.

George Frank Preble was a fisherman who lived on the shore of the Bay behind the woods on the other side of the cross channel southeast of our house. He had three sons about Vining's age, two much younger daughters, and later a somewhat retarded son. Near the eastern edge of the woods, in a two story house, the roof and chimneys of which we could barely see above the treetops, lived Mike Heath and his family of three sons and a daughter. One Saturday morning in May of 1907, one of the Preble boys, fifteen-year old Sydney, came to our place to visit Vining. He was still there at noon and accepted Mother's invitation to join us for dinner. I barely remember the unusual experience of having another boy at our table but the folks remembered the humorous remark Sydney made when they asked about his neighbor, Wesley Williams. "He's still keeping chairs warm," Sydney said. It was only a week later that our neighborhood was shocked by the finding of eighteen year old Norris Heath fatally shot near the highway that passed through the woods a short distance west of his home. His body was found near the spot where the path to the Preble's house branched off from the dirt highway. Both young men had been working that week at the sawmill. They were walking home together on pay-day. At five years of age, I was too young to ask questions about such incidents but I listened intently to conversations. Pa told Mother, "They went to George Frank's house and Sydney admitted the deed." He was sentenced that fall to life imprisonment at Thomaston State Prison, where he died some three years later. This was the only violent crime that I knew about in our town.

Most of our local infractions of the law were of a minor nature such as disturbances of the peace. Al told me of an incident that occurred soon after he graduated from high school. He became involved when one of Old Santy's grand-children came to our house around midnight complaining that her father, Old Santy's son-in-law, had been drinking too much and had gone berserk, chasing people around the house and threatening to kill their cow. Pa told Al to hitch up the horse and drive to the Village to tell the town constable, Bert Cornish. Sheriff Cornish responded to Al's knocking at the door of his Pleasant Street home by appearing in his upstairs bedroom window. He told Al he could not drive two miles into the country at that time of night for a case of drunkenness. "You go back and get your father and Ed Denham and the three of you go up there and take him," the sheriff told Al. Dismayed, Al returned home. By that time, I guess things at Old Santy's had quieted down. "Take him" was a frequently repeated phrase in our household after that.

One forenoon some years later, Pa came home from the Village and told us how he and Will Given had helped the Sheriff arrest a fellow who had been on an intoxicated spree earlier the night before. "It was Joe Maloon, the fellow who lives in that houseboat on the Cathance tied up just below the West Branch bridge," Pa said. "When Joe saw the sheriff, he crawled right into the mud underneath his flat-bottomed houseboat that was grounded on the high flats at low tide. The three of us had all we could do to pull him out, feet first. We took him to jail."

The village jail was a low square brick building on a vacant lot near Puddle Dock on the east side of the Village. Most of its inmates were held for only brief periods. If serious charges were to be brought against them requiring detention for an extended period, they were taken by train to the county jail in Bath. There they would be close to our county court of law. The jail also provided overnight lodging for down-and-outers who were trying to escape the rain or cold. One night, two men were locked up as thievery suspects. In the morning, the jailer found the building empty although the door and windows were still locked. The pair had pushed the roof up far enough above the brick walls for them to crawl out beneath the eaves.

In the years when we were walking to high school along the railroad, we met tramps quite frequently. Usually they were men around fifty years of age or older travelling alone, or occasionally in pairs, rarely in trios. I had an uneasy feeling when I met these hoboes on a lonely section of the tracks, but none ever tried to interfere with my walks to school. Usually, we passed with a friendly "hello." The hoboes had two campsites between our farm and the village, where they rested, built a campfire, and perhaps enjoyed a snack. One of these spots was beneath a clump of spruce trees close to the railroad in the far end of our pasture. Another was under a big hemlock in the woods close to the tracks near Jellerson's Crossing. One often found a recently-opened baked bean can or sardine tin at these resting spots. It was while Vining was in high school that he learned from the railroad section crew that some wayfarer had met a tragic end not far from our farm. He was told: "The railroad investigators found pieces of clothing and parts of the unfortunate traveller scattered all the way from Amasa's pasture to Scott Davis' woods. He must have been struck by a southbound express rounding the bend through Amasa's woods. There's no way of telling who the fellow was. Those hoboes have no home, no family, probably no friends, and possibly, they don't even have a name, except a given one."

Chapter Twenty-Seven

Waste, Recycling, Wild Foods, Maple Syrup, Apples, Gum, Toys, Medicines, and Other Natural Resources

We never had a serious problem with the disposal of garbage or rubbish on our farm. There were too many omnivorous creatures around and anything combustible went into the stove. As for leftover table scraps and other food wastes, after the dog and cats had been fed, the pigs and hens consumed everything that was left. Egg shells were fed back to the hens for recycling, after they were completely crushed. If egg shells in their original shape were fed to the hens, they might acquire the habit of eating their eggs before we gathered them. Apple and vegetable parings were eagerly consumed by the pig. Cows were glad to get banana peels, corn husks and cobs, and the discarded wrapper leaves from cabbages. Clam shells were placed in a shorts sack and completely crushed with a heavy maul, then fed to the hens to provide gizzard stone for grinding food and calcium for egg shells. Buttermilk that had become too old for biscuit-making and soured milk of any kind went into the pig's pail on the walk in the wood shed.

There was little solid waste such as cardboard, glass and tin containers, since we bought few packaged things. There were no molasses or vinegar bottles to throw away because we had a gallon stone jug for molasses and a similar one for vinegar. When these became empty they were taken to the store to be filled from a barrel by a crank-type hand pump installed on the barrel's head. All pasteboard boxes that we had no use for were used for kindling the cookstove fire. Lard came in three-quart tin pails with a tightly fitting cover. These pails had a myriad of uses around the house and barn; besides, we used them for years as school lunch pails. Perhaps our commonest tin disposal item was the empty salmon can. We made good use of parts of it. The jagged edge of the opened cans was pounded down smoothly with a hammer to make many useful containers. We used them for watering cabbage plants when they were transplanted, for flower pots and for holding nails. The tin discs from the tops were used to tack over rat holes in the alleyway where we kept the grain. Glass Vaseline jars with their screw-on caps were washed and used for storing such items as copper rivets and carpet tacks, as well as vegetable seeds that we wished to save for next year's planting. Empty paint containers with their residual coating on the inside made the most durable containers for a variety of purposes. About the only containers that we threw away were patent medicine bottles and tin cans or pails after they had sprung a leak. We kept a wooden box for these in the woodshed and it required emptying about once a year – at the place where the riverbank was "falling in" near our north line in the river pasture.

Some of the patented feeds that we bought for calves and chickens came in cotton sacks that Mother eagerly converted into dish towels or pillow covers for the boys' straw mattress bed. The slip covers may have been a little rough at first, which we minded not at all, because, after a hard day's work, we paid little attention to smoothness of a pillow. The granular salt that was used in butter making also came in cotton bags, either five- or ten-pound sizes. Mother removed the stitching along the seams and was rewarded with a squarish piece of frayed-edged cloth that made fine handkerchiefs for home use. The salt bags had a brand name and other advertising material stenciled on the cloth, but these words soon faded after a few washings. When I first learned to read, I made out the statement "salt is not salt" on the front of the bag. I asked Mother what they meant by that. "They mean that some brands of salt have impurities in them," she replied.

A related product we called saleratus was Arm and Hammer baking soda that came in one-pound yellow boxes. We had no use for the empty box, but in the top of every package was a small card with a colored picture of a bird on one side and a description of the bird on the other. Mother saved all of the cards and after many years we had a good collection. When Vining shot a beautifully marked duck up river one fall while he was in college, we got out our bird cards and identified the waterfowl as a male wood duck. Vining took the trophy to a Lewiston taxidermist.

Besides making use of many things that ordinarily would be thrown away, we gathered wild plants, fruits and berries for food. In the years before the apple trees Pa had set when he bought the farm commenced to bear fruit, apples were gathered from non-grafted trees that grew wild along the river. They were "natural fruit" apples, produced on trees that had grown from an apple seed. Ungrafted trees of this sort vary greatly in the quality of the fruit. Some are small, sour and of little use except for pig feed or cider. Occasionally a wild tree bore fair-sized apples with an attractive flavor. Any nondescript apple provided important food for the ruffed grouse and we always looked for "partridge" around apple trees growing in or near the border of the woods. "Pa used to take us over to Preble Creek every fall," Minerva recalled, "to gather apples from a tree on the beaver dam between the creek and the river. We thought they were the most wonderful apples – good size, juicy with a real good flavor." There were two or three wild trees on the old Dankin farm near the head of the river that bore good apples too. Another tree that had highly edible natural fruit stood on the west side of the gully in our river pasture when I was a boy. Its large pinkish apples had a fine flavor. They were what we called "water core" apples and were excellent eating, although they were poor keepers under our storage conditions. We tried to gather them each fall before they dropped from the tall leaning tree and were eaten by the cows.

Like most thrifty Yankees, we utilized every possible natural resource. Few things went to waste. After foodstuffs had run the gauntlet of our table, the dog, cats, chickens, pigs and cows, there was nothing left. To supplement our farm-raised meats, eggs, dairy products, fruits and vegetables, and fish from the river, we picked wild berries wherever we could find them, and we had many meals of game birds during open season. As soon as the overwintered rosettes of dandelion leaves started to grow in the spring we had meals of this green, with wafers of hard boiled eggs for additional protein. A little later we collected the heart-shaped leaves of a wild aster plant that appeared beneath the oaks Up-under-the Hill. We called them "tongues" and cooked them for greens. We found fern fiddleheads that we called "bananas" and ate them on the spot as soon as they appeared along the edge of the upland by the river swamp.

In June, we found the first ripe strawberries along the railroad, on those warm steep banks where a cut had been made through a rise in the ground. A week or two later they became ripe in both of our pastures and in fields that had not been plowed recently. My sisters sold wild strawberries at the Village stores and bought cloth for new dresses with the money. It was a case of first come first served during strawberry picking times in our neighborhood. One June morning, Genevieve, Jeannette and I went to find some berries in our west field. A lady we'd never seen before was already there picking strawberries in a lower part of the field out of sight of our house. My sisters conferred briefly and Jeannette, the bolder of the two, approached the stranger, telling her, "We need all of the berries in this field." The lady made no reply but crossed the line fence into the neighboring field and continued searching for berries on the Cromwell farm. Of all the different kinds of preserves that Mother made, we liked those made from strawberries best of all. Because they were "slow picking," compared with other wild berries, we had fewer strawberries to put up for winter's use. Mother rationed them throughout the year.

Every time a woodlot was cut over it was sure to produce an excellent stand of raspberry brambles a few years later. The stems continued to bear delicious berries for several seasons. We gathered them by the pailfuls. Mother canned many quarts of raspberry preserves every summer. She added enough sugar to make the berries appetizing and with lots of juice. A tablespoonful of raspberry preserves made the best follow-up to a dose of Epsom salts. They were often used as a bribe to get us to take the purgative. Fortunately the tart liquid quickly washed away that god-awful taste of the salts. A spoonful of raspberry juice came in handy when we had not-too-bad a cold. Quinine tablets were also administered for colds. When the cold was a mild one, we were given only half a tablet. We never escaped the bitter taste of the cut-in-half pill. The follow-up of preserves helped to wash away that unpleasant taste.

Two or three times a year, on a cloudy day in midsummer, when there was little chance of making hay, we made a picnic lunch and crossed the Bay in the motorboat to gather blueberries. The common low-bush type was abundant on the rocky, partly wooded sloping land along the eastern shore of the Kennebec. It took only a short time to pick a pailful of the clustered berries. After each of these trips to the Woolwich shore, we ate blueberries with sugar and cream for several days, and Mother made fresh blueberry pies. She also preserved a lot of the berries. We held the canned blueberries in less esteem than the strawberries or raspberries. Even so, there were few left by the end of the winter.

On the blueberry trips to Woolwich there were not always enough of us to fill the boat, so we asked some neighbors to go along. One day Abby Denham (Sherman's wife) went with us. She brought her eleven-year-old nephew, Wallace Cromwell. After we had spread out in different directions to gather blueberries, Wallace decided he would pick huckleberries instead, since there were a lot of these shiny black berries on two-foot-high bushes in the same area. When we met at the riverbank for midday lunch, Abby asked Wallace to show her how many berries he had picked. "I have my pail over half-full of huckleberries, Aunt Abby, just see, all that many." A look of disgust came over Aunt Abby's face. "We came here to pick blueberries, numbskull," she scolded. "What did you want to pick these things for? There's a worm in every one of them." Abby took a berry from Wallace's pail and broke it open. "See that little white worm, right there beside those seeds. Now dump all of those huckleberries right here. After we've had lunch, you pick some blueberries! Hear me?"

On another of our trips to Woolwich, we asked Aunt Etta if any of her family would like to accompany us. Her oldest daughter, Cousin Bertha, was visiting there at the time, together with her husband, Rev. Kern from Minneapolis, and their son Leon. All three of them came along. By the time they started the boat ride home, a strong breeze had sprung up. The Bay was quite choppy and considerable spray was coming over the side. Jeannette stood up to change her seat to the other side of the boat. A roll of the launch caused her to lose her balance and she sat down quickly beside Rev. Kern. Unfortunately the Reverend had removed his straw hat and placed it in the vacant spot beside him. It was one of those rigid straws, sometimes called a skimmer, that everyone wore at the time. Jeannette was a well-built teenager; the straw hat collapsed beneath her weight.

One of Mother's favorite preserves was made with golden currants. We had four clumps of the four-foot bushes – two of them at opposite ends of the front door steps, one near the sink spout behind the house, and another downhill from the privy at the north end of the stable. Every year the bushes bore drooping clusters of fragrant yellow flowers in the spring that attracted hummingbirds. It seemed as if every individual flower in the cluster produced a currant. We picked them when the first ones started to turn black. At that time many were red and most were still green. Mother canned them in sweet syrup and we had them for dessert on special occasions only. They were rated highest of our many canned things. Since the bushes were an alternate host for white pine blister rust, State inspectors made us destroy them in the 1920's.

Halfway across the marshy meadow in our river pasture, there was a patch of cranberries around which Pa had driven some cedar stakes and enclosed the small area with a single strand of barbed wire to keep out the cows. We picked two or three pecks of cranberries there each fall. In the early years, when the open season on waterfowl began September first, we used to come across cranberry patches in the meadow pastures upriver while snipe hunting. Often, on the following Sunday, the whole family went to the spots with pails and brought back several quarts of cranberries. Those that were not eaten by Thanksgiving were kept under water in stone jars down cellar and were used for making sauce during the winter months. Mother served cranberry sauce quite regularly with our frequent meals of fresh pork. After Weymouth's swamp near our schoolhouse become frozen over in November, we often went to the places where frozen cranberries were dangling from the tops of the vines above the ice and ate the watery fruit at recess time. When frozen, the flesh of the cranberry lost all of its firmness, and the fruit became a spherical sack filled with liquid. The frost-affected berries had an intriguing way of popping when squeezed between the teeth, and the liquid inside the tough outer skin was rather pleasant to the taste. As school children we ate many cranberries that way every fall.

With the exception of Concord grapes produced by a single vine that climbed over a low arbor in the orchard, our only cultivated fruit was the lowly apple. We enjoyed several different varieties. Unfortunately, the kind we liked the least was the one that we had the most of – Ben Davis, a dark red apple shaped something like our present-day Delicious and endowed with remarkable keeping qualities. We often referred to the fruit as "cork stoppers" and, although they were good for cooking, we hardly ever ate them except in late spring and early summer after the better-eating sorts were gone. Unusually free from insects and diseases, Ben Davis apples bore abundantly every year; it was certainly not one of the alternate-year bearers. Pa said the reason we had so many trees of this kind was that everyone was extolling the Ben Davis as a superb variety soon after he bought the farm, so he planted several young trees to supplement the scattered trees of other sorts. Previous owners of our place must have had a yen for good apples for there were some old trees that bore delicious fruit within easy walking distance of the buildings. Close to the old cellar hole in the orchard were two large spreading Bellflower trees that produced some of our tastiest apples. They yielded bumper crops every other year, with a small yield in between. They were longish apples – some people called them "sheep's nose" – light yellow in color with an occasional reddish cheek and they had a truly remarkable flavor when fully ripe in winter. Our earliest apple was the Wealthy, of which we had two trees that stood near the opposite ends of the orchard. I took along a few Wealthies on my way to the Shore and placed them on the shell rack of the gunning float to enjoy during an hour or two of duck hunting after coming home from high school. Every time I taste a Wealthy apple now, I am reminded of the early fall along the river; a partridge flying back to the woods at sundown after stuffing its crop with wild rose hips on Newell's meadow and ready to roost till dawn on some hidden balsam limb; also, wild rice bending with the tide, their tassels heavy with those slender kernels that duck enjoy so much.

At the south end of our orchard was a medium-sized tree with many small tart greenish apples we called the Wallbridge variety. They were juicier than the Ben Davis and kept even longer in the cellar. We ate a few of them along in April after the better tasting sorts were gone and the Ben Davises had begun to shrivel. The Wallbridge flavor was not attractive and most of them were carried from the cellar in late spring and fed to the pigs. At the north end of the orchard stood the Grindstone Tree – so called because when Pa bought the farm Ben Sedgeley's grindstone still stood beneath it. The top of the tree had been grafted to Tolman Sweets; one of the large lower branches to Baldwins. A pair of kingbirds nested every year in the Grindstone Tree. Perhaps the oldest apple tree on our farm was the Old Greening Tree that stood near the northwest corner of the ledge back of the house. Most of its main trunk leaned almost horizontally three feet above the ground, possibly the result of its encounter with the tornado back in the 1890's when the old barn blew down. The low sloping trunk made it one of our favorite trees to climb. Only a few yards away, on the west side of the ledge, was a group of five large Tolman Sweet trees. Their annual crop of medium-sized pale yellow apples provided some of our best fruit for eating and cooking; they were relished, too, for their sweetness by both pigs and chickens. We stored more of these sweet apples than of any other sort. On the east side of the ledge, due north of the stable, stood Mother's apple tree – one of the older trees of the Ben Davis variety.

Some of our best eating apples were produced at the edge of the woods Up-under-the-Hill. At the southern tip of the woods was a large tree that forked near its base. The west side bore Baldwin apples and the other had Northern Spies. Another Northern Spy tree stood at the corner of the larger henpen Up-under-the-Hill. This variety was one of our favorites. The Northern Spies on the half Baldwin tree were only medium-sized and a fairly deep red in color, while those on the henpen tree, somewhat shaded by a young oak and some poplars, were much larger and light green in color with some reddish streaks on their side exposed to the sun. The fruit from both trees had that exquisite Northern Spy taste, however. Directly in front of the big henpen Up-under-the Hill was a cluster of five Ben Davis trees that grew from a common stump. They were the largest and most productive of all of our trees of this sort. Apparently these trees became dependent on the high fertility associated with their nearness to the henpen. A few years after we stopped using the pen, all five trees died, for no other obvious reason. "It's not going to look the same Up-under-the-Hill anymore," Pa said after I had cut down the dead Ben Davis trees and hauled them to the house for firewood.

Notwithstanding the fact that we had some delicious apple varieties, we thought none of them equalled two kinds that grew in our neighbors' orchards. We were extremely fond of the late fall apple, the Garden Royal, that Amasa raised on one of the trees in the orchard behind his house. It was a small light reddish brown variety with a delicious flavor. Among the several apple trees in front of the Cromwell house was one we were told was Maiden's Blush. When ripe, there were none finer for eating. Some way or other we managed to obtain a few of both of these most desirable apples every fall. During high school years, I secured scions from both of these varieties and grafted them onto small natural fruit trees that had grown from different seed at various locations around the farm. Eventually we had some of these cherished fruit of our own. Likewise we had McIntosh apples – the progeny of scions that Al sent me from Harvard, Massachusetts. We also grew some big Golden Balls from scions taken from an almost branchless tree Mother used to call hers. It stood by itself in a grassy area south of Grandfather Williams' house.

At housing time every fall, much of the space in our cellar was taken up with apples, potatoes, rutabagas and cabbage. Some years there were a few beets and carrots left over from summer raids on the garden. High up, two long shelves made by suspending long wide boards from overhead floor timbers, were laden with Mother's preserves. In the dark northeast corner, Pa kept the bow section of an old rowboat partially filled with moist ready-mixed mortar for use in repairing chimney and stone masonry. Occasional moistening with water kept the mortar from hardening and ready to use. Next to the mortar box was the big molasses barrel half full of salt pork in concentrated brine. There were two large permanent wooden bins for potatoes. We stored our apples in a variety of containers – tubs, boxes, barrels and sawed-in-two boats. Since the Ben Davis apples were such good keepers and required but little attention during the winter, they were mostly kept in flour barrels. Our Tolman Sweets were stored in two halves of an old weather-beaten skiff that had drifted half-submerged into our river. The boat had too many decayed spots to be repaired, so Pa sawed it in half, boarded up the open ends, and the two halves held all of our Tolman Sweets. Bell Flowers, Northern Spies, and Baldwins were kept in hogsheads that were made by sawing a vinegar barrel in two. Other kinds of apples, in small quantities, were placed in boxes and baskets of various sizes. One of our orchard trees had a single large limb that bore Black Oxford fruit. These apples were exceptionally fine eating after they became thoroughly ripe along about May. We were careful to protect these from the rats by keeping them tightly covered in a discarded wash boiler. To keep the apple bins out of the mud, we placed them on pieces of cedar railroad ties.

By keeping the different kinds of apples in separate containers, it was easy to find the kind we were looking for when we went to the cellar with a tin pie plate on a cold winter evening to get some apples to peel and eat beside the sitting room stove. I often ate five or six apples of selected sorts on a single winter's evening. If I ate too many, Mother became concerned. Up to the time I was seven or eight, she frequently cautioned me saying, "I wish you wouldn't eat so many apples before going to bed. It makes extra work for your mother every time the blankets have to be changed." Besides serving as bins for storing apples, the portable tubs, boat sections and large boxes provided us with some navigational sport once in a while. Some years we had early spring rains before the ice had melted away from the outer end of our cellar drain. Rain plus the melting snow near our house caused a couple of feet of water to accumulate in the cellar. This was a transitory condition that we made the most of on the first day we had at home. Using pieces of board as paddles, Genevieve, Jeannette and I maneuvered the empty apple bin boats into every corner of the cellar, in the dim light provided by the two small windows set in the brick foundation atop the stone walls. Our boats were by no means water tight. Frequent bailing with a tin pail enabled us to keep our feet dry and the ships afloat. If we were fortunate, the water might remain in the cellar for two consecutive weekends before the ice melted in the ditch out in the field allowing the cellar to drain dry. Boating in the house cellar was a pastime requiring Mother to call us twice for dinner.

It was sometimes as late as June before our last apples of the season, the Ben Davises and the Wallbridges, were all eaten or fed out. We did not have to wait three months to have more apple pies, however, even though the Wealthies wouldn't ripen until September. For days in the preceding October Mother had peeled, quartered, strung on cotton string, and dried more than a bushel of our Tolman Sweets. She used her dried apples during the summer for turnovers, pies, sauce, and brown betty. Dried-apple pie and a glass of milk was a frequent dessert in haying time. Mother also made a delicious dessert, which she called bird's nest pudding, from either fresh or dried apples. It was a sort of an oversized turnover that entirely filled a biscuit tin. The top crust incompletely covered the apple filling, as it sort of floated on the sweetened filling.

Homemade maple syrup was a delicacy that we obtained as one of the farm's natural resources. Both sides of our driveway were lined with maple trees that Pa had set out in the late 1800's but they were still too small to be tapped. However, we did have several large maples Up-under-the-Hill and along the east side of the Point. Two or three of the trees in the former location were rock (or sugar) maples; the rest were red maples, which people said had less sugar in their sap. We tapped them all. We started about the same time the snow cover in the fields and pastures had melted enough to reveal bare patches on elevated spots where winter winds had prevented deep accumulation. We used Pa's bit-stock and a half-inch bit for making the holes in the south side of the maple trunks. Our assortment of spiles consisted of two metal ones, that had hooks for hanging a pail, and several handmade wooden spiles from which the sap dripped into a vessel on the ground. Some of the spiles were split from a soft pine board; we cut a groove along the top side to carry the sap to the end where it dripped into a glass jar, metal pan, or sometimes a large lard pail. We also made hollow spiles by punching the pith from a short section of elderberry stem. On sunny days following a cold night, we collected the sap twice a day to avoid the overflowing of some of the smaller containers in our motley collection of sap buckets.

One day in late March when the sap was running, Sherman Denham came down for a brief afternoon chat with Pa in the kitchen. Pa glanced out the window as Sherman walked home along the east side of our hill. He said to us, facetiously, "Sherm might take a drink of your sap when he goes past those maples up there. I remember what they said about Fred Cheney over in Woolwich. There was this neighbor who used to drink a lot of Fred's sap every chance he got. Fred put an end to that by putting some jalops into the sap buckets where the fellow had been drinking. According to what I heard, he physicked the devil out of the swigger."

Mother kept two large kettles on the cookstove into which we poured the maple sap as we brought it from the trees. No extra energy was needed in evaporating the sap since we kept a fire going in the stove all day at that time of year to keep the house warm. When the flow of sap tapered off, after about a two-week run, we usually had three or four quarts of thick maple syrup in the kettles. "If we kept it on the stove long enough, we'd have maple sugar," Mother said. But we liked the syrup so much to have with fritters for Sunday breakfast now and then that we never allowed the process to go beyond the heavy liquid stage. Mother sealed the syrup in quart Mason jars and kept them on the shelf at the top of the cellar stairs.

Most of our medicinal items came from Lorenzo Small's drugstore in the Village. Among these were Epsom salts, tincture of benzoin, quinine tablets, spirits of niter, and Johnson's Anodyne Liniment. There were, however, a few therapeutic items that were gleaned from the farm. For years, in the corner of a drawer in the pantry we kept four or five dry brown puffballs about the size of tennis balls. They were useful, we were told, for stopping nosebleed. Several puffs of the dried spores into the nostrils were supposed to encourage the formation of an effective clot. None of our nosebleed cases were ever serious enough, however, to bring this treatment into play. At the start of the trapping season each fall Mother requested of us, "The first good fat skunk you catch, dress out the carcass and bring it in and I'll try to get out the grease." We used a pint or more of skunk's grease every winter for chest colds and the like. A mature skunk in late fall had a thick layer of the whitest fat beneath the skin. Two animals would provide enough soft white practically-odorless grease to fill a quart Mason jar. In the days when we removed the entrails from the chickens we dressed for market, we removed the yellow fat imbedded in the mesenteries and kept that also for medicinal purposes. In contrast to the white fat of the skunk, chicken fat was bright yellow. Pa claimed that the skunk's grease was more effective than that of chickens for alleviating congestion in the nose, throat, or chest, in the case of colds. My sisters, however, would have none of the skunk medication; they opted for the chicken. "I'll add a digit of turpentine to some chicken fat for you to use on your sore throat," Mother told Jeannette. "It might make the ointment a little more penetrating." When she suggested doing the same for Pa's chest cold, he said, "Don't put any turpentine in that for me. Skunk's grease is good enough without any additive."

Mother must have had a premonition about the effectiveness of activated charcoal before it came into popular use. When we called her attention to a burned place on a molasses cookie, she told us, "That's good for you; the burned part will help sweeten your breath." For a sore throat she suggested we tie one of our used black stockings around our neck after applying the skunk's grease before going to bed. To help alleviate Pa's asthmatic problem while sleeping, Mother filled a small pillow each year with balsam boughs from our discarded Christmas tree. Strictly speaking, this was not always a resource from our farm since we often got our Christmas tree from the woods across the river, thus allowing all of our young firs to grow into log-sized trees. Regardless of the source, the fragrance from the pillow, Pa thought, helped him to breath more easily at night. It served as a follow-up to the inhalation, before retiring, of smoke from burning saltpeter-impregnated papers. Two or three times a year, Mother prepared a batch of saltpeter paper by tearing up brown paper bags, soaking the pieces in a strong solution of saltpeter and drying them on the top of the stove. Pa kept a large flat six-inch oyster shell (at least that's what he called it) on the high sill of his bedroom's dormer window, in which to burn a piece of the paper that gave off smoky fumes as he inhaled them.

Every time we picked chickens for market, the feathers dropped into an old discarded wash tub and were carefully saved for filling mattresses. Likewise, when we picked wild fowl, we sat around one of the same tubs with a newspaper on our laps to funnel the feathers into the tub. Feathers from wild ducks were considered the best and we kept them separate for making pillows. In filling a pillow or mattress, Mother carefully passed the feathers through her fingers as she placed them in the tick. Any feathers with long sharp quills were removed, otherwise they might pierce the ticking and annoy the sleeper. Our bed in the boys' room never knew the luxury of a feather mattress. We had a straw mattress that was very comfortable, but it had a tendency to become packed and hard with every week of use. The straw had to be renewed at threshing time each fall. Straw mattresses had to be fluffed up every time the bed was made, to maintain that restful spongy support.

Like all children, we were always looking for chewing gum. Once in a while we were given one of those flat sticks of store gum that were four inches long, three-quarters of an inch wide, wrapped in paper and cost a penny. Most of the time we chewed spruce gum right from the tree and never looked for any other kind. With a little experience in gathering spruce gum, we learned to avoid pitchy exudations that one sometimes finds on spruce trunks as well as on pine. We sought hardened globules attached to the bark where they had been secreted as a sticky syrup. Every time we were in spruce woods, we collected a lot of this gum and placed it in a blue tin tobacco box with a hinged cover that was kept on the kitchen shelf above the woodbox. The gum we collected during the winter supplied us for a long time because we made it last for several chewings. Each of us had a special spot where we deposited our gum on the up-and-down wainscoting in our kitchen. There was a thick horizontal molding at its top. The rounded upper edge of the molding had a semicircular gouged-out place at the end where it fitted against a door casing. These little recesses in the woodwork made perfect places to deposit our gum when not in use. Each of us had his own depository. It was a serious offense to deposit gum in another's spot or to take someone else's gum from its resting place.

On one of our trips to the woods each winter, Mother gave us a small glass vial for collecting balsam from the blisters on the smooth bark of fir trunks. It was a slow task, squeezing the clear balsam from a broken blister and collecting it in the vial held below. Mother used the balsam on our cuts and scratches, with a piece of paper pressed onto it to cover the stickiness. Although the balsam was very sticky, with a glue-like consistency, we seldom used it as an adhesive, probably because of its slowness in drying. Whenever we needed to stick something like clippings in a notebook or a steamed-off postage stamp to another envelope, we made a few drops of paste with flour and water. For mending chairs and broken dishes, we got out the paper bag of dry granular glue tucked away in one of the pantry cabinets and dissolved a bit of it in hot water.

We made toys and tools from appropriate parts of trees growing on the farm. In the spring, we broke off a low-hanging branch from one of the three willows back of the house and made an excellent whistle. A five-inch section was cut from a small limb, somewhat thicker than one's thumb. The bark was loosened by tapping with the handle of the jackknife held by its open blade. The cylinder of bark could then be easily slipped off and, with a little carving and whittling, a whistle was finally produced that had a shrill tone and a lifespan of several days. From stems of the elderberry shrub we made miniature popguns. The large soft pith was punched from an eight-inch section of the stem. Small wads of chewed-up paper, spit balls, were pressed firmly into both ends of the opening that was formerly filled with pith. A stick, somewhat longer than the elderberry section, was whittled down to make a plunger. With a quick shove one of the wads was pushed into the tube, compressing the enclosed air and causing the wad in the far end to be expelled with a loud pop. If the front wad was firmly seated, the soggy projectile often flew all the way across the schoolroom, with a remarkably flat trajectory and sometimes with considerable accuracy.

Among our homemade tools were two wooden mauls that saw a lot of use.

One of these was kept at the Shore and was used in driving stout leader stakes for the weir, and also for driving sucker net stakes in places where the river bottom was firm blue clay or packed sand. This heavy maul was made from a piece of yellow birch trunk that Pa cut across the river. We kept the other maul, made from an apple tree, in the stable for driving fence stakes and crushing bagfuls of clamshells for the hens. Another much-used tool that Pa made before I was born was the flail used for threshing peas and beans. The heavy head of this tool was a thirty-inch section of heavy hornbeam, two and a half inches in diameter, that Pa cut from Up-under-the-Hill. A hole was bored through a flattened end of the piece of hornbeam so that it could be fastened to a long rake handle with a dried eel skin. The flail was operated with a sort of semicircular motion and the heavy hornbeam head was very effective in smashing dried pods of cultivated legumes. While Pa was threshing beans on the barn floor one rainy day, he told us about an ancient battle (I think he had been reading Josephus, the historian) in which the defenders of their homeland used scythes and flails in warding off invaders. In the hands of a skilled person, either of these tools could prove effective even against a sword.

The cattle stanchions in our barn were small hardwood posts cut on the farm. They were fastened between the cow and her crib. The tie-chains were fastened to an iron ring that slid up and down the stanchion. No two-by-four sawed timber was deemed strong enough for this purpose. An extra-large oak stanchion was selected for the bull and his tie chain was much stouter than those used on the cows.

In the henpens, the first roosts were made from spruce weir stakes. After our pens became infested with feather mites, the spruce poles were replaced with green alders. The alders dried without the formation of seasoning cracks which were so numerous in dry spruce. After getting their fill of blood from the chicken's feathers, the mites left their host and massed together in cracks along the perch to digest their meal. It was much easier to see and paint with creosote the masses of mites on the surface of the smooth alder bark than was the case when the insects were hidden in deep fissures of the spruce.

There were two sawed planks upstairs in our stable that Pa was keeping to make a pair of runners for a new horse sled. They were about fifteen feet long and one end of the planks had a right angle projection three feet in length. "I had those runners sawed from a leaning spruce that grew on Harvey Preble's river bank," Pa told us. "One winter when Al was in college, I paid Harvey ten dollars for all the wood and timber on his bank from Preble's Creek to the Spar Landing and a rod back from the river. We cut more than ten cords of firewood and had a few thousand feet of lumber from just that little area. The spruce that those runners were sawed from leaned so low over the bank that the lower limbs touched the water at high tide. The tree had a big root that grew straight up towards the top of the bank. That root made the bend for the sled runners." But the old blue horse sled that Pa used for years lasted as long as he had any need for this type of transportation. Maybe one day someone will find a use for them.

Chapter Twenty-Eight

Social Life: Picnics Up-under-the-Hill, May Baskets, etc.

We had few community social events in our part of town. For several years prior to 1910, our farm was host for one day every summer to an outdoor get-together. It was a picnic staged in August by the Eastern Star society in the Village and held in our moss-carpeted oak grove Up-under-the-Hill. The picnic ground, as we called the shaded area, was a small level space under tall red oaks on the west side of the hill, a few yards from the highway. Pa gave permission for the asking. The spot had been used for some time, even before there were two long tables and a few waist-high shelves fastened to the tree trunks. Since the trees had over-grown the ends of the attached boards, the installation must have been there for twenty years of so. There were no amusements for adults but a swing was set up for the children. I remember attending with Mother one of the last picnics held on our grounds. It was before I had started school. Everyone had come for a good time, talking and eating and drinking homemade lemonade. Each had brought something in the way of food as the tables were filled with sandwiches, cakes and pies. There were several pails of lemonade – plenty for the thirty or forty people in attendance. Uncle John operated a small candy, gum and peanut concession on one of the wide shelves between two oaks at the south end of the grove. His items were the only ones that had to be purchased. Jeannette told me about the time when she went to the picnic as a small girl. Mother had given her a nickel to buy something at Uncle John's stand. Unfortunately she lost the money along the way and had to go without her all-important candy. Minerva recalled seeing Uncle Ed stretched out on the ground with his head propped up on an arm and telling something about each new arrival.

Most of the oak trees, a few with a scar or two in the rough bark where the boards were once attached, still stand in the picnic grounds but the wooden tables and shelves have long since disappeared. Untrodden moss still holds the soil in place, just as it was seventy years ago. The narrow field that Pa used to plow for a garden and for hay has grown up to hardwood trees. The low wooden bridge across the roadside ditch, with its hemlock planks and two railroad ties for stringers, has disappeared and left no trace. Only a gap in the stonewall beside the road marks the spot where the driveway turned in to the picnic ground. This quiet area, once the site of sociability on a happy day, will probably never again hear the friendly chatter of people gathered for a moment's respite from their daily chores.

Another annual event was a "box social" held on an August evening in the school house at the Corner. Sometimes there were as many as twenty participants. Each lady brought a box lunch, adequate for two, that was auctioned off to the highest bidder. The males did the bidding. Each winner enjoyed the privilege of sharing the contents of the box with the lady who brought it. I remember one of the socials that I attended during one of my last years at the Jellerson School. It was held, I believe, for the purpose of raising money to purchase window shades for the school. To make sure that I did not become too involved in the bidding and spend more than I should, I took with me only fifty cents (approximately the gross income from two dozen eggs). When the auctioneer, Sherman Denham, called for bids on the third box I started the bidding at twenty cents. It was one of the prettiest boxes of the evening – large, wrapped in pink tissue and decorated with frilly curlicues. I wanted that box the worst way. Bidding against me was our bachelor neighbor, Charles Holbrook, who went to twenty-five immediately. When I said forty, he topped it at forty-five. At this point I hesitated for a moment, hoping to give Charles time enough to wonder if he might be going too high. But he topped my last-ditch with a let's-get-this-over-with bid of sixty cents. If he had correctly guessed the state of my finances, he could have saved a nickel.

With Sherman's next offering I was more fortunate. There were only one or two bids against me and the box was mine for forty cents. The lady who brought the box was Earl Brown's attractive young wife. I felt highly elated as we shared the delicious sandwiches and pastry, sitting side by side in one of the large back seats of the schoolroom. I don't think I even took the pains to notice who the partner was that Charles drew with his fancy box. After squeezing into the single-desk with Mrs. Brown, I couldn't have cared less. Her husband, Earl, was at the party also. He may have been drinking hard cider for he kept coming around while we were eating, holding out his hands cupped together and wiggling a thumb between them, saying, "See the little green snake!"

In Maine, early May evenings were among the loveliest times of the year. Sometimes there were even the faint odors of apple blossoms and flowering currants in the air. A continuous chorus of frogs and toads filled the evening stillness. Occasionally a snipe made his spirit-like winnowing noise high above some nearby swamp and a whippoorwill called from the top pole of a pasture fence. The temperature was ideal for perfect comfort. This was May basket time. While Genevieve and Jeannette were in high school, we were the recipients of a May basket every spring. Also, each year, we took part in hanging a basket to a few youngsters in the neighborhood. It was imperative that the recipient family be kept entirely in the dark as the group planned; the basket had to come as a complete surprise. May baskets represented cooperative efforts; several children contributing a few cents apiece towards purchase of a couple of pounds of assorted candies. Someone took the initiative to prepare the basket, which usually was a shoe box with a sewn-on cardboard handle and elaborately decorated with colored crepe paper, the edges of which had been fancifully frill-curled with scissors. One of the boys in the group was assigned the task of quietly approaching the recipient's house, after the others had had time to select a convenient hiding place nearby, leaving the basket on the doorstep, and giving two or three loud knocks on the door.

It was half an hour after dark. The supper dishes had been washed and put away. My two sisters were doing their homework at the kitchen table. Pa was whittling some scraps of pine board for kindling next morning's fire. Mother was darning socks and I was sitting on the oven hearth looking at the last issue of *Hunter-Trader-Trapper*. Suddenly, the house almost vibrated from three loud bangs on our front door. "May basket!" Genevieve and Jeannette shouted together, as they dropped their pencils and dashed into the night. I slipped into my shoes and followed them. It was before any of us owned a flashlight. Before searching for the visiting guests, we had to wait till our eyes became adjusted to the darkness. The first hiders we found were Blanche Emerson and Alice Bates, the two girls who lived up the road with Abby and Sherman Denham. They were squeezed against the woven wire fence behind the cedar hedge. Jeannette next found Merton Webber squatting in the corner of the pump house in the tie-up. It was he who had banged on the door. Genevieve found Maurice Pratt and Rena Kimble sitting on the pile of lumber in the dark recesses of the barn cellar. Finally, the captured ones told us there were only two more to find, Forrest Douglas and Helen Denham. It took a lot more searching but we eventually located them under the grape arbor in the orchard. The group gathered in our kitchen for a few minutes. There were too few chairs to go round and hardly enough room for everyone to stand while the May basket was passed amongst the group. Mother brought a plate of molasses cookies from the pantry, and, after a few minutes of pleasant chat, the basket hangers departed for their homes.

The May basket that I remember best was the one we hung to Helen Hackett's older brother and her younger sister the year I was a junior in high school. Helen joined the outsiders that evening and was one of the hangers to be caught. Her classmate, Florence Small, was staying with her that night. They told Helen's folks that they were going for a short walk soon after dark. By prearrangement Wallace Hunter and I met the two girls a short distance down the road and we waited for the rest of the group to arrive. Zina Maxwell was given the task of hanging the basket. I don't know where Wallace and Helen chose to hide, but Florence and I went into the juniper- and fir-spattered pasture across the road from the Hackett's residence. It was a beautiful evening, mild, absolutely calm, and with that certain softness in the air so characteristic of a mid-spring night. Florence looked charming in the pale light of the first quarter moon. Her straight black hair was neatly parted in the middle and rolled into a pug in the back. We were among the last caught that evening. The Hackett children found us only after we whistled to Lawrence as he was searching along the stone wall with its strand of barbed wire fence beside the road. Next day was Saturday. No one had to hurry home. We spent most of the evening playing drop-the-handkerchief on Helen's front lawn.

Chapter Twenty-Nine

Natural Disasters and Fires

In southern Maine, we felt an uneasiness at times concerning possible disastrous effects of natural phenomena, such as floods, lightning and windstorms. We had them all at one time or another, but substantial losses were, generally speaking, rare. On only one or two occasions can I remember a spring freshet high enough to flood our low east field near the river. Such a rise of water occurred one spring near the turn of the century and washed out the Bay Bridge across the lower part of the Androscoggin between Topsham and Bath. For Bowdoinham farmers who sold their produce in Bath, the loss of the bridge meant a much longer trip to market by way of Brunswick. Some of the old pillars still remain, but the structure was never replaced. More recently, a new bridge across the Kennebec just above Richmond Village was carried downstream by an ice jam accompanying an early spring freshet and deposited on the upper end of Swan Island. This highway bridge was later rebuilt. At the height of one of our greatest freshets, Pa drove a stake at the water's edge in front of our old fish house. That was the closest approach flood water ever made to any of our buildings. It would have taken a deluge of biblical proportions to wash away our house, which was some twenty feet above high water mark.

Although Pa was usually calm and collected in moments of excitement, he became uneasy during severe thundershowers. If one developed during the night, he dressed and went downstairs. "If lightning should strike the barn, I'd want to get the animals outdoors before fire could make much headway," he said. One evening during an intense electrical storm, an exceedingly bright flash of lightning was followed instantly by a loud snap and a terrific clap of thunder. Vining was looking out the kitchen window. "It struck the barn!" he shouted. He and Pa dashed through the stable and alleyway to see what had happened. Next day, we found that lightning had struck the willow tree on the edge of the swamp in Amasa's east pasture near the Old Wharf. Another summer, lightning struck Amasa's barn while he was out of town. After the shower, Pa visited the barn to see if there was any damage. "It apparently hit the weather vane first," he said, "and opened up a crack in the ridge pole the whole length of the building. It's a wonder there wasn't any fire started, with all of that dry hay up there."

There was never any serious damage to our buildings from high winds, as far back as I can remember. However, about ten years before I was born, the folks lost the old barn to a tornado. Ordinarily one does not associate tornadoes with Maine but they had one that year. It happened when Minerva was a pre-school child and Vining was a baby. Pa was away at work. Al and Lois were at school. During the early afternoon, Mother and Minerva were gathering kindling wood back of the house. When a heavy black cloud appeared in the northwest, Mother said to Minerva, "We'd better go inside. It looks like a thundershower coming." They had been in the house only a few minutes when the terrific wind began to blow. It did not last long. As soon as the sky lightened, Mother saw that the barn, which stood on the ledge about hundred feet north of our house, was gone. She was too frightened to investigate the damage, fearing the safety of the house. Soon after the wind subsided Uncle John came to see if Mother and Minerva were all right. Mother asked him to see what had happened to a young calf that was kept in the old barn. The other cattle were in the pasture. The calf was found alive and uninjured standing on a bare scaffold that had been blown fifty yards into the field. The folks later learned that two barns were destroyed in the town of Litchfield shortly before the twister hit ours. The loss of the old barn was not too serious, since it was inadequate in size. It had been built when the Sedgeleys lived in the house in the orchard. Soon after the tornado, Pa started accumulating lumber for the frame of our new barn, which was erected in a communal barn-raising a few years later.

A few years before the old barn was blown away, it came close to being burned down from a fire started by a kerosene lantern. One evening in January, Pa got home from work soon after dark and went directly to the barn to do the chores before supper. It was during a cold spell, so, without removing his overcoat, he set the lantern on the barn floor and climbed the ladder to pitch down hay for the night's feeding. He threw down several forkfuls of hay, assuming that he was building a pile close to the ladder. Presently he saw smoke rising from the barn floor. His stack of loose hay had toppled over against the lantern and some of the hay was ablaze. By the time Pa climbed down the ladder, the flames had reached the edge of the high mow. He quickly removed his overcoat and with it beat out the fire thereby preventing almost certain destruction of the barn. I remember the singed places on the old tawny overcoat that we later used as a lap robe on cold trips to the Village.

With Bowdoinham's only piece of fire-fighting equipment, the hand operated Water-Witch, housed in the Village more than two miles away, Pa was always cautious to avoid creating any fire hazards around the house or barn. Had a fire broken out in our house, we would have had to be our own volunteer fire department. Pa insisted that we hold a kerosene lamp with both hands when moving it from one location to another. In the barn, he told us never to set the lantern where it might get accidentally knocked over. One was constantly reminded of the possibility of fire from the lantern by the peculiar, not unpleasant odor that it caused, possibly due to combustion of hay dust particles which were thick in the barn air. I noticed the odor of burning dust every time Pa asked me to hold the lantern for him as he gave the cows a late feeding of hay on winter nights. In the house, we were careful about wood fires even in our well-constructed stoves. All fires were carefully extinguished when we left the house for a day. Chimney fires were one of our biggest worries. Since we burned a considerable amount of "green" wood as well as some pitchy kinds like pine and spruce, there was a tendency for our brick chimneys to become lined with a deposit, besides becoming saturated with brown liquid creosote. Although we religiously scraped down the inside of our chimney at least once a year, we did have occasional chimney fires. They were allowed to run their course and burn out, but we kept a close watch of the chimneys in the upstairs rooms and attic. The roar of a chimney fire and the dense cloud of black smoke drifting over the fields were frightening to say the least. We wondered if the house might be going next! One day the kitchen chimney caught fire while we were eating dinner. After taking a look at the outside chimney and making sure that there was no smoke in the shed chamber, we returned to the midday meal. Shortly, the horizontal part of the metal flue, that passed through the kitchen wall into the chimney, became red-hot in one spot. In a matter of seconds, the wallpaper beside the circular flue collar caught fire. All of us sat motionless for a few seconds watching the tiny flame spread slowly on the paper. Jeannette, then a teenager and sitting closest to the stove, was the first to make a move. She arose from the table, picked up her glass of water and splashed it on the steadily advancing blaze. As we finished our dinner, the black smoke from the chimney drifting across Amasa's field gradually diminished as the sooty deposits burned up. "We didn't get around to scraping out that chimney quite soon enough this year," Pa said. I remember him saying that the fire which destroyed the old Sedgeley house in the orchard was caused by a faulty flue pipe.

When I was ten we had a vivid demonstration of how merciless and dreadful a house fire can be. It was a calm pleasant forenoon a week before haying. Al, Vining and I were working on the motorboat as it swung at its mooring near the Point. We were busily polishing the brass parts of the engine, filling the glass oil cups and pumping out the water from beneath the floor. One of us happened to see a billowing cloud of black smoke above the oaks just below Cromwell's ledge. "That must be the Cromwell house!" Al said. "Let's get up there!" We quickly paddled to Cromwell's landing, tied the skiff to a tree, and scrambled up the wooded hillside toward the fire. We were not the first to arrive at the scene. Pa was already there. He had found a ladder in the barn, an axe in the woodshed and had chopped a hole in the roof above the kitchen. We saw him pour a bucket of water into the hole out of which smoke was billowing. He had seen the smoke behind our Hill as he reached our driveway on his way home from the Village. After tying the horse to a tree beside the driveway, he had run across the field and was one of the first to reach the burning building. By the time the three of us arrived, Old Santy and two or three other men were there but they were too few to form an effective bucket brigade from the well to Pa on the roof. As we reached the dooryard, Pa came down the ladder. "It's no use!" he said before reaching the ground. He told us afterwards that the chamber over the kitchen was filled with a swirling mass of flames. "Get everything you can!" he advised us. Old Santy, hearing what Pa had said, went around telling people, "'Tis no use, I do tell you. It's no use."

Abby Denham was picking raspberries in their garden back of the barn and was unaware of the fire until Pa had made a hole in the roof. With uncontrolled emotion she told the men where the valuables were and what to bring out first. Billy Brown, who lived in the old Pratt house at Pratt's Crossing, and I carried a box of canned goods and some other things from the shed next to the kitchen. The dooryard was soon filled with furniture and all sorts of things hurriedly removed from the burning building. Sherman had gone to Richmond with market produce that morning. When he returned, it was practically all over. He left his horse beside the road, and, open-mouthed, ran up the short driveway, staring at the tall naked chimneys and the fallen timbers still burning in the cellar. By that time, Mother had learned of the fire and come to offer Abby consolation. She found her behind the barn, weeping, and tearing her apron to shreds. There's so many things we'll never be able to see again," she told Mother. It was past noontime when the last of the flames had subsided. Sherman came down to our house for a late dinner in mid-afternoon, but Abby did not accompany him. Mother took some food to her, which she ate somewhere in the barn.

It was a day or two before we had a clear picture of the cause of the fire. The weather had been hot for several days and there had been no need for a fire in the kitchen stove. The stove had been used as a convenient place to dispose of waste paper and other combustible material. A lot of rubbish had accumulated. Abby's aged mother, Liza Cromwell, was living with her daughter and son-in-law. She was alone in the house that morning, and, feeling cold, she lit the kitchen stove as she had done so often for many years. The roaring fire ignited the winter's collection of soot in the chimney and tongues of flame must have carried sparks through masonry cracks in the brick structure. Landing on combustible material on the dry attic floor, they started the inferno which Pa saw when he chopped a hole in the roof. I did not see Liza at the fire. Someone took her to the home of another daughter in the Village.

Once or twice, I remember running downstairs half asleep when Pa called us in the middle of the night to see the sky lit up by a fire. The most spectacular of these sights was the pre-dawn blaze when one of the big Kennebec ice houses burned. The entire northeast sky was brilliantly aglow. "It's so light in here you can read a newspaper," Pa said as my two youngest sisters and I entered the kitchen. "That must be the Clark and Chapman icehouse where I used to work." It was a bit more frightening the night when he called me to look out of his dormer bedroom window to see Amasa's mill ablaze. The mill's smokestack was clearly visible from our house in the daytime and that night we could see the flames flashing above the trees at Scott's Point. The mill was a total loss and was never rebuilt. The fire started on a cold snowy night in the winter. It was thought possibly to have been accidentally set by someone who sought shelter from the storm and who tried to spend the night in the warmth of the boiler room. On another winter night, we saw a fire slightly to the west of the mill site. It was Mrs. Call's brick house at Jellerson's Corner that time, the fire started from live coals in wood ashes removed from the fireplace and dumped in the woodshed. Glowing coals retain their fire-starting capacity for several hours sometimes, when covered with a thin layer of ashes. For this reason, ashes removed from a stove or fireplace in which a fire has been burning recently must be disposed of with extreme care.

Chapter Thirty

Snow Tracks

We saw many different kinds of tracks in the snow around our farm. There were those of the fox, the squirrel, some small rodent that had scurried from hole to hole, and possibly a shrew. Among the birds, we saw tracks of crows, partridge, snow buntings, blue jays, and perhaps a few footprints of goldfinches beneath a pigweed plant where the bird landed to retrieve some seeds that dropped as it fed on the ripe heads above the snow. These were the single tracks. The maker had passed on with no intention of following those tracks again. We had a couple of animals, however, that, like us, kept travelling again and again in their own footprints to make a well-beaten path in the frozen snow.

When the deep snows of winter came to Maine, people living in the country reacted much like the white-tailed deer and snowshoe rabbit. Deer kept their trails through cedar swamps open by frequent travelling in the same tracks. This enabled them to reach their main source of food – cedar browse – throughout the winter and provided avenues for escape from predators. Somewhat similar were the snowshoe rabbit paths in Amasa's pasture. After following their trails with bow and arrow one day, I said to Pa, as he sat by the stove after supper, "There must be an awful lot of rabbits in those firs, they've made paths everywhere." "No, there aren't so many," he replied, "they're on the go all night. One pair of rabbits can make a lot of trails in a single night."

Muskrats had the right idea, I thought, when it came to avoiding the accumulated snows of winter. They had their dry, grass-lined dens in the highland at the edge of swamps, with openings underneath the ice. They gathered food beneath the ice and ate it in their frost-proof houses, the only openings to which were also well beneath the ice. Even in the severest winters, muskrats were oblivious to the depth of snow. "After all," said Pa, who often expressed dislike for Maine winters, "all this region's good for is bears and woodchucks. They know enough to hibernate."

When it came to obtaining our weekly supply of groceries throughout the winter, we were in sort of the same fix as the deer. Our road to the Village, the source of groceries and other supplies, had to be broken out after every snowstorm. Likewise the horse sled road to Aunt Emma's woodlot across the river had to be kept open all winter. Like the deer and rabbits, we didn't plow the snow aside, we merely kept packing it down and maintained a passable road. Besides, we always had a couple of footpaths that had to be maintained through the deepening snows of winter. One of these paths followed the leeward side of our south line across Amasa's field and meadow onto the river's ice. We followed the same path every day to tend the sucker nets when low tides came. Another snow trail was the path across the pasture as far as the railroad tracks on the way to school. Like the horse sled roads, our frequent walking kept the snow packed down and the footing became more solid day by day. The longer the period of good weather between our storms, the easier the travelling along our paths became. Drifting snow sometimes filled the paths and this blown-in snow was often firmly packed – we just walked on top of it. In contending with a fresh fall of snow, unlike the shoveling of today's sidewalk, we rarely used a shovel except to clear our doorsteps or to improve the narrow path to the henpen door. We merely walked back and forth in the same path until the snow became packed down. Whenever anyone said "snow plow," he meant the heavy V-shaped iron blade attached to the "cow catcher" of steam locomotives that the Maine Central kept going during every storm to prevent accumulations of snow on the railroad tracks.

In early days, slow but efficient oxen were used to open our snow-blocked roads. For the blizzard winter of 1887-1888, the Town had engaged Uncle Everett to "break out" the roads from Center's Point to Hall's Corner and from Mike Heath's to the meeting house near Clay Hill, after every snowfall. The Big Blizzard occurred in March that year, and Minerva was born on the third day of the storm. It was on the morning of March 13th that Mother told Pa she was certain their third child was on the way and that he should go for Mrs. Blair. Pa had to drive down the road a mile to get Ellen Blair, who took care of Mother on such occasions. Uncle Everett knew that Mother was expecting any day. Consequently Pa hoped that he would open up our part of the road the first thing that morning. Uncle Everett had spent the forenoon breaking out the road between his house and the Village. Returning home around eleven o'clock, instead of opening the road from his house northwards, he stopped for dinner and let the rest go till afternoon. Like time and tide, the process of giving birth for no man waits. Twelve o'clock came with a slackening of the blizzard snowfall but with no sign of Uncle Everett and his oxen. Mother told Pa he shouldn't wait any longer. Provoked by Uncle Everett's delay, Pa hitched old Dick into the sleigh and made the first track between our house and Uncle Everett's, on the way to the Blair's. Al recalled how, as a boy of four, he was barely tall enough to look over the kitchen window-sill and watch Pa in the pung drive old Dick through the three day's accumulation of snow in our dooryard. "The snow was so deep in our dooryard," Al said, "that the horse had to make long leaps to get through." Pa had to make the first track not only out of our driveway but also down the road as far as Uncle Everett's. On the way back, he had to hold up one side of the pung to get past a deep drift on the road and keep the vehicle from tipping over and causing Mrs. Blair to fall out. In spite of the extreme depth of the new snowfall, and the fact that it was a late season blizzard with many deep drifts already here and there along the road, Pa made his way to Mrs. Blair's and back with no undue delay. Fortunately her arrival preceded that of Minerva's by a full half hour. "Your father never quite forgave your Uncle Everett for breaking out the other roads first that forenoon and for stopping to eat his dinner before doing the part up past our house," Mother told me years later.

Chapter Thirty-One

Meadow Hay and Flats Hay

In the latter part of the 1800's and early 1900's, meadow hay was a highly prized commodity. It was harvested on swampy lowlands all along the Abbagadasset and on swamps farther inland. It was one crop farmers could count on every year, and there were no expenses whatsoever for seed and fertilizer. No matter how severe the summer drought, there was always enough moisture in the meadows to produce a good mixed stand of vegetation. It wasn't all grass but many bog-loving plants – low sedges and bulrushes, buckbean, water avens, cotton grass, blue iris, sweet flag and an occasional clump of pitcher plants – comprised the mixture and, when dried, were relished by the cattle in winter. Here was a commodity that cost nothing to produce, that Nature provided year after year, and the only expense to the farmer was the labor of the harvest. Since hard work and hand labor were the order of the day, every patch of meadow along the river was eagerly harvested as soon as the upland crop was in. Years later Pa said, "We were foolish to go so much all out to harvest the meadows in those days. If we'd only plowed and fertilized a couple of acres of highland, they would have raised ten times as much hay, and better quality too, than we could have gotten from ten acres of meadow. And with a lot less work too." But meadow hay was some sort of fetish to the local farmers. With their conservative, self-sufficient attitude, they felt that no available free feed for their livestock should be allowed to go to waste. Perhaps such thrifty habits were among the reasons farm people succeeded in their frugal ways.

By the time I was old enough to help with the farm work, most of the meadows in our area had been relegated to pasture. Uncle Everett's marshland was one exception. He continued to mow meadow hay by hand for years after his neighbors quit. I can remember Pa and Al mowing some of our meadow with scythes a year or two before Pa fenced the swampy land along the river. One summer was unusually dry, so dry in fact that Vining mowed parts of our meadow with the horse-drawn machine. This could be done only rarely. When it came to hauling the dried hand-raked hay onto the upland, we had a set of four wooden ten-inch square bog shoes that could be strapped to Dandy's feet enabling him to work in the marshy places. It was sometimes possible for the horse to pull an unloaded cart onto the meadow when he could not pull a hay-rack load of dry hay. Under these conditions we let the horse pull the empty hay rack to some central spot in the swamp where it was loaded. The horse was returned to firmer ground and he then pulled the load of hay to dry land with a long rope.

As far as nutritive value was concerned, Pa considered meadow hay only slightly better than oat straw for cattle feed. "It's good enough for a bull," he said, "and it's all right for overwintering young stock. But try to feed it to your cows and you'll end up without much milk in the pail. Upland hay, even from an old worn-out field, is a lot better. I can't understand why people ever got so worked up over meadow hay; they'd travel for miles to harvest the stuff." Two abandoned barns that stood on Preble's Island when I was a small boy bore testimony to the correctness of Pa's evaluation. Nothing ever seemed more out of place than those two well-built barns with their tight walls and shingled roofs standing on a swampy island around the bend at Kil's Point. Exceptionally high tides frequently covered the entire island every spring and fall. Yet, the Prebles swam their oxen across the river every summer and filled both barns with meadow hay. Come wintertime, the same oxen teams hauled the hay on the ice to their homestead barn where it was consumed by cattle old and young. Both barns collapsed during the years I was in grade school, either from wind or from decay of the foundations on the boggy soil. Later, the fallen roofs provided excellent spots to make snow-free sets for mink, with a frozen tomcod nailed to a levelled rafter for bait.

When Pa decided to cut no more meadow hay and turned all of our marshy land along the river into pasture, I was more than pleased. Not because there would be no more meadow-haying to be done – I always liked working in the meadow where the variety of mown vegetation had a fragrance all its own – but because we would have a bigger area for hunting snipe. Wilson's snipe are attracted to marshes where cattle have grazed, perhaps because of the hoof prints in the muddy soil where the squat and shy birds can hide at the approach of danger, or possibly somehow the cattle may help to improve the food supply in the soft earth, where the snipe probe for worms with their long flexible-tipped bills.

Besides meadow haying, there was the cutting of "flats hay" that grew in the intertidal zone along the river. This was a more aquatic venture than the haying in the semi-dry swamps. It involved wading in the deep mudflats at low tide and scythe-mowing all vegetation that one came to. The growth was generally much taller than that in the meadows but the stands were not as dense. Most of the flats vegetation was head-high wild rice with a colony of yellow pond lily here and there with its broad flat leaves that frogs sometimes sat on when the tide was high. This is the plant with cup-shaped yellow blossoms on thick stems. The almost spherical blossoms, open at the top, have an attractive shade of deep yellow but the odor is by no means a perfume. Along the outer edge of the flats was a band of pickerel weed with long cone-shaped heads of bluish-purple flowers. Scattered among the pickerel weed and often advancing into the open water were clumps of tall, perfectly round, dark green stems of one of the bulrushes. Each curving stem had a small cluster of brownish flowers near the top. Along the inner edge of the flats, near the beaver dam that bordered the meadow, was a strip of coarse erect plants, mostly blue flag and sweet flag, interrupted occasionally by patches of foot-tall horsetail plants we called pipes, with fluted hollow stems and blackish nodes. This whole group of water-loving plants was harvested for hay.

If farmers went to a lot of trouble in harvesting meadow hay, they outdid themselves when it came to haying the flats. After mowing by hand in the mud that was a foot or two deep, they had to gather the crop by boat when the tide was high. The floating hay was pushed into small rafts and lifted, dripping wet, into a boat. The green wet hay was taken to some landing place where it was spread out on high ground and allowed to cure in the sunlight. When thoroughly dry, they hauled the hay to the barn and stored it away in mows. Although livestock ate it readily during the winter, according to Pa, flats hay was no better than that from the meadow when it came to making milk.

The farmers held meadow hay in high esteem and the inflated value once placed on the swampy land in which it grew indirectly resulted in our belief that three acres of wetland in the southeast corner of our farm did not belong to us. The plot extended northwards from Amasa's line for more than a hundred yards along the far edge of our lower field, then its boundary went due east to the river. We always referred to it as Newell's Meadow, because the last owner was Newell Purington. During the last years that our meadow to the north was being mowed every summer, Newell's plot was growing up to bushes. Pa religiously avoided mowing any further than the straight border line. Wilson's snipe no longer frequented the area because of its shrubby cover, and partridge came from across the river to eat the rose hips from bushes scattered amidst the other shrubs. The last time they cut the hay on Newell's plot must have been years before I was born. Minerva told me that Pa gave Newell permission to haul the hay across the field to the highway.

Years earlier, my folks had learned how these three acres of meadow came to be set apart from our farm. It went something like this: one of the former owners, back before the Sedgeley's time, made the mistake of serving smoked ham at noon to a man they had hired to do some plowing for a day. Unfortunately for this owner, the plowman did a lot of talking about the excellent ham dinner he had enjoyed while on a job in the eastern part of town. The highly complimentary remarks reached the ears of another farmer who lived on the next road about a mile to the west of our place. This man had lost some hams he had smoked and was holding for market in an outlying smokehouse. After a bit of elemental sleuthing, he accumulated sufficient evidence to accuse the former resident of our farm, who raised no pigs himself, of larceny and had him brought before the Justice of the Peace. The decision was against our former owner who had no money with which to pay the fine. He was forced to relinquish some real estate to compensate for the hams. To surrender the smallest acreage possible, he settled the case by giving the plaintiff three acres of this most valuable land – a corner of the meadow. Sometime in the late 1880's Pa offered the Puringtons, heirs of the plaintiff, a hundred dollars for the piece of swampland in an attempt to reunite it with our farm. His offer was refused. Years later, neighbor Amasa, who had once been a selectman, told us there was no record of anyone ever having paid taxes on the plot of land we called Newell's Meadow. When Newell Purington died, his property went to Charles Randall, a resident of the Village. Upon returning from the Village in 1915, Pa told us he had met Charles on the street that day and had offered him ten dollars for a piece of the meadow. Charles said he could have it, but to keep his money until he could furnish a deed for the property. Charles told Pa to go ahead and to fence the land or use it in any way he wanted. As soon as haying was over that summer, we removed the river-pasture fence across our swamp and the fence along the inner edge all the way to Amasa's line, giving our cattle free range over all of Newell's Meadow. When we sold our farm in 1969, the lawyer in Brunswick who searched the deeds found no record in the County Clerk's office in Bath of any legal transaction whatsoever pertaining to Newell's Meadow. If a deed ever passed on this parcel of swampland, it apparently was never recorded.

Chapter Thirty-Two

Utilities and Hygiene: Fertilizer, Outhouses, Baths and Chamber Pots

"Public utilities" was a term that meant little to us on our farm in Maine. Practically the only such services that we enjoyed were maintenance of our road by the town and R.F.D. mail. Our horse-and-buggy mailman had postage stamps to sell, money-order forms, and he gave us receipts for registered mail. We had no telephone until I was a sophomore in high school, although Uncle Ed had installed one several years before. Kerosene lamps supplied our lighting needs; we had no electricity until I finished college. For water, we had our well and the rain barrel. In those days, water played an insignificant role in waste disposal, and the only plumbing involved in the disposal process was the four-foot piece of curved lead pipe that extended from the kitchen sink through the outer wall and a few inches beyond the clapboards on the north side of the house.

My folks used to talk about the red outhouse that stood in a dip on the ledge a few yards north of our buildings. They said, in the old days, people directed strangers to our place by telling them to "look for a white house with a red outhouse behind it." It was gone long before I came on the scene – moved to a spot near the barn and used as a coop for "breaking up" broody hens. When Pa built the stable, he attached a two-hole back house to the east end, where the floor was about four feet above the ground. Mother referred to the addition as "the privy" and called her visits there as "making a call on Mrs. Jones." To Pa it was always "the backhouse" or a more explicit term. In the winter, I can say truthfully that it was the coldest place on our farm. Below the floor, it was boarded up very loosely, allowing cold northeast winds to blow upwards with undiminished circulation straight from Quebec. As children we hated to go there on cold wintry nights. This led to certain disciplinary problems with our parents. With several persons crowded around the airtight stove in our small sitting room, any impolite indiscretion on the part of the younger folk was sure to bring a rebuke from our elders. Our diet, involving a few meals of baked beans each week and the consumption of much fresh pork during the winter, tended to exacerbate the problem. Mother usually looked around disapprovingly at us when we sometimes lost control of ourselves but she was too polite to make remarks. Pa, on the other hand, became very quiet and stared at us with a stern look, then, when he had become thoroughly disgusted, he sometimes said, "I don't know which one of you it is, but someone had better take the lantern and go to the backhouse."

Besides being as cold as the North Pole in winter, our privy had another disagreeable feature – it had to be cleaned every year. This was done soon after haying when there was ample sodland far removed from the house where the fertilizer could be spread with plenty of time for complete decomposition before we harvested the next hay crop. Choosing a day in August when there was a strong wind from the northwest, we backed the horse cart up to the structure behind the stable. With handkerchiefs tied over our noses, and with long-handled dung forks, we went to work. After the cartload was spread in the field, we loaded it with cow manure from the barn cellar and spread it also, to "clean" the cart body. One summer, Pa decided to grow cabbage on the fertilizer from the backhouse. We placed a shovelful of the fresh material every eight inches in open furrows and covered each mound with soil. Pa had already started a lot of cabbage seedlings in a short section of a garden row. We transplanted these on the next day that it rained. Pa knew that seeds of young plants should not be placed too close to fresh hen manure in the row; that material was so strong that it burned tender roots. He had not used fertilizer from the privy before. We set all of the rows with young cabbage plants, placing one in the top of each of the covered mounds. When the skies cleared a day or two later, practically all of the seedlings withered and died. Like hen manure, the privy product proved too much for them. We had to reset the entire patch, placing young cabbage plants between the mounds at a safe distance from the fertilizer. "That's the best lot of cabbage we've ever raised," Pa decided when he harvested the crop in October.

After everyone else had retired for the night, our kitchen served as a bath-room, in which we took turns for our weekly, bi-weekly, or more distantly placed baths. The big dishpan placed on spread-out newspapers between the cookstove and sink took the place of a bathtub. Whenever someone asked to take a bath, Mother had the teakettle full of hot water as well as the tank on the end of the stove, and an extra pail of rainwater was placed accommodatingly in the sink. My sisters were careful to pull the shades but the male members of the family never bothered about the unlikely possibility of a Peeping Tom.

Just as our agate-ware dishpan served as the bathtub, so did the heavy china mug beneath each bed make flush toilets superfluous. It was a convenient item of bedroom furnishing; the inconvenience was the need for someone to empty the receptacle every morning. However, we were not like the unkempt people in Dresden that Pa told about. Their white house had a yellowish splattered streak down the side beneath the bedroom window where they emptied their pots into the flowerbed below. Disdainful of such laziness, we kept what we called the "slop pail" exclusively for emptying the bedroom pots. This daily chore was assigned to Jeannette. Pa asked her not to pour the slop pail down the backhouse, except in cases of emergency, because it made more seepage towards the well. During the warmer months Jeannette carried the pail to the hayfield between the house and road where she emptied it onto the grass. We could tell how far she carried the pail by the dark green in the field where the hay grew dense and tall. When there was snow on the ground, she took the pail to the barn and poured it down the third scuttle in the gutter behind the cows. This scuttle was the one nearest the horse stall. The pile of manure in the barn cellar below was always hot and steaming with the semi-dry horse manure. Daily moistening of the manure helped to pre-vent excessive decomposition of the fertilizer. George Blair told us once that they had hatched chickens by placing the eggs on a pile of "het-up" horse manure. One cold mid-winter morning, Jeannette was late for school and Mother told her not to take the time to empty the pots. "I'll empty them for you sometime during the day," she said. As usual Pa was the first to go to bed that night, leaving the rest of us in the warmth of the sitting room. We heard his footsteps in the chamber overhead as he got ready for bed. After a while Pa's loud voice came down the ventilation hole in the ceiling above the stove: "Where's the pot? There's no pot up here!" Startled, Mother looked up from her knitting and said, "Oh heavens, I left it out in the stable. Jeannette, you go out and get the pot for your father. It's on the stairs by the privy door. I forgot to bring it in this forenoon." The pot was delivered and Jeannette had scarcely settled in her chair when Pa's booming voice came again from upstairs. "Where's this damn pot been anyway? Cussed thing's colder'n ice!"

Ever since childhood I have never liked to use the word pot. I've disliked hearing the word. I felt that way after I had finished graduate school and was on leave from my job in New Haven. I was working on a research problem in seedling nutrition with Dr. Burton E. Livingston at his laboratory of Plant Physiology, Johns Hopkins University. We had completed one phase of the study and I had submitted to him a rough draft of the paper we would try to have published in a journal. After he had returned the manuscript, I noticed that every time I had used the word "crock" to describe the plant containers we used, it had been crossed out and the word "pot" written above it. In discussing the changes with Dr. Livingston, I told him I realized the containers we used were clay flower pots waterproofed with varnish, but I disliked the word because it reminded me of the vessel we kept under the bed in Maine. "Oh, you're thinking of thunder mugs," he said and laughed. When our paper was sent off, the term "pot" appeared throughout.

Disposal of our barn wastes involved a lot of hard work, but there were no sewage lines to clog. An area about fifteen feet wide along the south side of our barn cellar was partitioned off to retain the manure that was dropped through the overhead scuttles behind the cows. The pigs and hens were free to roam over the stored manure. Towards spring, the manure piles became so tall they tended to clog the scuttles in freezing weather, making it difficult to clean the gutter, as had to be done twice daily. To clear the scuttles, someone had to put on rubber boots and, with a potato hoe, tear down the tops of the piles – sometimes a difficult task when the weather was cold enough to solidly freeze the surface of the pile. We usually tried to have the barn cellar cleared of manure each autumn before the snow became too deep to drive the loaded horse sled over the field. Spreading manure was one of our less enjoyable jobs; we tried to put it off as late as possible. Consequently, some years, there was considerable carry-over from one winter to the next. Near the southeast corner of the barn, where the swinging doors opened to the manure piles, there was a puddle in a low spot only a few feet across where liquid collected as it was forced from the piles by pressure. This was a favorite feeding place for swallowtail butterflies, both black and yellow. They moved their wings slowly up and down as they imbibed the dark brown liquor. From the puddle, a foot-deep ditch led to the brow of the hill at the south end of the orchard. For fifty yards further down the sloping field, there was a dark band of timothy and witch grass that became wider as it extended down the hill. The tall dense stand of hay was unmistakable evidence of the abundance of plant nutrients in the barn wastewater being carried by the ditch.

Chapter Thirty-Three

Butchering

Like the traditional weekly washday, we had certain days each year when everyone's efforts were directed towards some specific task. One of these was pig-killing day. An air of urgency existed from the time we got up until the job was finished. Pa did the chores early and breakfast was over by seven-thirty. "Anyway, there was one less chore this morning – we didn't have to feed the pig," he said. First of all, the wash boiler was placed on the stove and filled with water, as were all of the sizeable kettles that we had. Mother kept a hot fire going in the cookstove with dry hardwood, so that all the water would be boiling within the hour. Pa sharpened the butcher knife. The horse's grain box was brought into the stable where it was used to hold three pounds of rosin while we pulverized the coarse crystals with a wooden mallet. Two boards were removed in the stable chamber floor so that a chain could be wrapped around one of the overhead beams from which a block and tackle could be suspended. The rainwater barrel was emptied and placed beneath the hoist. Short pieces of plank were placed across two wooden horses to make a table on which to lay the scalded pig while we scraped off the bristles. The actual killing took place in the barn cellar and the freshly killed pig was dragged up around the barn and into the stable by the horse and whiffletree. That ended the duties of the horse for the day. He was returned to his stall. As the pig lay on the stable floor, Pa spread powdered rosin over it, and melted the rosin into the bristles with hot water from the teakettle. The rosin helped to stick the wiry bristles together so that they could be scraped off in bunches with a sharp knife. A slit was made behind the pig's hind ankles exposing the tendons beneath which a homemade ash gambrel was forced. The iron hock of the block and tackle was fastened to the gambrel with a short loop of rope and the pig was hoisted head-down until the two blocks met at the overhead beam of the stable. Next came the ticklish job of bringing boiling water from the stove to the dunking barrel until it was nearly half full. After both ends of the pig had been soused in the scalding water, all of us turned to with some sort of a knife and scraped off the bristles from head to tail, and down to the hooves. "If we get the head and legs clean, now," Mother said, "it will be that much easier when I get around to make the hogshead cheese and pickled pig's feet."

It didn't take Pa long to remove the innards from the strung-up pig. "Hand me that stick with the pointed ends over there on the workbench," he asked, as the last of the internal organs were removed. Pa spread the pig's flanks apart with the stick and draped the two leaves of lard from the back of the abdominal cavity over the horizontal stick. During one of the pig killings, Minerva was home from college and she pointed out to us some of the anatomical structures we didn't know, like the spleen, pancreas and appendix. Pa knew the gall bladder. He cut it off from the liver at once. "Those are the lungs, that you call the lights," Minerva told Pa, "and that sheet of muscle you call the skirt is the diaphragm." I waited to get the bladder which we inflated immediately with a bicycle pump to make a football. The only internal organs that we used for food were the liver, heart and skirt.

"Some people eat the kidneys," Pa told us, "but I wouldn't eat one of them if you paid me to." They went into an old wooden tub, along with the stomach, intestines, lights and windpipe, to become frozen solid after a couple of cold nights. All of the tub's contents were chopped, finely and a little at a time, during the next few weeks for the hens. It would all be fed out long before the weather became warm enough to thaw the frozen organs in the tub. "When can we have some pig to eat?" I asked Mother during my first pig killing. "Not until tomorrow," she replied. "It has to hang in the cold overnight to lose all of that animal heat before it's ready to eat." It turned colder that afternoon, so Pa wrapped the heavy yellow horse blanket around the dressed pig to prevent freezing. "Freezing dries out the pig's skin and makes the pork rind hard."

Breakfast on the morning after pig-killing day was the best of the entire year. There's nothing as tasty as crisply fried slices of fresh belly pork from a newly killed pig. Mother filled the black iron skillet several times with the thin strips of untreated bacon to make enough of this delicacy for all of us. "We'll have to have liver for breakfast for a few mornings now," she said. "No one likes liver after getting a taste of fresh bacon. One year the liver hung out there in the stable frozen for weeks before we ate it."

The dressed pig hanging in the stable took up so much space that the horse and pung could not be driven inside. For this reason, Pa cut up the pig after it had hung for only a day or two. All of the meat that would be roasted or made into chops was cut into chunks and hung on the overhead beams in the stable chamber. They froze solid in a day or two and all that was not consumed remained frozen until March. Along towards April the last of the meat developed a slight but not objectionable taste, that, as in the case of slightly rancid butter, we actually enjoyed. The pig's legs with the feet attached and the head were carried into the house and placed on the table in our north dining room where they kept cool until Mother could tend to them. Our unheated dining room was as good as a walk-in refrigerator during the winter months. Pa packed the fatback in the wooden molasses barrel in the cellar. For making it into salt pork, he packed it in the barrel with a lot of rock salt between each layer and added a few ounces of saltpeter. I'm not sure he knew why the saltpeter; it was just traditionally used. I cannot recall that he ever told us what the purpose of this additive was; it was one of those things that "they did." A wooden lid weighted down by a heavy fieldstone was placed over the pork to prevent it from floating when he added enough rainwater to cover the barrel's contents. Some years, we salted the hams and shoulders by soaking them in brine for a month and hanging them in the smokehouse for a week or two when the herring were being smoked. If we didn't want to smoke these parts, we hung them in the stable chamber with the rest of the fresh meat and sliced them as needed for frying. It was during one of those winters when we ate the hams fresh that we discovered the pig had apparently injured, some way or another, one of the hind legs in the hip region, possibly by climbing the step from the manure storage section of the barn cellar into the dry pig pen. When we came to slicing the ham, we discovered, as I remember, that the bone was not completely fractured but there was a local bloody area at one spot near the center of the ham. That year, Al was at home at pig-killing time and he had used his revolver to stun the animal in the killing process. While Mother was cutting out the affected meat before cooking, Minerva asked if, perhaps, the injury might have been caused by the bullet. "They shot him first, didn't they, Pa?" she asked. "Silly, don't you know anything?" Mother replied. "They wouldn't shoot him in the ass!"

Somewhat less exciting than pig-killing days were the days we spent picking chickens. On these more frequent occasions, again, everyone in the family became involved. The fowl to be slaughtered were selected the night before, usually following a request from Chase's store in Bath for a specified quantity of dressed poultry. The birds that were marked for slaughter were placed in a confined space in the barn where they could be easily caught the next day. Like the row of crosses in the movie *The Seventh Cross*, there were four rope yarns dangling from the beam above the gutter behind the cows. My string was considerably longer than those used by Pa and my brothers. The nooses were fastened around the feet of the birds, allowing them to hang down while being killed and plucked. A paper-lined tub or box was placed beneath each string to collect the feathers that were saved for pillows and mattresses. Pa complained about some birds being so much harder to pick than others. Broilers always were more difficult than older fowl. Their tender skin often became torn when the feathers were too hard to pull. In the case of bad tears, Mother sewed the ruptured skin back together with a needle and thread. Pa often remarked, "This bird's going to be a bad one to pick, he's so slow about dying. Maybe we're not sticking them in the right way, I don't know. Perhaps we ought to keep the ones we're going to kill on soft feed for a few days beforehand – some say that makes them easier to pick." At one time, we plunged the freshly-killed birds into a pail of hot water to make the feathers come out more easily. This treatment often damaged the appearance of the skin and Chase's store said they preferred dry-picked birds.

Mother and my sisters brought chairs into the tie-up, placed shorts sacks over their laps, and "pinfeathered" the chickens as soon as we had removed all of the older feathers. During the years I was a small boy, Pa removed the crop and innards from all the dressed poultry but later on the store wanted to buy the whole chicken and do the cleaning themselves when the birds were sold to their customers. That was several years before the stores sold chickens already cut up.

As soon as all of our fowl were prepared for market, we tied them in bundles of four or five and hung them in the house cellar to cool. Next day they were sent to market. In the summer, we usually took the poultry to Bath by boat. At other times the dressed birds were packed in crates or boxes and sent to Bath by railway express. When Pa was hauling hay to Bath in winter across the Bay, he sometimes took dressed poultry along on top of the load. Occasionally, we lost a chicken or two in transit. The rope yarn around the chickens' legs once broke while Al was passing a bundle of dressed birds from the motorboat to Pa standing on the wharf at Bath. In accordance with Murphy's Law, the string let go just as the chickens were directly above the open water between the boat and the dock. Al caught one of them as it splashed but two or three quickly went to the bottom. A dock-side loafer who was watching us came over and asked if we had lost some of the chickens. "We got them all," Al told him. The fellow might have wanted to dive for them.

Life on the Abbagadasset

One day in late spring, less than a year after we had the telephone installed, Mr. Stilphen, manager of the meat department at Chase's, called up to place an order for some fowl for the weekend. We dressed the poultry the next day. Since Al had not yet come home for the summer, the motorboat had not been launched, so Pa sent the fowl to Bath by railway express. Early the following week, he received payment by check in the mail. Our mail carrier usually came up our road about eleven o'clock and it was getting along towards noon when Pa opened the envelope with the check from Chase's store. The weight that they had paid Pa for was five or six pounds less than we had found them to weigh. "Those steelyards of ours aren't that far off," Pa said. "They must have made a mistake down there." Pa had not become accustomed to talking over the telephone but this was the one time he would use the thing and talk to Mr. Stilphen in no uncertain terms. He asked Jeannette to make a toll call to Bath. The store was reached and Mr. Stilphen was on the line when Pa took over. "You know, Stilphen, those hens weighed more than you allowed us for," Pa shouted into the phone. Pa listened intently but had difficulty understanding what Mr. Stilphen was saying. "I didn't get that," he said, "what did you say?" Pa was trying hard to hear. He moved the receiver to his other ear. "Now what was that you said, Stilphen?" At that moment it was high noon by our clock on the mantel. It started to strike in its slow deliberate fashion. Pa knew it was near midday and the strike would be a long one. Lowering the receiver, he turned to us in complete disgust and said, "Throw that cussed thing out the window!" Pa had no better success understanding what Mr. Stilphen was saying after the clock stopped striking than before. He said to me, "Here, take this and see if you can make out what he's trying to say." "Ask your father if he nailed down the cover of the crate. You know, hammer and nails, like that," Mr. Stilphen said. "Tell him we tied down the crate with rope yarns," Pa directed. All I can think of," Mr. Stilphen replied, "someone must have taken one of the birds on the way down here."

Once a chicken-picking day saw one of the few occasions that we failed to go out of our way to accommodate a neighbor. It was a Sunday forenoon while we were halfway through the job of dressing out a batch of poultry. Someone looked out our driveway and saw Jerry Hall approaching with horse and wagon and the family cow in tow. It was one of those years that Pa had a bull. He was hitched in a stanchion at the far end of the tie-up beyond our line-up of chicken strings. "He would have had to bring a cow here just as we're busy picking chickens," Pa remarked. I am sure Pa would have had us push the feather tubs aside and take a break for a few minutes, while Jerry tied the cow to the ring behind the front tie-up door and Pa turned the bull loose. Al was the one, however, who became particularly disturbed at the thought of interrupting our work. "We can't hold up all this just for him," Al said. "Let him take his cow down to Uncle Ed's." "Ed doesn't have a bull right now. He'd have to take her over to Sam Wilde's," Pa replied. One thing was certain, Pa didn't want to lose the fifty-cent breeding fee. But he decided not to overrule Al. As Jerry drove up to the barn, Pa went to the tie-up door in his blood spattered overalls with feathers sticking to them. "We're not standing the bull anymore, Jerry. You'll have to take her over to Sam Wilde's place." Jerry looked at Pa without speaking. As he turned around in the dooryard, he looked back and could see all of us involved in picking chickens. He may have thought, "Why doesn't he say he doesn't want to be bothered?" It was nearly two miles to Sam's farm.

Chapter Thirty-Four

Insect Pests and Lice

Few areas of the world are free of noxious insects. In southern Maine, mosquitoes were so numerous in June that we refrained from going to the Shore after sunset and sleeping on our unscreened porch was out of the question. At that time of year if a mosquito got past the screened door and started humming around the kitchen or sitting room, it was immediately chased down by someone with a folded newspaper. Pa was particularly annoyed by the sound of a mosquito anywhere in the house at night. During late May, all of June and early July, mosquitoes were so thick in the woods across the river that we seldom tried to go there, even on days when the sun shone brightly. It was at that time of the year that young crows became fully fledged and left their nests. Every year Pa made a practice of going across the river to get a young crow to hang in our corn patch. He could usually bag a young bird but the mature crows were far too wary for him to approach within gunshot. To repel the mosquitoes, he purchased an ounce of oil of citronella from the village drug store to apply to his face and hands when he entered the woods.

After the mosquito menace had subsided, we were frequently bitten by the ox fly, a blackish insect with spotted wings, a little larger than a house fly. This and the much larger horse fly were most aggressive towards humans – both were described as being "sharp bitten." In addition to these two larger-sized insects, our cattle were pestered by small black horn flies that clustered around the base of the cows' horns and also behind their shoulders. They preferred black cattle or those with black patches in the right spots, but lacking such colored areas landed anywhere on a bovine of any color. Unlike the larger ox and horse flies, these small pests remained on the cows after they entered the barn for evening milking. To prevent being constantly whacked by cows' tails at milking time, we got rid of the flies by spraying them with a hand sprayer containing Eureka Fly Killer, a product made and sold by J. H. Ames in Bowdoinham Village. Cows stopped switching their tails as soon as they were sprayed. Unfortunately there seemed to be little residual benefit from the spray, as the horn flies returned in numbers after the cows were returned to pasture.

I do not remember any great annoyance caused by ants on our farm. The mounds they built here and there in the hayfield were somewhat of a nuisance when the cutter-bar of the mowing machine struck one of the low ant hills, possibly clogging the knife or stopping the machine. When we had some brine to discard from the pork barrel or the herring tub, we often poured pailfuls of the liquid on ant mounds in the field. That controlled the pismires. Another social insect, the bumblebee, however, was a much more serious threat and, once in a while, troublesome. One summer, Al was mowing hay in our east field with the horse-drawn machine when the mower passed over an underground nest of bumblebees. The insects swarmed out of their hole in the ground in a mad frenzy and several of them stung the horse. Paying no attention to Al's shouts nor to his yanking of the reins, Dandy took off at a 45° angle to his original path. He had fled the hayfield and was crossing our potato patch with the mower still in gear before Al could bring the horse to a stop. Another time it was I who had a run-in with a nest of bumblebees. The previous fall, Pa had plowed a piece of land in the west field between the Tolman Sweet trees and the road. He had been too busy fishing and carpentering away from home in the spring to harrow the land as he had planned and to sow it down with grass. The plot of rough, plowed ground had produced a bumper crop of coarse weeds by August. "Take the scythe and mow some of those weeds for the pigs," Pa told me one day after haying was over. "You can cut some of them every day or two and the pigs will eat all that stuff in a couple of weeks." It was the second day before I came to the first bumblebee nest. The rough ground with the sods standing on edge, nearly perpendicularly, and with the remains of last fall's grassy second crop in every furrow, made ideal spots for the bees to make their nests. I knew enough to leave the area as soon as I came to the bees' nest hole and the defenders started sizzling out. Back at the house, I told Pa about the bees. "We'll fix you so that you can clear them out of there," he said. "Pull a shorts sack over your head and shoulders. I'll cut holes for your arms and others to see through. Put on a pair of long gloves and take a broom and swat every one of the cussed bees as they come out of their hole. That's the way we dressed when we harvested that bee tree across the river, and we never got stung once. They can't sting you through that burlap." I went forth to do battle with the bees as Pa told me. When I started swinging the broom bees appeared from everywhere all around me and, although I was getting some of them, they soon found openings between my shirt cuffs and the gloves. After they had stung me three or four times, I took out for the house. "Let them go till night," Pa said. "We'll pour some kerosene on them after dark and set them afire." We came across two more bumblebee nests in the same plot of ground during the next few days.

In the vegetable garden, we had many of the same insect pests that are around today, such as the green cabbage worms, potato bugs, striped cucumber beetle and cutworms. "I've quit setting out early cabbage," Pa said. "The root maggots took them all two or three years in a row. Since then I've planted only late ones. Cabbage grows better in the fall anyway, and late crops miss the maggots." As children, we never saw a corn earworm. The European corn borer had not reached our area although we were warned about them by U.S. Department of Agriculture posters with their colored pictures in the waiting room at Harward's Depot, along with posters concerning the white pine blister rust. Black and yellow striped cucumber beetles attacked the cotyledons of our cucumber, pumpkin, and squash seedlings as soon as they showed above ground. Wood ashes sprinkled on the young plants repelled most of those active little bugs. Dusting with powdered lead arsenate took care of cabbage worms and those big horn worms that defoliated tomato plants. We prevented too much loss from cutworms by digging them from the soil near plants they'd cut off the previous night. Cutworms have tough skins and it took a lot of pressure from one's heel to squash them into the dirt. Our biggest insect problem with vegetable insects was the Colorado potato beetle. We called them potato bugs. When the potato plants first emerged, I was sent as a preschool youngster to the potato patch with a tin can half full of kerosene and instructions to find as many of the bugs as I could and drop them into the can. "If you see any patches of yellow eggs on the potato leaves, pick the leaf off and drop it in too," Mother told me as I started for the field the first thing after breakfast. Hand picking like this kept the potato bugs under control for a while. As the plants grew larger, Pa took over the work of bug control by splattering the leaves with a water suspension of Paris Green. He used a worn-out broom with the handle sawed off for shaking the water onto the plants as he walked along the row.

We felt much animosity towards the tent caterpillar. They made unsightly white nests in the crotches of cherry and apple trees and defoliated the branches within crawling distance of their nests. But most of all we despised the half-naked larvae that crawled around everywhere after they became full grown and left the nest to find a place to pupate. We were able to control them on our apple trees by rubbing out the nests with a stick while the small worms were inside. Since our wild cherry trees were almost worthless, we didn't hesitate to apply a torch to worms' nests on them. One night every spring, along in May, we went on a tent caterpillar burning spree. First, we tied a rag to the end of a light pole and saturated it with kerosene. When we reached the group of young cherry trees behind the henpen Up-under-the-Hill, we lit the torch and held it flaming beneath the worm nests. Immediately, we heard the plop, plop of the roasted worms as they fell on the dry leaves of last year beneath the bushes.

For some reason, our area in Maine was free from black flies such as pestered stream fishermen and outdoorsmen "up-country." We were sometimes bitten by a tiny black midge that we could hardly see, but I was never troubled by a black fly in Bowdoinham. Like most every household, the common housefly was a perennial problem. They were also a nuisance in the barn and stable as well as in the house. At the end of every chicken-picking day we hung the dressed poultry in the cellar as soon as possible to prevent their becoming flyblown. Flies were always getting drowned in the pans of milk that Mother set away for the cream to rise. She kept a black-handled three-tined table fork handy to fish any floating flies from the sticky cream. Everyone used rectangular sheets of sticky fly paper around their houses. We hung strips, bought rolled up in a cardboard cylinder, in the woodshed, stable, and on the porch. After a couple of weeks they were entirely black with entrapped flies. The late Governor Cross of Connecticut told a story about a man who asked the waiter behind the bar in a restaurant for a piece of the blueberry pie on the shelf behind him. As the waiter turned around he said, "I think we have no blueberry pie." With a swish of his hand, he said, "It's apple." It always seemed to me to be in defiance of the law of gravity but wherever a fly roosted overnight on our kitchen ceiling there was a cluster of fly specks in the morning. Before going to bed on summer nights, one of our parents often took the kerosene lamp from the table and held the open chimney close to the ceiling directly under a hapless fly that had chosen the spot to perch for the night. None of us young folk were allowed to use this fly-control method because of the danger of setting the house on fire.

It must have been too cold for cockroaches around our house. At least I never saw one. We had a few silverfish around the mop boards and shelves. They ate the dried flour paste where we had fastened pictures into notebooks. We never tried to exterminate them. I never saw a carpet beetle or its larvae until I got to Connecticut. Clothes moths, however, were always a problem and we had to place moth balls in woolen goods that were put in storage. We killed all tiny moths we saw flying around the house. After mashing them between our hands, we could tell clothes moths by the satiny appearance of the scales. At bedtime my sisters sometimes said, "Good night, sleep tight, don't let the bedbugs bite," but I have yet to see, or feel, my first bedbug. One parasitic insect with which I did have a single bit of experience, however, was the head louse. An outbreak of pediculosis at the Jellerson School occurred one fall, and when I started scratching my head, Mother took a close look and found both nits and lice. She gave me a thorough shampoo with extract of quassia chips added to the soapy water; that ended the infestation. There was speculation as to which family was responsible for the initial infection, but opinions lacked any substantial proof.

Among the most annoying insect pests that we encountered were the chicken lice that got on us every time we picked our fowl. Wild ducks had them too. Although these parasites lived on us only for a day or so, they could be annoying. Mother showed us the best way to crush a louse between two thumbnails. Wild black ducks seemed to have the most active and bothersome lice. They were elongated in shape and nearly black, while the chicken louse was yellowish. They lost no time in running up one's arms and reaching the hair while we were picking the game bird. Lice from our fowl were a little slower in getting around than the black wild ones.

For extreme annoyance the tiny feather mites that we acquired from the chickens were probably the most elusive. We were likely to get some of the mites on us every time we plucked one of our fowl and we were sure to end up with a few if we entered the henpen during the summer. The mites were barely visible to the naked eye and they often were unnoticed until they began their slow trek up the back of our necks or through our hair. It was a matter of luck if one was able to locate and remove the mite with the fingers. Often they merely stopped moving when we tried to brush them off but as soon as things became quiet near them, they started crawling again. Such tactics could cause insomnia. One year when Genevieve was teaching in the Winsted, Connecticut, high school, she brought Ruth Butler, one of the teachers, home with her for a week's visit at the beginning of summer vacation. While we were gathered in our backyard one evening, I set up a teeter board using a two-by-six inch plank that had recently served as a roost in the henpen. Ruth enjoyed the see-saw but the next morning she complained of a bout with chicken mites. She was reminded, she said, of the song, "Thanks for the Buggy Ride."

Chapter Thirty-Five

Evening Adventures

It was a happy occasion whenever Pa took me with him on one of his evening errands. So different from the daytime, it was fun riding with the horse and wagon on a dark night when the whole countryside was still and calm but dimly visible. The barking of a dog, a great horned owl hooting 'way off somewhere in the woods, and the distant whistle of a locomotive sometimes broke the stillness. We needed no headlights for, no matter how dark it was, the horse could always see the way. We did have a lantern, nevertheless, tied to the inner end of the seat, to prevent a collision if we happened to pass another team. When the roadbed was rocky, sparks flew haphazardly when the horse's iron shoes hit the stones.

One of my first rides at night was on an hour-long visit to Ira Allen who lived on the Newell Purington place on the road to the Village a little way past the schoolhouse at Jellerson's Corner. Pa wanted to borrow Ira's heavy iron hooks that grabbed the lower part of the roof just above the eaves and supported a block and tackle at each end of the horizontal ladder-and-plank staging. Charlie Allen and I played on the floor while Ira cranked up his phonograph. It was the first time I had ever heard canned music. I expect that Ira's was one of the few talking machines in town at the time. I thought the music was delightful. The records he played were small hollow cylinders. I listened to a talking record as if the voice were from outer space.

Another trip was on a Saturday night to the Village. Pa wanted to get some shells for his double-barrel 10-gauge shotgun. It must have been around the middle of October, for the fall flight of black ducks had started to move south. Pa discovered his ammunition was running low, and he'd not be making his weekly trip to town for a few days. By Monday morning, there could be a lot of ducks on the river. "Sure as anything, there'll be a flock light in the cove below the sandbank if I don't have shells enough for the gun," Pa said. Saturday evening was the only night of the week that the stores were open after supper. It was a thrilling sight to see the well-lit streets, the open stores, and so many horses with wagons tied to hitching posts all along Main Street. Some farmers brought their own hitching device – a heavy iron disc placed on the ground with a leather strap fastened to the horse's bit. It was an effective anchor to the animal. I believe many of the farmers came to town that night just to sit around and talk. There were several small groups wherever they could find a place to sit and smoke. Pa went to Cornish's general store for his shells. I remember the shiny square box of twenty-five factory-loaded shells that cost fifty cents. Pa's heavy hammer gun had Damascus twist-steel barrels that were considered unsafe for smokeless powder. So the shells he bought were Winchester's Blue Rival with a low brass base. They were loaded with four and a half drams of black powder and one and a quarter ounce of No. 4 shot. Every time one of these shells was fired there was a cloud of smoke in front of the hunter. On a calm day one sometimes had to wait a minute to see if he had bagged his game. On the way home that night, as we rounded Jellerson's Corner, we could hear the constant quacking of ducks feeding in Merrymeeting Bay. "I hope some of them stay around for a few days," Pa said as he slapped a rein over Dandy's hindquarters entreating him to start trotting down the slight grade towards the narrow bridge over Mrs. Call's swamp.

Another evening ride, I recall, was in the spring of the year. That time, Pa took our non-fertile eggs to exchange with John Maxwell for two settings of hatching eggs from their full-blooded Rhode Island Reds. Pa stopped at Elliot's roadside spring at the foot of Maxwell's Hill and unhooked Dandy's check-rein so he could have a drink. A tree toad made his rattling chirp in the branchy willow tree above the pool while Dandy drank his fill. In the farmhouse at the top of the hill, John's wife, Jenny, brought in a milk pan full of eggs and placed them on the kitchen table. She selected the brownest and best-shaped ones to swap for ours, tapping each one gently with her fingernail to make sure none of them had cracked shells. She placed them carefully in the pail of sawdust that we had brought. "We put some sawdust in that pail to keep them from getting jiggled too much on the way home," Pa told Jenny. "How about that? Would too much jarring keep eggs from hatching?" At that point John broke in with his opinion. After raising the stove lid and squirting tobacco juice into the fire, he said, "Naw, you can't hurt eggs that way. Remember the time, Jenny, I got that setting of eggs up at the Hall boys'? That skittish bay mare I had got scared of their stationary engine and raced all the way home. Every last one of those eggs hatched!"

I used to like to go with Pa when he visited neighbors and hear him tell of things that he never mentioned at home. He told John, that night, how they weathered a gale in the *Sea King* off Cape Hatteras. It was a stormy night and the vessel had been blown off course, too close to the mainland. Suddenly the sailor on lookout shouted: "Breakers ahead!" Captain Ben Adams ordered all hands on deck to swing the big ship towards deeper water. He stood there with his rifle and threatened to shoot if they didn't bring the vessel around. A turkey gobbler on board was in the wrong place at the wrong time. The bird belonged to Captain Ben who planned to have it for Christmas dinner. The crew detested the bird all the way from Bath. They had to clean up after it every day. In the excitement and commotion that night, the bird started fluttering right in front of one of the sailors who was working frantically to loosen one of the ropes that controlled the jib. Exasperated no end, the sailor rapped the old gobbler on the head with a marlinspike and the bird disappeared over the side.

Another evening we went up the road half a mile beyond John Maxwell's. It was to the Hall boys' farm that time to get two young pigs that Pa had spoken for when the litter was born three weeks earlier. Joe and John Hall were doing the milking when we arrived. Pa sat on a stool on the walk behind the cows and talked with the two brothers while they milked by hand. When the last cow was stripped dry, we moved to the milkroom near the front of the hay barn where the cream separator was located. John placed a full half-pail of warm milk on the floor while he proceeded to fill the tank of the separator. One of his hungry cats started eagerly to lick the froth from the pail, tipping it over and spilling all of the milk. John shooed the cat out of the barn and continued filling the tank. At this point Pa asked if they had a problem with rats. "We raise cats, not rats," John replied. Most separators at that time had a good-sized crank that someone turned by hand. The

Hall boys, however, had a novel source of energy for operating the machine. Joe brought in a husky ram and shut him in a treadmill beside the separator. The work of separating the cream from the milk was done economically and effectively by sheep power; no energy from petroleum, imported or otherwise, was required here.

As soon as John had washed the equipment, we went to the pigpen at the open end of the barn cellar where Pa, in the lantern light, selected two female piglets which we placed in a shorts sack and carried to our wagon. Pa formerly bought castrated male pigs to raise for meat, but one year a pig he purchased had been incompletely altered. It turned out to be a "blind boar" whose meat had an unpleasant strong taste. After that, he bought only sow pigs. "You're surer of having something good to eat if you raise a sow," he said. On the way home, the full moon was fairly high, and just before we came to Pratt's Creek, we saw a small dark animal run across the bridge and disappear in the alders on the side of the dike. "Did you see that animal?" "What was it?" I asked. "I couldn't see it very well from this side," Pa replied. "It was behind the horse from me most of the time. Could have been a stray cat. More'n likely though it was a mink, in that kind of place."

Chapter Thirty-Six

Business Ventures

A couple of unprofitable business deals convinced me that we were not too shrewd in the buying and selling of farm creatures. As I remember, it was in the fall of 1910 that Pa bought twenty white pullets from Jim Pratt. They were attractive large pure-white birds with single combs that were already becoming red, indicating that they should be getting ready to lay. "A dollar apiece is a big price to pay for a flock of pullets," Pa said, "but if we can get some eggs from them this winter, while eggs are high, we ought to make some money from them." Pa built a new roosting place for the birds in the east end of the barn. They had the run of the barn floor and tie-up. This gave them a lot of space for exercise and should have encouraged egg production. Late February came and nary an egg from the new flock. Some of our pullets had been laying well for a month or so. About that time, Pa began to wonder if the purchase had been wise. Consequently, when Chase's store asked for some dressed fowl, Pa said, "Let's take a look at those white pullets." I held the lantern while Pa and Mother examined them the night before chicken-picking day. "These birds are as fat as butterballs," Pa said. "Maybe they're too fat to lay. I'll bet we won't get any eggs from them before May. Let's let Chase have them, and take our lickin'. They've cost us a lot for grain already." As I remember, Pa got back the purchase price of the pullets, but it was doubtful if there was any profit, figuring the cost of their keep from Thanksgiving to March.

The next fall, Vining engineered a deal that left Pa a little poorer than he was before. It was Vining's last year in high school and he was doing homework at the kitchen table after the rest of us had gone to bed. I was awakened when he called up the hallway:

"Pa, are you there?"

"Yeah, what is it?"

"Alden and Young Santy dug out a den of skunks and they want to sell us the skins. Can you come down?"

"Oh, I guess so. Be down in a minute."

Alden Avery was our next door neighbor at the time, having rented the Cromwell house. He and Young Santy Pratt had dug out a den of skunks in the woods behind Preble Creek that afternoon. There were eleven skunks in the den. It was early evening moonlight by the time the two men had finished the skinning. When they climbed the bank at Cromwell's landing place, they saw the light in our window and, being anxious to turn the pelts into money as quickly as possible, they decided to try to sell them to us. Through my bedroom wall I could hear Pa moving around while he was getting dressed. I wondered what Pa was thinking, for I had heard him say once, "People must be pretty hard up when they dig out skunks." Soon he was going downstairs. By that time, the potent skunk odor had diffused upstairs. The temptation to see the pelts was too great. I slipped into my clothes and joined the group in the kitchen. Vining had spread newspapers on the floor and was already sorting the pelts into four groups according to how much white they had on their backs. The most valuable furs had only a white patch on top of the head and the usual white tip on the tail. This was Grade No. 1. Grade No. 2 had two short stripes from the head to the vicinity of the shoulders. Skunk furs with narrow white stripes down the back were Grade No. 3, and those with two broad white strips were No. 4. In our trapping experience, we had noticed that the skunks we caught in the woods across the river tended to be of relatively high grade. They seemed to have less white on them than those from cultivated areas. A large percentage of the skunks we caught around the open fields on our side of the river were broad stripers, No. 4's. This lot was typical of our woods' skunks. Three-fourths of the furs Vining graded as Nos. 1 and 2. But the two men had struck it lucky that day. Often times, one digs out a den to find only a single skunk or none at all at the end of the burrow. There were eleven skunks in this one. "Piss was flying in every direction when we dug into their nest," they told Pa. The stench in the kitchen left no doubt that they were telling the truth!

A few days earlier, Vining had received his returns from a small trial shipment of furs sent to Funsten Bros. in St. Louis. Before this, we almost always sent them to G. R. Hunnewell in Auburn. He was well pleased with the prices Funsten had paid him and he thought their grading had been very generous. With the good prices he had received as a guideline, he figured the amount he could afford to pay Alden and Young Santy. He soon stated the figure he could offer for the furs – a little more than twenty dollars. It was quickly accepted by the sellers. Since Vining had no money, Pa paid for the furs. Pa also spent two hours the next day, while Vining was at school, turning the skins flesh side out, fastening them onto drying boards before hanging them to dry on the east side of the barn. We had only four skunk boards, so Pa had to make some new ones to stretch the eleven skins. Ten days later, Vining removed the dried skins, wrapped them in several thicknesses of brown paper, and shipped them via railway express to Funsten Bros. We shipped muskrat and mink pelts by mail, but skunk skins were a different matter. It was two weeks before payment arrived from St. Louis. The envelope was large size and elaborately engraved, the invoice sheet was also a big one with all different fur-bearers listed and with a few spaces under each kind for recording the number of furs received of that species and the grades into which they were sorted. Although the check was a relatively large piece of paper, the amount was dismayingly small. Vining scanned the grading and pricing sheet with a look of disgust. "We lost some money on that deal," he told Pa. "Maybe they were just baiting me with the good prices they paid on the first lot – trying to get us to send them more furs. They graded these last ones down pretty badly too." Pa was the loser but he seemed to take the matter philosophically. At least he didn't scold Vining for his lack of business acumen. Perhaps he thought it would teach him a good lesson. Funsten's check allowed Pa to get back about eighty cents on each dollar he spent. Telling Al about the deal later on, Vining admitted, "We paid too much for those furs."

It was only three or four years later that I felt the full force of Pa's low regard for St. Louis fur buyers. At Thanksgiving time I had a mink pelt and several muskrats ready for the market. Vining was home from college for the four day weekend. "Seems like Hunnewell didn't pay you any too well for those last muskrats you sent him," Vining said. "Why don't you try sending this to that Taylor company that's been mailing us their price lists every so often? They might pay real well on the first lot of furs you send them." The F. C. Taylor Company, another buyer of raw furs based in St. Louis like Funsten Bros., had us on their list for mailing their seasonal prices on raw furs. I don't know how we came to receive their offerings, unless Vining had requested their price list sometime earlier, or possibly they had obtained our name from the list of subscribers to the magazine, *Hunter-Trader-Trapper*. Anyway, with Vining's urging, I sent the mink and eight or ten muskrats to Taylor's. Two weeks later, I received payment. I opened the letter with the check from them one afternoon in December as soon as I got home from school. A few minutes later, Pa asked me to help him roll the baggage wagon into the barn. He pulled on the thills while I was pushing behind. "Taylor paid $3.50 for the mink," I said. Pa was apparently shocked and became angry. He stopped pulling the wagon and turned to tell me: "They only paid you three-fifty for that mink! That's a damned low price, I think. Hunnewell paid you four dollars and a half for that mink you caught on Newell's meadow, after he'd laid in the trap for a week. I tell you, those fellows out west there are no one to do business with." The stern tone of Pa's voice got to me. I felt that I had done a shameful thing by sending the furs to St. Louis. Knowing that I was about to start to cry, I forsook my job at the rear of the wagon for an out-of-sight place inside the barn. Noticing my predicament, Pa gave a half-hearted laugh. "That Vining's responsible," he said after he pulled the wagon into the barn by himself. "He ought to know better by now."

Chapter Thirty-Seven

Aunt Emma Maxwell

Aunt Emma was our only well-to-do relative. She made a big impression on us children, probably because we knew she had a lot of money and she gave us so many things. She was a portly good-looking woman, with a pleasant face and curly blonde hair done up almost African style. She spoke rather hesitantly, with a pleasant voice. She had some sort of nervous ailment that caused a noticeable shaking of the head, particularly when she talked. She must have been an unusually attractive girl, and, I've been told, had several suitors. When it came time to marry, she asked Pa which of two men, Albion Maxwell or Al Hillman, she should favor. Pa advised her to take Al Maxwell, which she did. As it happened, Al Hillman married another of Pa's sisters, Carrie. We ended up with two Uncle Als. Uncle Al Hillman became a harness maker in Bowdoinham Village. Uncle Al Maxwell owned a farm on the Kennebec with a woodlot that extended westward to the Abbagadasset, almost directly across the river from our Shore. Many years after he had inherited a small fortune from a rich uncle, Pa told us that he first knew Al Maxwell as a poor dairy farmer, making a living from the land. Pa must have had a great deal of respect for Uncle Al, however, for Mother said that it was Pa who wanted my oldest brother named Albion.

Sometime after receiving their inheritance, Uncle Al and Aunt Emma bought another home close to the Kennebec in Richmond Village. Later they purchased a house in Portland, on Chadwick Street near the Western Promenade. They kept the Richmond house and the farm in Bowdoinham for several years after moving to Portland. They sold the farm to a lumber dealer around 1912. Several years later, in the late 1920's after the timber had been cut, Vining bought the old Maxwell farm and restored the buildings. The Maxwell's only child, Irving, was a year younger that Vining.

The windfall that the Maxwells enjoyed came from the estate of their Uncle Noble, a sea captain and ship owner who made a million in coastwise trade. Noble was a bachelor uncle. It was common knowledge that he was once in love with a beautiful girl from Bath and he was expecting her to meet him at the dock upon his return from a voyage. She met him as planned; but she was with another man. Noble grew wealthy all by himself and remained single for the remainder of his life.

Visits from the Maxwells were important social events for us. They drove up from Portland once or twice each summer, sometimes just for the day, occasionally they stayed overnight. Along in May after our road had settled, Mother received a note from Aunt Emma saying they would like to visit us the coming weekend. "We'd better kill two hens this time," Pa said. "With their chauffeur, there'll be four of them. One roasting fowl isn't enough for all of us and for them too. I can't get but two or three good servings from each side of a hen. That doesn't leave much for the rest of us." There was always a lot of excitement when the Maxwells' shiny touring car drove into our dooryard. The first of their autos that I can remember was a five-passenger Thomas Flyer with a fold-down top and open sides. I was particularly interested in the big brass horn that was operated by squeezing a rubber bulb beside the steering wheel. On the running board was an acetylene generator that produced gas for the headlights. A match was used to light the gas. They started the motor with a crank.

This was the car in which I had my first auto ride. I almost didn't get it the day they went to Richmond to see the house where they used to live. Feeling sad at the prospect of being left at home, I asked Mother if I could go with them. Mother in turn asked Aunt Emma if there might be room for me. "Why, of course," came the anxiously-awaited reply. "We should have asked Bert in the first place." The Maxwells and their chauffeur wore long light-weight coats to protect their clothing from the road dust. The rest of us paid little attention to the dust; we just enjoyed the fast ride at twenty-five miles an hour.

There was much excitement every time the Maxwells came for a visit. Aunt Emma always brought many good things to eat. The packages covered the kitchen table. Besides a big box of candy, she brought cakes and cookies from her neighborhood bakery shop. One unforgettable item was the cluster of bananas. It was one of the few occasions that we had a banana to eat. Mother always found a five dollar bill in the sugar bowl after Aunt Emma left. One year she sent us a turkey for Thanksgiving, and we received a goose for Christmas several times. She always sent a big box of presents at Christmas, too. My first and only sled was a Christmas gift from Aunt Emma. It had a dark blue top with painted scroll and a high steel frame. I named it "Rena" for the girl next door. When I penciled the name on the underside of the wooden top, I spelled it "Rener." Vining saw the name and remarked, "Rena is spelled the same either forwards or backwards, isn't it?"

I remember Pa's saying how shocked he was when we learned of Uncle Al Maxwell's death, when I was about five. He died suddenly and unexpectedly from a heart attack, I believe, which was then often diagnosed as acute indigestion. It happened during the winter. Pa and Mother went to Portland for the funeral by train. After Uncle Al died, Aunt Emma, Irving, and the chauffeur continued to drive up from Portland two or three times each summer; when Irving became old enough to drive, they no longer hired the chauffeur. By that time, they had purchased a Packard. One visit was in September, during the open season on waterfowl, and Vining took Irving up river in the gunning float. They joked that evening about Irving's missing the one shot they had at a duck as it jumped from the shoreline grass. He was using Pa's heavy 10-gauge shotgun and Irving complained that he could not support the gun long enough to take careful aim. After the guests had retired, Vining told Pa that Irving wanted to see their woodlot the next day before returning to Portland. Vining was concerned that Irving might see some of the freshly-cut stumps where Pa had cut a tree for lumber. Aunt Emma always told Pa to cut as many dead or scrubby trees as he needed, anytime, for firewood. Along with the firewood, Pa had taken the liberty of cutting some pine, spruce, and hemlock for logs to take to the sawmill. "Take him through the south side of their woods, along the Dunning line. You can take him across Preble Creek Swamp and all the way to their house. I'd keep away from the old wood road on the north side where we've done most of the cutting," Pa told Vining.

For a year or two, while Irving was in high school, Aunt Emma hired my sister Lois to help with her housework and to tutor Irving in Latin and mathematics. A few years later, Jeannette stayed there for several days while recuperating from her breast tumor operation at the nearby hospital. I received several articles of clothing that Irving had outgrown. Aunt Emma gave me a practically new, dark blue sailor suit with knee-length trousers that he had worn very little and which I wore as a dress-up suit for at least two years. I wore a pair of Irving's low tan shoes for an entire fall and again throughout the following spring. My older cousin, Helen Denham, who often walked with me to school at the corner, tried to make fun of me once for wearing "those walking shoes" in all kinds of weather. "They're not made for roads like this," she said, "and mud and water will splash right into them. They're not waterproof either." "These shoes are perfectly all right," I told her. "They're comfortable and I like them."

Had it not been for Aunt Emma, Minerva and Genevieve would have had much greater difficulty in meeting their college expenses. Pa was paying for most of Vining's education at about that same time and he contributed little towards either of my sisters' bills. They were able to borrow enough from Aunt Emma to supplement their income from part-time teaching and waiting on tables at Poland Springs so that they were able to continue their college careers.

Chapter Thirty-Eight

Winter, Ice and Cold

When winter came in Bowdoinham, some things were not far behind. Some came with it. The things one could always be sure of were ice and snow and cold weather. Some of the things winter brought we regarded with mixed emotions. Take ice for example. When it plugged the outdoor sink spout, it was a nuisance; it also was when we had to chop it out from the chickens' troughs and from the cattle's watering tub each day. We cussed the ice that built up beneath the stable door and kept it from opening easily. But how we enjoyed the ice when it formed a crust on the snow thick enough to bear our weight and we could go sliding in the gully. We had no lollypops but icicles broken from eaves of buildings served the same purpose, perhaps a healthier one, and tasted just as good. When winter temperatures turned the sap in our beech and maple firewood to ice, the wood was much easier to split than it was in summertime. We used to marvel at the frost pictures, merely ice in a different form, on our kitchen windows in the morning following a frigid night. It was fun, too, to draw pictures and write by scratching on the frosty panes.

Probably the greatest benefit we derived from winter's ice was the natural bridge sheet it formed on all our waterways, thus making transportation possible, either by foot or sleigh or sled, to those places that were reached only by boat in summertime. Because of the thick ice sheet formed on Merrymeeting Bay, farmers in our area had a shortened route to Bath for selling hay and other farm products. Aunt Emma's woods across the river with all its firewood and standing timber trees was readily accessible by river ice in wintertime. We were able to set sucker nets through the ice and drive to the fishing sites with the horse to gather up the fish on shipping days, because of the ice sheet on the Abbagadasset. During the winter when I was in the seventh and eighth grades, I was able to set muskrat traps over a wide area during Christmas and spring vacations because I was able to use skates to get to trapping areas some distance from our farm. Not only were Cromwell's and Beal's meadows, Pratt's Creek, and the swamp behind our west woods within easy reach, but I also skated from Amasa's pond, across his pasture, across that of Uncle Everett and Uncle Ed, to Scott's Pond, Mrs. Call's meadow and the swamp on the Newell Purington farm, west of the Jellerson schoolhouse. It would have taken too much time to reach all of those places on foot when the swampy places were ice-free bogs or open water. At the same time, ice on our rivers had its drawbacks. All shipping on the Kennebec and Cathance rivers had to be suspended as soon as cold weather took over in December. Before the Kennebec started to freeze over, government boats took up all channel buoys and stored them away until spring. Offsetting these adverse effects, however, subfreezing weather brought employment for hundreds of workers who helped to fill the big storage houses with cakes of heavy ice. And, come summer, there were further benefits from the winter's cold. The stored ice had to be loaded onto sailing vessels that carried it to distant ports. River ice was big business in our area before the electric refrigerator came on the scene. But, just as the advent of cement idled the granite quarries along New England's coast, so did the advent of electricity sound the death knell of the ice industry on the Cathance and Kennebec.

Although Pa "put up" more than enough ice for our own use every winter, enough to last us until the river froze again, we scarcely had any income from its sale. Occasionally some neighbor bought a ten-cent block for making ice cream or to keep some special fresh food cold for a day or two. Oddly enough, however, no one in our town, as far as I know, used a standard ice chest for preserving food. Most farm families kept their perishables down cellar during warm months, or some suspended perishable items in their wells. For us, ice was more or less a necessity from the last of April till Thanksgiving. Pa added chopped ice to barrels of shad to be shipped to Boston in May, and to boxes of suckers bound for New York City in October and November. On those sweltering hay-making days of July and August, we enjoyed icewater as a sort of luxury. On hot days in the hay field there was nothing like a drink of icewater to offset the oppressive heat. The Abbagadasset was sufficiently free of pollution at that time so that there was no need to fear contracting typhoid from drinking water that was cooled with its clear blue ice. When our weekly summertime fish peddler had seafood at bargain prices, we often bought more than we could consume in the next day or two. On such occasions, someone then made a trip to the Shore with the wheelbarrow and returned with a chunk of ice for packing round the excess haddock, mackerel, or clams in a paper-lined box down cellar. If churning day was unusually warm, Mother asked one of us to get some ice for cooling the butter and making it firm in its final washings. "It makes the butter a bit more solid and a lot easier to stamp out," she said. On every Fourth of July and often on a Sunday later on, we made a batch of ice cream in our gallon hand-crank freezer. Coarse rock salt was added to the crushed ice around the central cylinder in the wooden freezer pail. This made a quick efficient freezing mixture that shortened the time we had to turn the crank.

Our windowless old fish house near the tip of the Point with its double-walled bin in the back end was where the ice was stored. The space between the walls was filled with sawdust for effective insulation. Fishing lines complete with sinkers and hooks hung from nails in a post at one corner of the bin. One cold day in early spring, before I was old enough to go to school, I was examining the fishing gear when a fishhook got caught in one of my mittens. Try as I might, I couldn't remove the fishhook. Pa heard me crying while he was sorting weir stakes outside. He came to see what my difficulty might be. He pushed the hook completely through the cloth and cut the line with his jackknife. "You can't pull back a fish hook out of anything," he said. "You have to push the hook on through then cut it off and tie it on the line again. They're bad things to play with anyway."

After Al built his motorboat, a new building was needed to house it during the winter. One was constructed east of the Point not far from the old fish house. The new boathouse had extra space for our boating and fishing equipment, plus the variety of tools that were formerly kept in the old fish house. Pa tore down the fish house and used much of the lumber to build a new ice house close to the boathouse. Hard pine timbers, discarded into the river when the railroad bridge was repaired, provided long-lasting sills for the new ice house. It was a tall building, high enough to hold several tiers of thick ice, plus a thick blanket of sawdust.

Its walls, like those around the ice bin in the old fish house, were double and filled with sawdust. There were two doors, one above the other, making it possible to stack ice cakes clear to the roof. After the new ice house was built, there were two winters when we harvested no ice at all because the building held enough ice to last for two years. Sawdust insulation prevented excessive melting during the summer. For some reason, the three or four inches of white snow ice comprising the top layer of each cake melted more slowly than the thicker layer of blue ice underneath. We had some snow ice left after the clear bottom layer had been completely melted.

Harvesting ice on the river was not the easiest of our winter tasks. However, it was pleasant work. One year we had a lot of cold weather early and the ice was thick enough to put up during the last days of the Christmas vacation, before Al had to return to his teaching. Usually, however, Pa waited until the river ice had reached its maximum thickness and the weather was a little warmer towards the end of March. At that time of the year, the days were getting longer, too, and there was still plenty of snow on the ground for using the horse sled. "There's a good flat stretch of channel ice between the breakages, just above the sandbank this year," Pa said one morning in late winter. "That'll be a good place to start cutting today." As a first step, Pa chiseled two holes two feet apart through the thick ice, large enough for him to use the coarse-toothed ice saw – a heavy tapering steel blade, five feet long, with a horizontal handle fastened to the wider end by a curved rod. From these holes, two parallel saw cuts were made about thirty inches apart. Pa split this peninsula of ice into approximately square blocks with the heavy wood-handled ice chisel. It was difficult to get the first cake out of the water onto the surrounding ice. If it could not be raised easily it was sometimes pushed down and out of the way beneath the surrounding ice, to be retrieved later, after a sizeable hole had been created. Later blocks were then easily slid upwards out of the water on an inclined eight-inch plank. The same plank was also used for sliding the cake of ice onto the horse sled. Six heavy cakes made a load for Dandy to pull to the icehouse door. The spruce plank again was brought into use for sliding the blocks of ice from the sled into the house. We used five-foot ice picks that had a sharp iron hook for pulling the ice cake and an equally sharp forward-pointing prong for pushing. The ice went into the house easily until a couple of layers had been stacked away. After that it was hard work sliding the ice up the incline to form higher tiers. It was during this operation one year, I remember, that Pa became disgusted with the way Vining was moving the ice. It was one of those weekends when Vining was home from college and he was helping us put the last of the season's ice in the icehouse. Pa was standing on an upper tier of ice near the door waiting for Vining to start an ice cake up the incline far enough for him to reach it with a pick. Vining got the cake of ice onto the plank but it seemed to stick there and he had difficulty getting it to move upwards on the plank. "Can't you get that ice up here any faster than that?" Pa asked. "When I was your age, I could snake that cake of ice up that plank like nobody's business." Vining made no reply. With a lot of turning and pushing, he and I finally shoved the ice up the incline within reach of Pa's waiting pick.

Some years, when there were unusually high broken ice sheets pushed upwards along the river bank, Pa harvested ice from these thick breakages instead of getting it from the level sheets floating on the water. It was much easier to saw and remove the ice cakes from these breakages than to pull the blocks up out of the water. The harvesting of breakage ice, however, sometimes required longer hauling distances, since we often had to go down river as far as Preble Creek where the river was wider to find breakages of a desirable height. We had to be careful in selecting ice in the breakages, to make sure it was free of flats mud. Since they formed along the edges of the shoreline flats, the ice pushed upwards in them was sometimes contaminated with flecks of mud.

Some years, in the late fall, ice on the river became a few inches thick before we had any snow. It was badly cracked near the shores where it lay on the sloping channel bank at low tide but the breakages had not begun to heave. At such times, it was interesting to walk along the channel and watch floating debris drift along with the tide beneath the ice. Sometimes we saw small schools of smelts swimming along close to the ice. Al told us how, sometimes, on inland lakes, it was possible to stun fish swimming beneath the ice by hitting the ice a heavy blow with an ax. The stunned fish could be caught, he said, by cutting through the ice and grasping the fish before it regained consciousness. He tried to get some of the smelts that way but none appeared to be affected by the blow. Had he stunned any of them, it is doubtful we could have been reached them before the tide carried them away.

Aside from the river, the big expanse of glib ice that formed on Cromwell's meadow before the snows came made the whole swamp a marvelous place for skating. Fall rains usually flooded the lowland from our back pasture to the railroad culvert over Pratt's Creek. Cold nights around Thanksgiving made ice a few inches thick over the entire area. It was here, one cold night in early December, that I received my first frostbite. It was one of my big toes. We thawed it out when I got home, with no lasting effects except some peeling a week or two later. We built a fire on the ice but its warmth was felt only for a distance of a few feet. Irving Maxwell's hand-me-down, ten-inch leather boots that I was wearing were notoriously cold and they were too tight to allow for good circulation. I wore the boots so many times and the heels became so badly worn that the skate clamps could not get a good hold. I was a freshman in high school that year. One Friday after school I stopped at the village cobbler's shop to get some leather for rebuilding the run-down heels. Charles Staples, the shop's owner, looked at me indignantly when I explained my needs. His expression as much as said, "Why don't you bring your boots in to me and let me fix them?" With his sharp knife he cut two small squares from a big sheet of thick orange-tan leather. Each of the two pieces was about equal in area to the top of a teacup. "How much?" I asked him. "Ten cents apiece," he replied. The price was a slight shock to me, but he had already cut off the leather pieces. Twenty cents was all I got for the skin of an undersized muskrat. After dinner that Sunday I brought into the kitchen our iron shoe last, brass shoe nails and a hammer, and started to chisel off the outer layers of leather on the boots. Pa came close to see what I was doing. "You'd better let me fix them, hadn't you?" he asked, and he took over the job. I showed him the pieces of leather I'd gotten at the cobbler's. "That's not the right kind of leather to make heels out of," he said. "It's too soft. You need sole leather for that. What'd he charge you for them?" "Ten cents apiece," I told him. "Ten cents for a squib of leather like that?" Pa held the pieces of leather up so that Mother could see them. "Look at what the Staples charged that boy twenty cents for," he said. "That man ought to have his arse kicked!" Pa went into the shed and found a pair of Al's old discarded shoes with heels still in good shape. He removed the outer layers of the heels and fitted them to my boots, fastening them on with clinched nails. "You've got something there that will hold your skates," he said. "If that Charles Staples wasn't one of our good butter customers," he continued, "I'd tell him what I thought of him the next time I see him."

Besides skating, another sport that we enjoyed in the late fall was running and then sliding stiff-legged on the smooth newly-formed ice, with extended arms for better balance. This activity apparently brought into play the same leg muscles that are used in descending a mountain. For a while following either of these activities, the muscles in the front part of the leg became quite sore, making walking uncomfortable for a day or two.

Everyone knows that water expands when it freezes causing burst pipes, cracked glassware or ceramic vessels, and bulged bottoms in tin pails. Also, heavy sheets of ice floating in the river's current can, from its own momentum, do a lot of damage to boats that are jammed against a ledge or some other solid object. Ordinarily, however, we think of stationary ice as being quite static and staying put. But on the tidal river, certain changes take place during below-freezing weather that tend to make the ice sheet wider and wider as long as low temperatures prevail. This is due to the tendency of the cracks in the ice along the bank of the channel to open up at low tide, when the sheet of ice over the main channel falls to a lower level than that of the flats ice resting on the muddy shore. With the incoming tide, the rising water in these cracks freezes immediately on the super-cooled edges of the ice sheets. As a result, the river's ice sheet becomes a little wider with every high tide, maybe an inch wider than it was the day before. Any significant increase in the width of the ice layer is opposed by the containing riverbanks. But something has to give, just like a rock can split when water freezes in a crack. Two things do happen, in varying degrees. One of these, a temporary seasonal effect, is the formation of pressure ridges, the "breakages," where the ice sheet cracks close to the channel bank and a broken edge of one sheet becomes pushed upwards. This is the way, they tell us, that mountains were formed, when giant sheets of the earth's crust jammed against one another. By late winter the breakages along the Abbagadasset were often taller than a man, several feet or even yards in length, pushed upwards on edge at angles frequently approaching vertical. When springtime comes, one of the first indications that the ice is getting ready to "go out" is the flattening of the breakages.

The other change brought about by movement of the winter's ice, with a more lasting effect on the shoreline, is the formation of those low ridges along the shore that we called "beaver dams." They were formed along the outer edges of swamps bordering the river. Pressure of the ice as it pushed mud and debris against the shore each winter, year after year, eventually formed a low firm ridge along the river's edge. These "beaver dams" were breached here and there by creeks, guzzles and drainage ditches. Alders, elms, gray birch, red maples and occasionally a white pine tree grew on the beaver dams. They were favorite places for muskrats to end their burrows with a nest. Once in a while, a woodchuck dug a summer home in the top of a beaver dam. These ridges were found only along stretches of the river where low level marshy land lay barely above the high water mark; a firm highland bank effectively resisted the pushing effects of the ice. The small swampy island a stone's throw across the channel from our Shore was completely bordered by a beaver dam. There was also one on our marshy meadow, half way between the upland and the river. It extended southward, with occasional interruptions, across Newell's, Amasa's and Uncle Everett's meadows, a distance well back of the river all the way. This inner beaver dam paralleled the river, and it suggests that at some time, perhaps centuries before, the channel of the river may have been located a considerable distance further to the west of its present location.

Travelling on slick ice was difficult and sometimes even downright hazardous for man or beast. Oxen were fitted with iron shoes for improved traction on the ice. In early December each year, Pa took our horse to the blacksmith to have its summer shoes removed and sharp cocks welded onto them in place of the flatter summer ones. Under the weight of the horse, the stout chisel-like cocks cut into the slippery ice and prevented the animal from slipping on icy hilly roads or while travelling on the river. The winter cocks were removed from the horse's shoes in early spring. "Those sharp cocks," Pa said, "wear out the flooring of the horse's stall." For his own safety Pa bought a pair of metal creepers that were fastened to the instep of his boots by a leather strap that buckled above the foot. The creepers were made from a rectangular piece of thin metal with all four corners turned downwards. The sharp corners pierced the ice at every step. They were necessary for tending sucker nets in the winter since the ice around the hole through which the net was hauled was dangerously slippery due to the smooth ice formed by water from the dripping net.

Freezing temperatures in late spring were helpful to us in the seeding of new hayfields. A real cold night in March, after the snow was gone, caused the water in the upper layers of soil to freeze and the many small columns of ice produced a porous soil surface temporarily. Pa often took advantage of this honeycombing effect and sowed his grass and clover seed on ground that had been plowed and harrowed in the fall. While we were having breakfast he said, "That was a good freeze we had last night. I'll put out some grass seed before the sun has time to settle the bare ground again." The tiny seed fell into the multitude of cracks and crannies in the soil surface. When the sun melted the fragile ice columns, the seed became buried at an ideal depth for germination and seedling growth as soon as favorable temperatures prevailed a few weeks later. In this way, the little pillars of ice saved Pa and Dandy many hours of work, first of harrowing the ground to prepare the seed bed and then, after sowing, to cover the seed.

One effect of freezing of the soil, however, was less welcome to the farmers. "It's funny," Pa said. "You plow a piece of land and pick up every stone you can find. Then, after you lay it down to hay, and mow it four or five years, you plow it again. I swear, after the second plowing, there are just as many rocks to pick up as there were the first time. The freezing of the soil seems to bring the stones to the surface. I don't know why it should, but it does." As a boy, I always wished the buried stones would stay put. Picking up rocks and throwing them into the horse cart was one of the least enjoyable of the jobs on our farm.

With the ice sheet that formed over Merrymeeting Bay in December, Nature provided farmers in East Bowdoinham with a short route for hauling hay to Bath. Around 1910, there was always a ready market for hay in all the cities, for the work now done by trucks and cars and taxis was then done with horses. So many horses ate a lot of hay. Our local farmers took their hay to Bath on certain days so that, partly for safety's sake, they crossed the Bay together. "I'm going to take along a fifty-foot piece of stout rope tomorrow," I heard Pa tell John Hall one day when they were planning the first trip to Bath. "That ice isn't any too thick yet, out there over Cathance channel. If anyone breaks through, we'll probably be able to pull him out." Pa loaded the sled with loose hay the day before going to market and tied it down securely with a rope along the top of the load. He left home before daylight and joined the other farmers at Jim Pratt's landing at the northwest corner of the Bay. The Abbagadasset channel came close to shore at that spot and it was an easy place to get onto the solid ice. They followed this channel to the Cathance then proceeded to the Androscoggin channel and to an old highway that came down to the edge of the Bay, in North Bath. Some mornings at sunrise, from our kitchen window, we counted from ten to fifteen loads of hay crossing the Bay one behind the other with a good distance between the loads. It was like a caravan; the dark loads of hay against the white background of the snow-covered ice. If the wind was right, we might hear the faint tinkling of the brass bells that dangled from the horses' collars.

Before the Bay Bridge over the lower Androscoggin was washed out in a spring freshet sometime around the turn of the century, farmers did not have to wait for the Bay to freeze over before hauling their hay to Bath. With this bridge gone, the shortest land route to Bath was via Brunswick, a distance they considered too far for a horse to haul a heavy load. Sometimes, when the Bay was late in freezing over, farmers in our part of town crossed on the thicker ice that had already formed across the Androscoggin at the site of the former bridge. Once across the river, they entered North Bath at the usual place. This route was longer than the one across the Bay and it went through Bowdoinham Village, then southward along the road to Topsham. This was the road on which Martha Robinson's home was located. While Al was courting Martha, he often drove down to see her with our gray horse, Dandy.

Dandy also hauled loads of hay to Bath. On one of the hay caravans via the old bridge site, Pa hitched Dandy's reins to the pitchfork on top of the load and let the horse follow the load ahead, while he sat on the rear of the load of hay and talked with Amandus Borjesson, the driver of the load behind. When they reached the Robinson residence, Amandus pointed ahead excitedly, saying "Look where your horse now goes, Jimmy. You going to see Mrs. Robinson?" Before Pa could get back to the reins, Dandy was heading up the Robinson's driveway. By the time he had turned around and driven back to the highway, the other teams had passed and Pa was the last of the group to reach the market.

Some winters the weather became cold enough to freeze sufficiently thick ice across the Cathance and Androscoggin channels in the Bay, but it was a risk to transport loads of hay across those treacherous spots where the swift currents sometimes delayed the formation of thick ice. Test holes chopped in the ice sheet had to show it to be eight or more inches in depth before farmers would dare crossing. During very mild winters, Pa sold little or no hay in Bath. Instead, come spring, he sold his surplus to Will Given, a hay merchant in the Village. Mr. Given had a hay press that he set up in our barn floor and compressed the hay into heavy rectangular bales that were bound by strands of hay wires fastened lengthwise of the two-hundred pound bales. The hay press was a tall heavy structure that required two men to operate. With the heavy bottom lowered to the barn floor, the press was filled with loose hay that the operators pitched from the barn mow. If Pa wanted to sell only half a mow of hay, he borrowed Wilbur Douglas's hay knife – a heavy one-piece iron blade and handle that had a shallow undulating cutting edge on one side. With this the men sawed the mow of stored hay straight in half, leaving a wall of cut hay stems at the side.

Power to squeeze the hay into a compact rectangular block was furnished by a horse in the dooryard that walked around and around, hitched to the end of an eighteen-foot wooden lever. The lever turned a big spool around which a wire cable was wound. The cable raised the floor of the press, thereby condensing a bulky mass of loose hay into a tight block at the top. After hay wires were fastened around the bale, it was removed from the baler and stored in the barn scaffold. The driver of the horse then pushed a short lever that released the spool, allowing the cable to unwind and the heavy bottom of the press dropped with a big thump to the barn floor. To prevent this pile-driving weight from breaking the floor timbers, Pa shored up the barn floor with extra posts in the barn cellar beneath the press to absorb the shock of the falling press. One winter in the early 1930's, slippery ice on the road resulted in a fatal accident to two local men who worked for Mr. Given on the hay press at our farm. They were on their way to work when they were killed at Jellerson's Crossing. Their car skidded on the icy spot and was struck by the morning southbound passenger train we called the "Seven O'Clock." An automatic signal now helps to prevent such accidents at Jellerson's Crossing.

It takes cold weather to make ice, but you don't have to have ice around to be cold. The coldest feet I ever had were experienced as, barefoot, I drove the cows to pasture on frosty mornings in the fall. I stopped every ten steps or so and placed one foot on top of the other to get the soles warm. Someone wrote about purposely stepping in warm cow manure on such occasions. I never did that. Besides a warm "meadow biscuit" is seldom around when you need it. As for the whole body becoming chilled through and through, I remember only two occasions in particular when I was about eight years old that I thought I was just going to freeze for sure, one with Vining, the other with Pa. On both occasions I was sitting in the skiff on the river with little to do but keep warm. Both times it was an overcast late fall day and a cold wind blew from the northeast.

The first incident took place the day after Thanksgiving, while Vining was having his first long weekend at home in his freshman year at college. He asked me to go upriver with him to set some muskrat traps, since he would have two days to tend them. Vining rarely asked me to go anywhere with him on the river and I eagerly accepted this invitation that gray November day. It was low tide when we reached the shore. Although it was late in the fall, there was shell ice along the shore but the weather so far had not been cold enough to freeze the river completely over. The river banks offered some windbreak, but the disagreeable wind drew down the river, like all our northeasters seemed to do. Vining did the rowing while I sat in the stern of the skiff with a paddle and tried to keep the old square-ended boat from grounding on the low flats. Steering the skiff involved a minimum of activity – not nearly enough to keep me warm. By the time we reached Kil's Point, I was half-frozen. From then on, Vining stopped frequently to go ashore and look for muskrat holes along the high water mark. I was left to hold the boat against the flats and was getting colder every minute. When he had set the last of his traps at the foot of the grassy bank near the east end of the big railroad bridge, I was more than half-frozen. The return trip was slow because we were going against a strong flood tide, although the wind was in our backs and therefore helped us make faster progress against the incoming tide. After landing at our Point, I was numb with cold but I did manage to walk from the Shore up across the field and to our warm house. Mother must have been working in the field or perhaps in the barn that day, for Lois was the only one around when we reached the kitchen. She noticed my predicament and helped me remove my jacket and shoes. I sat close to the stove with my feet on the hearth as she rubbed my hands and feet. "You shouldn't have let him get so cold," Lois told Vining. "His feet are like ice." I don't think I accompanied Vining when he tended his traps on Saturday and Sunday. I'm sure it took more than two days to forget how cold I had been on Friday.

It's a wonder I didn't come down with pneumonia, or something worse, one December when Pa took me along to steer the skiff while he towed a raft of six or eight logs, picked up around the river during the fall, to the sawmill. "I hadn't planned to have the logs sawed until spring," he said, "but since the river's still open, we might as well take them down today before she freezes over. There's always a lot of work we'll be busy with in the spring. It's high tide today around noon so we can take them to the mill on the first of the ebb right after dinner." Again the day was cold and gray with a northeasterly wind – the kind that's coldest on the river. Again I was sitting almost motionless on the stern seat of the skiff moving the paddle blade from right to left, while Pa pulled on the oars to make the logs move a little faster than they would drift with the tide. As we were passing the sandbank, a great blue heron flew past us, heading upriver. "What's that old harn doing around here this time of year?" Pa asked. "I've heard that it's a sign of an open winter when they stay here so late. Maybe this will be a mild one. Lots of years, the river is frozen over solid by this time." As we proceeded a hundred yards further downstream, a lone black duck quacked as she flushed far ahead of us in the bend of the river at the Spar Landing. "That's the way with these late season birds," Pa said. "They've been shot at so much they get wary and jump away a mile ahead of you. That one was sitting there in the bend of the river where she could see a hunter coming from either direction. A black duck is a wary bird but they get really smart this time of year."

The chill in the air on that raw December day was getting to me, and the sawmill was yet a half a mile away. By the time the logs were tied up at the slip, I was barely able to stand. "I'm cold," I told Pa. He took me first to the boiler room where Old Santy was feeding the fire with slabs and sawdust. "Climb on top of the boiler and get warm," he told me. The arching layer of bricks that covered the boiler wasn't the warmest place I'd seen but I did become thoroughly warmed there after several minutes and descended the short ladder to look for Pa. He was giving Charles Holbrook instructions as to the dimensions of lumber he wanted from each log. "Let's make mostly two-by-three's out of this one," he told Charles as the endless chain brought a small ten-inch spruce up the slip from the water to a point in front of the big circular saw. It was interesting to watch them saw the old pine that we had found adrift. Apparently it was once a part of a log boom, perhaps somewhere on the Kennebec. It had a half-inch hole in one side that might have been made for an iron bolt or spike. Charles probed the hole with his jackknife blade before sawing off the first slab. He repeated the probing of the mud-filled hole before each successive cut was made, to make sure there was no iron deeply imbedded within the log. "Amasa doesn't like to have us saw logs that have been used for something like this one," Charles told Pa. "You never know when you'll run onto iron and ruin some teeth on the saw." It took less than an hour to saw our few logs. Pa and I were soon heading back upstream. With no logs in tow, I did a lot of paddling to keep warm while Pa gave the skiff good momentum with the oars. Although we were going into the cold wind, the extra activity kept me much warmer than was the case on the way to the mill. I was reasonably warm when we reached the house.

Another occasion the cold really got to us was during a ride in the horse-drawn pung to the Village on a cold day. Sitting still for half an hour when the temperature was well below freezing and a blustery northwest wind was blowing all around us brought chills through our warmest clothing. To keep our feet warm we had a heated brick beneath the seat. The brick was effective on the way to the Village but of little use on the way home. Pa often dropped the reins over the dash-board and walked behind for a ways "to get his blood circulating," on some of the coldest trips. He showed me how to keep my hands warm by swinging my arms and pounding my shoulders. Strangely enough, although we were exposed to zero temperatures on many occasions, I cannot recall that any of us ever had a serious case of frostbite, either while riding to the Village or while outdoors at home.

We often complained about the ice and cold of winter, yet there were times in the summer when we looked back on those frigid days and wished for an hour of their coolness. Some of the most uncomfortably hot conditions that we worked under were associated with haying. One stifling summer job that first comes to mind involved the stowing away of hay when the barn mow was nearly full and one had to work partially stooped over beneath the roof. When a load of hay from the field was brought into the barn, the horse was removed from the thills and hitched to a whiffletree at the end of the rope which hoisted big forkfuls of hay from the load onto the mow. One of the womenfolk drove the horse in the dooryard. Vining operated the big steel fork that carried one-sixth of a load at each setting and released the hay high up on the haymow. Pa was waiting, pitchfork in hand, to tear apart the hoisted mound of hay and pitch it to the back of the mow. It was my job to spread these smaller forkfuls around, on top of the mow, and tread the loose hay tightly against the eaves. There was little ventilation so close to the roof and the heat was oppressive, to say the least. On such occasions I sometimes thought of winter days when I would climb the ladder to pitch down some hay for the cows, and wisps of vapor would appear in front of my face every time I breathed. Right then, I would have opted for a winter's day. Likewise, the chunks of ice floating in the pail as we took a drink before going to the field for the next load of hay were much more appealing than similar chunks we had to scoop out from the stake holes of the sucker net on a freezing January day. Obviously, circumstances greatly alter the way we look upon that solid state of water known as ice

Chapter Thirty-Nine

Roads, Ferries, Railroads and Traffic Accidents

When it came to transportation in Bowdoinham's early years, a study of our farm was like reading a page from a history book. It was always intriguing to trace visible relics of one of the first roads in town. Years before the railroad was put through, an old road entered the west end of our pasture and we could see a short remnant of the old highway where it cut through a low rise of ground about fifty yards east of the Maine Central right-of-way. The short narrow gully, worn down by road travel, had grown up with young firs, a couple of small pine trees and a lot of juniper bushes as far back as I can remember. The gully ended at the low-level swale that ran across our pasture from Amasa's woods to our back swamp. It's a well-known fact that dirt roads in the country tend to cut into the ground wherever they cross a hill. Horses' hooves and wagon wheels, especially in muddy times, tend to dig up the roadbed soil, much of which will soon wash downhill in the very next rain. Oftentimes, road maintenance involves the plowing of ditches along both sides of the road to provide better drainage and to increase the firmness of the center of the roadbed. Such activities, year after year, tend to dig the road deeper and deeper into the hillside.

In the case of the old road in our pasture, there was no depression left where it crossed level ground, because there was less tendency for the loosened soil to wash away. Proceeding eastwards, as soon as the ground began to rise to form the big hill in our west pasture, another gully was worn several feet into the blue clay subsoil. One could easily follow this old roadbed to the top of the hill where it crossed our farm boundary into Amasa's pasture. The old road gully was traceable all the way down the east side of the hill to the level land near the outlet of Amasa's pond. Here, again, there was no evidence of the old road for thirty or forty yards of level ground. As soon as the land began to rise again, however, towards our present highway, the old road gulch reappeared and continued up the hillside until it reached the present road. Directly across the highway, one could see the old roadbed depression for a short distance in the narrow strip of hayfield between our driveway and the south line. The old roadbed washout faded when it reached the flatland approaching our dooryard. From this point, we were unable to trace the old road any farther. But we do know, from Silas Adams' history of the town, that it continued to our shore, where travellers continued on their way across the river by ferry. On the east side of the stream, the ferry landed at the terminus of an old wood road at the upper end of the sandbank. It is difficult to imagine what sort of a boat served as a ferry – probably a small flat-bottomed scow that was paddled and poled by hand. Old Santy told the improbable story he'd heard years before about a bear that tried to board the ferry in midstream one day. The operator held the attacker under water with the paddle forced down his mouth. Before timber was cut on the old Dunning farm, it was possible to follow the wood road all the way to an open field on the Kennebec. I often wondered who the people were who travelled the old road and wore the gulches in the hillside. Early resident farmers on the way to market, old settlers on horseback, pairs of oxen with heavy loads, a country swain taking his sweetie for a Sunday evening ride in a light one-horse carriage.

Traces of the bridges where the old roads crossed creeks or the river were as discernable as the washed-out gullies on hilly terrain. In the old days, when they bridged a waterway, it was apparently customary to dump a lot of rocks all the way across a streambed before building the bridge itself. Constant washing by the tides prevented the rocks from becoming buried with silt and they remained exposed to view for years. Permanent too are the stone and loam dikes across marshy land at the ends of the old bridges. As a boy, one such old bridge site and the associated dike held a fascination for me. They were part of a long-forgotten road that crossed Pratt's Creek near the present railroad culvert west of Pratt's Crossing. Like all impediments of this sort in a watercourse, this old stone bridge bed across the shallow channel of Pratt's Creek had caused a deep basin to be washed out on the downstream side of the bridge. Here Merton Webber and I found our perfect "swimmin' hole." It was a completely safe place to learn to swim – dog-paw at first, later discovering more graceful strokes. At high tide the water was over our heads in the middle of the basin, but we could easily wade across the deepest part when the tide was out. Another bridge and dike, vestiges of an old road, could be seen up-river at Charlie Hill's shore, about half a mile below the Mill Pond. Here, at low tide, one could see the stones all the way across the bottom of the river. A low dike extended inland from the high flats near the west end of the one-time bridge. Since the channel ran close to the steep bank on the east side of the river, there was no dike needed on the eastern side. Charlie Hill had his "haul-up" there and his cows came down to the stream to drink. One Sunday afternoon in late May, Jeannette and I rowed up river on the first of the flood tide. The water was still very low when we reached Hill's shore. We paused awhile at the site of the old bridge. The rocks were there all right. There was scarcely enough depth of water to float the skiff above them. Looking closely, we saw a number of lamprey eels clinging to the rocks by their suctorial mouths and their long slender bodies swinging with the incoming tide. Apparently this was part of their spawning process. I pulled several of the snake-like creatures from the rocks and placed them in the boat. They were strange looking fish, three feet in length with a mottled gray-green skin, and a row of "port holes" on each side of the throat where other fish have gills. Next day Mother boiled them in the old cast iron kettle, stirred in some cornmeal and fed them to the hens.

Equally as interesting as the remnants of the former bridges were the old corduroy roads that farmers had built across swampy places, some of them two or three generations ago. The nearest, and most recent, of these was Amasa's wharf, a dike-like structure across his marshy meadow from the highland to the channel's edge. Amasa and Charles Holbrook built this low roadway, I was told, for unloading seaweed that they had loaded on a scow in Sheepscot Bay. They envisioned a profitable enterprise transporting this commodity for use as a fertilizer on Amasa's farm and for sale to neighbors. Economically, the undertaking never proved a success, but the old dike across the marsh still remains as a monument to their dream.

I walked along it every morning while tending muskrat traps before leaving for high school.

Another nearby structure of this sort was Cromwell's bridge – a long firm roadway across the wide meadow northwest of our farm. It was used for years for driving cattle to and from the pasture beyond the railroad and for hauling firewood and timber from the pasture woodlot. Its one weak spot was the floating bridge of railroad ties with planks nailed crosswise. The bridge was in mid-swamp over a boggy creek bed that was one of the upper reaches of Pratt's Creek.

In the woods across the river, we knew of four of these corduroy roads over the alder and maple swamp that drained southwards into Preble Creek and reached almost to the highway east of the Harward's Depot. The first and southernmost crossed the swamp at the head of the open area of the creek. It was on the Stephen Preble farm and had not been used for years. Whatever kind of bridge once crossed the narrow creek channel had been washed out years before. But the old dike, mostly overgrown with sedges, grass and alder bushes, was still in evidence across the swamp to the wooded peninsula below the Old Pine. A pathway followed the top of the dike and it could be followed with more or less ease, all the way across the swamp. It was used by partridge hunters wearing ankle-high shoes, rather than hip boots, who wished to cross the swamp with dry feet. The swamp was a likely place to flush a partridge, for there were many wild rose bushes with their attractive red hips scattered rather frequently among the alders.

Farther up the swamp, one came to the second corduroy road on the old Dunning farm. This was part of the onetime town highway that met the ferry at our Point and ran eastward to the Kennebec. This old swamp road was shaded by tall maples that kept it from supporting impenetrable vegetation. The full width of the road was clear and open all the way across the swamp, which, at this point, had narrowed to thirty or forty yards. The surface of the corduroy road was not much higher than the level of the swamp, and water during springtime thaws flowed freely over it. But it was a serviceable passageway across an otherwise impassable swamp. The old road was covered with sphagnum moss and other ground-cover vegetation, the tallest of which were different kinds of ferns. In spite of many years' accumulation of leaves and humus, the outline of some of the old logs placed parallel to the swamp could still be seen in certain spots. It was the corrugated appearance, due to the many logs laid close side by side, that gave these roads across the swamp their name – corduroy.

A few hundred yards up the same swamp, on Aunt Emma's farm, was another of these old log roads, across which Albion Maxwell hauled meadow hay from the Abbagadasset with his oxen and brought in firewood and saw-logs from the deeper parts of his woodlot. Still further north, on the next farm, Kil Maxwell's, was yet another corduroy road; this one was not quite as long as the others because the swamp became narrower the farther it went from Preble Creek. Kil hauled meadow hay, cordwood and logs over the corduroy dike. In addition, he brought upland hay from the two cleared fields situated deep in his woodlot, hayfields that have long since been abandoned and now support a stand of some of the tallest pines in town. But the old wood-bed roads to this day defy the boggishness of the swamp and are there ready to serve anyone who wants to use them. Farmers found it profitable to build them, in days when every potential asset the land produced had to be harvested and turned to cash.

Why is it that wooden structures such as these old corduroy roads are still there after so many years? Over a period of several generations they have remained as firm as if they had been made of rocks or soil or gravel. We know that certain kinds of wood, like cedar or chestnut or locust, are exceedingly durable under almost any conditions. But farmers in that area had limited numbers of cedar trees to cut, and practically no locust or chestnut. They had quantities of durable red oak, but the logs used in these old roads were of poorer quality soft woods like sapling pine, shaky hemlock, knotty spruce, and the less valuable fir. The answer to the long life of these corduroy roads probably lies in the fact that most any kind of wood that is kept continuously wet doesn't decay so fast. Timber that is kept under ordinarily dry conditions, but is subjected to intermittent wetting, is most readily attacked by wood-rotting fungi and suffers most rapid decay. The lower bridge on the Abbagadasset rests on wooden piers made with criss-crossed logs sometime around 1800. Repairs have been made to the bridge's superstructure but the old round logs below high water mark have never been replaced. The wood that has been perpetually wetted by the tide has remained impervious to decay.

One summer, we saw an example of how well a tree trunk can be preserved if the wood is kept continuously wet. It was after Vining had become curious about a slight twenty-foot ridge in the muckland behind our icehouse. Probing the ridge with a crowbar, he discovered a log a few inches below the surface of the spongy soil. He worked for two or three days digging out the main stem of a large white pine about two feet in diameter at the high end. The jagged end of the log showed that the trunk was broken when it fell. The butt was missing. Some of the larger limbs had apparently been cut off years before, others appeared to have been broken off. We rolled the log from its muddy bed onto some skids and allowed it to dry for a couple of weeks. We pulled it ashore with block and tackle, aided by wooden rolls beneath the tackle. Vining hoped that the log would be worth sawing into boards. But after splitting a short section from the big end, we found the wood was discolored throughout and that it had lost most of its former strength. "That's not worth taking to the mill," Pa said. However, the old pine trunk that had lain in the swamp for probably a hundred years or more still retained its firmness. We manufactured it into stove wood and it baked a lot of beans.

A road of any sort usually involves travel, transporting, and various kinds of traffic. Traffic often meets with occasional accidents. Probably the worst accident any of the old corduroy roads across Preble Creek Swamp ever saw was not more than the sidewise sluing of a sled-load of logs. This could happen following a heavy rain in winter. With a sharp drop in temperature, the road might become glazed with two inches of slippery ice. One of the sled's runners may have broken through the ice at the roadside and become mired in the black muck of the stagnant swamp. Such an accident brought the peavey into play. The logs were rolled onto the ice. The sled was pulled back into the road and the logs reloaded. On our dirt roads in the country, traffic moved too slowly for accidents, and horses had too much sense ever to collide. Of course, there were those once in a lifetime things like the time Scott Davis came home drunk from Bath and drove his horse straight ahead at Jellerson's Corner instead of turning up the road towards his house. The obedient horse walked unhesitatingly into the river at the Town Landing near Amasa's mill.

The only vehicular accident I witnessed as a boy occurred on Main Street in the center of Bowdoinham Village. Bill Raymond and I were on our way home from high school. We were on the sidewalk in front of Cornish's store when we heard the clatter of horse's hooves coming nearer fast and the shouts of "Whoa! Whoa!" behind us. We had scarcely turned to look when two heavy sorrel horses hauling a high load of lumber on wheels streaked past down the hill. The hatless driver was standing on top of the load yelling to the horses and yanking frantically on the reins. A hundred yards ahead, the street crossed the railroad. Twenty yards beyond the tracks was the Cathance River. A half block beyond Cornish's store, another street intersected, at which point the load of lumber ordinarily would turn right on the way to the loading ramp at the railroad station. At this point, the driver abandoned hope of halting the runaway load. The breeching strap had broken at the top of the hill and the rough ends of the heavy green lumber were prodding the horses into a mad dash forward. The animals had no intention of slowing down, to say nothing of stopping. Even before he passed me, the driver must have been weighing his chances of meeting with serious injury or even death if he stuck with the barrelling load. If the team kept straight, he might crash into a passing train, or, if the tracks were clear, plunge into the river. Should the stampeding horses try to make the usual right turn at the first intersection, they would never make it. They would surely crash into the post office building at the corner. Immediately after passing Bill and me, the driver dropped the reins, jumped from the load, and landed inside the sidewalk on a grassy area near the town's Civil War cannon. He picked himself up at once and limped towards his team. The horses started to make their right turn, but sensing that they might crash into the single-story post office, they veered back into Main Street. The horses missed the post office but the load smashed into the corner of the building. The two terrified animals stood wild-eyed on the town scales in front of the damaged weigher's office. The town's barber shop was in the far corner of the building only a few feet beyond the scales. Charles McEwen, the barber, came out of his shop at once, dressed in his white coat and with a straight razor held high in his right hand, to see what had caused the terrific jolt that nearly shook his customer from the chair. McEwen faced two trembling but uninjured horses that were only a few feet from his door.

Although the trains were not quite as fast around 1910 as they are today, I remember three railroad accidents within sight of our house. The biggest one was a pile-up of fourteen freight cars in the shallow cut near the south end of the dike on Cromwell's meadow. It happened before breakfast one morning, while Pa was in the vegetable garden west of our house. Pa called to us in the house to come and see the wreck. "There was a crackling noise while the train was crossing Cromwell's dike," he said. "When I looked up, there was a cloud of dust above the cut in Fred Beals' field. A number of freight cars and the caboose were standing stock still on the dike. I could hear the engine and the front part of the train still going down the tracks behind Amasa's woods." When we reached the west field, the engine had continued on to the Village to report the accident. Later that forenoon, after wrecking crews arrived, a northbound passenger train arrived and the passengers walked past the wreck to board another train that had backed down from Gardiner. Later trains between Portland and Waterville were rerouted via Lewiston. As soon as the work of clearing the wreckage was underway, I waded barefoot past the muskrat house in Beal's swamp and watched the operation from the side of the railroad cut. I was curious about the contents of the wrecked cars; most of them were loaded with lumber. At dinner that noon, Genevieve asked Vining, "Why don't you go over to the wreck and see if you can get a job helping to clear it up?" "Yeah, I'd probably be working under some big burly Irish boss," Vining replied. It took the crews with their derricks until the next afternoon to clear the road, repair the tracks, and have normal traffic restored. We heard later that a broken axle had triggered the wreck.

A less serious accident happened on a cold morning a few days after Christmas. A single freight car, loaded with Aroostook potatoes on the way to Boston, broke loose from a long train as it was crossing the dike on Hall's meadow only a few yards west of the big railroad bridge. We noticed the unusual performance of the train just before we sat down to breakfast. From our north window, we saw a number of stalled cars on the dike, and the engine with several cars coupled to it was stopped on Cromwell's meadow. After breakfast, Pa, Al, Vining and I walked up the river on the ice to see what had happened. A Bangor and Aroostook freight car was lying on its side on the frozen slough at the foot of the dike. The car had broken apart in a couple of places and solidly frozen potatoes were scattered over the ice. Although each carload of potatoes had its own stove to keep the tubers from freezing in transit, there was no fire started when the car crashed at the foot of the ten-foot embankment. We were told that there was a man on the train who kept the fires going in several of the cars. Fortunately he was in one of the other cars when that one left the tracks. We filled our pockets with frozen potatoes to take home. They became somewhat soft when thawed. The ones we cooked were too sweet to enjoy. We fed them to the pigs. All along the shore of the river, the following spring and summer, we saw empty inflated potato skins floating at high tide.

The *Flying Yankee*, a fast express, sped past our farm around five every afternoon. Between Gardiner and Brunswick, it ran non-stop. Only once did we see the long passenger train, with its mail and baggage cars, sleepers and coaches and dining cars, motionless on the tracks. One day we were amazed to hear it come to a sudden stop only seconds after the powerful locomotive had crossed the dike on Cromwell's meadow. Our neighbor, Francis Hutchins, was talking with Pa in our dooryard when we heard a blast of the locomotive's whistle, seconds before grinding brakes brought the train to an abrupt halt. The three of us hurried into the driveway to get a better view of the train. The engine was hidden behind our pasture woods. The line of dusky cars stretched up the tracks across the swamp all the way to Old Santy's woods. We saw a white-jacketed porter appear in one of the car's doors. Someone in a dark uniform and vizored cap walked alongside of the train and disappeared into the cut. We watched for several minutes. There was a sharp report that sounded like a gun. "What was that?" Pa asked. Francis was a short stocky man, with an expressionless face. You sometimes wondered if he ever had a thought. But he came up with a likely suggestion. "Do you suppose they could have struck some animal on the tracks? That's what it must be. They shot it to put it out of its misery," Francis replied. Pa was skeptical and said, "But they wouldn't have any gun." "Oh yes they would," Francis said. "They carry shooting irons on those trains." Curiosity got the best of me that evening. Towards dusk I walked out to the railroad and up the tracks. There was a red and white heifer lying on the sloping wall of the cut. One of her hind legs had a compound fracture. The next evening there was a mound of fresh earth at that spot, where the section crew had buried the victim of the fast express. So Francis was right. The train had hit one of George Hackett's heifers that had found a hole in the fence along the right of way and had wandered onto the tracks. Francis told us later that the railroad had reimbursed George because it was Maine Central's fence where the animal left the pasture.

Chapter Forty

Herding and Fencing

"Don't Fence Me In" would have been an unpopular song in our neighborhood when I was a boy. Being a good neighbor depended to a large degree on whether or not the farmer kept his livestock within bounds. Allowing a horse, cow or pig to wander onto neighboring property was a serious breach of farmer's etiquette, and the owner of the vagrant animal was looked upon with disfavor. "Why don't they keep their pigs at home?" Pa complained when Sherman Denham's hungry brood sow came down to our orchard and ate all the fallen apples she could find. Such an attitude demanded adequate fencing almost everywhere – not just any old fence but good ones, capable of restraining all sorts of domestic creatures. When Mother was a girl, she said they had many stump fences. Pine and cedar stumps were used a lot. Sometime within a few years after a tree was cut, the stump with the larger roots still attached was partially dug up by hand, then pulled free by oxen. To make a fence, the disks of roots were placed on edge, close together in line, as one might arrange a lot of old wagon wheels to protect a garden plot. Before I can remember, most of the old stump fences on nearby farms had been burned as firewood and replaced by barbed wire or woven wire fences. There were a few short sections of the durable stump fences still remaining, however, here and there when I was a boy. One such section was the only barrier along the farm line between Uncle Ed's and Scott Davis' pastures. It was a formidable structure even for a person to get over and I used to walk past it to a section of new mesh wire that was easier to cross.

Between our farm and the Cromwell's, in the wooded area Up-under-the-Hill, there had never been a fence – only a low stone wall that livestock could easily step over. When Sherman Denham and Abby were living there, he used to turn their dappled gray horse loose to graze in their hayfield. Often the long-legged beast came into our barn and had to be driven back home. Al told me about the cow that Liza Cromwell and her son, Oliver, kept some years after Jere died. The cow had the habit of visiting our farm and Pa once found her among the vegetables. Jokingly, he told Oliver that he'd have to shoot the cow if she came down to our place again. On a cloudy day a while later, a skunk showed up in our field in the daytime. Pa dispatched the skunk with his 10-gauge shotgun that made a boom like a cannon. Elderly Liza heard the shot. Minutes later Liza appeared on the east side of the hill, raising her arms and shouting, "He's shot the cow! He's shot the cow!"

Amasa Williams pastured his sheep in both the river pasture and in the one west of the road when he went to Boothbay Harbor for the summer. He had an arrangement with Ira Allen to keep an eye on the flocks while he was away. But Ira lived over a mile away and was seldom around when any of the sheep got out. On several occasions one or two sheep wandered onto our farm. There was a bit of excitement in it for us when it came to catching the stray sheep and lifting them over the fence into their pasture. Pa claimed he detested sheep and vowed he'd never have one on his place. He complained a lot whenever one of Amasa's sheep got through the fence, but he never said anything about it to Amasa upon his return in the fall. Since Amasa never raised any fuss when our hens crawled through the big meshes of his sheep fencing and foraged in his field, Pa probably felt that he should overlook occasional trespassing by a sheep. We objected most to the sheep because it seemed as if there were always two or three dead ones every summer, and our dog Snipe could not resist the temptation to lie down and roll on the over-ripe remains. We never could figure out why dogs take such delight in getting so smelled-up. We took Snipe to the river and forced him to swim for awhile.

On the whole, we had much more trouble with our own livestock getting loose than we had from visitations by neighbors' animals. One summer morning at breakfast I listened to Pa, Al and Vining tell about rounding up our young cattle that had got out of the river pasture and come up to the house. Snipe's barking sometime around midnight awoke Pa who heard the cattle rummaging around in the dooryard. They were in the backyard when the men got downstairs. Al ran into our wire clothesline that caught him below the chin. Finally they were able to drive the five heifers and young bull back to the pasture. They found two of the four poles in the barway were dropped at one end allowing the cattle to crawl between the top and bottom bars. Pa explained how cattle "always like to rub their necks on everything they come to. They stick their heads through a barway and rub until one end of a sliding pole drops. Then they start rubbing on the next one. With a couple of bars down, they can crawl through." As I listened to the talk about the excitement of the previous night, I had the feeling I'd been overlooked, since no one had awakened me to help in the roundup.

More excitement, accompanied by real fright, was in store for us later that summer when our three year old Jersey bull shook loose his heavy stanchion chain and, the first we knew, was cavorting in our front yard. Pa and Al, at the time, were shingling Uncle Ed's stable. Teenage Vining was at home. Since we had heard that bulls are afraid of pitchforks, he boldly got one from the barn and tried to shoo the anticking bull back into the tie-up. The bull had no intention of being driven anywhere. Mother sensed the danger of the situation and told Vining to get Pa and Al. Vining slid the pitchfork onto the porch and, with rapid strides, took off across Amasa's field. That was before there was a line fence in front of the house. With the open field in front of him and with somebody running across it, it was a wonder that the bull didn't take after Vining. But the animal was too busy goring the earth. Those of us in the house watched half-coweringly as the bull ran back and forth in the dooryard, stopping now and then to drop to his knees and, with outstretched tail, dig up the turf with his stout horns. It was the first time since the previous November that he had been outdoors. Apparently the fresh air plus discovery that he was no longer tied to a stanchion made him frisky. When the menfolk arrived, he was goring the trunk of the apple tree at the corner of the barn. He had hooked deep grooves in the young tree's smooth bark. Armed with an oak club, a baseball bat and a pitchfork respectively, Pa, Al and Vining were able to jockey the bull back into the barn and into his stanchion. After that day, Pa kept the toggle that passed through the ring of the heavy bull chain tied in place with a piece of rope yarn. After supper that evening, I helped Pa smear green cow manure on the injured apple tree and we wrapped the treated trunk with strips of burlap to keep the exposed wood from drying out and encourage healing. "We'll have to sell that old bull as soon as the young one gets a little bigger," Pa said. "He's been getting a little difficult to handle lately. I don't trust him anymore."

There were occasions when our ordinary four-foot fence seemed inadequate to contain an animal that had its heart set on getting to the other side. Livestock such as cattle, for instance, which are gregarious creatures, tend to become frantic when alone, as in the case of an individual becoming separated from the herd. It takes a high fence, and a strong one, to keep an isolated animal from joining his mates. This behavior was clearly demonstrated to us one summer by an eighteen-month old Guernsey bull that Pa decided to turn out to pasture with the milking herd during the day. The first time out, he followed the cows down the driveway and the pasture lane with no trouble whatsoever. He grazed peacefully with the cows during the day. In bringing the cows in that evening, all went well until the dooryard was reached. The trouble may have been partially triggered by the presence of the fish peddler with his smelly horse and wagon outfit in front of the house as the herd filed up the driveway. The cows walked calmly past the peddler and entered the tie-up door as usual. The young bull, however, bringing up the rear, hesitated in the middle of the dooryard and refused to approach the barn. "You keep him here," Pa told me, "until I can get the cows tied up. We'll see if we can drive him in then." One of my sisters came out to help. She stood in the driveway with the broom. Mr. Catlin, the fish peddler, aware of our problem, also came to our assistance. He stood weaponless in the narrow field between the driveway and our south line fence beside the foot-deep cellar drain. Catlin was a tall man, slow-moving, with a roundish head that seemed to set squarely and directly on his broad shoulders. He had never lived on a farm and, like many non-farmers, was deathly afraid of a bull. When Pa and I tried to get the animal to enter the barn, the bull turned and dashed past us and started back to the pasture. At the sight of Minerva and the waving broom, he left the driveway and cut across the field, towards the pasture lane. He was headed straight for Mr. Catlin who waved his outstretched arms to stop the beast. The bull acted as if he saw no one at all and held his unswerving course to the pasture. Catlin jumped deftly across the ditch as the bull rushed past. The bull never stopped running all the way down the lane and back into the west pasture. "Put up the bars and let him stay there tonight," Pa said. "We'll get him when the cows come in tomorrow."

Next day, we looked for the bull among the cows. At noon the herd was lying in the sun on the hillside but there was no bull in sight. "He may be hiding in the woods out by the railroad," Pa suggested. "If he doesn't show up by milking time, we'll take a look out there to find him." It was mid-afternoon when Helen Denham phoned saying that our bull was in their pasture and that her father would bring him in with the cows at milking time. Along towards five o'clock, we hitched the horse to the baggage wagon and went town to Uncle Ed's. At first, it looked like a repeat performance of the day before. The bull followed Uncle Ed's cows until they entered the barnyard but he refused to go through the gate. "He's an ornery cuss, ain't he, Jim? You wait there a minute," Uncle Ed said. "Soon's I get the cows fastened, I'll lead one of them out here. Maybe he'll follow her into the barn." The plan worked nicely and the bull followed a short distance behind the cow through the big doorway. One of the sliding doors was open and Pa positioned himself so that he could push it shut. As soon as the bull's hindquarters were inside the barn, Pa started to close the door. Sensing that the door was closing behind him, the young bull spun around with the agility of a kitten and caught the door with one of his horns just as it was within two feet of closing. Pa had given the rolling heavy door plenty of momentum and it closed with a thud. We had the bull trapped in the barn floor. I walked behind as we led the animal back home, hitched to the back of the wagon. As far as I know that was the last time we let the bull outdoors, for the following year or two that we kept him. It was a puzzle to us how the young bull got through, over, or under the three fences between our pasture and Uncle Ed's. We walked the entire length of our south line looking for some place he might have broken through Amasa's fence without finding any point of exit from our pasture. The fretfulness of the bull, upon finding himself isolated in the approaching darkness, plus the fact that he may have sensed the presence of three non-milking heifers that Uncle Ed allowed to stay out overnight, may have given him the urge to jump three fences that separated him from others of his kind.

We often noticed the most flagrant disregard of fences shown by a mature heifer, and occasionally an older individual, when they came into heat in a pasture where no bull was kept. Females in this condition often showed unbridled determination to escape from their enclosure to join some other herd, possibly a half mile away. "Once in a while, you'll find a cow that all hell can't keep in a pasture when she comes into heat," Uncle Ed said when one of his unbred heifers showed up in the field behind our barn one day. Our bull was tied up in the barn and his bellowing may have had something to do with the cow's coming to our place. We not only had difficulties with cattle during their estrus periods, but once we had a female pig that rooted her way out of her portable pen and reached the river before we knew she had escaped. It was a pleasant Sunday afternoon in late summer. Uncle Al Hillman had walked over from the Village that morning to have dinner with us. After dinner the menfolk sat talking back of the stable. Uncle Al and Pa puffed leisurely on their pipes. The tide was high so that one could see the water at several places on the river. Uncle Al sat on the chopping block, facing the Shore. His eyesight must have been good for a man of seventy. In the midst of the conversation, he took his pipe from his mouth and stared at the river. "What's that white object in the water down there?" he asked. We all looked in the same direction. Sure enough there was something swimming towards the sandbank. The river's surface was perfectly smooth and, in addition to the ripples the animal was making, Al thought he saw an ear projecting above the water. "Looks like a hog, don't it?" Pa asked. "Couldn't be ours, she's down in the orchard in the pen. Take a look, Bert, and see if she's still there." The pen was empty! Before I could return to the house, all hands had started towards the Shore. Uncle Al and I stayed behind to keep an eye on the pig from the hilltop near the pasture bars while Pa, Al and Vining went for the boat. We watched the animal approach the sandbank as if she intended to go ashore there. Apparently the bank was too steep and brushy at that point so the pig returned to the middle of the river and continued downstream. Our skiff soon appeared, moving fast, with Vining at the oars and Pa paddling vigorously. They overtook the shoat near the Old Pine and guided her towards our meadow. Vining removed his shoes and stockings, rolled up his pant legs, and drove the pig across wet marshland to the lower end of our field where we kept her surrounded until Pa and Al joined us after returning the boat to our landing. Pigs are stubborn things to drive when loose in the open, but there were enough of us to drive the young sow back to the orchard and into her propped-up pen. Pa drove a temporary stake on both sides of the pigpen and nailed the lower boards to them, to prevent the pig from lifting the pen with her snout. We would not have had this trouble with a female pig if Pa had continued his former practice of buying male piglets to raise for meat. No one had an explanation as to why our pig took to the river. Perhaps she thought there might be wild razorbacks in the woods beyond. Or perhaps she heard someone's pig beyond the woods on one of the farms along the Kennebec. I became worried when we saw the pig in the river because Mother had told us that it was fatal for a pig to try to swim. "Their sharp front hooves cut their own throat as a hog paws the water," she said. Ours, however, showed no injury from her half hour swim in the Abbagadasset.

Our problems with livestock on the loose were not always a matter of pigs or cattle. Dandy, the old gray horse, was most difficult to catch when he occasionally escaped from his stall in the barn. The stall was too narrow to allow him to turn around and we never kept him tied with a halter. All that kept him from backing out of the stall was a piece of stout rope hooked across the open end of the stall four feet above the floor. Dandy actually sat on the rope sometimes when he dozed on three feet in relaxation with a haunch propped against the boarding. We never were concerned about him in this position for the rope always held and he never did a backwards somersault over it. It was a different matter, however, when somebody failed to hook the rope, or, perhaps in fly time, the horse might unfasten the hook by a violent switching of the tail. When he discovered himself loose and prancing around in the dooryard or field, Dandy was no tired old nag. He held both his head and tail high like a thoroughbred as he cut capers in the open. When we tried to approach him with a halter while he was nibbling grass, he paid no attention to us until we got within a few feet of his neck. Then, knowing full well what the rope was for, he frisked away emitting a loud pop at every jump. Having moved a safe distance away from us, he resumed his feeding. Our last resort, and the technique that usually worked, was to approach him with his grain box containing some cracked corn and oats. Once we got the horse to take a mouthful of the grain, he willingly followed us as we carried the box back to the stall.

While hunting woodchucks in our east field one spring afternoon, I was surprised to flush a young calf from the bushes along our south line. The veal-aged animal managed to scramble over Amasa's woven-wire fence that had not yet been straightened up after slanting with the weight of a recent snowdrift. The calf took off across Amasa's lower field. I returned to the house immediately. Pa called Uncle Ed to see if he knew who the owner of the calf might be. "Foss Pratt had a calf get away the day before yesterday. It's probably his. I'll call him about it," Uncle Ed told Pa. Foss lived next to George Hackett on the other road. How the calf managed to cross the railroad and Cromwell's meadow to reach our field no one will ever know.

Foss soon arrived at our house with horse and wagon. He brought Sherman Denham with him to help catch the calf. Uncle Ed came up also and the five of us soon flushed the calf again from a patch of the bushes at the end of the hayfield. This time, it headed up Amasa's sloping field towards our road. Barefoot, I gave chase to the bull calf, while the others came along at a fast walk. Before it reached the road, the calf turned south, running between Amasa's house and the road. By this time it had slowed considerably and I was following not far behind. Uncle John Williams had converted a low spot in his field into a cranberry patch. The calf headed straight for this. Here, I thought, might be a good chance to catch it when it slowed down a bit in the muddy footing. I got close enough to grab the fleeting calf's tail, but it slipped through my hand without appreciably slowing the young animal. A few bounds and it regained its speed on dry land beyond the bog. Within minutes, we had the calf cornered against a fence on Uncle John's Island. As the pursuers closed in, the frightened animal dashed straight towards Sherman, who may have appeared to the calf to be the person least able to move fast. Sherman lunged for the calf, bowled it over and pinned it to the ground. "I've got 'im, Foss," Sherman said. After tying the calf's feet and placing it in the wagon, Foss said, "I was going to alter him into a steer and raise him for beef. I dunno now, all this chasing may make him too wild to keep." "Oh, he'll be all right, Foss," Uncle Ed replied. "Keep him hitched for a while and feed him well. When you castrate him, that'll help to take any of the wildness that he has out of him, too."

Fences are not the only barriers that cattle sometimes cross when they want better grazing or companionship of other cattle. After Amasa sold his sheep, he rented his river pasture to Uncle Ed, who pastured several dairy heifers there. During the winter, Uncle Ed noticed that one of his best yearling heifers was pregnant and would probably have a calf by turnout time. He was greatly puzzled and no less provoked. He didn't like to have his heifers start milking before they were two years old. There seemed to be no explanation since the only bull we had that year was in the barn all summer and no one else on the road had one. It was some time after Christmas before Uncle Ed learned the truth. He was talking with Sam Raymond at the sawmill. "One day the last of August I was putting out some early eel pots up by Preble's Creek," Sam told Uncle Ed. "It was low tide and I saw that Holstein bull of Preble's swim back across the river from Amasa's meadow to Harvey's shore. He walked across the mud flats and joined Harvey's cows at the edge of the woods just below the creek." "By God, that explains it!" Uncle Ed replied with an air of consternation. "I wish Harvey'd build a fence along the river and keep his damn bull at home." Uncle Ed had not reached the height of indignation, however. A few weeks later, Harvey Preble got wind of the fact that his bull had sired a calf for Uncle Ed. He called at Uncle Ed's one day and tried to get him to pay the customary fifty-cent breeding fee. Uncle Ed was always an excitable loud-spoken man, over six feet tall in his rubber boots. "I'll never pay you a damned cent," he told Harvey, throwing up his arms and stomping the stable floor. "That heifer was too young to be bred anyway. And what's more I didn't want her bred to any cussed Holstein. They throw too big calves and that young heifer'll probably have trouble calving!" The next time Pa talked with Harvey at the Village, he learned of Harvey's failure to collect the fee. Harvey complained, "It's getting so nowadays a man can't collect an honest debt anymore."

It always seemed as if Harvey Preble had difficulty every day rounding up his cattle for the evening milking. We used to see his herd grazing along the river on warm summer afternoons. There they were, a long ways from Harvey's barn, having travelled a couple hundred yards through dark spruce woods. When it came time for Harvey to drive the cows home, they were often scattered along the riverbank or lying down in the shady woods. We could hear Harvey's shouts echoing beneath the canopy of trees, loud and clear, all the way from beyond the river and across Amasa's fields to our house. One Sunday afternoon, while Harvey was busily calling his cattle, Genevieve and I participated in a bit of amusement that I'm sure our parents would have disapproved of. We stood in the small door on the south side of the barn that opened into the barn cellar henpen and shouted repetition of Harvey's words as he called his cattle. It was a warm calm afternoon and the sound travelled back and forth with exceptional clearness. After we repeated Harvey's shouts several times, he paused for a moment and hollered, "You come over here and drive 'em yourselves!"

Although the trespassing of dogs and cats was not related to faulty fences, difficulties with pets did occur occasionally, even in our wide-open countryside. Stray dogs occasionally killed a few of Amasa's sheep. When Uncle Everett discovered that three sheep in his pasture beyond the railroad had been attacked by dogs, he immediately came up the road to see if Snipe might have been involved. Snipe was lying on the porch when he entered the dooryard. The dog started at his approach. Uncle Everett looked for tell-tale signs of wrong-doing around Snipe's mouth as the dog greeted him in the dooryard. Later, our cousin Nat told Al that he would not have let his father come to our house if he had been at home just then.

We were afraid we might have jeopardized Amasa's good will once when his cat became caught in a steel trap we had set for rats in our barn cellar. Vining saw the cat heading for home across Amasa's field, clumsily dragging the trap and chain. Pa was reading the newspaper when Vining ran to tell him. "Take a pitchfork and stick it into the ground over the cat's neck," he told Vining without lowering the paper. "That will hold him so you can take the trap off without getting scratched." I watched Vining as he followed Pa's instructions. The trap had caught only the claws on a couple of the cat's toes. He took off rapidly across the field for Amasa's barn as soon as Vining released him. He walked with no difficulty when we saw him the next day. Our neighborly relationship with Amasa was exceptionally good and we tried to keep it that way. We tried to avoid hard feelings over all such unfortunate incidents as this that might cause them.

I felt guilty once of almost causing a quarrel between two of our neighbors, the brothers Ed and Sherman Denham. In a way, the U.S. postal service was to blame. When they instituted R.F.D. in our town they placed a limit on the number of highway miles each route could cover. In order to keep our Route One within limits, they allowed our carrier to come up our road only as far as Amasa's driveway. This meant that our mailbox and Sherman Denham's had to be placed down the road a ways beside Amasa's. We often went to the mailbox to await the carrier.

One summer afternoon Alice Bates, one of the two state ward girls who lived with Sherman and Abby, and I were waiting at our mailboxes for the mailman Bob Ferguson. She told me that their big part-collie dog, Rodney, had left home again on one of his two- or three-day absences. We had already waited half an hour or so for Bob and the prolonged wait was becoming a little boring. To create some excitement, I facetiously and untruthfully told Alice that I'd heard Uncle Ed say he'd do away with Rodney if he showed up around his slaughterhouse again. Alice appeared to take no stock in what I was saying and I pursued the fabrication no further. Bob finally arrived and we walked mail in hand up the road to our respective homes. Soon after arriving with the mail, I was sent by Pa to chop alder bushes in our west pasture. As I started out our driveway, Sherman was walking rapidly down the road swinging his arms in an agitated fashion. We met at the end of the driveway. The angry look on Sherman's face frightened me somewhat. I'm sure his blood pressure was 'way up there too. There had always been a degree of animosity between Sherman and Uncle Ed. Maybe Sherman was a bit jealous of his brother because Uncle Ed, through his marriage, got a much better farm than the old Cromwell place. "Did Ed say he was going to kill my dog?" Sherman asked explosively. It had been a long time since I had felt such a cringe of guilt. Almost trembling, I assured Sherman that I was only teasing Alice and that my statement about Uncle Ed's intentions were entirely imaginary. "Well, all I can say is he'd better not! He killed my cat! I'll be damned if he's going to kill my dog!" Sherman said as his frown subsided a bit and he turned to walk back home. I could have put Sherman straight about the cat and possibly might have left Uncle Ed in somewhat better light. I knew that Sherman's black tomcat had been caught in the act of catching Uncle Everett's chickens that spring and it was he who gave the predatory feline his due. But then, had I told Sherman that, Uncle Everett could have become the target of Sherman's wrath. I felt that I'd caused enough mischief for one day, and remained quiet. However, I would have liked to vindicate Uncle Ed's gentle nature towards pets. Although he was a butcher by profession, he never mistreated a cat. Only when someone brought him a tom to be altered, being an accommodating person, did he cause the slightest pain by chucking it head first into a rubber boot and quickly performing the operation free of charge.

Chapter Forty-One

Friends

When I was a pre-schooler, there were no boys of my age in our immediate vicinity for me to play with. Rena Kimball lived next door with Amasa and Ella, but they went to Boothbay Harbor every summer. During the winter, she and I went sliding in Amasa's east field and we played around the big old willow tree half way between our homes. We were within sight of Mother and Rena's "Auntie." Sometimes, Aunt Angie Thomas and her daughter Elizabeth came down from Richmond to spend the day with Mother. Elizabeth and I were the same age. Perhaps it was just as well that there were no young boys of my age around, for I had long yellow curls that boys probably would have teased me about. One of the members of Mother's church, Mrs. Palmer, came from Gardiner and brought along her young son, Edgar, who was more than a year older than I. We played in the churchyard after the morning service while our mothers were preparing the baked bean dinner upstairs. One day, after a squabble, Edgar ran upstairs and told his mother, "She hits me. When she hits me she makes me mad." Mother scolded me and we went outdoors again to play.

At school, there were other boys to play with at recess time and during the noon hour, but none of them lived near enough for spending time with after the school day was over or on weekends. By the time I was in sixth or seventh grade, Merton Webber began visiting his Aunt Abbie Denham on the Cromwell farm and he was my most frequent playmate for several years. We went swimming and fishing after I had done the chores and could slip away from home for a while. After starting school, I seldom saw any of the neighborhood girls outside of the schoolroom. In the eighth grade, I had a crush on a new girl whose family had moved to our town from Orr's Island. Her first name was Pearl but I cannot remember her last name. She was a seventh grader and I thought she was the prettiest girl I'd ever seen. I had the thrill of my young life when I got to hold her in my lap for a minute while we were playing some sort of a game in the schoolroom during the noon hour. I was a junior in high school, however, when I had my first date. Classmate Bill Raymond and I had been close friends all four years in high school, and, since Bill, a year older than me, had no use for girls, I remained under the influence of his philosophy during the freshman and sophomore years. During my junior year, when school let out, I started walking as far as Pleasant Street with Florence Small, who was then a sophomore. Pleasant Street, where she lived, was on the east side of the Village and we both followed the same street out of town on the way home. Bill lived east of town also, but he usually went on ahead when I walked with Florence.

It was springtime before I mustered sufficient courage to ask Florence to go to a minstrel show that was being given by local talent in the Town Hall on Friday evening. She agreed and the stage was set for a memorable first date. I remember little about the minstrel but I will not forget a few minutes standing on the porch when I took Florence home. There was a bright moon and her straight dark hair looked even darker than it really was. What I do remember most was the clean odor of the soap she used. Returning home on the bicycle, the three hills that always seemed steep and required hard pedalling were no more than gentle knolls. As I approached our driveway, late season frogs sounded unusually peaceful in Amasa's pond and toads were still singing in Cromwell's meadow. A whippoorwill called from the top pole of the fence along our swamp. That bird's call never sounded so sweet to me before. Could it be the near midnight calmness of a May countryside that made things seem so different? No, it wasn't that. The straw mattress never felt as soft as a feather one before.

Florence and I had a couple of more dates that spring. One of them was the hanging of a May basket to Helen Hackett. The last one was the senior reception dance in the Town Hall on graduation night. After the dance, we strolled to the baseball field back of the high school and sat in the bleachers for a while in the moonlight. Along towards midnight we were walking through the center of the Village towards Pleasant Street when we noticed a lady coming towards us. "It's all right, Mother. We're coming," Florence told her as soon as she recognized who it was. Mrs. Small turned around and went back home. "She worries about me so much," Florence said.

Florence was away from home during the summer, at a girl scout camp somewhere north of Augusta. We corresponded at weekly intervals. In September the opening of high school coincided with the start of duck hunting. On school days I often set the alarm clock to go off before daylight and I went to the river for an hour's hunting before getting ready for school. Every Saturday I spent the forenoon hunting from our gunning float; in the Bay if it was ebb tide before daybreak or up river if the morning tide was coming in. After mid-October I had the trap line to tend, plus late season hunting. That fall, I talked with Florence frequently at school, but there seemed to be little time for dates. Even on the day the armistice was signed and I went to school only to find it closed for the day, I did not stay in town to take part in the celebration but returned home to set some more muskrat traps while the tide was low. In December I was confined to the house for two weeks with virulent Spanish influenza that was so prevalent in the fall of 1918. My folks allowed me to have no nights out for a while after that. My last date with Florence was sometime in January of my senior year. There must have been a lot of snow on the ground, for I remember walking to the Village along the road sled tracks and listening to the cold dry snow crunching at each footstep. I do not remember the occasion of the date, but it may have been some school function to raise funds for the junior class.

Later that winter someone told me that Florence was going with Arthur Carr, who lived near the Bowdoin border and was graduated two years before. I tried to make no more dates, although we were friendly and sometimes walked home together as far as Pleasant Street. It came as a distinct surprise at our graduation exercises, when Grace Brown, our donor of class gifts, presented me with a Bausch and Lomb hand lens (I still use it) which she said was "to make big things out of Small."

When Florence's graduation took place, I was at home after the first year at Bates. Bill Raymond and I went to the graduation reception in the evening. I talked briefly with Florence in the receiving line. She sent me one of her graduation pictures with a note saying her affair with Arthur began when he took her home from a school function in her junior year – one that I did not attend. They were married soon after graduation. The next time, and the last, that I saw Florence was twelve years later. The occasion was a holiday weekend when both of us had returned from out of state to visit home, she from Beverly, Massachusetts, and I from New Haven. On my way back to Connecticut I had driven into Gil Brown's garage at the edge of town to get gas for my secondhand 1930 master-six rumble-seated green and yellow Buick sport roadster that I'd bought at the bottom of the Big Depression. At the cash register in the garage, I recognized Arthur talking with Gil. We shook hands and I asked if Florence was in the car outside. She was there with her three children. Florence politely acknowledged my greeting but she seemed to have little to say. She appeared deeply occupied with her youngest child that she was holding in her lap in the back seat. After exchanging a few pleasantries we said goodbye and I drove away. That was in 1932. On another visit home in the late 1940's, Jeannette told me that Florence had died from cancer a year before.

Chapter Forty-Two

Gadgets: Camera and Flashlight

While in the sixth grade, at the age of nine, I saw an advertisement in *Hunter-Trader-Trapper* offering a free camera for selling twenty packets of gold-eyed needles at ten cents per packet. I asked Mother if I could answer the ad and try to sell the needles in our neighborhood. She did not encourage the project, saying that Pa did not like to have us selling things that way. I must have persisted until I got her consent, for I sent for the needles which arrived in midwinter. I soon learned that a salesman's task is not an easy one. Most of our closest neighbors bought a packet, usually, I felt, because they were family friends and wanted to help me out, rather than because they needed the needles. On the way to school one morning I called at Scott Davis' house to make a sale. It was the only time I had been inside their home. Scott was not around, but his maiden daughter, Ina, graciously bought a packet of needles. "What do you get for selling them?" she asked. "I'm getting a camera," I replied. The farther away from home I got, the harder it was to make a sale. One Saturday morning I rode to the Village with Pa. He dropped me off at the corner near the top of Clay Hill and I was successful in selling two or three packets to Mother's church sisters who lived on the other road. Returning to Clay Hill on foot, I called at the Staples' residence where Pa had delivered the weekly pound of butter a half hour earlier. Mrs. Staples, the cobbler's wife, was sitting near her front window sewing when I called. She showed me the many needles she had in her sewing basket and said she had no need for any more. One cold wintry day in early February, I tried to sell some after school. When school let out, I decided to contact the homes down the road from the schoolhouse, towards Center's Point. It was a blustery day with blowing snow. Walking was so difficult that Lois drove to the Village with horse and pung to bring Genevieve and Jeannette home from high school. They stopped at the Jellerson School to pick me up on their way home. Only the teacher was at the school and she told them I had gone down the road to sell my needles. They found me as I was leaving the Welch's residence about half a mile below the school. "You shouldn't strike out selling needles in weather like this," they told me. But I justified the difficult walk to them. "I've made two sales," I told them. "One at Jim Allen's and the other to Mina Welch."

The small camera that I received was an extremely simple device. It was a black box a little over two inches square and about four inches long. It came apart in the middle, the rear half telescoping over the front part. A small lens about a quarter of an inch in diameter was installed in a hole in the front end. A thin metal tab protruded above the lens. When one pushed the tab with the finger, it acted as a shutter. Length of exposure was regulated by the speed with which one moved the tab. For time exposure, one held the tab in "open" position for the desired length of time. To load the camera, one dropped a plate into the back half of the box, the front half of the camera was then pushed against the plate to hold it in place. A few two-by-two sensitized glass plates came with the camera, along with some photographic chemicals and sheets of blue paper for making prints. I exposed all of the plates and got fairly good negatives but the printing was not successful. Prints were made by placing the negative plate over a piece of the blue-print paper in direct sunlight on our porch. In this step we ran into difficulty and for some reason failed to get any clear prints. None of them were good enough to keep. I never bought additional plates for the camera.

A few years later, I obtained a Kodak camera as a premium for metal tags saved on the square plugs of Everyday Smoke tobacco that Pa bought for chewing. It was also a box camera that used a 2¼ by 3¼ inch film pack. Al's wife Martha had taken a lot of pictures as a girl and she taught me to develop the film and do my own printing. For a darkroom, we lowered all of the shades in the kitchen after nightfall. The film was developed in the kitchen sink. For a safe light, I cut a hole in a wooden box and pasted a piece of red paper over the opening. A candle inside the box provided sufficient light for processing the film and for loading the printing frame with photographic paper. Exposure of the sensitized paper was made by holding the printing frame a few inches from our kerosene lamp. I took many pictures with this Kodak and still have a lot of them in good condition.

Another cherished item obtained with Pa's tobacco tags was a flashlight. It held a pair of size D batteries, had a thick convex lens, and operated by pressing a flat spring at the back end against the screw-on metal cap. I remember how thrilled I was the first night after it came in the mail. As soon as it was dark enough to use it, I took the flashlight into the field west of the house. Its instantaneous beam reached all the way to the woods Up-under-the-Hill. I was able to study closely a glow-worm that I found in the hayfield stubble. The flashlight was kept under my pillow for weeks. It was the most useful thing for locating the makers of amphibian noises in the springtime swamps. Pa called it "the buglight" and often used it to locate things in places where the kerosene lantern would be awkward and unsafe. When Jeannette told Al that I took the flashlight with me to a revival meeting at the schoolhouse one evening, he facetiously accused me of shining it on Jim Allen's bald head as he knelt in prayer, asking, "Oh, God, let there be light." The flashlight was a durable one; it lasted until I went to college. Finally its case became rusted through in spots and the holes were wrapped with friction tape.

Chapter Forty-Three

Dogs, Cats and other Pets

Pa told us about a dog he had during the early years on the farm. I do not know much about it except that it was black, but nonetheless it must have been a big help in driving cattle. At that time, Pa was raising more young cattle than he had pasture for. Also, most of the non-cultivated land on neighboring property was not fenced, so there was no pastureland nearby for him to rent. The nearest available pasture was eight miles straight up on our road in a section of Richmond called Goshen. With the help of his dog, Pa drove eight or ten head of heifers and young steers the entire distance in the pre-dawn darkness and returned home in time for breakfast. It must have been a difficult task to keep the several young cattle moving along an unfenced road in the dark. Although Pa's dog helped drive the cattle to pasture, some other dogs did him no favor by harassing the cattle during the summer. When it was time to bring them home in the fall, one of the heifers was so wild that they had to leave her in the wooded and brush-covered pasture until winter. Some weeks after the first snowfall, a trap pen was built, baited with hay and the animal was captured. Although in excellent condition, thanks to her ability to browse, the heifer never recovered from her dog-provoked wildness and they had to sell her for beef.

Mother told me about old Tom, a dog they had when Vining was a boy. One hot summer day, the dog bit Vining who had stepped over him as he lay in the kitchen door. Our parents feared that the incident might lead to worsening relations between Vining and the dog, so old Tom was summarily destroyed. "We decided then to have no more dogs," Mother said. They had none until December of 1907, when Al brought an English setter puppy with him from Greenville, when he came home for Christmas vacation. We all remembered the existing rule about no more dogs in the family, but anything that Al did was looked upon with favor and so we did have a dog. The puppy, which Al had already named Snipe, was homesick right away. Soon after dark on one of the first days we had him, he disappeared. Al came in from the woods a short time later and was able to follow the dog's tracks in the snow. He tracked the puppy up the road towards Harward's Depot where they had left the train the day before. When he reached Pratt's Crossing, half a mile from our farm, Al heard a low growl from the ditch beside the road. It was Snipe cowering in the snow. Apparently he was trying to trace his way back to his litter mates in Greenville. We were careful to keep him confined around the house for a few days. He didn't attempt to leave again. After he became a few years of age, Snipe left home for a day once in a while but always returned. The year Vining was at home, when the river ice was breaking up, in late March of 1914, Snipe was gone for two days. Towards evening of the second day, Vining was at the Shore when he saw Snipe across the river whining to come home. The ice was moving in the channel and he didn't dare to try to come across the floating cakes. Vining walked up the river, crossed the railroad bridge, and went down through the woods on the other side to where Snipe was waiting. He followed Vining home. "He must have followed another dog over one of the bridges," Vining said, "and didn't know how to get back."

Snipe was a close companion all the years I was growing up. Al always considered him to be his dog, but I spent much more time with him than did anyone else in the family. His help in flushing game birds, finding wounded ones, and in retrieving was invaluable. Snipe also kept woodchucks under control around our farm and he caught many field mice every summer. He was always at hand when the last forkful of hay from every field stack was lifted onto the wagon; the mice took refuge beneath the stacks at haying time. When I returned home after the first two weeks at Bates, Snipe had passed away.

Along with the dog we always had a cat on the farm. We never considered either the dog or cat strictly as a pet. At the best, they were regarded as utilitarian pets that at least partially paid for their keep. Some of our neighbors kept two or more cats – one that spent most of its time in the kitchen, who was the housecat. Those that roamed outdoors were "barn cats." Because of the quantity of food they ate we considered it uneconomical to have more than one. He was a tom that spent a lot of time during the day under the cookstove. For a few daylight hours and at night he hunted mice and rats in the barn and stable, and birds whenever he found them. At milking time, morning and night, he showed up for two or three helpings of warm milk straight from the cow. During the winter, whenever we saw a rat had eaten into a pumpkin or some apples for the seeds, we put the cat down cellar for a few successive nights until the trouble stopped. When an unopened bag of grain was eaten into by a rat, we shut the cat at night in the alleyway where we kept the feeds. On those nights, we had to cover the grain barrels with boards to prevent the cat from using them as litter boxes. Our Johnny bread was made from the same cornmeal that we fed to the pigs and cows. Pa and I were greatly surprised one winter evening when our cat caught a big rat on the walk behind the cows. It all happened quickly while I was holding the lantern for Pa as he spread fresh sawdust for the night's bedding. "That's a smart cat," Pa said. "Caught that rat while we were working right here. The rat couldn't have gotten more than a foot from his hole, back there against the boarding."

In dealing with cats around the house, Mother was quick to hear the first muffled cough coming from beneath the stove. Grabbing the broom, she flung the kitchen door open and shooed the cat into the woodshed before he had time to regurgitate anything on the floor. "Scat! Out of here! Quick!" she shouted as she pushed the broom under the oven hearth.

Although we lived over two miles from town, on a seldom-travelled dirt road, we had the problem even then of people from town slyly leaving unwanted cats at our farm, assuming, no doubt, that people living in the country would welcome an extra cat or two. Such "gifts" aroused no little resentment. Our dog and cat were fully capable of consuming all of our table leftovers and as much milk as we could spare. If there was any discarded food the pets didn't want, there were flocks of chickens and a pig or two anxious to devour them. We couldn't afford to feed any donated felines. I remember two instances when such abandoned animals had to be disposed of. Once a female cat and a sub-adult kitten appeared out of nowhere. Their presence called for donating more milk at milking time and providing them with solid food besides. When both cats were in front of the barn one evening before dark, Pa told Al that this was a good time to get rid of them. Al reached for the shotgun, which was always available, in the till by the stable door. I watched as they buried the cats in the henyard between the barn and the big hen-pen. Another time, a pregnant cat suddenly made her home with us one summer. Before anything was done with the intruder, she gave birth to a batch of kittens in the stable chamber's eaves. Before the kittens were a week old, Genevieve and Jeannette were assigned the task of disposing of both the cat and her kittens.

The customary method of disposal was by drowning in the river. I tagged along as my sisters carried the doomed ones to the Shore in a burlap shorts sack weighted with a used brick. The spot they chose for the ceremony was on the west side of the Point where the channels came close to the sloping ledge. As they swung the sack back and forth between them, Genevieve intoned a simple prayer and, with the last word, the sack sailed to the middle of the stream. A lot of bubbles arose after the burlap bag sank beneath the surface. A few of the bubbles persisted long enough to float downstream a short distance with the tide.

We were always dismayed at our cats' bird catching habits. One black tom we had was a common offender in this respect. The barn swallows dive-bombed him on his way between the house and barn. He was much annoyed, as he crouched low and lashed his tail from side to side. He often jumped high into the air after the pestering birds. Only once did I see him catch one in mid-air. One summer night, Genevieve was awakened near midnight as she slept on the porch by the cries of a robin that had a nest in our elm tree. By the time Pa got down-stairs, the cat was making off with the mother bird and a partially fledged young robin was sitting near the base of the tree. The nest was empty. We placed the young robin in a bird cage on a chair on the woodshed walk. It ate earthworms the next day. By late afternoon, the cat apparently became hungry again. As we were eating supper, there was a rattling commotion in the shed. We rushed to see what was going on – the bird cage was knocked off the chair, its door was open and the cat had disappeared beneath the walk with the fledgling bird.

Pets of a different sort were enjoyed by Vining as a teenager. He spent hours at a time feeding live flies to spiders that spun their webs in the upper cor-ners of the square windows along the tie-up walk. If Vining was not around at dinnertime, we knew right where to look for him; someone was sent to the barn to tell him things were on the table. Vining never talked very much about his spi-ders, although he did say that he could maneuver them into fencing duels. During the summer, many large horse flies entered the barn and ended up on the tie-up windows. Vining held them buzzing in the predator's web until they were firmly enmeshed by the hungry spider.

Somewhat envious of Genevieve with her ageless "Beauty," a short-legged Rhode Island Red hen, for a pet, I chose one of our most friendly hens for mine. She was a large single-combed hen, sort of off-white with darker markings. She had a lot of indistinctly barred feathers indicating Plymouth Rock inheritance, mottled whitish patches, and here and there, a faint brownish wash. I called her "Hawkbill." Her Plymouth Rock ancestry may have led to her being sent to market before her time. Barred Rocks were always getting too fat on the diets we fed them. One night when I was five years old, I was holding the lantern while Pa and Mother selected a dozen hens to be dressed the next day for Pa to take to Bath with his load of hay. Searching for the fattest individuals, Pa lifted Hawkbill from the roost, noted that she was unusually heavy. He handed her to Mother to get her opinion as to the hen's fitness for marketing. "That's my hen," I protested. Whereupon Pa took the fowl from Mother and examined her a second time. "She's getting too fat to keep any longer, Son," he said. "Hens as heavy as that sometimes drop dead right off the roost." Mother agreed with Pa. She told me that I could have my pick of any of our pullets for another pet. They realized the situation was a delicate one. After a moment's pause, Pa made one of his unusual offers – he would put the money he got for the hen in a savings account for me in their bank in Bath. With both parents on the other side of the fence, and with the prospect of a bank account of my own, I consented to Hawkbill's demise. Two days later, the bank made one of their infrequent mistakes in starting my account and credited me with four dollars instead of the three which the hen brought. Pa received a letter regarding the error and he gave the bank an extra dollar on his next trip to Bath.

The new pullet I selected as Hawkbill's replacement was a large double-combed dark (almost chocolate colored) Rhode Island Red. She turned out to be a layer of dark brown eggs and we raised several of her progeny. An unusual thing happened to this hen two or three years later. While Mother was feeding the flock, she noticed that kernels of corn the hen swallowed dropped to the ground. After the supper dishes were stacked in the pantry, we went to the barn to examine the hen, who had then gone to roost above the cows on a horizontal plank that held the tops of the stanchions. My parents examined the hen and discovered that there was a hole in her crop. Theories were proposed as the how the injury might have occurred, such as flying against a protruding nail upon leaving the roost or being hooked by a cow if the hen happened to land in the manger. We never were sure as to how it happened. The hen was carried to the kitchen, where Mother threaded a needle with clean white thread fresh from a spool and, while Pa held the bird back-down on the table, sewed up the hole in both crop and skin. A period of convalescence was then prescribed for the hen while her operation healed. She was placed by herself in the winter henpen in the southwest corner of the barn cellar. I was given the responsibility of caring for my hen until she could be returned to the flock. My folks told me it might be well to give the hen something soft like bread crusts soaked in milk to eat for a few days, and to keep milk or water available all of the time. They cautioned about feeding her too much hard grain that might swell and cause undue pressure where the lining was stitched together, if her crop were too full.

During those early years in school, I frequently had depressed feelings early in the day. Such attitudes were pronounced when I first awoke and sometimes persisted a few hours. I had some of those feelings after awakening one morning a few days after my hen's crop had been sutured. The intensity of my feeling was accentuated when I realized that I had forgotten to feed her the afternoon before, after returning from school. I was afraid she might have died from starvation during the night. When Mother called me for breakfast I told her, for perhaps the only time, that I did not feel well enough to go to school. Having raised several children, Mother apparently decided it was one of those circumstances that are best overlooked. I was allowed to stay in bed. Minerva was at home at the time. After a while she came upstairs, sat on the side of the bed, and asked me why I didn't want to go to school. She told me the reason why she, as a young girl, did not attend school on a couple of occasions and then said, "Now I've told you my reasons, why don't you tell me yours?" She might as well had talked to the Sphinx. After school had already been in session for a couple of hours, I went downstairs, had breakfast, and went fearfully to the barn. I looked in the outside window of the barn cellar henpen. There was the recuperating hen busily scratching in the litter, in search of grain. Sheepishly, I did a lot of extra chores around the house that day.

Chapter Forty-Four

Egg Business

The daily gathering of eggs was a task assigned to us children. It was one of our least objectionable chores, although, like the milking of cows, it had to be done every day, rain or shine. Since eggs were one of our major sources of farm income, it was a considerable responsibility for us to gather them and pack them for shipping to Boston. I remember one unfortunate occasion when I failed to bring in the eggs in good condition. It was during the early years before I had my own flock of layers Up-under-the-Hill. I had gathered the day's offering and was returning to the house for supper. I wore long overalls and was barefoot. Halfway across the field, I started to run. My big toe on one foot became caught in the opposite pant leg and I went sprawling in the path. The egg pail flew from my hand. Of the dozen or so eggs I probably had in the pail, only two or three were retrieved unbroken in the hayfield grass.

Hens do most of their laying in the forenoon, but there were always some that seemed to prefer to lay later on in the day. Consequently we waited until 'long towards suppertime before gathering up the day's production. We usually combined egg gathering with the evening feeding of the flock. Really cold days in winter presented a problem because in our cold hen houses an egg might freeze in a few hours after the hen left the nest. If an egg freezes solid, a longitudinal crack opens up the entire length of the shell; someone had to collect the eggs at mid-day. Frozen eggs could not be sold and had to be used at home. When we were at school, Mother had to see to it that no eggs got frozen. Although it was too cold for the eggs, the hens never seemed to mind the cold temperatures. "Their coats beat ours," said the cartoon in Park and Pollard Company's *Year Book and Almanac*.

Gathering of the eggs also involved removing from the nest any "setting hens" that had become broody that day and refused to leave the nest after laying the last egg of their intended clutch. These broody hens had to be "broken up" by placing them immediately in a cage especially constructed for this purpose. They were confined for three to five days until they got over their broodiness. Following their return to the laying flock, they started laying a new batch of eggs within a week or two. One September day I was gathering the eggs after getting home from school. There was a setting hen in a nest on the high scaffold in the barn. I was not big enough to carry the hen in one hand as I descended the perpendicular ladder. I secured a length of stout twine and a wooden spool. After tying one end of the string to the hen's leg and the spool to the other, I tossed the hen off the scaffold. She flew gracefully downwards to the barn floor and ran immediately to join the other hens in the dooryard. It was there that I caught up with the spool and started to reel in the squawking fluttering hen. As I reached down to grasp her, there was a great commotion and something hit be above the eyebrow. It was our ornery two year old Rhode Island Red rooster, full of fighting fury, that beat me with his wings and tried to spur me at the same time. Racing into the house, I had Mother put some benzoin on the scratch. Before the antiseptic, or the tears, were dry, I had dashed back to the stable, taken the horse whip from the wagon, and was taking after the rooster. Mother said she saw a near flash as we disappeared around the barn.

Mother insisted that we pack the eggs in a shipping case each day as soon as we had collected them, otherwise some might get broken if they were left lying around in pails or pans. Most of our cases held thirty dozen eggs. We had a couple of fifteen-dozen cases for use in the fall when production was way down and the eggs would become too old if we held them until we had enough to fill a larger case. A fifteen-dozen case had a single compartment, and the thirty-dozen cases had two, each deep enough to hold five layers of thirty-six eggs, with a half-inch layer of shock-absorbing excelsior in the bottom. Each egg was held on end in a square made by crisscrossing thin strips of cardboard so fitted together that each egg was held upright in its own little space. Each holder held six eggs to a side, and the thirty-six-egg layer was separated from the one beneath by a square flat sheet of the same thin cardboard.

We were told to make sure that every egg was perfectly clean before packing it in the case. Our parents wished to take no chances of getting a reputation of sending dirty eggs to market. Cleaning the eggs was the most unpleasant part of egg gathering. It seemed that some hens were prone to enter the nest with dirty feet, and since several hens often used the same nest, a number of eggs might be soiled by one individual. Occasionally a hen became exceedingly untidy and defecated in the nest. We had to clean all dirty eggs with a damp cloth and dry them with a towel before packing. Barnyard dirt, or even the common whitish hen manure, was easily removed from the eggs, but once in a while, an egg became partly covered with one of those odious dark brown droppings that we called "black hen manure." This kind of feces was sticky and moist, about the consistency of salad dressing. It emitted the most vile of odors. Stepping in one while barefoot was one of our occupational hazards. Although the dark substance could be entirely removed by washing, the foul odor remained.

Another equally unpleasant surface contaminant of the fresh-from-the-nest eggs was actually a result of our unwillingness to pay good money for artificial nest eggs when we had perfectly good natural ones that for some reason had failed to hatch. Some sort of nest eggs were considered essential to encourage hens to continue laying in their nest from which every newly laid egg was soon removed. If it weren't for the nest egg, hens might abandon the chosen nest and start laying in another "stolen-away" spot where we wouldn't find the eggs. The least attractive nest eggs were a couple of wooden ones that someone had whittled from soft pine, something like the wooden nutmegs of early Connecticut fame. Our best source of nest eggs was the brooding clutch; there were always a few that didn't hatch. Regardless of the reason why these didn't hatch – whether they were infertile or aborted development – they became in due time what we knew as rotten eggs. A completely rotten egg was easily identified by shaking it close to one's ear and listening for a slopping of the liquid contents. By midsummer these leftovers from spring hatching became thoroughly deteriorated within. Sometimes internal gas pressure from putrefaction caused the egg to burst spontaneously. Sometimes the careless movements of a hen shuffling around in the nest would crush the fragile shell of the overripe egg. Anyway the odor was most offensive. The decomposed egg material stuck to the new eggs like glue. We detested cleaning for market any eggs that had become spattered with the contents of a broken nest egg. Worse yet, we had a down-deep fear of what might happen if, by mistake, one of the deteriorated nest eggs got placed in the shipping crate.

After examining each egg for cracks or stains, we placed it in the marketing case. As our hens were of mixed breeds they laid eggs that varied greatly in color. We were told to save out the large brown eggs each day for filling the top layer of the packing case. This was the layer the commission merchant in Boston examined when he opened the case and decided on the price he would pay us for the lot. On the Boston market, large brown eggs always brought the highest prices.

During the summer, we maintained the freshness of the eggs by keeping them down cellar, the coolest place available, until the case was ready for market. In the fall, winter and spring, we kept them in the back dining room. On the coldest winter nights, Pa brought the partially filled case into the sitting room before going to bed, to prevent freezing. If the day was very cold when he took the eggs to the express office, he covered the case with a heavy blanket for the half-hour ride in the horse-drawn pung. For years we sold all of our eggs to Goldsmith, a commission merchant, who deducted shipping charges, and the fifteen-cent fee for return of the empty case, from our check. Some of the egg cases that Pa had made withstood many round trips to Boston over the years. One day we received a letter from Magoun Square Creamery in Medford, Mass., saying that they had been handling our eggs at retail for some time and suggested that we save the agent's commission by sending the eggs directly to them. My folks did this for a year or so, until, for some reason there was a long delay in payment by the Magoun Square Creamery and they resumed shipment to Goldsmith. A month or so later, another letter came from Magoun Square saying that they had received no eggs from us for some weeks but they had again obtained our eggs from the commission merchant. Was there some dissatisfaction? Pa asked Genevieve to write the Creamery telling them that we did not like to wait so long for payment. The matter was resolved and shipments to Magoun Square were resumed.

Chapter Forty-Five

Hazards

Our parents always cautioned us about hazardous things. We were not to play near the river, with its slippery banks and swift currents. Matches were not made for play. "Don't ever run with a pair of scissors or a glass in your hand." But there was one hazardous thing they never warned me about, probably because it never occurred to them that I would be dare-devil enough to attempt it. At the age of seven or eight, I played in the barn on days when I was not at school, especially during the winter. Punching a swinging bag of threshed bean pods, or climbing a tall ladder to the great beams and jumping into the haymow, became common-place. I looked for more exciting things to do. Mother would have been horrified had she known that I even contemplated walking the great beams that stretched across the barn floor twenty feet up. But this gave me a thrill and the feeling of self confidence, as if I'd mastered tight-rope walking. The beams were rough sawed hemlock timbers eight inches square. Pa walked across the barn on them in hay-ing time, carrying a steel "grab" with iron pulley and two dangling lines of heavy hay fall, when he changed the hay drop from one side of the barn to the other. But Pa did that only when there was a load of hay standing directly beneath the beam waiting to be unloaded. My stunts were performed with nothing but the hard barn floor two stories down. The reason for wanting to walk across on the beam was probably like that of the mountain climber scaling Mount Everest – "because it was there." I was somewhat unafraid walking the beam because I felt that I could grasp it should I lose my balance and in some way crawl to the ladder. A few such crossings were made every winter. I never mentioned the accomplishments to anyone, however, knowing full well the reprimand which would be in store in case my parents found out.

Danger lurked, also, in a game we played on floating logs at Amasa's saw-mill during the school noon hour. Every spring, following the log drives on the Kennebec, Amasa purchased a few hundred cull logs from a big mill at Gardiner. The logs were a motley collection of soft woods made up largely of short logs, crooked ones, conky pine, shaky hemlock and knotty spruce. Many of them were small in diameter, such as today would be cut into four foot lengths for pulp. The logs were cut up-country during the winter, along with better quality timber, and all were brought down stream in the big spring drives. The busy mill at Gardiner sorted out many of the cull logs, considering them uneconomical to saw, and it was glad to sell them in the water to anyone, at a bargain price. Amasa used some of the longest logs to make a boom around his raft and towed it with the *Nellie G.* down the Kennebec to Merrymeeting Bay and up the Abbagadasset channel to his mill. The raft was anchored at high tide on the flats just below the mill where the logs were available for sawing whenever convenient.

It was only a short dash from our school house along the road straight to the river's edge where the logs were kept. Towards the end of the school year in June when everyone was barefoot, we raced to the river on days when the tide was high at noon, as soon as we had finished lunch. We played Follow the Leader on the floating logs, many of which were too small to stand on but they would support our weight temporarily if we kept moving. One day while in the sixth grade I was racing across the rafted logs close on the heels of eighth-grader Forrest Douglas. He stepped on a small log that sank out of sight beneath his weight, a foot or two beneath the water. My body's momentum demanded that I take the next step even before the log resurfaced. I misjudged its exact position and went down feet first between the logs. Fortunately we were on the high flats not far from shore. I found myself standing on the mud in water just below my armpits. Had we been close to the channel, I would have gone completely under. Such spills might result in catastrophe. I scrambled back onto the larger log in front and continued the chase. The blouse and short trousers reached a half dry condition in time for afternoon session. During the afternoon they dried out. At home, I was standing beside the warm stove when Mother remarked, "Look at that streak across your blue blouse!" She asked for no explanation and I volunteered none. The incident was one of those experiences that are part of growing up. Maybe it made me more cautious sometime later on. Mother may have thought that someone pushed me off Mrs. Call's bridge into the drainage creek from the swamp.

Besides something that might be dangerous to myself, on a few occasions I recall committing acts that could have injured someone else. The most flagrant incident of this sort occurred one afternoon while I was walking home from high school with Bill Raymond. Our homeward paths separated after we crossed the bridges over the West Branch. He followed the highway up Clay Hill and I climbed the railroad embankment to follow the tracks to our pasture. After reaching the top of the embankment, I picked up a small stone and tossed it carelessly high in the air in Bill's direction. Fortunately Bill was wearing a heavy woolen cap, for the stone, coming down with much acceleration, glanced off his head. I hastened back to see if Bill was injured and to apologize. He shrugged off the incident. However, next day, he told me his head ached while he was studying Cicero that evening. Sometime later, I did the same accidental thing to a snowshoe rabbit. It was early spring, after the rabbits had turned from white to brown, as I was walking along the high railroad embankment just below Jellerson's Crossing on my way to school. I spotted the rabbit crouching motionless and almost invisible from camouflage in the brown pasture grass beyond the railroad fence. For the sake of amusement, I wanted to let the hare know that he was detected and frighten him from his hiding with a nearby thud. Here again the rock that I tossed straight up in the air came down with fatal precision on the rabbit's head. It was with repentance and unhappiness that I continued down the tracks to school.

Vining used to caution me about throwing stones into trees because bruises in the bark might cause later decay of the wood and impair the health of the tree. Likewise, Pa reminded me once that there was a fine for breaking glass insulators, when he saw me throw a rock at a telephone pole one day. One fall, I felt that I could use stones instead of bow and arrow for hunting. I traipsed the swamps and meadows with a small white salt bag of rocks hunting snipe and rails, as soon as the season opened. Strangely enough, I never bagged a single piece of game with either the bow and arrow or the rocks in all the years I hunted with them, although a sad moment of my boyhood occurred one fall afternoon when I hit a small bird with a stone as it sat high in the top of one of the maples along our driveway. It was with deep remorse that I gave the bird a quiet burial.

It was my curiosity that almost killed our cat. I was checking on something I had heard Mother say about the agility of cats in general. In speaking of a feline's natural acrobatic abilities, she once said, "if you tossed a cat off the roof of a house, it would land with its feet on the ground." One cold winter day while I was playing in the barn, it seemed a good time to find out how well our cat could emulate the flying squirrel. I reasoned that if a cat could make it to the ground from a rooftop, a drop from our eight-foot scaffold above the barn floor should be easy. The cat twisted sideways in midair and landed on her four feet, but was unable to keep from bumping its nose on the barn floor. Fearful that it might be injured, I hastened down the ladder and held it in my lap while sitting on a mound of hay. The cat seemed a bit dazed and there was a slight hemorrhage from one nostril. I was sorry I'd tossed it from the scaffold. "Mother shouldn't have told me that," I thought.

Had our parents been in the habit of administering punishment, some of us children would probably have received spankings for many of our pranks. Minerva told me that Mother overheard her say something naughty while she was playing in the dooryard one day while the barn was being built. "Mother took me into the pantry and spanked me," she said. This was the only case of parental punishment of a physical nature that I ever knew about. However, I came close to receiving physical rebuke one day when I was about five. I wasn't quite old enough to be in school, and I spent a lot of time with Mother around the kitchen. She allowed me to stand on a chair in the pantry and use the doughnut cutter on the rolled out sheet of dough before she fried the doughnuts in a shallow iron kettle of hot lard. She also let me cut shitepokes in flight in her freshly rolled pie crusts, making openings to prevent the crust from puffing up when the pie was baked. This time it was on Tuesday, for Mother was standing by the kitchen table doing the ironing. I was on the kitchen floor in some sort of play. To make some small talk, I mustered up enough courage to ask Mother a question about the differences between boys and girls, a matter that had aroused in me a considerable amount of curiosity. Mother was obviously flustered. "Stop that kind of talk right now!" she told me. I was a bit taken aback by her reaction. Not wanting to accept defeat, however, I rephrased the question and asked it again. This time, she quickly stood the heavy black flatiron on its end and turned to me with her right hand opened threateningly. "Do you want me to box your ears?" she asked. There was a stern expression on her face. I knew she meant business. Realizing that I was getting nowhere in my quest for information, I closed the matter with, "I was merely asking a civil question."

As a small boy I remember how pleased I was when Pa occasionally picked me up and carried me around the room for several minutes. "Would you like to see your father again?" I asked him once. "Nope," he replied rather surprised. "What would I want to see him for? He hit me with a shovel once when I wasn't much bigger than you are." One of the few times that Pa ever threatened to punish me occurred one Sunday afternoon in late October when I was a freshman in high school. We were paddling down river in a skiff at low tide to tend the sucker net near the Old Pine. Pa was in the stern of the boat and I was up front. As we were passing the mouth of the big creek on our meadow, a duck suddenly flushed in the grass close to the beaver dam, about thirty feet across the high flats. From the bird's rusty brown color and white patch at the base of the bill, I recognized it as a female bluebill, a species that stayed mostly in large flocks in the open water of the Bay but were seldom seen on the river. The duck was wounded and unable to fly. It dropped back into the fringe of sweet flag and iris at the inner edge of the flats. Acting on reflex, I quickly pushed the bow of the skiff ashore and dashed across the soft mud after the duck. Back in the skiff with the captured bird, I tapped my shoes against the outside of the boat to get rid of the sticky gray-black mud. Pa was watching from the stern seat of the skiff, taken completely by surprise by the suddenness of it all. When he saw my tan ankle-high shoes that I wore to school all covered with flats mud, he became momentarily angry. "If you step into that mud again with your dress shoes on I'll give you a lickin'," he said. I wondered why he should become so concerned about the shoes that I had recently purchased with my own muskrat money. But Pa was no one to talk back to when he was feeling out of sorts. Instead of homework that evening, I prepared the bluebill skin for mounting. Every time I look at the bird, Pa's threat of punishment comes to mind.

Chapter Forty-Six

Music and Radios

Although none of us could carry a tune, we enjoyed occasional family sing-alongs. Sometimes, on a Sunday afternoon, everyone except Pa gathered around the small Cressy and Allen organ that Aunt Emma had given to my sisters. With Genevieve providing the music, we sang the best we could. We had two song books – a church hymnal, from which we sang selected old standbys such as "Jesus, Lover of my Soul," "My Faith Looks up to Thee," "Rock of Ages," and "Onward Christian Soldiers." The other was a collection of Civil War songs, all of which praised the Union efforts. There was also a thick-covered rectangular book with elementary lessons in organ playing. I tried to figure out how to play a few simple notes as given on the first page but learned only one scale; Genevieve taught me that.

In 1923 we heard our first radio broadcasts. When Minerva came home from Bound Brook, N.J., for summer vacation, in her new red four-cylinder Buick roadster, she brought Grace Lloyd, another teacher, with her for a brief visit. Miss Lloyd had a small battery-operated radio set which she left with us to use while she spent the remainder of the summer in eastern Maine. The radio was a varnished hardwood box about ten inches square, with a shiny black top on which were located a couple of dials and two or three adjustable knobs. Two headphones were a part of the set. We decided to place it on a small table in the southeast corner of the living room. Grace explained the aerial and grounding that would be necessary for its operation. For a good connection, we drove Pa's iron marlinspike into the dirt floor of the cellar and ran a piece of copper annunciator ball wire up through a hole in the floor. A similar piece of wire was passed from the radio through the window, over the porch roof, and fastened to a bedroom window casing. To get the best possible reception, we extended the aerial across the front dooryard to one of the windows high above the barn door. With these two installations completed, we settled down at the set to see what broadcasting stations might have listening areas that reached far away Maine. To our delight and surprise, above the catcalls, squeaks and squeals, we tuned in first thing on a program of music from station KDKA in Pittsburgh. I forget the call letters of another station that we heard quite clearly which broadcast from Aeolian Hall, New York City. We also received broadcasts from the Shepard Stores in Boston, others from Schenectady and Newark. One of the most exciting broadcasts was the one Pa and I listened to covering the Demsey-Firpo fight. The announcer's voice was not too clear that evening but it was particularly clear when the Bull of the Pampas knocked Dempsey from the ring. We were able to pick up the gist of the action every round. Towards the end of the summer, when Minerva would soon be taking the radio back to New Jersey, there seemed to be a decrease in volume. I connected the batteries in parallel instead of the usual series. Apparently that was not the thing to do. The set went completely dead and remained so for the last two weeks we had it.

Chapter Forty-Seven

Lois

For the most part, my boyhood years on the old river farm were happy. Except for the occasional drudgery of doing chores, haying or going to school, I entered into everything with eagerness and got a lot of fun out of such things as cutting wood, tending nets, and helping with the garden. In all these years there was one occasion of extreme sadness. Tragedy befell during the winter of my sophomore year in high school when we lost our oldest sister, Lois Ann.

Among my earliest recollections are those of Lois' loving care. She treated me most like a mother of any of my sisters and I can still recall times when she rocked me to sleep while reading some story or Mother Goose rhymes. It seemed as if she always had time to look out for me when Mother was busy with her work. She took me to a photographer in Brunswick when I was five years old to have my picture taken before I was to have my curls cut off and wear a "dutch-cut" instead. I wore my white suit that she and Mother made for me – mostly, I expect, to have "something nice to have my picture taken in." Lois also made most of my clothes during the first years in grade school – either by ripping up some of Al's or Vining's old suits or by using second-hand clothing that Attie Curtis used to send us in a barrel occasionally from Brunswick.

Like most of our family, Lois entered Bates. It was before I can remember but for some reason, probably financial, she went to college only a short time. When I can first remember, she was teaching grade schools at different points in southern Maine. She used to be at home for vacations and during the summer. During my last two or three years at the schoolhouse down at the corner, Lois was teaching in Hollis Center. There she met Walter Ingram, a sawyer in a portable mill. They were married during the fall of the last year I was in grade school. The next summer they used to drive up to Bowdoinham quite frequently on week-ends. After one of those visits, Minerva rode back with them for a week's visit. The next time they came up I went back to Hollis with them for a week. I rode in the high back seat of their Stanley steamer up over the rear wheels and with a relatively low back rest much like our baggage wagon. The Stanley took about half an hour to get up steam when one wanted to go somewhere but it was one of the fastest cars on the road – doing up around forty miles per hour with the throttle well open.

Lois and Walter were living in a small cabin in a pasture somewhere in the Hollis Center-Bar Mills area. There was a small brook nearby that drained a cranberry bog. As I was wading along this brook one day underneath the low alders, I saw a brook trout for the first time but I had no luck in catching it. I am still using the Miller's Falls crank-type hand drill that Lois and Walter gave me the first Christmas after they were married.

Although I never heard Lois complain about their living quarters, I am sure she was hoping they would soon be able to afford to have a larger home in town. The cabin had but a single room. I slept in a canvas tent nearby. There was a shallow well near the brook in which the perishable food was kept. One afternoon we set up a target on the edge and I showed Lois how to load and shoot the .22 rifle that I'd brought down from home with me.

The first inkling of trouble came one afternoon in early December of 1916. We had just had one of those early season snowstorms which had deposited about a foot of light dry snow on frozen ground. It must have been on a Friday, because I often used to take more time walking home from school on Friday afternoons. In coming home that day I had left the railroad track at the barway into Bub's pasture and had come out through Bub's woods, looking for partridge or their tracks in the new snow. When I entered the kitchen, Mother told me, "Minerva took the train down to Bar Mills today." (That year, Minerva was staying at home, instead of teaching.) "She got a telegram from Walter telling her to go to Lois at once. I can't imagine what it's all about. The more I think about it the more worried I get."

Minerva and Lois came home together the next afternoon on the two o'clock train. They walked down from the little depot at Harward's Road. Pa, Mother, and I were in the kitchen when they came in. Immediately, after a few words of greeting, Lois said, "Walter's left me. I can't understand it. He never spoke an unkind word to me in his life. We went to the bank where he kept his account and he'd taken out the two hundred and fifty dollars that he had there. I don't know where he's gone."

At that point Lois' voice became choked and she commenced to sob a little.

"I'd let him go and forget about him if it were me," Minerva stated flatly.

Lois held her face in her handkerchief and went into the next room.

"He was always taking them headache pills, every time he was here," Pa offered sort of in a way of explanation.

I was too young to have any knowledge of things of this sort but I did recall the incident that occurred when I was visiting in Bar Mills. Lois took Walter to task quite severely when a notice came from the bank that his account had been overdrawn. After listening in silence for some time, Walter said: "Well, I'll just have to get over to the bank and put in some money. I don't see why you should take it out on me like this. It isn't the first time by any means that someone has overdrawn his account."

Pa and Ma moved out of their bedroom upstairs so that Lois could have a quiet place to herself. There were too many people coming and going in the two heated downstairs rooms and the front bedroom over the living room got some heat through the hole in the ceiling. Lois stayed by herself most of the time, except when she came downstairs for meals. She talked very little to any of us. After a week or two she stayed in bed most of the time. Mother became afraid of some illness. She and Pa decided to have Doctor Irish come over from the village. Dr. Irish made the usual examination and then came downstairs to talk to Pa and Ma.

"She seems perfectly all right physically," he said, "but there seems to be some great mental concern that is depressing her. Perhaps you can help me out in understanding the case. Maybe there is something I can do, 'though right now I can't think of anything in my power to help much."

Pa and Ma both sat quietly and neither offered any of the information Dr. Irish had politely requested. After talking a while longer the doctor said, "I will talk to her a few minutes again and leave some sleeping pills which may help her in getting a little more rest and build up her strength a little."

While Dr. Irish was upstairs the second time, Pa said to Mother, "You may as well tell him the whole story. Then he'll know what he can or can't do. I don't know as it would do any good but he might as well know all about the case."

Even so, I don't think either of them told the Doctor anything about the cause of Lois' depression and she continued much the same for several days longer. Along about this time Pa said to me one day while we were sitting in front of the kitchen stove after dinner, "We'll have to fix up a little flock of hens somewhere for Lois so she can have something to look after and sort of take up her mind." I thought it was a good idea and indicated my approval. At that time I had two small flocks of hens in the two henpens Up-under-the-Hill that I tended regularly and took entire care of them. Mother had a flock in the big henpen back of the stable and some more in the barn cellar. Either of us would have gladly contributed some fowls for Lois' flock but no one ever took the initiative to set up a separate new flock some place and the good intentions never got any farther than Pa's suggestion. I suppose I should have talked with Mother about starting such a project for Lois but somehow I felt that the directive should come from someone who had more of a say about such things than I had. I'm not sure either that Lois would have cared about tending a flock of hens, although if she could have taken an interest in them it would have given her something to think about besides her own unfortunate predicament. She was always more interested, as I recall, in things around the house such as sewing, cooking and papering the kitchen. Except for helping with the raking of scatterings at haying time, I don't recall ever having seen her taking a hand in much of the farm work.

Lois' condition seemed to improve along towards Christmas time and she did enter into the gaiety of the Christmas tree. Soon after New Year's she decided that she and Minerva would return to Bar Mills, try to close up some of the things that Walter left unfinished and return sample tools and gadgets that had been sent to him for trial or purchase. She also planned to dispose of a device for automatically moving logs sideways on the carriage of the mill after each board was sawed from the log. Walter had either applied for a patent on this invention of his or a patent had already been granted. I'm not sure which was the case.

It was a Monday morning at the end of Christmas vacation that Lois and Minerva chose for their trip back to Bar Mills. I remember the occasion real well because, since Pa was taking them up to Harward's Depot to get the early seven o'clock train for Portland, I also went along with my lunch box to take the train as far as Bowdoinham Village on my way to school. Thus for fifteen cents I could avoid the two and a half mile walk out across the pasture and down the railroad track. Genevieve also took the train to Brunswick and Lewiston that morning on her way back to her senior year at Bates. With Genevieve was her high school friend, Gretchen Hulse, who had come over to our house on Saturday to spend the week-end. She was going as far as the Village only.

There must have been plenty of vacant seating space on the car we entered on Maine Central's seven o'clock south-bound local that morning because I remember we occupied two sets of seats for four persons – two sets of double seats, one seat of each facing backwards. Lois chose one of the forward-facing seats and sat down next to the window. Minerva took the seat directly in front of her facing the rear of the train. Genevieve and Gretchen assumed the corresponding positions in the other pair of seats almost directly across the aisle. Gretchen looked at me and smiled and I promptly sat beside her. Lois, looking over at me, said, "Sit with me, Bert," and she put her hand on the vacant seat beside her.

Not suspecting any of the things that were to happen in the next few weeks, I let my elation over the prospect of riding as far as the Village beside an attractive red-headed young lady sway my decision in the matter and I smiled beamingly at Lois without making any move to change seats.

"Oh well, never mind," she said as she turned and looked out of the window at the wintry woods and country road as the train started up from Harward's Crossing.

Lois and Minerva returned on the afternoon train the next day. On the whole, the trip had been disappointing for them and for Lois in particular. They had picked up many of the loose odds and ends, taken care of the accumulated mail and packed up a lot of things to be sent home. Lois' one big hope for some sort of recompense – the patented mill device – seemed to be entirely out of reach. Someone had informed her that any transfer or sale of the patent would have to be covered by Walter's signature. That was out of the question now. Lois seemed to go along for several days after that trip on the energy and good spirits she had built up over the period around Christmas time. I remember seeing her standing at the kitchen table ironing some clothes with a flat iron kept hot by alternating it with one of the several over the firebox of the kitchen stove. She was ironing slowly without taking her eyes from her work and making no conversation with Mother or me. After that her spirit seemed to fade away again. She spent most of the time in the upstairs bedroom – most of the time probably in bed. One Saturday afternoon, a high school classmate, Ethel Douglass, dropped in for a visit after learning that Lois was at home. "And I will see Lois?" I remember Ethel asking of Mother as she came into the house. They sat in the living room for some time. Ethel did most of the talking and Lois said very little. Such occasions did not seem to cheer Lois up very much; if anything they seemed to depress her emotionally.

Things wore on without much change for two or three weeks. It was the dead of winter and just at that time of the year when we were likely to get our coldest weather of the season – the last week in January. One morning that week – I think it was Tuesday or Wednesday – I was sort of half awake in my northeast bedroom waiting for the alarm clock to go off that I had set for about six-thirty. School began at eight-thirty and it took me a little over an hour to walk across the pasture to the railroad tracks, into the Village, and then up the hill to Coombs High School. That meant I would have to leave the house shortly after seven o'clock. At that particular time that morning, I knew it must be after six o'clock for a lot of light was coming in my northerly dormer window. Since the alarm clock had not yet sounded I realized it was probably around six-fifteen. As I waited to muster courage to get out of the warm bed into the below-freezing room, I heard someone walking down stairs. The footsteps sounded in the sitting room and I heard the door open at the foot of the stairs. Whoever it was, was then coming up stairs. As the footsteps reached the top of the landing just outside my door, Lois said to me, "Bert, are you awake?"

"Yup."

"You'd better be getting up. It's getting late, you know."

I wondered why she should tell me that it was late when I knew there was plenty of time to get ready for school. I waited a while longer until the alarm sounded. Then I got up, switched the silencer on the clock, and, taking my clothes downstairs, dressed in front of the coal fire in the sitting room. Pa had bought a Standard Oak coal stove for that room about a year earlier and installed it in place of the old "airtight" wood stove. When I was in high school, I was often the first one up on school days. Some mornings, however, Pa was already having his coffee by the kitchen stove when I came downstairs. Mother left the double boiler full of oatmeal on the coal stove the night before and she had also put up my lunch and left that on the kitchen table. Many days, while in high school, I often had completed dressing, eaten breakfast, and was off to school before anyone else was up.

That particular January morning, I reached Cornish's store about the usual time. I stopped there as usual to leave my canvas laced-up leggings, which were necessary for walking across the pasture through the snow, behind one of the radiators where I would pick them up after school. Apparently Mrs. Cornish had been looking for me, for she came to the front of the store as soon as I entered.

"Jeannette just called up and asked me to have you come back home this morning," she said in her friendly manner but with a deeply-concerned expression. "I'm awfully worried something is wrong over at your house," she continued.

I was much surprised at the call but could think of nothing right off to be particularly worried about. "I don't know what it can be," I said to Mrs. Cornish. "Pa's asthma has been troubling him lately. Maybe he's not feeling well and they want me to do the chores."

"Well, I hope it's something like that," Mrs. Cornish replied.

"Guess I won't take off my leggings now," I said as I thanked Mrs. Cornish for giving me the message and started out of the store.

Turning the corner towards home just below the concrete drinking trough, I met my classmate, Bill Raymond, going towards the old post office.

"Going the wrong way, aren't you, Bertie?" he said.

"Just got word to go back home," I replied. "Guess Pa must want me to do the chores today."

"See you tomorrow," he said. "Hope it's nothing serious."

For several minutes I took the matter lightly but by the time I got to the bridges over the Cathance Branch, I was beginning to feel worried. "They never called me back like this before," I thought. "With Jeannette and Minerva both at home, they could manage all the things that have to be done around the barn without my help. There must be something really serious about this." During the time that I took from the railroad tracks at the foot of Clay Hill until I got up to Jellerson's Crossing, I became firmly convinced that something must have happened to Pa real sudden. I remembered the time when, as a small boy, I saw Pa topple over backwards as he coughed while standing over the kitchen stove. Mother left her work at once and tugged at one of Pa's arms. "Jimmy, get up! Get up, Jimmy!" she said excitedly. In less than a minute Pa opened his eyes and got onto his feet again, apparently all right. "Something like that, but a little more serious, may have happened this morning," I thought. By the time I reached the crossing almost up to the Davis' south line, I heard a bell such as people hung on the horse's collar for winter travelling. Looking back I saw Uncle Ed standing up in his pung driving towards the village. He was looking down the track as he crossed the railroad and since I was nearly out of sight up the track he did not see me. I felt that possibly he had come over to meet me on the way home and give me a ride the rest of the way. At the same time, he was planning, I thought, to tell me the bad news, whatever it was. I kept on up the railroad and the nearer home I got the worse I felt. By the time I'd crossed our pasture and had reached the driveway I was quite certain of just what had happened. Yes, there were a lot of fresh runner tracks – like both sleighs and pungs – in our driveway. When I left that morning the last track was a day or two old. Of course, I reasoned that the Doctor must have been there and possibly the undertaker by that time. Within a minute or two, I was in our dooryard in the position to look through our kitchen. The north window and one of the south windows in the kitchen were directly opposite one another so that anyone near the stove stood out in profile as one looked straight through the two windows. What a relief! There was Pa standing over the stove with one foot up on the hearth and his forearm resting on the raised knee. I had seen him in that same position hundreds of times before when he was trying to keep his head and chest in the heat from the stove. After all that worrying on the way home and everything was all right after all! I expect my face must have shown at least a little happiness as I went into the house. Pa looked at me but did not say anything. There was no one else in the kitchen at the time. Soon Jeannette came out of the sitting room with a dusting cloth in her hand. Her face was sad and expressionless. I am sure by that time I wore a look of bewilderment. Here my thinking had been all wrong and I did not have time to start over again on a new line of reasoning. Jeannette beckoned me into the sitting room where she said to me:

"Lois is dead."

This was both a shock and a surprise, but at least I now knew why I had been called back home. I looked at Jeannette for two or three seconds to see if she was going to tell me anything more. Apparently not. I walked slowly back to the kitchen. Whatever I did for the next hour or so I cannot recall exactly. I must have changed into my work clothes and gone out to do some of the daily chores. I do remember, however, that I kept thinking about what could have caused Lois' death. In her condition of very low spirits, I figured, a sudden heart attack might have been brought on by so much depressed feeling. That was the best guess I could make.

It must have been along in the middle of the forenoon, and I was sawing and splitting wood out in the stable, when Pa came out of the house and stopped at the stable door. As soon as I had finished sawing the piece of wood I had in the sawhorse, Pa asked me, "Where do you keep the cartridges for your twenty-two?"

"I have them in a box upstairs on my bureau," I said. From the tone of

Pa's voice and the question he asked, I had the first inkling as to what had really happened that morning.

"Let's take a look," he said as he turned and started up the stairs over the coal bin to the shed chamber. I followed Pa through the open chamber into my bedroom.

"There is the box of cartridges there," I said. "But I had the cover on the box."

The small box of cartridges was now open and the cover was lying close by.

"You ought to keep them out of sight somewhere," Pa said. "But then," he continued, "it probably wouldn't make any difference if she was going to do away with herself she'd have done it one way or another, anyway."

He then went out into the upstairs hallway, walked over near to his bedroom door and came back with my rifle. He handed me the gun without saying anything. I immediately pulled back the hammer and opened the breech-block. Someone had already taken the empty cartridge.

"Where did you have the gun?" Pa inquired.

"Standing right over here in the corner behind the old cabinet," I said as I put the rifle back in its place.

"M-m," Pa mumbled as he started downstairs.

Albert A. Dunlap

Life on the Abbagadasset

Could you ere forgive me
for all that I have done.
Could I ask forgiveness
for my many wrongs.
You came to me so pure and sweet
You were my cooing dove.
Why couldn't I have rained
upon you worthy words of love.
Now in the scarlet autumn
when the leaves are going to rest,
I think of you so often and
wonder, was it for the best.
I hear the din of memories
ringing in my ear.
I wish with all my soul
and heart that you were only here.
The sun which shone upon
us both would guide our path as one
I wish with all my soul again
that you would only come.
Oh could I call you
Back to me and meet
your earnest gaze
of the lovely and the beautiful
The light of other days.

W.M.I.

(This poem was mailed to Lois in Bowdoinham from Walter Ingram in Philadelphia on April 1, 1920, some three years after her death.)

Albert A. Dunlap

Life on the Abbagadasset

GLOSSARY

Definitions mostly from the Oxford English Dictionary.

Spelling: Abbagadasset: This was an accepted spelling of the word in the early 20th century, although now the river is usually spelled "Abagadasset". Spelling of many names varies, within Bert's manuscript and among various sources. This edition has arbitrarily chosen one form for each name: for instance, Sedgeley, for what was variously written as Sedgeley, Sedgely or Sedgley. And a non-sequitor, Bert pronounced Cromwell as "Crummel."

Bluebill: in Bert's story, it probably meant a lesser scaup (*Aythya affinis*), although greater scaup, ring-necked duck and ruddy duck have also been called bluebills.

Duck hawk: local name for a marsh hawk/northern harrier/marsh harrier.

Fyke net: a bag net, made with hoops of decreasing size. From Dutch word, fuik.

Gambrel: a hooked stick used often for hanging meat or clothes. [See Hock, as both refer to a part of a horse's hind leg.]

Glib ice: glib meaning smooth or slippery, a Canadian expression for very smooth ice.

Guzzle: a gutter or drain.

Hackmatack tree: another name for the American Larch or Tamarack tree.

Hock: a rod, stick or chain with a hook at the end. [See Gambrel]

Jalops: also spelled jallop, jollop, etc. a purgative drug made from resinous tubers of *Exogonium purga*, from the Mexican city of Jalapa.

Keelic: term used by Santy Pratt for part of his seining equipment. Perhaps "killick or killock', a heavy stone used on small boats as an anchor. Origin obscure, but term used by earliest English settlers in Massachusetts Bay,

Mow: the pile of hay stored for the winter in a barn, also hay mow; rhymes with 'now'.

Pung: a one-horse (seldom two-horse) sleigh or sledge used in New England. From Indian word 'tompung' and etymologically related to toboggan.

Pumpkinseed: another name for sunfish or pond perch.

Shitepoke: a small green heron of North America.

Shorts sack: uncertain origin and meaning, but from context a rather large, burlap bag.

Skeg: a slanting part of the keel at the sternpost.

Sucker: any of several cyprinoid fish, in the carp family.

Thill: the pole of shaft of a wagon that attached the hauling animal to the vehicle.